St. Louis Community College

Forest Park
Florissant Valley
Meramec

Instructional Resources
St. Louis, Missouri

Morals, Reason, and Animals

Morals, Reason, and Animals

S. F. Sapontzis

Temple University Press
Philadelphia

Temple University Press, Philadelphia 19122
Copyright © 1987 by Temple University. All rights reserved
Published 1987
Printed in the United States of America

The paper used in this publication meets the minimum
requirements of American National Standard for Information
Sciences—Permanence of Paper for Printed Library Materials,
ANSI Z39.48-1984

Library of Congress Cataloging-in-Publication Data

Sapontzis, S. F. (Steve F.)
  Morals, reason, and animals.

  Bibliography: p.
  Includes index.
  1. Animals, Treatment of—Moral and ethical aspects.
I. Title
HV4708.S23   1987   179'.3   86-30221
ISBN 0-87722-493-5 (alk. paper)

For Toby, Duffy, and Georgie—
and for Jeanne, too

Contents

Preface   xi

Acknowledgments   xix

PART I: THE MORAL (IN)SIGNIFICANCE OF REASON   1

1 Why Should I Be Rational?   3

    I. "Rationality" and Its Alternatives   4
    II. The Methodological Counterattack   6
    III. The Moral of the Story   8

2 Where Reason Enters In—and Where It Doesn't   11

    I. Incidentally Good Actions   12
    II. Ulterior Motives   17
    III. Acting Out of Context   21
    IV. Moral Agents, Philosophers, and Judges   22
    V. Summary and Conclusion   26

3 Being Rational and Acting Morally   27

    I. What "Rational" Refers To   28
    II. Can Only Rational Beings Be Moral Agents? 30
        A. Acting for the Right Reason   32
        B. Acting on Principle and Acting Morally 36
        C. The Free, the Rational, and the Moral 38
        D. Everyday Freedom   40
    III. Pursuing Ideals vs. the Value of Virtue 41

4 People and Persons   47

  I. Metaphysical vs. Moral Persons   47
 II. The Humanist Principle   52
     A. The Logico-linguistic Defense of Humanism   54
     B. The Phenomenological Defense of Humanism   58
     C. The Transcendental Defense of Humanism   60
     D. The Consequential Defense of Humanism   62
 III. Conclusion   69

PART II: "ANIMAL RIGHTS"?   71

5 What Liberating Animals Is and Isn't About   73

   I. The Moral Sense of "Animal"   73
  II. Applying the Rhetoric of Liberation to Animals   76
 III. Applying the Concept of Equality to Animals   78
  IV. Applying the Rhetoric of Rights to Animals   82
   V. Is Animal *Liberation* an Affront to Human Liberation?   84
  VI. Summary   87

6 Three Reasons for Liberating Animals   89

   I. Liberating Animals and Developing Moral Character   90
  II. Liberating Animals and Making the World a Happier
      Place   96
 III. Liberating Animals and Being Fair   103
  IV. Conclusion   110

**PART III: ANSWERING SOME OBJECTIONS TO LIBERATING
            ANIMALS**   111

7 Can Animals Have Interests?   115

   I. Language and Interests   115
      A. "Having an Interest"   116
      B. Language and Desire   119
         1. Language and Belief   120
            a. The Psychological (In)Significance of
                Grammar   120
            b. Language and Truth   125
         2. Language and Self-Consciousness   127

C. Conclusion   129
II. Reason and the Moral Significance of Interests   129
     A. Being Rational and Having Interests   130
     B. Having Interests and Moral Standing   134

8 *Moral Community and Animal Rights*   139

     I. The Reciprocity Requirement   140
     II. The Agency Requirement   145
     III. The Relations Requirement   151
     IV. The Humanist Requirement   154
     V. Conclusion   157

9 *The Misfortune of Death*   159

     I. Why (Supposedly) Only Rational Beings Can Have a
         Right to Life   160
     II. Having vs. Taking an Interest in Life   161
     III. Having Interests and Having Rights   163
     IV. Having an Interest in Life and the Right to Life   166
     V. Suffering a Loss and the Awareness of Loss   170
     VI. Summary and Conclusion   173

10 *The Replacement Argument*   177

     I. The (In)Significance of the Replacement Argument   178
     II. Six Ways of Evaluating Moral Standing   179
          A. Describing the Six Ways   179
          B. Six Evaluations of the Replacement Argument   183
     III. Total Population vs. Prior Existence Utilitarianism   189
     IV. Prior Existence Utilitarianism and Obligations to
          Future Generations   194
     V. Summary   195

PART IV: A FEW CONSEQUENCES   197

11 *Vegetarianism*   199

     I. The Simple Answer   199
     II. Exploiting, Slaughtering, and Harvesting   201
     III. Exploiting, Killing, and Scavenging   206
     IV. Starvation   207

12 *Whither Animal Research?*   209

    I. Can Animals Consent to Research?   210
    II. Should Research Be Done Only with Those Who
        Consent?   213
    III. Are Humans a Superior Form of Life?   216
    IV. Should Superiors Exploit Their Inferiors?   222
    V. Summary and Conclusion   225

13 *Saving the Rabbit from the Fox*   229

    I. The Variety of Absurdity   233
    II. Ought Implies Can   239
    III. "Avoidable" Suffering   245
    IV. Conclusion   247

14 *Plants and Things*   249

    I. Environmental Ethics and Inherent Value   249
       A. Environmental Crisis and the (Supposed) Necessity
          of Inherent Value   250
       B. The Variety of Goodness and the (Supposed)
          Necessity of Inherent Value   253
       C. Conclusion   258
    II. Environmental Ethics and Ecological Holism   259
       A. The Biotic "Community" vs. Animal Liberation   260
          1. The Arbitrariness of Total Holism   261
          2. Environmental Ethics vs. Personal Preferences   264
          3. Morality and the Affirmation of Life   267
          4. Summary   268
       B. The Good of Nonsentient Things   268
    III. The Environmental Ethics of Animal Liberation   270

Notes   273

Bibliography   291

Index   297

Preface

THIS BOOK explains what I, at least, think "liberating" animals from human exploitation refers to and would amount to, why the standard justifications of this exploitation are inadequate, and why, consequently, we ought (morally) to liberate animals from that exploitation. So you may be excused for wondering, why bother writing or reading this book? Haven't Peter Singer, Bernard Rollin, Tom Regan, Stephen Clark, Michael W. Fox, Mary Midgley, et al. amply developed the philosophical foundations of animal rights? Philosophers, however, are reluctant to admit that any issue is ever settled—that's how we've kept in business these many years. The seminal writings of animal liberation philosophers have not met with universal acclaim, leading to a general philosophical endorsement of animal rights. Quite the contrary, those writings have been sharply, variously, and extensively criticized. These criticisms have drawn responses, leading to a lively, ongoing discussion that, over the past fifteen years, has at least moved animal rights from the lunatic fringe to the respectable periphery of contemporary philosophy. This book is intended to be a second-generation contribution to that discussion. That is, it focuses on what have come to be the pivotal issues of that discussion and responds to the objections to animal liberation that have arisen with the detail and precision that years of discussion permit.

Nevertheless, this book is not intended to be a work of comprehensive, "systematic" philosophy in the tradition of, for example, John Rawls's *A Theory of Justice* and Tom Regan's *The Case for Animal Rights*. Personally, I find the "bits and pieces" approach to moral philosophy and the less systematic reflections of moral philosophers like Aristotle and David Hume to be more congenial and compelling than such systematic productions. Consequently, this book is written with the idea that it is not so much specific moral principles as enlightened, responsive, coherent beliefs, attitudes, concerns, and commitments that are the goals of moral philosophy and the wellsprings of progressive moral practice.

Also, other than trying to keep in close touch with current, common moral beliefs and practices, I have no theoretical moral ax to grind. I am neither a utilitarian nor a rights theorist (presuming, as advocates of each generally seem to presume, that these are exclusive positions). That is because I do not find that our moral tradition is either (exclusively) utilitarian or (exclusively) rights-oriented and because I believe that compelling moral arguments must build upon currently accepted moral tradition. I agree with those who emphasize the complexity of morality, many of whom have criticized advocates of animal rights for trying to oversimplify morality, for example, by suggesting that there is only one criterion of moral considerability. However, I disagree that taking the complexity of morality into account counts against animal liberation. In Chapter 6 and throughout Part III, especially Chapter 8, I show how the many different tracks of everyday morality all point in the direction of liberating animals.

I think that this makes the animal liberation argument of this book significantly different from those of Singer and Regan, for example. I also think that the argument here improves on the arguments of those philosophers. While Singer's argument is, in my opinion, masterfully constructed and an outstanding piece of utilitarian reasoning, it may be too exclusively utilitarian to satisfy any but the most dedicated of utilitarians. The argument of this book has strong utilitarian dimensions—because everyday morality has such dimensions—but it includes other considerations as well. Regan is so zealously anti-utilitarian that he goes to the opposite extreme, whence his argument will likely satisfy only the most dedicated of anti-utilitarians. His argument is an immense and impressive edifice, but, unfortunately, it is founded on dubious slippery slope objections to utilitarianism and perfectionism and on what may very well be a mirage, namely, "inherent value." By contrast to Regan's work, this book is modest, but at least its foundation is actual, everyday moral practice and ideas, not theoretical disputes and contrived concepts.

As mentioned, this work focuses on what have come to be the pivotal issues in the animal liberation debate during the 1970s and 1980s. Those issues themselves focus on the question of the moral (in)significance of reason and the moral implications of being or not being a "rational being." By far the most common defense of our exploiting animals—and the one that is best supported by our moral tradition—is that we are rational beings, while they are not. Other animal rights philosophers have, of course, attempted to overcome this defense, but this has been only one small part of what concerned them in their books. Too often, these refutations have been little more than reciting the now famous "argument from marginal cases," that is, pointing out that we do not consider it morally acceptable to exploit nonrational humans, such as the severely retarded and brain-damaged. Unfortunately (for the animals), the argument from marginal cases is not that compelling; basically, all it does is show that most of us are sentimentally attached to members of our own species to a degree greatly exceeding our attachment to members of other species and that morality is more complex than one might have thought (see Chapter 8 for a discussion of the argument from marginal cases).

By contrast, this book is all about the moral (in)significance of reason and what follows therefrom. Part I seeks to give the reader a feel for how concepts of "reason," which refer to quite a variety of different things, actually function in everyday moral practice. Mainstream, Western moral philosophers, such as Plato and Kant; have made reason the source and focus of morality. Even such noted animal rights philosophers as Singer and Regan have given reason a similar pride of place in morality by agreeing that only rational beings can be moral agents. Everyday moral practice, however, does not confirm this preeminence of reason in morality. Consequently, Part I is intended to be a bit of an eye-opener, questioning some of the least questioned presumptions of mainstream, Western moral philosophy. (These are issues that are not limited to questions concerning the relation between humans and animals; so the analyses in Part I are not confined to human-animal examples and questions.)

Chapter 1 discusses the obligation to be rational, arguing that that obligation is not an overwhelming, all-pervasive one. There are morally acceptable alternatives to being rational—irrational as that may sound. Now that the bloom is off existentialism, there are probably not many moral philosophers who would rise in defense of irrationality, but once we go beyond the emotive, evaluative meaning of being "rational" and look into some of the cognitive, descriptive meanings of the term, such as being calm rather than emotional, we can see that there are viable alternatives to being rational and that labeling and condemning these as "irrational" is just name-calling.

. Chapter 2 discusses where we do and where we do not require information about an agent's "rationality" when establishing the moral value of his or her actions. The action considered in Chapter 2 is the foiling of a bank robbery, and while the agent's motives and understanding of the situation will ordinarily be considered in establishing the moral value of such an act, his or her capacity for "reasoning" will not. There is greater variety to the relevance of reasoning to the moral value of actions than moral philosophers, who have often focused on the making of moral judgments, have generally recognized. While we certainly want our judges to be moral, what is central to a judge's being moral can be peripheral to the moral value of a hero.

Chapter 3 discusses, and challenges, the commonly accepted proposition that only rational beings can be moral agents. That is a particularly important proposition in the animal liberation debate, since many of those who argue that there is a morally crucial difference between humans and animals, a difference that entitles us to exploit animals for our benefit, do so on the grounds that we are moral agents but animals are not. In spite of the ubiquity of that argument, few animal rights philosophers have investigated the concept of moral agency or challenged the claim that animals are not moral agents. Chapter 3 remedies that, arguing that being a moral agent is not an all-or-nothing condition and that some animals are virtuous agents, even if none are fully moral agents.

Finally, Chapter 4 explores the relation between being a "person" in the descriptive sense (i.e., being human or a rational animal) and in the moral sense (i.e., a being who ought to be respected or who is a holder of rights). The commonly accepted position on this issue today (except where human fetuses are concerned) is simply to identify being human and meriting respect: all and only human beings merit basic moral rights, which have, consequently, come to be known as "human rights." It is argued here that this identification is gratuitous, is contrary to some well-established principles of moral reasoning, and encourages a deplorable conception of morality.

The conclusion of Part I is that morally, reason is not as crucial as mainstream, Western moral philosophers have made it out to be. It does not follow that reason has no place in or is detrimental to morality and that we should exchange our moral traditions for sentiment, instinct, breaking the iniquitous inhibitions of civilization, and returning to the golden age of the unfettered, noble savage. As in politics, so in moral philosophy, the all-or-nothing approach is out of touch with the way things are and work. Although rationality is not the be-all and end-all of morality, neither is it irrelevant to nor destructive of morality, and, as mentioned earlier, throughout this study, I will be trying to resist the allure of the simple and to give all the diverse elements and the overall complexity of everyday, contemporary morality their due. Consequently, the purpose and conclusion of Part I is not to provide an alternative to reason as *the* source of morality but to raise doubts about the traditional emphasis on the crucial and comprehensive importance of reason for morality. It is that tradition that has been repeatedly invoked to make our exploitation of nonrational animals—those "dumb brutes" —respectable; so it is that tradition that must be brought into question before people will be able to question that exploitation and put an end to it. Thus, Part I does not establish a foundation for later deductions; instead, it is intended to undermine the complacency that would otherwise simply dismiss what follows and thereby to inspire a bit of the wonder that, as Aristotle says, is the beginning of philosophy.

Part II develops a general conception and defense of animal liberation that are consistent with the idea that

> we are rational beings in ways animals are not:
> this is a morally important difference; but
> it does not justify our exploiting animals.

That is the proverbial "in a nutshell" version of the position argued for in this book.

Chapter 5 provides reasonable, defensible interpretations of such key terms in the animal liberation literature as "animal," "liberation," "rights," and "equality" and explicates and defends the analogy that animal liberationists have drawn between their movement and the campaigns against such prejudices as racism and sexism. William James says that the first, knee-jerk reaction to new ideas is ridicule, and the reaction to animal liberation has certainly confirmed the accuracy of that remark. Even today, with the animal rights movement nearing the end of its second decade, many of its opponents still seek to refute it through ridicule. That effort usually proceeds by constructing straw-man exaggerations and misrepresentations of what liberationists are seeking for animals and then blowing over these straw-men with a hearty laugh. The purpose of Chapter 5 is to provide a more weighty interpretation of animal liberation, so that the discussion of it can proceed to more serious issues.

Chapter 6 places the burden of proof on those who oppose liberating animals. I do not think that we need to consult Eastern religions or rely on novel moral terminology or concepts, such as "*telos*" and "inherent value," in order to indicate that we ought (morally) to liberate animals. I think that our everyday moral tradition and concepts, such as our well-established concerns with fairness and minimizing suffering, provide a sufficient basis for that argument. Chapter 6 develops that argument through reviewing the concerns with happiness, fairness, and virtue that are contained within our everyday morality. I describe this as "putting the burden of proof on the opponents of animal liberation" because our general moral concerns with being fair, minimizing suffering, and so on do not, like axioms in geometry, provide a foundation for knock-down, drag-out proofs. Rather, they establish the standard to which a moral person should adhere, unless he or she can provide sufficiently morally weighty reasons to do otherwise in a special situation. Consequently, the best a general moral argument for animal liberation can do is to show that it is the exploiting of animals, not the liberating of them, that should be regarded as morally deviant and in need of justification.

Part III then discusses and challenges in careful detail arguments that opponents of animal liberation have offered in their attempts to shoulder that burden. These arguments all focus or rely on our being and animals' not being rational.

Chapter 7 deals with the claim, made most notably by R. G. Frey in his extended "case against the animals," that only beings with interests can have rights and that only rational beings can have interests. Although environmental ethicists seeking rights for trees and rivers would challenge the first of those claims, I agree with Frey that only beings with interests can have rights. Consequently, the argument of Chapter 7 is directed to the claim that only "rational" beings can have interests. I show that "having an interest" does not require the intellectual, linguistic accomplishments opponents of animal liberation would have us believe it does.

Chapter 8 deals with four arguments against animal rights intended to justify the most common, gut-level response to calls for animal rights: But they're *just* animals! These arguments are based on the following four claims: only those who respect the moral rights of others are entitled to moral rights; only moral agents are entitled to moral rights; one is entitled to moral rights against others on the basis of his or her (capacity for) familial, personal, political, economic, or other such relations to them; and moral rights are a creation of, by, and for human beings. Each of these four criteria for being a holder of moral rights is a way of detailing the idea that moral rights originate in a community of similarly interested, rational beings. This would, presumably, make it impossible for animals to have moral rights, since it is impossible, presumably, for them to be members of that community. While the idea that morality is the product of a community of interests is a vintage one enjoying renewed popularity today, none of these four restrictions on possible moral rights–holders is confirmed by everyday moral practice. The idea that moral rights derive from the need for mutual inhibitions, if we are to avoid lives that are, as Hobbes said, "solitary, poor, nasty, brutish, and short," cannot account for a primary function of moral rights, namely, to protect the weak against the strong. Similarly, moral agency commonly entails responsibility for, not license to exploit, those who are not moral agents, such as children. Also, our morality includes ideas of moral communities, for example, "the brotherhood of man," that are not tied to, and, indeed, are intended to counterbalance, communities of personal, economic, and other interests. Finally, although our moral concepts have been created by us, they can (logically) be applied to others besides us.

Chapter 9 deals with the question of whether killing animals is itself morally objectionable. Our current "humane" concepts and practice are based on the belief that while making an animal suffer can be morally objectionable, painlessly taking its life is not. In the philosophical literature concerning not only the morality of exploiting animals but also the morality of abortion, this belief is bolstered by arguing that life is valuable for individuals only if they "value" it. It is that argument that is disputed in Chapter 9. We can have a morally significant interest in life and can suffer a morally significant loss in painless death, even if we do not explicitly consider and evaluate life and death. That is because, as far as we know, life is necessary for happiness.

Finally, Chapter 10 deals with what has come to be known as "the replacement argument." Roughly, this argument contends that as long as animals that we kill are given a decent quality of life beforehand and are replaced with equally happy animals afterward, there is nothing morally wrong with our raising and killing them. This argument has seemed so powerful when directed against utilitarian defenses of animal liberation that Peter Singer has accepted it in principle, although he argues that it applies to relatively few animals, since factory-farmed and laboratory animals are very seldom provided a decent quality of life. The argument of Chapter 10 goes far beyond this, showing how the thrust of this argument is limited not only to utilitarian moralities but even to a particularly dubious form of utilitarianism.

The concluding section of the book discusses some of the practical, more or less specific consequences of the animal liberation position developed here. There are chapters on vegetarianism, the (im)morality of animal research, whether liberating animals would require us to inhibit predation, and the relation between animal rights and environmental ethics.

Chapter 11 discusses the dietary implications of liberating animals. While the humane tradition does not advocate vegetarianism, most contemporary animal rights advocates are vegetarians. However, it is argued here that vegetarianism is not entailed by animal liberation, although the dietary consequences of liberating animals will closely approximate vegetarianism. Except for eating eggs, the use of other animal products like leather and wool is not discussed here, but the consequences of animal liberation for these uses of animals are clearly the same as the consequences for meat-eating.

One of the traditional and hottest targets of animal liberationists is animal research. Liberationists attack this research both because of the great suffering it inflicts on animals and because animals do not consent to participate in this research, a fundamental requirement for all research on human subjects. Researchers respond that this research is essential for making scientific, medical progress that greatly enhances the quality of human life. Chapter 12 begins with a discussion of animals' (in)ability to consent to participate in research and the moral implications of this. It is argued that animals can show whether or not they desire to participate in research and that a consent requirement could be meaningfully applied to animal research. The remainder of the chapter then focuses on the pivotal presumption that underlies the researchers' justification of their work, namely, the idea that since human life is "morally superior" to animal life, we are justified in humanely sacrificing animals in research that benefits humans. That presumption is faulty, because the only sense in which humans are clearly morally superior to animals could not, without self-contradiction, be employed to justify our exploiting them. I then conclude that the moral to be drawn from the loss of that presumption is that animal research should be governed by the same moral principles that govern research employing human subjects.

Chapter 13 discusses the common complaint that extending moral rights to animals would entail the preposterous conclusion that we ought to protect prey animals from predators. Hardly an animal rights lecture passes without someone rising to say that if they really are dedicated to saving animals from suffering and premature death, liberationists should be out there saving the little fish from the big ones. The comic futility of such an endeavor is supposed to show the absurdity of animal liberation. The argument of Chapter 13 first questions whether this conclusion really is preposterous. I show that although our massively and beneficially interfering with predation is not feasible, neither is it absurd. There is a role in morality for unattainable ideals. The argument then turns to whether liberating animals entails interfering with predation. I think it does, but only if doing so would not cause more harm than good (understanding "harm" and "good" in some utilitarian manner). The argument here (sections II and III of Chapter 13) is as much concerned with the logic of moral reasoning as with the issue of our obligation to prevent predation. Seeking out extreme, implausible consequences is a popular way of trying to refute moral principles, and a considerable part of the discussion in Chapter 13 is aimed at laying to rest this tactic on the grounds that such cases are irrelevant in a "practical science" like ethics.

The book concludes with a discussion of the relation between animal liberation and environmental ethics. Chapter 14 discusses both Tom Regan's and J. Baird Callicott's interpretations of this relation and disagrees with both. Basically, Regan's attempt to incorporate animal rights within an environmental ethic is unattractive because of the long-since discredited value theory he employs. In order to convince us that we should try to resurrect such an antiquated value theory, Regan would have to show us that that is the only way to cope with the dire environmental problems confronting us, but his argument fails to do that. Callicott's attempt to show the superiority of environmental ethics to animal liberation is crippled by his inability to distinguish a moral from an aesthetic value. This leaves his environmental "ethic" nothing more than a personal preference for the outdoor life. The chapter concludes with a sketch of an environmental ethic derived from the principles of animal liberation developed in Part II.

When there are already excellent studies in the field, it is always reasonable to wonder why a new book on the same subject is appearing. And there already are excellent books advocating animal liberation, especially those by Rollin and Singer. I hope that this Preface has made clear the contribution this book is supposed to make to the discussion and cause of animal liberation. Whether it accomplishes what it is supposed to, you can discover only by reading further.

Acknowledgments

THIS BOOK derives from a series of articles published between 1979 and 1985 in *American Philosophical Quarterly, Between the Species, Environmental Ethics, Ethics, Ethics & Animals, The Journal of Value Inquiry*, and *The Monist*. I would like to thank the editors of those journals for publishing those articles and for permitting me to include material from them here.

Although many of the following chapters are based on one or two of those articles, the book is not a collection of essays. All those articles have been rewritten, updated, refined, expanded, harmonized, and otherwise reworked to create an integrated study. Also, considerable new, previously unpublished material has been added.

I would like to thank the following people for reading my manuscript in its entirety and giving me their comments on it: Jeanne Gocker, James Nelson, Bernard Rollin, Mary Anne Warren, and those who reviewed it for Temple University Press. I would also like to thank the following for their comments on parts of the manuscript or on the papers that were incorporated into this book: J. Baird Callicott, Arthur Caplan, Lawrence Finsen, Sidney Gendin, Harlan Miller, Evelyn Pluhar, Kenneth Shapiro, Bonnie Steinbock, and some of the anonymous referees of *Ethics & Animals*. I am grateful to California State University, Hayward, for granting me sabbatical leave during 1984–1985, which is when the bulk of the writing of this book was accomplished, and for financial assistance for the preparation of the index for the book, which was ably constructed by Charlotte Shane. Finally, I would like to thank Temple University Press for publishing this book, and in particular Jane Cullen, for wanting to publish it, Doris Braendel, for getting it into print, and Ed Cone, for editing it.

Part I

The Moral (In)Significance of Reason

FROM PLATO through Kant to such contemporary writers as Alan Donagan and John Rawls, many mainstream moral philosophers have insisted that morality is a product of reason. The purpose of the four chapters in Part I is to bring that insistence into question.

These four essays do not provide a comprehensive, compelling argument for an alternative source for morality. Given the diversity of everyday moral practice, I doubt that morality has a single source and that any philosophical analysis that aims at demonstrating such a source can provide more than mental exercise. The method of these essays is to follow everyday moral practice, noting what "reason" and related terms mean and refer to here and there. In this way, we can arrive at a fair picture of reason's place in actual moral practice. For better or worse, this picture is rather different from the one a person would get by reading Plato, Kant, and many other Western philosophers. Perhaps this is because these philosophers have been more intent on showing us how morality ought to be practiced than on showing us how it actually is practiced.

Many people, not all of them philosophers, cite the human possession of reason vs. animals' lack of it when trying to justify the preferred moral status we commonly enjoy over animals, for example, to justify its being morally acceptable for us routinely to eat animals and to kill them in research for our benefit, although it would not be morally acceptable for them to feed on us or for us to be killed in research for their benefit. If reason is *the* source of morality, then that justification can seem plausible and can be formulated in the following way:

A1: Since morality aims at the realization and proliferation of moral values, those who can produce these values are morally entitled to preference over those who cannot.

A2: Only rational agents can produce moral values.

1

> A3:   Human beings (ordinarily) are rational agents, but animals are not.
>
> A4:   Therefore, human beings (ordinarily) are morally entitled to prefer-
>   ence over animals.

On the other hand, to the degree that reason is *only one among several* weavers of the complex tapestry of morality, A2 is false, and citing human reason as moral justification for our sacrificing animals for our benefit takes on the appearance of an excuse. Thus, the following descriptions of the roles actually played by reason in our everyday morality point toward questioning the moral status we commonly assign to animals, a questioning we shall pursue throughout the subsequent parts of this volume. (Along the way, especially in Chapter 8, we shall be questioning the significance of A1. A3 will come up for discussion in Chapter 3.)

Chapter 1 discusses the idea of a moral obligation to be rational, a common presumption of many, if not most, mainstream, Western moral philosophers. Various senses of being "rational" are discussed, and it is argued that there are morally viable alternatives to being "rational" in each of these senses. Chapter 2 discusses what we would have to know about an individual's reasoning in deciding whether he or she deserves a commendation for heroism. It is argued that while issues concerning the agent's motives and practical understanding of the situation would be relevant here, issues concerning her or his capacity for moral reasoning would not. Chapter 3 discusses the concept of moral agency and the relation between being a moral agent and meriting moral respect. It is argued that being a moral agent is not an all-or-nothing condition and that being virtuous, even if not a fully moral agent, is what ought (morally) to be considered when questions of meriting moral respect are at issue. It is also argued that animals can be virtuous. Finally, Chapter 4 develops metaphysical and moral concepts of being a "person" and discusses the relation between being a rational animal and meriting moral respect. The humanist, egalitarian principle that all and only humans merit basic moral rights—"human rights"—is shown to be unjustified on four different grounds: logico-linguistic, phenomenological, transcendental, and consequential.

"No man is an island," the saying goes, and the same applies to moral issues. The following four chapters range far from explicitly animal liberation issues. This is because animal liberation issues arise in the context of a complex tradition of moral concerns, concepts, principles, and theories and must be resolved within that context, if calls for liberating animals are not to seem pretentious moral garb for personal preferences and affections. Consequently, we must begin by under-standing that general context before we can fruitfully focus on specifically animal liberation issues, and, as just indicated, the dimension of that context that it is most important for advocates of animal liberation to explore and test is the moral (in)significance of reason.

1

Why Should I Be Rational?

ALTHOUGH IT seems straightforward enough, "Why should I be rational?" is actually a rather peculiar little question. As a philosophical question, it seems to beg the question, for it presumes that we should be rational. "No, you shouldn't be rational" is a relevant answer to "Should I be rational?" but not to "*Why* should I be rational?" The question thus seems insincere, even unphilosophical. It asks for a rationalization of a commitment already made. It seeks reasons to cover a commitment not based on those reasons. But isn't that hypocritical? Isn't basing our commitments on the reasons offered to justify those commitments an essential part of being a rational person? Surely, sincerely rational people do not go fishing for supportive reasons after they have made their commitment. Thus, "Why should I be rational?" is a self-destroying question. Someone asking this question is not acting rationally.

On the other hand, if we ask the real question, "Should I be rational?," how would we go about answering it? Would we offer reasons in support of a positive answer? But if we are not already committed to rationality, of what relevance are reasons? Offering reasons in support of the conclusion that we should not be rational is even more absurd. We could turn to threats and fine rhetoric, of course, but are these *answers* to the question? Only reasons *answer* "Should I . . . ?" questions. Consequently, if we ask "Should I be rational?," we have either already answered it for ourselves or are asking a question that cannot be answered. Asking questions that answer themselves or that cannot be answered at all is foolish. So someone asking this question is also acting irrationally.

Thus, to ask "Why should I be rational?" or "Should I be rational?" is to be either a hypocrite or a fool. That is not a pleasant pair of options. Perhaps that is why Aristotle sagely advises us not even to bother trying to talk to someone who is not precommitted to the laws of reason and why Kant simply presumes, at the foundations of morality, that rational is what we ought to strive to be. But,

3

curiously enough, "Hypocrite or fool?" is also not an uncommon dilemma; the history of moral philosophy is studded with people who must be either hypocrites or fools. These are people who commit themselves to absolute moral principles. As soon as moralists say, "You should always . . . ," they are deluged with counter-examples that force them either to start making myriad exceptions to their rules or to hold to those rules by staunchly maintaining that what is obviously wrong is right. Perhaps the would-be rationalist is just beset by the devils of absolutism. Perhaps "(Why) should I be rational?" is such a peculiar question because we presume "Thou shalt be rational!" is an eleventh, absolute commandment chiseled on those famous tablets by some wandering, irreverent member of Socrates' tribe. Perhaps the proper response to the question is "Sometimes I should be rational, and sometimes I shouldn't." That's not very exciting, but it may be rational.

I. "Rationality" and Its Alternatives

But what are we going to be when we're not going to be rational? Certainly the answer cannot be simply "irrational." That would be preposterous. Do we ever sit down and weigh the pros and cons of being rational, then conclude, "All things considered, I think it would be better for me to be irrational"? Of course not. Rational vs. irrational is—except, perhaps, for surrealistic artists—just a comical straw man.

If we set aside the straw man, in what contexts might we really be counseled to stop being or doing X and to be rational instead? What could be the alternative Xs where being rational or not being rational is a real issue? And what would "rational" refer to in opposition to these alternatives? Only if we can answer these questions will we be able to make sense of "(Why) should I be rational?".

Like "moral," "rational" still usually has a strongly positive evaluative meaning. It is an honorific term (especially among philosophers). So if a proponent of Y can succeed in getting it labeled "the rational alternative," that is tantamount to winning the debate. Consequently, there are few, if any, cases where the alternative of rational vs. X would actually be debated with "rational" being used to designate one of the options. However, there are some cases where, before even getting to the evaluative issue, Y would be a much more natural candidate than X for being labeled "rational." Consider the following:

1. Being calm vs. being emotional. The opposition of reason to emotion is not merely part of philosophical lore. It is common to counsel someone who is letting her feelings or desires dictate her beliefs and actions to stop that and be rational.

2. Facing facts vs. hoping against hope. A mother who, ten years after her son was reported missing in action in Vietnam, still keeps his room clean, sets a place for him at dinner, and expects him home soon may be accused of not being rational.

3. Being a professional vs. being a crackpot. Someone who does research following procedures not respected by certified experts in the field or who develops theories using categories and hypotheses not accepted by the relevant professional community may be considered eccentric, possessed, to have lost his scientific perspective, or otherwise not to be rational.

4. Debating the issues vs. relying on rhetoric. We may accuse our opponent's speech, at least, of not being rational, if the opponent relies on rhetoric rather than facts and logic to sway the audience.

5. Being tough-minded vs. being tender-minded. Certainly, those who condemn belief in unverifiable propositions and reliance on revelation, intellectual intuition, and other such mystical sources of "truth" consider themselves to be the Swiss guard of rationality.

These cases give us something concrete to work with. The contexts of opposition give content to being rational and indicate what may be presented as evidence for and against "the rational alternative." These are real issues, without the foolishness of trying to sway an irrational person with reasons or of presenting reasons in defense of being irrational. Advocates of emotion, hope, revolution, rhetoric, or tender-mindedness can, without making fools of themselves, respond to the imperative "Be rational!" with the irreverent challenge "Why *should* I be rational?"

How might we try to answer such a challenge? What sorts of reasons are there for the rational alternative in each case? Old, reliable self-interest is a likely candidate for all five cases. If we can show that someone's emotion, hope, revolution, rhetoric, or tender-mindedness is more likely to lead to failure, frustration, and unhappiness than the relevant rational alternative, we will have given that person good reason to take that alternative. If the challenger is a utilitarian, we could appeal to the adverse consequences of nonrational attitudes or actions for the general welfare in any of these cases. Questioning the consistency of proposed nonrationality with an individual's other beliefs and actions and the appeal to "What if everyone did that?" could also be made in each case. Fairness and respect for the audience might be additional issues in the case of rational vs. rhetorical.

Thus, we could argue for the rational alternative in each case on the basis of its superior contributions to self-interest and to attaining the goals of traditional moral principles. The only logical exceptions to this are traditional moral principles, such as Kant's categorical imperative, which presume we should be rational and would, therefore, yield only circular arguments. With these exceptions, however, there are no peculiar conceptual problems with arguing these cases of rational vs. *X*.

But must there always be a compelling argument in favor of the rational alternative? Is it always counter to self-interest and to moral principles to be emotional rather than calm, to hope against hope rather than facing facts, and so forth? Obviously not.

Revulsion, anger, and the actions born of them are appropriate responses to atrocities. Calmly calculating the likely consequences for your own or the general happiness of the possible responses to rape, sadism, and genocide could be immoral. "That *must* be stopped!," we say; "those who won't take risks to stop such savagery are cowards," and "we'll worry about the consequences later!" The idea, let alone ideal, of a calm, calculating morality stripped of emotion is what so appalled Charles Dickens about the utilitarians. Outside the philosopher's study, calm calculation is not always preferred over emotional commitment and exuberance. Out there, rational vs. emotional is an open issue to be settled by the specifics of differing cases.

The same is true in our other four cases. Hoping against hope is sometimes the only way of preserving sanity, struggle, and life itself. How can we be faulted (*ceteris paribus*), on the basis either of self-interest or moral principle, in holding fast to hope in such circumstances? Such hope can be the stuff of which heroes are made. Again, pursuing crackpot ideas can lead to scientific revolutions, and inspiring but unsupported rhetoric may be the only way to move an audience in an emergency. Finally, if believing in something that is unverifiable (e.g., the existence of a benevolent God) merely comforts and inspires people, what is wrong with such belief? Those who condemn such belief *a priori* simply convict themselves of being intolerant, evangelical positivists.

Being rational is in any of these cases at best a *prima facie* obligation. It may not even be that. Being intellectuals, philosophers are predisposed to believe that taking the rational alternative will usually lead to maximizing self-interest, the general welfare, and/or the attainment of other moral ideals such as justice and respect for human rights. But is that obviously true? If we did not repress our emotions, would we be worse off? Rousseau, Marcuse, and others all argue we would not. They maintain that the repression of emotion is not the answer to immorality but the source of it.[1] Again, if we encouraged anarchy in scientific research, would that cripple such research? Paul Feyerabend claims the opposite.[2] Finally, if we took away people's religions, would we increase the general happiness? That certainly is unlikely. Even the *prima facie* status of an obligation to be rational may simply be a prejudice cherished by philosophers and others who have already committed themselves to the life of reason.

II. The Methodological Counterattack

But now we must face the philosopher's revenge, the step up to a higher level of abstraction. Even if we are not morally bound always or even *prima facie* to be rational in the above senses, what about the procedure used to decide when we should and when we should not take the rational alternative? Is there not a moral duty to make this a rational decision, one based on good *reasons*? Is there not another, more general, methodological sense of rationality, one having to do with the systematic, impartial gathering and logical use of evidence, to which we have a categorical obligation?

No. Once again, consider the alternatives. What would we be doing, if we were not basing our beliefs on systematic, impartial, logically organized evidence? We might be letting our emotions run away with us, which is the first case above. We might be engaging in wishful thinking, case two, or being swayed by rhetoric, case four. We might be relying on uncertified evidence, case three, or we might be relying on intuition, revelation, mysticism, or simply our will to believe, case five. Of course, there may be other alternatives as well; there is no way to guarantee that a list of contexts of opposition for a concept is complete. However, there is no reason to believe that any contexts not considered here are logically different from the five we have considered. Emotion, hope, rhetoric, eccentricity, and intuition are all ways of determining what we are going to do, no less than is reason. Even if some philosophers might hesitate to label such determinations "decisions," we have been working at "the methodological level" throughout this discussion; how could a discussion of contexts of opposition for reason do otherwise? Consequently, the conclusions of the previous section do not stand in jeopardy of being overturned for neglect of that level.

Nonetheless, we must acknowledge that there is a bit of truth to the idea that there is an abstract level to reason at which a categorical obligation exists. As already noted, in spite of romantic and existential inroads, "rational" is still an honorific term with a strong prescriptive punch. While this prescriptive meaning is constant throughout its uses, the descriptive content of the term will vary with the contexts in which it is employed. Consequently, if one takes a Platonic turn and identifies the "essence" of rationality with this unvarying meaning of the term, then one will readily discover an abstract level containing a categorical obligation. At this level, "Be rational!" is every bit as categorical as "Be good!" and "Do right!" And for exactly the same reason: all three of these imperatives are pure and, consequently, vacuous prescriptions to do what one ought to do or be as one ought to be. Of course, "rational" is not as purely a prescriptive term as are "good" and "right," but as soon as we start filling out the term's descriptive meaning, as we did above, "Be rational!" loses its categorical standing. Many philosophers have suspected that categorical obligations are always trivial and significant obligations are never categorical. What we have seen of rationality here confirms those suspicions.

Still, how do we tell whether a case is one where we should be calm or emotional, orthodox or revolutionary, tough-minded or tender-minded, and so on? Like so many other practical matters, it is a case of guesswork beforehand and "Did it work?" afterward.

There is no way to be certain that today's crackpot will not be tomorrow's laureate, that someone's life would not be even more crippled without futile hopes, that emotion will lead to disaster, that a great orator will not save the day, or that religious beliefs will not inspire extra courage and even lead to scientific discoveries. Instinct, dispositions, common sense, educated intuition, emotional ties, and moral commitments all play major roles in determining what we notice, what we recognize as relevant information, and what we take to be its significance when opting for the rational or the nonrational alternative. And since we seldom get a chance to try it again the other way, even hindsight can usually tell us only whether what we did worked well or ill. It can seldom tell us whether taking the other alternative would have fared better or worse. Not being rational is risky business, but then, so is being rational. Rationality is, after all, still a part of life.

III. The Moral of the Story

Well, what does all this amount to? We have found a way to make sense of "Why should I be rational?" As a challenge, it may be irreverent, but it is neither insincere nor foolish. It is an aggressive way of asking the honest question, "Should I be rational?" This is an open question. In different contexts, being rational is being different things, is opposed to different things, and is not always the best alternative. Rationality is not always the most effective way to further self-interest or to achieve the general welfare, justice, the maintenance of human rights, or whatever other general moral principles have led one to ask a moral "Should I be rational?" in a particular context.

People can, of course, commit themselves to "the rational way of life," that is, a life of moderate emotion, tough-mindedness, professionalism, facing facts, and eschewing purple prose. Remaining faithful to this way of life can itself become a moral principle and a point of honor. Some of us are predisposed by temperament and training to see this as a, even the most, respectable way of life. Those of us educated in the history of philosophy, which expressly opposes rationality to "animal desires," "womanish sentiment," and the Sophist's forked tongue, have certainly been conditioned to see the life of reason as the ideal of human existence. For people committed to the life of reason, "Should I be rational?" is not a question of the best means to a moral end but a question of which they value more, the ideal of rationality or the other moral principles (or self-interest) with which it has come into conflict. The answer to that question obviously must vary from person to person and from conflict to conflict.

To say that we cannot prove that there is a categorical moral obligation to be rational is not to criticize commitment to the life of reason. Dedication to the ideal of rationality is no more unjustifiable than dedication to the general welfare, fair play, human rights, or any other moral value. Morality, too, is still a part of life and, consequently, shares its uncertainties. As Kant recognized but misinterpreted, a being who is never in doubt as to what is the right thing to do would not be a "moral" being. In our world, where the quest for certainty is out of place, not all prejudgments are bad; some are even essential for daily life, morality, and certified judging itself to get started. Freed from the compulsion to hide commitments behind deductions, definitions, and intuitions and accompanied by a tolerant appreciation of life's diverse values, the rational way of life can make its contribution to the well-being of those who cherish it without unduly disturbing others. That may well be rationality's most general and surest virtue.

2

Where Reason Enters In— and Where It Doesn't

JOHN ALEXANDER entered the Powell Street branch of the San Francisco Savings Bank shortly after 2:00 P.M. yesterday. When he reached the window of teller Jane East, he quickly took a pistol from his pocket and began to order her to give him all the money in her cash drawer. Just as Alexander started to make his demand, Barney Gleason, a bank customer, rushed up to East's window, shoved Alexander aside, and simultaneously knocked Alexander's pistol to the floor. Bob Mann, the guard on duty, saw the gun, quickly scooped it up, and turned the tables on Alexander, who was soon handcuffed and taken off by the police. James Metzger, the bank manager, warmly thanked Gleason and said he would recommend him for a "San Francisco Certificate of Merit." These certificates are awarded monthly to citizens who risk their lives for their fellow San Franciscans.

Suppose you read this little story in the *San Francisco Chronicle* one morning, and your reaction is "Hold on there! I know Barney Gleason, and I was in the bank that afternoon and saw what happened, and Barney doesn't deserve any certificate of merit!" What might you have in mind? It could be any of the following:

(i) Barney was as startled as the rest of us when he saw that pistol pop out. We had no idea a robbery was in progress. Barney thought Alexander had cut in front of him in line, and having already had a trying day, he just blew his cool and stormed up to the teller to demand that he be served first. That's why he pushed Alexander out of the way and, incidentally, knocked the pistol to the floor.

(ii) Barney wants to get a loan from that bank and for some time now he's been trying to find a way to get in good with Metzger, the bank manager. Barney has confided to me that he figured that stopping the robbery would make Metzger feel obligated to give him the loan. After all, Metzger certainly wouldn't want the papers to hear that he had refused a loan to someone who had risked his life to stop the bank from being robbed.

(iii) Barney has told me that he believed that Alexander's pistol was only a toy and that he was much stronger than Alexander. Consequently, Barney figured that he could stop the robbery without putting himself in any danger. So he wasn't acting courageously at all.

(iv) Stopping that robbery was just a reflex action for Barney. He's not a reflective person at all; he's one of those people who just follow orders and carry on tradition. I'm sure he never thought about the danger he was putting us all in or wondered whether foiling the robbery was the right thing to do. After all, Alexander might have been some kind of Robin Hood, and that bank has been charging usurious interest rates and making an indecent profit for years now. Such considerations would never enter Barney's little mind; he wouldn't have the slightest idea how to deal with them. Since Barney didn't really evaluate the situation for himself, he doesn't really deserve any praise for what he did. You might as well praise the bank camera for taking Alexander's picture!

All these cases exemplify ways in which we refer to someone's "reasons" for acting when we wish to establish the moral value of an action. What do these cases tell us about the relation between "reason" and the moral value of action?

I. Incidentally Good Actions

In case (i), Barney inadvertently foils the robbery by accidentally knocking the gun from Alexander's hand. Not only does Barney not act for the purpose of preventing a crime; he does not even realize a robbery is in progress when he pushes Alexander aside and, coincidentally, knocks the gun to the floor. Under these conditions, it would be inappropriate to say that Barney acted courageously, and he certainly would not deserve a certificate of merit for what he did.

Nonetheless, it would not be nonsensical, bizarre, or even unusual to evaluate what Barney did—that is, knocking Alexander's gun to the floor, thereby contributing significantly to the foiling of the robbery—as the morally right thing to do. The honest people in the bank would surely agree that what Barney did was the right thing to do and would be relieved that he did it, even if inadvertently. If asked, "Did Barney do the right thing?," ordinary people would not answer, "We can't tell until we know why he did it." Nor would they say after learning that what Barney did he did only accidentally, "No, it wasn't the right thing to do, because he didn't do it on purpose." While Barney's not knowing the moral significance of his action and his lack of moral purpose in doing what he did would disqualify his action from being courageous and deserving special commendation, what he did remains the morally right thing to do in that situation and would commonly be recognized as such.

That actions can have moral value independent of their agents' understanding of what they are doing and purpose in doing what they are doing (henceforth, "agent-independent value") is readily understood on the basis of several moral theories. For example, according to classical act-utilitarianism, the moral value of what is done derives from its consequences for the general welfare. Assuming that foiling the robbery contributes more than other courses of action would have to the general welfare, what Barney did was the morally right thing to do. Since the direct consequences of what Barney did are the same whether he did it purposely or inadvertently, the moral value of what he did that derives from those consequences cannot depend on whether he purposely or inadvertently foiled the robbery.

I say "direct" consequences for there will be indirect consequences for the general welfare that will differ depending on the agent's understanding of and purpose for doing what he or she does and on the public's knowledge of the agent's understanding and purpose. For example, the public's sense of well-being will be enhanced if it believes that there are still courageous people about who are willing to get involved and prevent crimes. Of course, this contribution to the public's sense of well-being will not be produced by the accidental foiling of a crime (presuming the public knows of its accidental nature). Nonetheless, such indirect, agent-dependent differences do not affect the point being made here, which is simply that actions have agent-independent moral value. That this is not their only moral value will be abundantly acknowledged, indeed, emphasized, as we proceed.

Another way of understanding this agent-independent dimension of the moral value of actions is provided by some recent moral philosophers who argue that actions that can properly be described in paradigmatically moral ways have moral value.[1] What Barney did is properly described as "foiling a bank robbery" and "contributing significantly to the prevention of a crime." Both of these are paradigmatically moral descriptions.

It might be objected that these descriptions are ambiguous, since "foiling" and "contributing" may refer to purpose as well as to behavior. As the discussion of case (ii) will make clear, such ambiguity is to be expected in descriptions of action, since we commonly do not clearly separate motivation and behavior in our interpretation of action. However, even if we conscientiously scrub "foiling" and "contributing" clean of any hint of motivation, what Barney did retains moral value. Even at a strictly behavioral level, foiling robberies and preventing crimes remain paradigms of morally right action; they are exemplars of the kind of action that ought to occur in a just world. So on behavioral-paradigm grounds, as well as on act-utilitarian grounds, we can understand how Barney's inadvertently foiling the robbery has agent-independent moral value.

There is a real difference between acting in accordance with a rule and acting

according to a rule, and moral philosophers have often made much of this difference. Aristotle claims and Kant insists that only in the latter case, where one's
action is motivated by recognition of and respect for the moral rule, does the
action have moral value.[2] Such a limitation on moral value amounts to claiming
that whenever we evaluate the morality of an action, what we are concerned with
is the moral character of the agent. It is not what he did nor the consequences of
what was done but the good or evil will of the agent that is the source of the moral
value of his action and the object of our concern as we try to judge that moral
value.

Such an analysis represents a considerable oversimplification of common
moral experience. There is no denying that ordinarily right actions and good
consequences can be discredited by being motivated by an evil will, as when a
con artist sets up a mark for a later, larger kill with small acts of friendship and
self-sacrifice. However, there is also no denying that ordinarily good will can be
discredited if it leads to evil actions, as when someone sincerely seeks to save a
friend's soul, which has become endangered by a sinful way of life, by killing that
person before she totally damns herself. R. M. Hare's famous, fanatic Nazi con-
centration camp guard, who would throw himself into the oven if he discovered
that he is Jewish, is another example of how good—here, impartial, universalizing, dutiful—character cannot make what is ordinarily a wrong action right.[3]
What is morally wrong with exterminating people is not merely that you could
not will it to be done to you.

Furthermore, when morally evaluating an action, we may be primarily concerned not with an issue of character but with what was done or with the consequences of the action, as when we try to find out whether some tools were bor-
rowed or stolen or try to decide whether to enforce a law the enforcing of which
we suspect will be more injurious than the crimes the law was intended to prevent.
While attempts to restrict the moral value of action to agent-independent, utilitarian and behavioral-paradigm considerations are mistaken because of their
omission of the issue of character, so attempts to base the moral value of action
exclusively on an evaluation of the agent's character are also mistaken, because of
the agent-independent dimensions of the moral value of action. The moral world
contains wonders undreamt of in all such simplifying philosophies.

That evil will can discredit the moral value of ordinarily good consequences
does not entail that moral value derives from the will. An alternative explanation
of this discrediting effect is that motive is one among several contributors to the
overall moral value of action, with consequences being another contributor. This
alternative also explains how the moral value of action motivated by an ordinarily
good will can be compromised by bad consequences. As we shall see, this multi-
dimensional view of moral value accords well with and provides plausible explanations of many other of our common moral practices.

However, at the moment, it may be objected that even if actions may have moral value independent of their agents' character, this is not relevant to the present case, for Barney did not *act* when he inadvertently knocked the gun from Alexander's hand. Barney's foiling the robbery in case (i) is "a mere event," a natural occurrence dictated by the laws of nature. Barney's accidentally knocking the gun from Alexander's hand is no more an action and, therefore, no more a proper object of moral evaluation than would be an earthquake shaking the gun loose.

Another distinction frequently encountered in moral philosophies is that between "action" and "event," that is, between things which (under the relevant description) were done on purpose and things which (under the relevant description) were not done on purpose. Undeniably, this distinction is morally significant in some contexts, such as those of fixing guilt and commending valor. However, when the agent-independent value of what was done is what is at issue, as is the case here, a distinction based on the presence or absence of purpose in the agent must be irrelevant.

Furthermore, although this action/event distinction is a useful tool for certain analyses, it does not provide an accurate analysis of the ordinary meaning of "action." For example, assume that you are an eyewitness to Alexander's attempted bank robbery and that a reporter asks you to give her an account of the action in the bank that afternoon. You say, "Alexander waited in line, walked up to the teller, and pulled out a gun; another man rushed up to the same teller and pushed Alexander aside; and the guard picked the gun up from the floor and handcuffed Alexander." The reporter will certainly ask you, "But how did the gun end up on the floor?" If you say, "Oh, the second man knocked the gun from the robber's hand, but I believe that was inadvertent, so I don't include it as part of the action," you will certainly sound strange. Once again, there is more to "action" than the traditional, simple action/event dichotomy would lead us to believe.

Nevertheless, if philosophical tradition precludes labeling inadvertent doings "actions," so be it, but it will not follow from that stipulative definition that inadvertent doings are not proper objects of moral evaluation. While inadvertent doings cannot be objects of moral evaluations that directly or indirectly refer to character, they can, as just demonstrated, still be objects of agent-independent moral evaluations. Refusing them a favored label cannot change that.

Indeed, all sorts of things besides purposive actions can be objects of moral evaluation. Words and gestures are obscene. Paintings, statues, pictures, and films are pornographic. Interest rates and clothing are indecent. Being an unwed mother is disgraceful. Being illegitimate or unemployed is dishonorable. And the murderer being struck by lightning as he makes his escape is poetic justice. (I am not claiming that all these moral evaluations are correct, only that they are common and comprehensible.) Since moral commandments, principles, rules, impera-

tives, and prescriptions are concerned with directing action and since moral philosophy has been primarily concerned with providing or analyzing this moral
equipment, it is easy for those working in this field to get and give the impression
that all moral evaluation is the evaluation of action. However, as the examples
above remind us, this is not so.

Furthermore, it will not do to say that things, conditions, states, relations,
and the like take on moral value only because they encourage or inhibit moral or
immoral actions. Sometimes the relation is quite the reverse. For example, the
activity of dividing a widow's estate among her surviving children according to
how much each child cared and sacrificed for his or her mother is the morally
right thing to do because it leads to a just distribution of the estate. It is from the
fairness of the resultant condition that the activity here derives its moral value,
not *vice versa*. Again, the activities of slave trading are morally wrong because
they contribute to a condition that is an offense against people's moral dignity,
that is, against that "minimal self-respect" to which all innocent people are morally entitled.[4] We do not disvalue slavery in order to discourage slave trading;
rather, we disvalue the activity of slave trading, because we disvalue the condition
of slavery. Thus, even if influencing purposive action is a particularly common
and important function of making moral evaluations, inadvertent doings and
other nonactions can also have certain kinds of moral value and can be the primary objects of our moral evaluations.

Through our everyday moral experience, and especially our popular moral
literature (e.g., religious teachings and edifying stories), we develop an image,
albeit a rather nebulous one, of a morally good world. Philosophers from Plato,
in his *Republic*, to Rawls, in *A Theory of Justice*, have tried to focus and enhance
this image. One thing that is clear about these common images of moral utopia is
that here morality is not restricted to people behaving properly; rather, here "all is
right *with the world*." Consequently, when we morally evaluate the real world, it
is often in terms of how much or how little it conforms to our image of a morally
good world. This gives rise to evaluations of nonactions as readily as to evaluations of actions. For example, we question the justice of someone being born
blind or being killed by lightning. Perhaps such ideal evaluations are not as
purposeful as moral imperatives for action, but they are undeniably a part of
common moral practice. Apparently, and contrary to the desires of those who
would make of morality a pragmatically tight enterprise, common moral practice
does not recognize an obligation to confine itself to the purposeful, either for its
objects of or occasions for making moral evaluations.

In concluding this discussion of the moral value of inadvertent doings, I think
it is worth emphasizing that acknowledging that actions and nonactions can have
agent-independent moral value should not be confused with claiming that some
actions and nonactions are "intrinsically" morally right or wrong or good or bad.

I think the agent-independent moral value of foiling a robbery, aiding someone in need, goods being distributed fairly, and many similar actions and nonactions can be adequately explicated by a combination of utilitarian and behavioral-paradigm considerations. While these two moral theories explain how actions and nonactions can have moral value regardless of an agent's purposes, character, or reasons (if any) for acting, they leave this agent-independent moral value dependent on moral tradition and on the action's or nonaction's effects on the feelings of sentient beings and our estimations and evaluations of these effects. Thus, acknowledging the existence of agent-independent moral value does not require postulating any sort of mysterious, objective, intrinsic value-property that certain actions and nonactions possess and others lack. It requires acknowledging only that the agent's reasons (if any) for doing what he or she did are but one among the several sources of the moral value of what was done and of other things.

II. Ulterior Motives

Turning to case (ii), here Barney does recognize that Alexander is robbing the bank. Furthermore, he understands that this will customarily (and especially by the bank manager) be considered a bad thing and that foiling the robbery will be considered a good thing, and he purposely moves to foil the robbery. The question that is raised about the moral value of Barney's action in this case is the question of ulterior motives, for Barney acts to foil the robbery in order to make Mr. Metzger, the bank manager, feel obligated to give him the loan he wants. The question of ulterior motives provides several insights into the complexity of moral evaluation.

First, this issue shows that utilitarian and behavioral-paradigm considerations cannot provide an adequate explication of the moral value of action. If we come to believe that Barney had ulterior motives for foiling the robbery, the moral value of what he did will be seriously compromised. But the consequences of what Barney did and the propriety of describing what he did as "preventing a crime" are not affected by his motive for what he did. Consequently, there must be another, nonutilitarian, nonbehavioral-paradigm dimension to our initial moral evaluation of the action that is discredited by the discovery of ulterior motives.

Utilitarians might object to this conclusion by reminding us of the above-mentioned indirect consequence of what Barney did (i.e., our enhanced sense of well-being due to our belief, after witnessing Barney's heroics, that there still are courageous people about). Utilitarians might claim that this indirect consequence of his action is affected by Barney's motive and that it is this effect that compromises our initial moral evaluation of his action.

However, while it is true that discovering that Barney acted from ulterior motives would eliminate this indirect, beneficial consequence of Barney's action, it is not this elimination that leads us to lower our moral evaluation of Barney's action when we discover that he acted from ulterior motives. Rather than this indirect consequence being the source of this agent-dependent dimension of the moral value of Barney's action, this indirect consequence and the subsequent elimination of it are the results of our understanding and evaluation of Barney's motive and the subsequent change in that understanding and evaluation. It is because we place a higher moral value on moral motive than on ulterior motives and have lowered our moral evaluation of Barney's action, because of discovering his ulterior motives, that our sense of well-being is not enhanced in case (ii) by what Barney did. This relation is just the opposite of what our supposed utilitarians are claiming. Consequently, this attempt to incorporate this agent-dependent dimension of moral value into utilitarianism will not work.[5]

Second, this additional dimension is not adequately explicated in terms of intentionally acting to do what is morally right. Barney recognizes the moral significance of foiling a robbery and moves to do something that will have that significance. He purposely acts to do what is morally right. But ulterior motives will compromise the moral value of Barney's action in spite of its being intentionally moral. Therefore, although this agent-dependent dimension requires acting intentionally, knowingly, purposely doing what is moral does not suffice to fulfill the requirements for this moral value.

Third, this insufficiency is not due solely to the agent's doing something he believes others will consider moral but that he does not so value. When we discover that someone had ulterior motives for acting morally, we feel misled, and this feeling will be particularly acute if we discover that the agent did what he did because he believes others consider that sort of thing moral, even though he does not. However, even if the agent holds the common moral evaluation of what he did, the issue of ulterior motives remains. We do not need to presume that Barney does not really consider bank robbery to be a moral offense in order to understand that in case (ii) he has ulterior motives for what he does and to find that these motives compromise the moral value of what he does. If Barney were being denied a certificate of merit because of his ulterior motives, he could not adequately defend himself by saying, "But I believe bank robbery is a crime; I wasn't acting hypocritically when I foiled the robbery!" Just as morally proper motivation requires acting intentionally (i.e., knowingly, purposely doing what is moral), so it requires acting sincerely, but just as acting intentionally is not enough to meet the requirements of proper motivation, so acting intentionally and sincerely does not suffice to meet those requirements.

Fourth, there is a morally significant difference between doing something that is morally right for no reason (inadvertently) and doing the same thing for the wrong reason (from ulterior motives). Discovering that Barney only accidentally foiled the bank robbery would imbue what he did with a kind of innocence. Since he is a human being, presumably capable of acting in a morally properly motivated manner, the question of motive is relevant to evaluating what Barney did, even if he did it inadvertently, while that question would not be at all relevant to evaluating a light fixture's falling and knocking the gun from Alexander's hand. Consequently, discovering that Barney only accidentally foiled the robbery denies his action a moral value it might have had, a moral value the falling light fixture could never have. Nevertheless, Barney's accidentally foiling the robbery has the kind of innocence concerning motive that the falling fixture's fortuitously foiling the robbery would have. If it was all an accident, we were mistaken in believing that Barney acted courageously and will be disappointed to discover that he did not so act, but we will not feel misled in the way we do when we discover ulterior motives. Discovering inadvertence closes the door on evaluating motive; it indicates that although this looked like a case where motive was to be evaluated, this is not really such a case. Discovering ulterior motives keeps that door open and leaves us evaluating this case as one where a person understood the moral significance of the situation and his action, could have acted for the morally proper reason and seemed to do so, but actually failed to do so and acted on the basis of some other motive instead.

But how are we to understand this failure? I propose the following: when morally evaluating actions, we commonly consider them to be expressions of character. By "character," I mean the values a person holds, including his priorities among those values, and his readiness to act on those values and priorities. If we see someone risking his life to prevent a crime, we interpret that action as expressing (1) the agent's recognition of the moral wrongness of the crime, the moral rightness of preventing the crime, and the high priority of preventing the crime, and (2) the agent's willingness to risk personal harm or loss to do what is right. Having this expressive value is an important part of what is meant by calling the action "courageous." This expressive value indicates what we must add to intentionality and sincerity in order to have an adequate analysis of morally proper motivation: an action is morally properly motivated when the agent is moved to act by his commitment to the moral rightness of the action (this rightness may be based on utilitarian, behavioral-paradigm, religious, or other considerations). An action so moved can be said to have been "done for the right reason."

When we discover that Barney had ulterior motives for foiling the robbery, we discover that we have been misled about his character. Although his foiling the robbery was not inadvertent this time, it still fails to express the commitment to acting on moral value even in the face of clear and present personal danger that we originally thought it expressed. In some cases such misleading is unintentional, as when someone foils a bank robbery simply to protect his own money and does not care what others think of what he is doing. In such cases, our initial moral evaluation of the action is certainly deflated but not as much as in a case, like Barney's, where the misleading is intentional. When ulterior motives involve this dimension of using moral value for personal gain, misleading takes on the added dimension of deception, and the deflation of the initial moral value of the action is severe.[6]

Whether mild or severe, the deflation of moral value due to ulterior motives teaches us one more thing about the moral value of action: moral motive is not the same thing as prudence. While "ulterior motives" need not refer to instances of self-interest—logically, any other motive than the apparent commitment to moral value that seemed to motivate the action will be an "ulterior" motive—in common moral practice, when we raise the question of ulterior motives for an action, we are asking whether the agent "had something to gain" from an apparently self-sacrificing, selfless, noble, charitable, courageous, or otherwise similarly virtuous action. Discovering that the agent had something to gain from the action does not, of course, prove that the action was motivated by the prospect of such gain, but if we take the further step and conclude that it was the prospect of personal gain that motivated the action, the moral value of the action will be seriously compromised.

Theories of enlightened self-interest may be able to show that prudence can sometimes motivate the same actions that moral character would motivate. Since these actions will have some of the same consequences and fit under some of the same moral-behavioral paradigms as morally motivated actions, these prudent actions will have some of the same agent-independent moral values as the morally motivated actions. Nonetheless, the common moral question of ulterior motives shows that prudence and moral character are different motives and are of significantly different moral value.

Furthermore, prudence will not always lead to the same action as moral character. For example, no matter how much we may abstractly recognize that keeping promises, being honest, and the like are important for social existence and that social existence is important for our personal well-being, we still know that when a cashier accidentally gives us a twenty-dollar bill in change instead of a ten, and we must face the issue of being honest and returning the extra money, our society and general well-being will not crumble if we keep the twenty, any more than they have been destroyed by the myriad other petty crimes that are a part of everyday life. In this, as in so many other everyday moral situations, morality is opposed to self-interest. Consequently, the agent-dependent dimension of the moral value of action cannot be adequately derived from self-interest, no matter how enlightened, educated, or otherwise "rational" it might be.

III. Acting Out of Context

Turning to case (iii), we may assume that Barney intentionally acts to foil the robbery and is motivated to do so by his belief that (*ceteris paribus*) we should try to prevent crimes whenever we have the opportunity to do so. So here Barney does the right thing, on utilitarian and behavioral-paradigm grounds and also does it for the right reason. The issue here is whether his action is courageous. Obviously, moral actions, such as acts of charity, can be right and done for the right reason yet not be courageous. The question of courage is not relevant to all moral situations. But foiling a bank robbery is ordinarily a situation to which the question of courage is relevant. Seeing someone rush up and knock the gun from a robber's hand, as Barney did, we would immediately interpret his action as expressing courage, unless and until proven otherwise.

An action is courageous only if it expresses the agent's commitment to moral value and his or her willingness to act on that commitment even when doing so has a significant chance of leading to serious personal loss or harm. It is the requirement of willingness to act *even in the face of personal danger* that forces us beyond the issue of motive when evaluating courage and forces us to consider situations and the agent's understanding of his or her situation as well. For an action to be courageous, it must be done in a dangerous situation, and the agent must believe the situation is dangerous for him or her.

If the agent believes the situation is dangerous, but it is not, his or her action may be judged theatrical, comic, or embarrassing, rather than courageous. Suppose that Alexander is clearly drunk and attempting to rob the bank with a red plastic water pistol. Everyone around notices these facts except Barney, who rushes up and knocks Alexander's water pistol to the floor as if it were a real gun in the hand of a dangerous criminal. Barney would certainly be congratulated for being a decent person willing to get involved, but it would also be thought that he overreacted to the situation. He would probably feel embarrassed at having missed the obvious, and the other people in the bank would probably be somewhat amused at his misplaced heroics. Barney would certainly not be awarded a certificate of merit in this situation. Even if the situation were not one in which there obviously was really no danger—suppose Alexander appears to be a serious robber and his pistol is a convincing imitation—Barney's action would still not quite be courageous. This time there would be relief rather than amusement among bystanders, and Barney would not be embarrassed and would be more warmly congratulated and recognized as the kind of person who is capable of acting courageously. But this particular action would not fully merit the label of "courageous"; people are not awarded certificates of merit for stopping robbers with toy pistols.

Since Barney is to be recommended for a certificate of merit, we may assume that Alexander was a serious robber with a real gun, but according to the extra information in case (iii), Barney does not believe that he faces any real danger in foiling the robbery. This belief is sufficient to disqualify his action from being courageous, because it undercuts the relevant part of the expressive value of his action. Since Barney does not believe he is in danger, his action cannot express his willingness to act on his moral commitments even in the face of danger. His action may initially appear to have this expressive value—unless he acts with a nonchalance that indicates he does not recognize any danger—but discovering how he understood the situation will discredit that initial impression. Depending on the situation, that impression might turn into admiration of Barney's supreme self-confidence, if he, like Achilles, coolly regards all opponents as his inferiors and all situations as within his power to control, so that he sees no danger where mere mortals like us start to cringe. Nevertheless, there would be a certain hypocrisy in his accepting a certificate of merit (should his understanding of the situation go undiscovered), for he would know that he had not put his moral commitments to the test and, consequently, had not earned such a certificate.

Courage is not the only moral value of action that requires a certain kind of situation and a relevantly adequate understanding of the situation. There are similar requirements for acting loyally, kindly, temperately, honestly, compassionately, fairly, and so on. Only the simplest, most widely applicable moral evaluations of action, such as right or wrong, seem to lack this situation-understanding dimension and to be adequately analyzed in terms of consequences, behavioral paradigms, and motives. When we progress to richer evaluative characterizations of moral action, the kind of situation in which the action occurs and the agent's understanding of the situation must be added to the analysis.

IV. Moral Agents, Philosophers, and Judges

Case (iv) raises a further question of understanding. Here, the moral value of Barney's action is challenged on the grounds that he is an unreflective person who merely follows moral custom. He has never seriously questioned the moral values he was taught as a child and would be unable to mount an argument to justify his moral beliefs. According to some philosophers, this would severely compromise the moral value not only of Barney's action in the bank but of his whole way of life as well. Here is how Peter Singer puts the matter:

> The notion of living according to ethical standards is tied up with the notion of defending the way one is living, of giving a reason for it, of justifying it. Thus people may do all kinds of things we regard as wrong, yet still be living according to ethical standards, if they are prepared to defend and justify what they do. . . . When, on the

other hand, people cannot put forward any justification for what they do, we may reject their claim to be living according to ethical standards, even if what they do is in accordance with conventional moral principles.[7]

I think that many philosophers would agree with Singer that being ready to offer reasons justifying one's action is an essential part of the moral point of view. After all, what this requirement amounts to is that only those who are ready to engage in moral philosophy (i.e., normative ethics) can occupy the moral point of view. Moral philosophers cannot be expected to argue with that! However, a significant portion of the general, moral public would not accept this close tie between being moral and (being capable of) doing moral philosophy. For example, a committee charged with awarding certificates of merit to morally deserving citizens would never say something like the following: "We know that Barney's action had good consequences, that it is properly described as 'preventing a crime,' that he acted intentionally, that he was motivated by his belief that we should prevent crimes when we have a chance to do so, that Barney put his life in danger through his action, and that he was aware of this danger, but we can't award him a certificate of merit until we have him in here to see if he can provide a moral justification for what he did."

Ordinary, ethical people concerned with the moral value of actions but not with doing moral philosophy would never demand a justification for what Barney did. This is not because it is presumed he could provide such a justification, if he were asked for one. Barney would get his certificate of merit, even if all he could say in response to a call for justification was, "It just seemed like the right thing to do" or "I just felt that was what I ought to do." Indeed, many people would find such responses exemplary expressions of Barney's moral character: such responses indicate a gut-level, immediate, firmly established, intuitive grasp of and commitment to doing what is right, a commitment that will not easily be undercut by fancy rhetoric or seductive, sophisticated argument. For better or worse, unswerving dedication, loyalty, and commitment to recognized moral values have been and still are commonly valued as highly as, or even more highly than, the mastery of "subtle moral reasoning." Comparing the Duke of Wellington with Napoleon, an historian once remarked that "the English have always valued character over intellect"; ordinary moral practice does not indicate that a facility for or readiness to engage in moral reasoning is a necessary condition for acting morally or for living according to moral standards.

Singer is also incorrect in claiming that the requirement of justification, where it does exist, is evenhanded. If one's action conforms to the well-established moral principles of those who are judging its moral value, the agent need not be ready to justify the moral value of his action in order to be judged without reservation to have acted morally. On the other hand, if what was done does not conform to such principles, then one will have to justify his action in order to have it judged a moral action. For example, if Alexander were to claim that his robbing the bank was a morally proper thing to do, he would have to provide a justification for that claim. Justification of unorthodox action is certainly possible; moral justification is not limited to locating particular actions under the most obviously relevant, well-established moral principles. For example, Alexander might argue that he had been swindled by the bank and could not get relief through the courts or that his action was part of a revolutionary socialist plan or that his action was the last, desperate attempt of a man trying to defend a poor neighborhood the bank was trying to redevelop into luxury shops and condominiums. It is because justifications of unorthodox actions can be convincing that reasoned moral change, such as the abolition of slavery, is possible. Still, moral justification is a requirement that operates not in some ideal, impartial vacuum but against the background of moral history, which removes the burden of proof from the shoulders of the conformist and places it on the shoulders of the nonconformist. This may seem unfair, especially to those of us, like Singer, who seek important changes in traditional morality, but it is the way our morality works.

Some may question whether it is possible to believe an action is morally right without being able to offer some justification for that belief. If this were so, then it would be impossible to be morally motivated without being able to offer a justification for what one did. However, I think it is quite possible, even common, to hold moral beliefs for which we have no justification, provided justification is distinguished from rationalization. For better or worse, we seem to have a great ability to come up with reasons for our beliefs and actions that have been brought into question. But these reasons are often merely after-the-fact rationalizations of what we did or believe; they do not provide an explanation or analysis of why we believed when we did it that what we were doing was the right thing to do or of why we hold the beliefs we do. It is only reasons that provide such explanation or analysis that I am calling "justifications." This is not an arbitrary limitation on the use of this term, for being able to rationalize what one has done or believes is of no great moral value. Being able to rationalize what one did certainly cannot support the weight of Peter Singer's contentions, cited above.

Consider the following example. I could offer both utilitarian and Kantian reasons to justify my belief that bank robbery is morally wrong; however, these reasons have nothing to do with why I believe that bank robbery is morally wrong and would not have anything to do with my acting to prevent a bank robbery, should I ever have the occasion and courage to do so. The immorality of bank robbery is a moral value I have never faced as an open, personal question— "an existential question"—so I have never even tried to base my belief about this moral value on reasoning. Nevertheless, I do not view bank robbery in a morally noncommittal way; I believe that bank robbery is morally wrong. Moreover, my many discussions of morality with students, neighbors, nonphilosopher friends, and others lead me to believe that I am far from alone in having such unreasoned moral beliefs. So I conclude that it is quite possible to hold a moral belief without being able to justify (not to be confused with rationalizing) that belief. It follows, then, since there is no reason to believe that unreasoned moral beliefs are any less efficacious in motivating action than are reasoned moral beliefs, that one can act morally without being able to justify what he or she did.

In line with the objection above to using "action" to refer to inadvertent doings, some might try to escape this conclusion by claiming that if it is not based on reasoning, it cannot properly be called "belief." However, such a stipulative definition would be so thoroughly out of touch with ordinary usage that it would clearly be a recommendation for, rather than a description of, the meaning of "belief." In everyday practice, a paradigm of "belief" is religious belief, which is notoriously unrelated to reasoning. Some common, unreasoned moral beliefs are notorious, too, such as those condemning homosexuality and inter-racial marriage, and this may seem to indicate a critical inadequacy in the position being developed here. However, if we keep firmly in mind that in labeling something a "moral belief" here we are merely describing it and not subscribing to it or otherwise commending it, we can overcome this connotative obstacle to recognizing the existence of unreasoned moral beliefs and actions.

Having recognized that, we can also acknowledge that while being able to offer reasons to justify the moral value of what one did may be irrelevant to the moral value of actions like Barney's, there are other situations where this would not be the case. For example, when we are asked to balance conflicting moral goods and claims, being able to justify our decision by laying out the reasoning we went through to sort out and evaluate the conflicting goods and claims and to arrive at our decision would enhance its moral value, and being unable to do so would undercut its moral value. Complex, problematic moral decisions are supposed to be thoughtful, careful, and well-reasoned; this is a moral obligation for the person called upon to make the decision. Consequently, when morally evaluating such decisions, in addition to knowing the consequences of and paradigms applicable to the decision, the motive of the decision-maker, and his or her understanding of the situation, we need to know the moral reasoning of the decision-maker in order to form a complete moral evaluation of his or her decision. This additional requirement also applies to morally complex, problematic situations in which the outcome of reasoning is not a decision handed on to others but direct action, as when we must decide how to balance our competing family, professional, and civic responsibilities. If family members, colleagues, or neighbors question the balance we have struck, we must be able to say more than "It just

felt like the proper mix" in order to win their respect. Still, this additional requirement does not hold for all moral action, since not all situations calling for moral
action are morally problematic.

V. Summary and Conclusion

In closing this discussion of Barney and the bank robbery, let me simply
summarize the major conclusions of this analysis of moral evaluation and reason.
Foremost among these is that there are many dimensions to moral value. It sometimes seems that moral philosophers are dedicated to reducing moral evaluation
to a single concern, for example, will the general welfare benefit, or is the action
universalizable? I think such attempts properly impress nonphilosophers (such as
students in introductory ethics classes) as oversimplifying their everyday moral
experience, wherein they find many different kinds of moral issues and values.

Second, there are agent-independent dimensions to the moral value of action.
These may be understood on utilitarian and behavioral-paradigm grounds. In
evaluations of these dimensions (which may apply to things, relations, conditions,
etc., as well as to actions), the agent's "reason," in any sense of the term, cannot
be relevant.

Third, "reason" becomes relevant when we move to the agent-dependent
dimensions of moral value. Here, the moral value of an action will depend on

1. whether the agent "knew what he or she was doing" (in the morally
    relevant sense), as opposed to accidentally doing what is morally right
    (or wrong),
2. whether the agent "believed in what he or she was doing," that is, be-
    lieved that what she or he was doing was the morally right thing to do,
3. whether the agent acted "for the right reason," that is, was moved to act
    by his or her belief that the action was the morally right thing to do, and
4. where the more specific moral evaluations, such as courageous and loyal,
    are at issue, whether the agent "understood what was happening," as
    opposed to overreacting or otherwise mistaking the facts of the matter.

Fourth, in morally complex, problematic situations, where decisions must be
made about competing moral goods and claims, there is an additional moral
dimension concerning "reason": was the decision made after thoughtful, careful
reasoning about the moral goods and claims involved in the situation?

Of course, I do not claim that this comprises a complete list of the dimensions
of moral value or of the ways in which "reason" is or is not required for actions,
events, and so forth to have moral value. I offer it only as a step toward describing
the dimensions of moral value and understanding the relevance and irrelevance
of "reason" to these various dimensions of our moral experience.

3

Being Rational and Acting Morally

NONHUMAN ANIMALS (whom I will call simply "animals") do many things that would ordinarily be considered moral actions if they were done by human beings. Seeing Eye dogs and guard dogs show considerable self-restraint and responsibility, and there are numerous accounts of other, untrained dogs acting courageously, loyally, and compassionately. Charles Darwin contends that "there can, I think, be no doubt that a dog feels shame, as distinct from fear, and something very like modesty when begging too often for food. A great dog scorns the snarling of a little dog, and this may be called magnanimity."[1]

There are also accounts of porpoises risking their lives to save the lives of members of their own species and caring enough to save the lives of human beings, too. Additionally, members of many species of animals show extended parental concern and devotion to members of their families. Mary Midgley offers the following report about wolves:

> Recently, ethologists have taken the trouble to watch wolves systematically and have found them to be, by human standards, paragons of steadiness and good conduct. They pair for life, they are faithful and affectionate spouses and parents, they show great loyalty to their pack and great courage and persistence in the face of difficulties, they carefully respect one another's territories, keep their dens clean, and extremely seldom kill anything that they do not need for dinner. If they fight with another wolf, the encounter normally ends with a submission. They have an inhibition about killing the suppliant and about attacking females and cubs. Our knowledge of this behavior rests on long and careful investigations by trained zoologists, backed up by miles of film, graphs, maps, population surveys, droppings analyses, and all the rest of the contemporary toolbag. Moreover, these surveys have often been undertaken by authorities who were initially rather hostile to the wolf and inclined to hope that it could be blamed for various troubles.[2]

Thus, if moral evaluations were confined to the behavioral level of describing what was done and determining whether it sufficiently resembles paradigm cases of courageous, kind, responsible and otherwise virtuous action, then it would be clear that many animals are capable of moral action. At the behavioral level, a .dog's pulling a child to safety is no less a moral action than a human's doing the same thing.

Nevertheless, animals are not commonly considered moral agents. If we set aside religious dogmas about creatures with souls vs. those without, being created in God's image, and so on, the traditional arguments to show that animals are incapable of moral action concern the relation between reason and moral agency. Basically, all these arguments take the following form:

A1: Only rational beings can be moral agents.
A2: Animals are not rational.
A3: Therefore, animals cannot be moral agents.

Such arguments entail that the courageous, kind, responsible and other morally virtuous actions of animals can only appear to express moral agency, as parrots and radios can only appear to speak.

Since this argument obviously is valid, questions about its soundness must concern the truth of its premises. Three such questions come quickly to mind:

(I) What does "rational" refer to?
(II) Why is rationality necessary for acting morally?
(III) Do animals really lack the rationality necessary for acting morally?

We shall deal with each of these questions in turn.

I. What "Rational" Refers To

According to David Hume,

next to the ridicule of denying an evident truth, is that of taking much pain to defend it; and no truth appears to me more evident, than that beasts are endow'd with thought and reason as well as men. The arguments are in this case so obvious, that they never escape the most stupid and ignorant.[3]

Apparently Hume underestimated the ability of philosophers and nonphilosophers alike to overlook the obvious when dealing with animals, for we have, since Aristotle's time, defined our species as *the* "rational animals," in contrast to those other, "thoughtless brutes." The "obvious arguments" this tradition overlooks are nicely summarized by Richard Watson:

Many animals show every sign of remembering past events and of anticipating future ones, as anyone's dog does, and they actively communicate their needs and desires to us through behavior that certainly appears to be intentional. Clearly these animals must be accepted as self-conscious on the same grounds that we accept the self-consciousness of other human beings. They have some rationality and intelligence, they communicate through sign systems that are much less versatile than is human language but are nevertheless as adequate for expressing many personal wants and desires as is human speech (particularly from a purely behavioral standpoint), and they give every indication of knowing when they are hurt. They understand general principles of various sorts.[4]

It is clearly false, and in this day and age even irresponsible, to suggest, without qualification, that only humans are rational animals. Animals recognize causal relations and can figure out how to use them to solve practical problems. Even if they are not capable of flights of abstraction, neither are they confined to mechanically responding to simple stimuli and gratifying primitive physiological needs. They do not, as Jan Narveson would have it, "experience only more or less isolated sensations and uninterpreted feelings."[5]

While Hume is surely correct and only species chauvinism can make all this worth repeating, we will work here within the limits of standard moral usage, both in moral philosophy and everyday moral practice. Both of these have developed a sense of "rationality" and "reason" that makes this practical intelligence of animals irrelevant to argument A and the moral issue it embodies. As discussed in Chapter 1, "reason" can refer to many different things, and in everyday morality and traditional moral philosophy, "rationality" and "reason" refer to normal, adult, human intelligence (henceforth, simply "normal$_h$ intelligence"). That, of course, goes far beyond the obvious intellectual abilities of animals.

When Plato, Aristotle, Kant, Mill, and other philosophers who subscribe to versions of argument A discuss practical reason, their examples show that it is the reason of normal, human adults they have in mind. Their examples almost always concern normal adults, seldom children or geniuses, and almost never the retarded, insane, senile, brain-damaged, or animals. Their references to common moral sense are inevitably references to the sensibilities and sensitivities of normal, human adults. Similarly, in everyday moral practice, animals, children, and the retarded, insane, senile, and brain-damaged are generally considered amoral. Because they lack normal$_h$ intelligence, their undesirable actions (e.g., tearing up the neighbor's garden or making off with some candy) are generally not considered criminal or immoral (e.g., vandalism or theft) but merely regrettable, unavoidable consequences of their not knowing better. If a normal, adult human were to act in the same way, however, she would be considered immoral, for it is presumed that she knows better. Finally, although solving a particularly complex moral problem may require a particularly wise or thoughtful person, such as Solomon or Socrates, the correctness of the answer, once discovered, is supposed to be apparent to all people of common sense (i.e., to all normal, human adults). Thus, both common moral practice and traditional moral philosophy indicate that premise A1 asserts that only beings of normal$_h$ intelligence can be moral.

Some common moral practices may seem to challenge this conclusion, most notably, our sometimes treating teenage delinquents as adults. However, these practices do not show that there is something else besides or instead of normal$_h$ intelligence to which "reason" refers. Rather, they are a consequence of the fact that normal$_h$ intelligence is a condition that can be attained to different degrees and to varying degrees in different areas. We all know otherwise normal adults who are still children when it comes to handling money, their parents, disappointment, and so forth. Some people, like "the good ol' boys" and the characters played by Dudley Moore, never seem to quite grow up, while others seem "mature beyond their years." These sorts of variations certainly can make it difficult at times to determine whether someone is mature enough to be a normal adult for the purposes at hand. However, since these are practical, rather than conceptual, difficulties, they do not challenge the point being made here, that in everyday morality and traditional moral philosophy, "rationality" and "reason" refer to normal$_h$ intelligence.

II. Can Only Rational Beings Be Moral Agents?

Arguments showing that reason, as just defined, is necessary for morality fall into two groups. The arguments in the first group take the following form:

B1: An action is moral only if the agent recognizes that it is the moral thing to do and does it because it is the moral thing to do (i.e., "does it for the right reason").

B2: Only beings of normal$_h$ intelligence are capable of such recognition and motivation.

B3: Therefore, only beings of normal$_h$ intelligence can act morally.

In order to avoid confusion in discussing this and the following argument, we must once again distinguish between the agent-independent and the agent-dependent dimensions of moral value. Henceforth, "moral$_{ai}$" will refer to the moral value of an action that is independent of the agent's relation to the action. As discussed in the previous chapter, fulfilling a promise, preventing a murder, aiding someone in distress, caring for a child, and other such acts have a certain moral value, on utilitarian and behavioral-paradigm grounds, whatever the agent's reasons for doing them or whether the agent is even aware that she is doing these things. Ordinarily, kind and honest actions, for example, are morally preferable to cruel and dishonest actions, even if the agent is unaware that her action is kind or honest or even if she has ulterior motives for so behaving. It is to this agent-independent moral value of actions that "moral_{ai}" will refer.

On the other hand, "moral_{ad}" will refer to the agent-dependent dimensions of moral value. As discussed in the previous chapter, these are the dimensions of moral value that depend on the agent's understanding of the situation and his action, including their moral significance, and on his motive for acting. Thus, while (*ceteris paribus*) an honest act done to impress a friend has equal moral_{ai} value with an honest act done because it is honest, the moral_{ad} value of the second action is superior to the moral_{ad} value of the first action. Finally, "moral" can be used in the ordinary, inclusive sense to refer to the moral_{ai} plus moral_{ad} value of an action.

Using these definitions, we can reformulate argument B in the following way to avoid the appearance of circularity in premise B1:

B1′: An action is moral_{ad} only if the agent recognizes that it is the moral_{ai} thing to do and does it because it is the moral_{ai} thing to do.

B2: Only beings of normal_h intelligence are capable of such recognition and motivation.

B3′: Therefore, only beings of normal_h intelligence can act morally_{ad}.

Although this formulation has a different conclusion than the original, "morally_{ad}" having been substituted for "morally," this is not important here. It was acknowledged above that the reason why animals cannot act morally, if they cannot, is not to be found at the behavioral level (i.e., at the moral_{ai} level), since their actions can have many of the same consequences and can fit under many of the same behavioral paradigms as human actions. So it is the moral_{ad} aspect of morality that concerns us as we ask whether animals can act morally.

Turning to the second group of arguments supporting the necessity of reason for morality_{ad}, and employing our new terminology, we see that these take the following form:

C1: Only beings that are free to choose what they will do can act morally_{ad}.

C2: Only beings of normal_h intelligence are free to choose what they will do.

C3: Therefore, only beings of normal_h intelligence can act morally_{ad}.

Both of these arguments obviously are valid. So if there is any fault in them, it must again lie in the truth of their premises. In each argument, the first premise asserts a commonsensical, necessary condition for moral_{ad} action, and the second premise claims that that necessary condition can be met only by beings of normal_h intelligence. Since animals lack normal_h intelligence, these arguments could be shown unsound by showing that the actions of some animals meet the criteria for moral$_{ad}$ action stated in premises B1′ and C1. This can be done without too much difficulty. Additionally, it can be shown that everyday moral practice does not confirm the reasons usually brought forward to support premises B2 and C2. Thus, for the purposes of the following discussion, we will accept premises B1′ and C1 but will show both that there are counterexamples to premises B2 and C2 and that the reasons traditionally given to support these two premises are faulty.

A. ACTING FOR THE RIGHT REASON

The commonsensical idea underlying argument B was discussed at length in sections I and II of the previous chapter. This idea is that in a moral$_{ad}$ action, it is the agent's recognition of and commitment to the moral$_{ai}$ value of the action that moves him or her to act. Such actions are "done for the right reason" and are commonsensically contrasted with moral$_{ai}$ actions that are either inadvertent or done from ulterior motives.

The moral$_{ai}$ actions of many animals meet this commonsensical condition. When a dog pulls a child from a fire, it is not acting blindly, like an insect reacting to a chemical mating stimulus. As noted in the previous chapter, we commonly deal with actions as, among other things, expressions of character, and many of the flexible, responsive, purposive, intelligent actions of animals seem to express such character traits as responsibility, courage, and compassion.

Furthermore, these expressions are seldom, if ever, compromised by the discovery of ulterior motives. Some animals are capable of feigning and deception. For example, some birds pretend to have broken wings in order to lure predators away from their nests, and while out for a walk, a dog may feign a need to relieve itself, which it knows its master will stop for, in order to have a few more moments to stare at the dog behind a neighbor's fence, which it knows its master will no longer stop for. Nevertheless, animals seem to be much less deceptive than humans, especially in moral matters; the simple straightforwardness of their compassionate, courageous and other such actions is virtually never an issue. The only real issue here is whether animals recognize the moral$_{ai}$ goods and evils of situations and respond to them or whether they simply react on the basis of instinct or reflex conditioning to morally$_{ai}$ insignificant aspects of the situation.

When instinct and reflex conditioning are mentioned, we usually think of cases like salmon compulsively swimming upstream in mating season and Pavlov's dogs salivating at the sound of a bell. If an act of courage or compassion is stimulated in either of these ways, that would seem seriously to compromise its moral$_{ad}$ value.

However, an action can be instinctual, in the sense of being directed by something we have inherited, or conditioned, in the sense of being directed by something we have been taught, yet still be a response to moral$_{ai}$ goods and evils. For example, maternal instincts are responses to the needs of the young. A wolf's care for its young is not mechanical nor carried out inflexibly, without regard to the actual needs of the young in particular situations. Similarly, when we morally educate children, we attempt to instill in them the *habits* of responding to danger courageously and to need compassionately. It cannot be correct to say that once we have succeeded in making courage and compassion "second nature" in our children, we have robbed their courageous and compassionate actions of their $moral_{ad}$ value. Yet that is what we would have to say if the fact that an action was conditioned made it impossible for that action to have $moral_{ad}$ value.

Such instinctual and conditioned behavior does not resemble that of an ant repeatedly following chemical paths, seemingly without comprehending how what it is doing contributes to the welfare of its community. Maternal instincts and $moral_{ai}$ habits are responses to the $moral_{ai}$ goods and evils of the situation and are directed flexibly to accomplishing those goods or alleviating those evils. Therefore, actions based on such instincts and habits meet the commonsensical requirement that $moral_{ad}$ actions be done for the right reason.

The belief that actions could not be both those of a $moral_{ad}$ agent and instinctual or conditioned probably derives from the Cartesian mind/machine dichotomy. If we believe, as Descartes does, that the mind is a different form of reality than the body and that instinctual and conditioned behavior springs from the body, while $moral_{ad}$ behavior is motivated by the mind, it follows that instinctual and conditioned actions cannot have $moral_{ad}$ value. However, during the three hundred plus years since Descartes wrote his *Meditations*, we have learned a good deal about both human and animal psychology that challenges this tidy Cartesian worldview that separates mind from body, humans from animals, and $moral_{ad}$ actions from instinctual actions so cleanly and completely. For example, in *The Descent of Man*, Charles Darwin writes: "It is a significant fact, that the more the habits of any particular animal are studied by a naturalist, the more he ascribes to reason and the less to unlearnt instincts."[6] For those who will leave their beds to study them, animals are not mindless automata but creatures with varying degrees of ability to recognize and respond intelligently to their environments.

Psychologists, including those who study humans as well as those who study animals, seem to have gradually come to recognize that instincts and conditioned responses are not all of a kind with those controlling homing salmon and salivating dogs. Rather, they range from such closed, reflexive mechanisms through Gestalt tendencies and motor coordinations to open, flexible, general dispositions and educated sensitivities.[7] The moral for $morality_{ad}$ of Descartes' dichotomy having been exchanged for a continuum is that the $morally_{ad}$ important point is not whether an action derives from inherited capacities, habituation, or individual discovery; the $morally_{ad}$ important point is whether the action derives from a recognition of the $moral_{ai}$ goods or evils in the situation and a straightforward effort to attain moral$_{ai}$ good or alleviate moral$_{ai}$ evil. The behavior of many animals suggests that such recognition and motivation are not limited to the rational extreme of that continuum.

Furthermore, not all moral$_{ai}$ actions of animals can be plausibly accounted for as products of instinct and conditioning. For example, there are cases of porpoises helping drowning sailors. There is no reason to believe that porpoises have developed an instinct for saving humans, and these wild creatures certainly have not been conditioned to perform such acts through training or repetition. It has been suggested that these porpoises were merely playing cetacean volleyball with these sailors and only accidentally deposited them safely on shore. But if that were so, there would be reports of porpoises kidnapping hapless, unendangered human swimmers to be their toys for the day. There are no such reports. Other examples may not be as striking, but unless one is predisposed to think that animals always act on instinct or reflex, there is at least no more reason to think that a pet dog pulling a drowning child from a swimming pool is acting instinctually or reflexively than to think that a human being doing the same thing is acting instinctually or reflexively.[8]

Some philosophers have suggested that some animals are even capable of dutiful action. For example, Richard Watson writes:

> But do some animals intend to act with reference to moral principles? I believe that the answer to this question—on behavioral evidence—is yes. Some chimpanzees, gorillas (probably orangutans and perhaps gibbons), dolphins (probably whales), elephants, dogs, pigs, and maybe cats and some other animals are sometimes moral agents. That is, there is adequate behavioral evidence that they have self-consciousness, capability of understanding moral principles, free will, understanding of specific duties, physical capability, and sometime intent to act with respect to moral principles.[9]

Ethological studies, cited and discussed at length in the works listed in the previous two notes, suggest that human moral$_{ad}$ agency is not an anomaly but an evolutionarily valuable ability that derives and differs only in degree from various forms of animal parental and social instincts or dispositions. If these suggestions are correct, then we must once again envisage a variable mixture of inheritance, conditioning, and individual determination in the motivation of actions, and quite a few animals may be capable of varying degrees of dutiful agency. So to the conclusion that some instinctual and conditioned behavior satisfies the criterion of premise B1′, we can add that the evidence points to there being some noninstinctual, nonreflexive (or, at least, not merely instinctual, not merely reflexive) cases where animals recognize and respond to the moral$_{ai}$ goods and evils of situations.

The only remaining question concerning whether or not some animal behavior meets the criterion for moral$_{ad}$ action set forth in premise B1′ is whether an animal acting kindly, for instance, recognizes that kindness is a *moral$_{ai}$* good. This question of recognizing the moralness$_{ai}$ of moral$_{ai}$ actions has two parts, which we shall treat in turn: what is really morally$_{ai}$ good (e.g., Christian or samurai values), and what is the nature of a moral$_{ai}$ value, as opposed to pragmatic, aesthetic, and other sorts of values?

Answering the question about what really is moral$_{ai}$ is the traditional job of moral philosophers. However, in everyday morality, being able to answer this question is not a necessary condition for acting morally$_{ad}$. As discussed in section IV of Chapter 2, someone who intentionally and without ulterior motives acts to prevent a robbery would be considered to have acted morally$_{ad}$ even if he does not know how to demonstrate that stopping the robbery was the morally$_{ai}$ proper thing to do. Justifications are commonly required only when an action does not accord with standard moral$_{ai}$ norms. For instance, while everyday morality requires that anyone maintaining that an airplane hijacking is moral$_{ai}$ must be able to demonstrate this, it requires no such justification of the morality$_{ai}$ of stopping a hijacking. Therefore, even though animals are incapable of demonstrating the morality$_{ai}$ of their actions, their intentional and straightforward kind, courageous, and otherwise virtuous actions can be moral$_{ad}$ actions, for they accord with accepted moral$_{ai}$ norms and, consequently, do not require justification to be moral$_{ad}$. It would be silly to require that animals, or anyone else, have the ability to do something that need not be done.

The second question asks whether animals distinguish moral$_{ai}$ values from other kinds of values. Drawing such a distinction is a difficult task; philosophers have argued over it for centuries, some contending that it is contributing to one's long-range well-being that makes self-interested actions moral$_{ai}$, others that enhancing the general welfare is what makes actions moral$_{ai}$, still others that it is being universalizable that identifies moral$_{ai}$ actions, and so on. Most nonphilosophers would probably not have the slightest idea how even to begin to draw this distinction and would doubtless see no point to worrying about it. It is, once again, a concern of moral theory, not of everyday moral practice. For example, if someone intentionally and without ulterior motives risks her life to save someone else, her courageous act would be considered moral$_{ad}$ without any further question about whether she is able to distinguish moral$_{ai}$ values from other kinds of values. Again, as long as our actions accord with accepted moral$_{ai}$ standards, we do not have to be able to answer this theoretical question in order to act morally$_{ad}$. Therefore, even if animals do not know how to distinguish moral$_{ai}$ values from other kinds of values, as long as their actions accord with accepted moral$_{ai}$ standards, this inability cannot discredit the moral$_{ad}$ value of their intentional and straightforward kind, courageous, and other such actions.

Suggesting that in order to be a moral$_{ad}$ agent, one must be able to distinguish moral from other kinds of values and to demonstrate that certain proposed moral schemes are superior to others is part and parcel of a mistake discussed in section IV of the previous chapter, namely, claiming that only those who are capable of doing normative ethics are capable of being moral$_{ad}$ agents. If being able to answer the questions of moral theory was a criterion for acting morally$_{ad}$, there would be very few moral$_{ad}$ actions. Although Kant was willing to accept as a consequence of his moral theory the possibility that there may never have been even one moral$_{ad}$ action, the conclusion that there are few, if any, moral$_{ad}$ actions is not confirmed by everyday experience. If people seldom if ever acted morally$_{ad}$, our everyday world would be a Hobbesian state of nature dominated by a terrible sense of anxiety. No matter how cynical we may sometimes feel about the contemporary "decline" of civilization, things do not, fortunately, seem to have reached that nadir. It follows that people do not have to be moral theorists in order to act morally$_{ad}$. Since it would be unfair to require animals to meet stiffer criteria of moral$_{ad}$ action than are required of humans, it follows that being able to answer philosophical questions about morality cannot be used as a criterion to show that animals cannot act morally$_{ad}$.

Thus, some of the actions of animals, who are creatures lacking normal$_{h}$ intelligence, can meet the criterion for moral$_{ad}$ agency stated in premise B1′. It follows that premise B2 is false and that argument B is unsound. However, before proceeding to argument C, let us consider the justification traditionally offered for premise B2.

B. ACTING ON PRINCIPLE AND ACTING MORALLY

Moral philosophers who subscribe to argument B usually link recognizing moral$_{ai}$ values to employing some fundamental moral principle or principles. For example, Kantians hold that in order to act morally$_{ad}$, one must determine what is morally$_{ai}$ correct by employing the categorical imperative. Utilitarians hold that only those who base their actions on the principle of utility can know what is morally$_{ai}$ good and intentionally and straightforwardly attempt to accomplish that good. Both these ways of determining what is the moral$_{ai}$ thing to do are fairly abstract, complex processes. Consequently, in either case, reason, rather than sensation, instinct, emotion, or feeling, is the faculty required for such recognition and, therefore, for acting morally$_{ad}$.

In this way, traditional moral philosophers have taken the commonsensical idea that moral$_{ad}$ actions must be based on a recognition of what is moral$_{ai}$ and a straightforward effort to be moral$_{ai}$ and tied it to possessing normal$_{h}$ intelligence through the mediation of some abstract, controversial, philosophical theory about the fundamental principles of morality. Reason is here required for moral$_{ad}$ action only because it is being claimed that determining what is the morally$_{ai}$ right thing to do requires employing principles that can be employed only by beings of at least normal$_{h}$ intelligence.

Common moral experience does not support that claim and, consequently, does not confirm this link between that commonsensical idea and possessing $normal_h$ intelligence. People like Job and Cephalus, for example, who do not employ the categorical imperative, the principle of utility, or other such abstract principles can and do intentionally and straightforwardly perform acts of kindness, courage, honesty, fairness, and the like. They may be acting on the basis of sentiment, intuition, religious belief, tradition, or some other nonphilosophical basis, but the kindness, fairmindedness, and so on of their actions is neither accidental to their intent nor merely a means for attaining some $nonmoral_{ai}$ goal. Consequently, following our analysis of the previous chapter, they are acting "for the right reason" and, consequently, their $moral_{ai}$ actions are also $moral_{ad}$ actions —which, of course, they would have to be to have earned the exemplary place they have earned in our edifying literature.

Philosophers who hold that, nonetheless, there is still something $morally_{ad}$ lacking in their acts again confuse morality with moral theory and (being capable of) being $moral_{ad}$ with (being capable of) doing moral philosophy. Such confusion might be due to being misled by the expression "acting for the right *reason*" into believing that so acting must require employing reason. As we have seen, this expression does not refer to the mental faculty employed in generating one's actions but, rather, refers to issues of $moral_{ai}$ goods being intentionally vs. accidentally accomplished and to straightforward vs. ulterior motives for accomplishing those goods. More likely still, this confusion is due to the desire of these philosophers not merely to describe but also to revolutionize, reform, or at least revise everyday moral practice. Being a moral *philosopher* has traditionally involved being a moral teacher as much as or more than a moral observer. But while it is fine to wear two hats, we should not let our desire for moral progress cloud our view of moral practice. And everyday moral practice indicates that although abstract reasoning and principles are necessary for constructing moral theories—and might even improve moral practice—they are not necessary for intentional, straightforward $moral_{ai}$ action (i.e., for $moral_{ad}$ action).

Whatever their other problems, intuitionist accounts of morality are successful at describing the way $moral_{ai}$ values are usually recognized and determined in everyday moral practice. Although in complex situations or in attempts to convince ourselves to do what is right we may turn to something like the categorical imperative or the principle of utility, in most situations we simply perceive or feel what is the $moral_{ai}$ thing to do and, if we are $moral_{ad}$, do it. If such actions do not count as $moral_{ad}$ actions—which, according to the justification given for premise B2, they do not—then $moral_{ad}$ actions are as rare as dragon's teeth. As already noted, everyday practice does not confirm this bleak estimate. This is sufficient to discredit the traditional justification for B2, since if that premise is to remain in touch with actual moral practice, an adequate justification of it must contain an accurate description of current moral practice, but the traditional justification for B2 can, at best, be only a positive recommendation for improving that practice. For better or worse, moral$_{ad}$ action does not now require the kinds of reasoning on which moral philosophers believe moral$_{ai}$ practice should be based.

Thus, the compassionate, courageous, and otherwise virtuous actions of some animals meet the commonsensical criterion for moral$_{ad}$ action asserted in premise B1′, and the justification for premise B2, which claims that normal$_h$ intelligence is needed to meet that criterion, is faulty. Consequently, the argument that animals are incapable of moral$_{ad}$ action because reason is required for recognizing moral$_{ai}$ values and motivating moral$_{ad}$ action is without justification and unsound.

C. THE FREE, THE RATIONAL, AND THE MORAL

Turning to argument C, premise C1 maintains that freedom is necessary for morality$_{ad}$, and premise C2 maintains that only beings of normal$_h$ intelligence are free. As Saint Thomas puts it, "the very condition of the rational creature [is] that it has dominion over its actions, . . . whereas the condition of other things [is] that [they] have not dominion over their actions." [10] There are two commonsensical ideas underlying premise C1. First, moral$_{ad}$ actions are something the agent is responsible for, and only a free being can be responsible for its actions. For example, a coin machine that gives the correct change is not responsible for this, since it could not choose to do otherwise. The serviceman who can choose to do a poor or an effective job of maintaining the machine is the one who is responsible for its performance. Second, moral$_{ad}$ action is a sensitive response to a complex situation, including antecedent conditions and future possibilities, while a determined action is a blind response to an immediate stimulus. Therefore, only free beings can recognize and respond to the moral$_{ai}$ values in a situation. For example, if a bird tends its young only because they have a certain smell, without understanding that certain smells signal hunger, disease, or other needs requiring certain responses from it if they are to survive, then that bird is not acting morally$_{ad}$. Forced by instinct to respond to this morally$_{ai}$ irrelevant part of the situation, the bird is not able to respond to the morally$_{ai}$ relevant parts of the situation with a course of action chosen for its moral$_{ai}$ value. Consequently, it is incapable of acting morally$_{ad}$.

The second of these ideas is part and parcel of the traditional opposition of moral$_{ai}$ sensitivity to instincts and conditioning and, therefore, has already been challenged. Freedom vs. mechanical instincts and conditioning is not a dichotomy but a continuum, and many animals have instincts and habits that are sufficiently flexible and responsive to the moral$_{ai}$ goods and evils of a situation to qualify them as moral$_{ad}$ agents on this ground. For moral$_{ad}$ purposes, they are not machines but free beings.

Turning to the other idea, if only free beings can sensibly be held responsible for their actions, we see that everyday practice indicates that some animals must be free, since they are commonly held responsible for many of their actions. The common activity of housebreaking a dog, for example, presupposes that certain of a dog's activities are not entirely determined by instinct or canine nature and that praise and punishment can be nonarbitrarily meted out to dogs. Thus, dogs can be sensibly and fairly held responsible for certain of their actions, which, according to this idea underlying C1, entails that they are free.

Similarly, when dealing with animals as well as with humans, we distinguish free acts from accidents, compulsions, and acts based on misunderstanding or coercion. For example, a cat may freely choose to take a vitamin pill offered to it, may have the pill forced down its throat, or may take the pill unknowingly, when it is hidden inside a meatball. That the cat who chooses to take the pill is not being determined to do this by some sort of instinct or conditioning is evidenced by the fact that some days it will take its pill, and some days it won't. Thus, in everyday practice, certain animals are not treated like machines or natural phenomena that cannot sensibly be held responsible for what they do. These animals are treated as responsible beings free to choose what they will do. Such treatment is restricted, of course, to those areas where we believe the animals' cognitive and conative capacities make such treatment sensible. In this, our application of these concepts to animals is very much like our application of them to children and is quite unlike our refusal to apply them in any but metaphorical ways to machines.

Thus, some animals satisfy the commonsensical ideas that establish freedom as a necessary condition for moral$_{ad}$ agency. However, these animals lack normal$_h$ intelligence. It follows that premise C2 is false and that argument C is unsound. We may also note, as a bit of an aside, that since animals are, nonetheless, not commonly considered moral$_{ad}$ agents, it also follows that in everyday practice, freedom is not the crucial "property" distinguishing moral$_{ad}$ from nonmoral$_{ad}$ agents. No matter how much philosophers and theologians have tried to make of the relation between freedom and morality$_{ad}$, animals are commonly treated as free but not moral$_{ad}$ agents. Consequently, the crucial difference between moral$_{ad}$ and nonmoral$_{ad}$ agency must lie elsewhere.

It might be objected here that since "freedom" is a controversial concept and since no attempt has been made in this discussion to define it, this conclusion about premise C2 and argument C rests on shifting sand. However, it is this objection that would be unfounded. Whatever "freedom" may mean, according to the commonsensical ideas underlying premise C1, it is supposed to refer to something that is *necessary* for sensibly applying concepts like "responsibility" to beings and for sensibly praising and blaming them. Since we do sensibly apply that concept to animals and do sensibly praise and blame them, it follows that if we accept C1, then C2 must be false and, consequently, that argument C is unsound. Therefore, for the purpose of this discussion of argument C, it does not matter exactly what "freedom" means. The above criticisms of that argument could be challenged by explications of "freedom" only if those explications also challenged premise C1. Such challenges would, of course, lead to the same basic conclusion, that argument C is unsound.

It might also be objected that the argument of this section is faulty because the ideas underlying C1 refer to a special kind of responsibility pertinent only to moral matters, while holding animals "responsible" for their actions refers to other kinds of responsibility. Such an objection would again be mistaken. Fixing responsibility is certainly often a complex and difficult matter, involving questions of whether the individual understood the facts of the situation, recognized applicable rules, was coerced, was in control of his or her conduct, can be held responsible on the basis of *not* doing something, and so forth. However, these complex issues are the same whether we are dealing with legal, economic, professional, moral, or other sorts of cases; they do not differentiate *kinds* of responsibility but *issues* of responsibility that apply to many different kinds of cases, including cases of moral responsibility. Thus, "moral responsibility" does not refer to a special kind of responsibility but to being responsible or being held responsible in moral$_{ai}$ matters in just the same way one may be responsible or held responsible in economic, professional, and other matters. Consequently, our conclusion stands: accepting premise C1, we must conclude that premise C2 is false and that argument C is unsound.

D. EVERYDAY FREEDOM

Once again, let us pause a moment to consider the justification traditionally offered for the rationalist premise we have just put into question. The standard justification for premise C2 is that only beings capable of "standing back" from the course of nature to reflect on it are free to initiate action. Here is the way Kant puts it:

> Man really finds in himself a faculty by which he distinguishes himself from all other things. . . . This faculty is reason. . . . A rational being must regard himself as . . . belonging to the world of understanding and not to that of the senses. Thus he has two standpoints from which he can consider himself . . . : first, as belonging to the world of sense and under laws of nature (heteronomy), and, second, as belonging to the intelligible world and under laws which, independent of nature, are not empirical but founded only on reason [autonomy].[11]

Kant and the many others who share his viewpoint claim that only reflective beings can develop concepts of how nature works and can be controlled. For example, while other species come and go at the mercy of the weather, geological shifts, and the other factors that govern evolution, human beings can discover the laws and mechanisms of evolution and can use this knowledge to direct evolution as we wish, through creating hybrids, using gene-splicing to combat genetic diseases, and so forth. It follows, if that claim is correct, that only reflective beings are free, since being able to initiate action is at least a necessary condition for freedom and since "initiating" action means basing one's actions on one's concepts of the environment and his or her relation to it.

However, since "reflective ability" here refers to having normal$_h$ intelligence, which animals lack, this traditional justification for premise C2 is clearly false. Many animals are capable of initiating action. As Watson outlined, they recognize and respond to situations of some complexity, solve practical problems, adjust their behavior to overcome obstacles to their endeavors, and so forth. For example, dogs learn, without being taught, to push open doors; deer find new paths around landslides; and wild chimpanzees use leaves to get at water they could not otherwise reach. Normal$_h$ intelligence may be needed to control and reconstruct nature on a massive scale, since this is something normal, adult humans do but animals do not do. However, such reflective ability is not needed to be sufficiently free of the "iron laws" and "mechanical clutches" of nature to initiate action.

Thus, both traditional arguments to show that only rational beings can act morally$_{ad}$ fail. Their flexible, responsive, purposive behavior indicates that many animals are sufficiently free and sensitive to the moral$_{ai}$ goods and evils of situations to be moral$_{ad}$ agents. And the commonsensical ideas and traditional philosophical justifications underlying these two arguments do not provide substantive reason to doubt what that behavior seems to express.

Nonetheless, there is still something about the courage, kindness, and the like of animals that distinguishes them in a morally$_{ad}$ relevant way from the moral virtues of human beings. Although the traditional argument concerning freedom, normal$_h$ intelligence, and morality$_{ad}$ is a failure, it does, incidentally, indicate where this difference lies: by and large humans do, but animals do not, devote themselves to controlling and reconstructing things, including themselves. The remainder of this chapter is devoted to explicating and evaluating the moral$_{ad}$ significance of this difference.

III. Pursuing Ideals vs. the Value of Virtue

One of the ways in which morality differs from sets of rules like our tax code is that rather than merely prescribing or proscribing certain actions, morality is supposed to be a worldview and a way of life. Moral$_{ad}$ actions are supposed to be guided by that worldview and to be dedicated to the fulfillment of an ideal way of life. This is evidenced in several ways. When we try to teach morality, what we set out to do is to develop "moral character;" that is, rather than simply trying to communicate some information or to make sure that certain rules have been committed to memory, we try to communicate and develop a complex psychological and ideological web of values, sensitivities, attitudes, and commitments. And our primary tools in moral education are examples, such as, the lives of the saints and heroes and particular actions that express good moral character. If we follow Aristotle's counsel, when we want to discover what is the right thing to do, we try to find a good man or woman and follow his or her example.

Again, this dimension of morality is shown by our insistence that a person not merely follow a moral$_{ai}$ rule but that, in order to be fully moral, she must do the morally$_{ai}$ right thing because of her commitment to its rightness. A person who merely follows moral$_{ai}$ rules to fit in, because it is expected of him, because it is the prudent thing to do, or for some other, nonmoral reason is a kind of hypocrite. As noted in Chapter 2, our everyday images of a fair, decent, loving, Christian, honorable, etc. world may be somewhat nebulous and even contain contradictions, but it is only when we see actions as expressing a commitment to the realization of that world that they can be fully moral.

Finally, I would speculate that it is their lacking this dimension that leads Kant to refuse moral$_{ad}$ value to the actions of naturally kindhearted people. Such people do not act out of respect for the moral$_{ai}$ ideal; they simply follow their nature. Kant, on the other hand, holds that

> the achievement of the highest good in the world is the necessary object of a will determined by the moral law. In such a will, however, the complete fitness of intentions to the moral law is the supreme condition of the highest good. . . . But complete fitness of the will to the moral law is holiness, which is a perfection of which no rational being in the world of sense is at any time capable. But since it is required as practically necessary, it can be found only in an endless progress to that complete fitness.[12]

Thus, for Kant, one can be moral$_{ad}$ only if he is committed to the ideal of a purely rational life and continually strives to approximate more closely to this unattainable ideal.

Now, effectively pursuing ideals requires taking control of and reconstructing things, since ideals are conditions that will not naturally or effortlessly come to pass. These things include oneself, especially in morality$_{ad}$. The literature of morality is dominated by stories, counsels, slogans, images, and other devices to inspire us to take control of those forces around and within us that lead away from the moral ideal and either to suppress them or to redirect them in ways conducive to attaining the ideal moral life. For example, men are usually taught that they must inhibit their sexual aggressiveness and not take advantage because they are generally stronger physically than women, and we are all taught not to gloat or to laugh at the misfortune of others, both of which, as the behavior of children indicates, are native human responses. Depth psychology, too, emphasizes that the formation of an inhibiting superego and an ego ideal are essential parts of the development of a moral$_{ad}$ personality. Whether one is dedicated to a life of love or one of duty, a life dominated by the sentiments or by reason, as a moral$_{ad}$ being, one has to screen the psychological and social forces that influence her actions and seek to remake society and her personality in a way that maximizes good and minimizes evil.

Animals generally do not try to control and reconstruct their world or, especially, themselves. Of course, many animals make nests and mark their territories in various ways; others clear "stamping grounds" and collect things with which to construct elaborate displays; and a very few, like the beaver, undertake engineering feats that change the environment to better suit their needs. Here again, we are dealing with a human/animal continuum, rather than a dichotomy. Still, by and large, rather than trying to reconstruct their environment to suit their needs better, animals usually just try to fit in with, adjust to, or get along with what they are given. Furthermore, and most important when considering questions of moral$_{ad}$ agency, animals do not seem to engage in programs of self- and social improvement directed to refining and extending what abilities they do have and what techniques they have mastered for altering themselves and their world to make a better life for themselves. Although they have social orders, there is no evidence that they have social reformers. Although they can be trained and disciplined, they do not seem to engage in self-directed programs of training, discipline, or self-development. That is why Jonathan Livingston Seagull was so much more like us than like his fellow gulls. Although they are curious, they do not appear to be dedicated to increasing their knowledge or perfecting their methods of learning. This apparent lack among animals of dedication and striving to fulfill ideals through control and reconstruction is the truth behind the old idea that while the human world is progressive, nature is repetitive. Although nature evolves, animals do not seem to initiate change in an attempt to attain a better way of life.

It follows from this and from the role of ideals in moral$_{ad}$ life that animals cannot be fully moral$_{ad}$ beings, in spite of their many admirable deeds. They are not fully moral$_{ad}$ beings because their actions are not part of an attempt to fulfill an ideal way of life. The goods and evils they respond to are not so evaluated because of their relation to an ideal life, and their good deeds are limited to being responses to the situation at hand, rather than being part of a program of fulfilling an ideal. Adopting the following terminology will help to describe the situation here:

kindness, courage, honesty, and the like are "virtues";

intentional, straightforward acts of kindness, courage, and the like are "virtuous acts"; and virtuous acts that are done as part of fulfilling an ideal way of life are "fully moral$_{ad}$ acts."

Thus, it would seem that while many animals are virtuous, none are fully moral$_{ad}$.

If "reason" (i.e., normal$_h$ intelligence) is what is needed to project and dedicate oneself to an ideal, then it will be correct to say that only rational beings can be fully moral$_{ad}$ agents. Consequently, we can formulate the following argument to support premise A1, which, it will be remembered, claims that only rational beings can be moral:

> D1: An action is fully moral$_{ad}$ only if the agent does it because he or she believes it will contribute to attaining an ideal way of life.
>
> D2: Only rational beings can project and dedicate themselves to attaining an ideal way of life.
>
> D3: Therefore, only rational beings can be fully moral$_{ad}$.[13]

This argument seems to be sound. Although many animals possess sufficient sensitivity and intelligence to recognize virtues and to do virtuous deeds, they seem to lack the ability to lead a fully moral$_{ad}$ life dedicated to the attainment of an ideal. This is the truth underlying the contention in argument B that animals cannot recognize the morality$_{ai}$ of moral$_{ai}$ values. What animals cannot recognize is how virtuous deeds contribute to creating an ideal world.

Of course, argument D does not exactly justify premise A1. That premise claims that only rational beings can be *moral*, leaving nonrational beings amoral. Argument D concludes that only rational beings can be *fully moral$_{ad}$*, leaving it open for nonrational beings to be less than fully moral$_{ad}$. This, we have seen, is what animals are, since their actions are moral$_{ai}$ and virtuous. As emphasized in the previous chapter, moral value is not a simple thing that is either wholly present or entirely missing. There are many dimensions to moral value; so that certain creatures are incapable of being fully moral$_{ad}$ does not entail that they and their actions lack moral value altogether.

Thus, the support argument D provides for argument A is decidedly equivocal. Indeed, since the intent underlying argument A is to exclude nonrational beings from the realm of moral agents, it would seem that the basic conclusion of this analysis, including that which has led to argument D, is that that exclusion is unjustified. While animals may be incapable of full moral$_{ad}$ agency, that some of them can be virtuous agents brings nonrational beings into the arena of moral$_{ad}$ agency in a substantive way.

To reinforce this conclusion, we may note that this condition of animals (i.e., being virtuous but not fully moral$_{ad}$ agents) resembles that of being holy, as Kant understands this, and that of being kindhearted. According to Kant, God is not a fully moral$_{ad}$ being, because He does not have to be commanded to do the right thing. Being purely rational, He does not have to overcome the temptation or inertia of a sensuous nature and does good without internal conflict, strife, or effort. God always acts virtuously, but He is not striving to fulfill an ideal way of life and, therefore, is not a fully moral$_{ad}$ being.[14] Similarly, as noted earlier, someone who is kindhearted or otherwise disposed by temperament or sentiment to do good will act virtuously without striving to do so. Such a person treats others kindly not because she recognizes an imperative to do so, believes it her duty, or judges kindness to be part of an ideal way of life. Rather, she acts kindly because her immediate response to the needs of others is a feeling of sympathy and a desire to help them out. Thus, such spontaneous, sentiment-inspired acts are also virtuous but not fully moral$_{ad}$, and insofar as someone is capable of such acts, she is capable of acting virtuously but not fully morally$_{ad}$.

Are the holy and the kindhearted utterly lacking in moral$_{ad}$ significance? Since God fulfills the ideal for which fully moral$_{ad}$ beings are striving, it would be strange, indeed, if His acts were considered lacking in moral$_{ad}$ significance. Even as just a thought experiment, the idea of the holy shows that it is conceptually possible for something not to be a fully moral$_{ad}$ agent yet still act in ways that have moral$_{ad}$, as well as moral$_{ai}$, significance.

The case of kindhearted people is a bit more clouded, at least in the history of moral philosophy. As noted above, Kant holds that the actions of such people lack moral$_{ad}$ significance. According to Kant, such people just happen to do good; it is a fortunate accident that their inclination ordinarily accords with the dictates of reason.[15]

However, common moral practice does not confirm this Kantian evaluation. The acts of kindhearted, spontaneously generous, compassionate, and otherwise virtuous people are not commonly considered to be lacking in moral$_{ad}$ value or even to be of lesser moral$_{ad}$ worth than the virtuous acts of those who act out of a sense of duty. Indeed, kindhearted people are commonly considered more morally$_{ad}$ worthy than dutiful people. A sense of duty is commonly considered of secondary value, something that those who unfortunately lack virtuous dispositions must fall back on to do good. The loving parent, for example, is considered superior to the dutiful parent, and saints are not people who recognize obligations to their fellows but those who love them. The person who *desires* to do good is commonly considered to be of morally$_{ad}$ better character than the person who does not want to do it but does it out of a sense of duty.

Finally, as the discussion of instincts and conditioning showed, and as common experience readily confirms, a person who is kind by disposition is not ignorant of the goodness of acting kindly. The goodness of a kind act is that it is kind, and a person who is kind by disposition does kind deeds because they are kind. In complex and borderline cases, one may have to ask himself, "What if everybody did that?" in order to determine what is the right thing to do. But if, like the good Samaritan, one comes across a suffering individual whom he can aid and responds to that need sympathetically, then he has recognized the morally$_{ai}$ significant factor in the situation (supposing things are as they appear to be) and has responded to the situation in a morally$_{ad}$ appropriate manner. No further, special moral value in the situation or moral understanding on the part of the Samaritan need be postulated; the need of the one person and the sympathy of the other are all we, as ordinary moral people, need to know in order to understand the moral$_{ai}$ value in this classic moral situation and the moral$_{ad}$ worth of the Samaritan's response. Therefore, kindhearted people do good deeds intentionally, and their actions in no way resemble accidental good deeds. Consequently, the common practice of according moral$_{ad}$ value to good dispositions is justified, even though actions motivated by such dispositions are virtuous but not fully moral$_{ad}$.

Of course, animals are not in exactly the same situation as are God and kindhearted people. They do not always follow the dictates of practical reason, as does God, and kindhearted people can, apparently, act in fully moral$_{ad}$ ways, in addition to their "merely" virtuous deeds. Still, many animals are in a morally significantly similar situation: they act virtuously. Although they may be unable to recognize how virtuous action contributes to the attainment of an ideal world, they do recognize the needs of others and respond to those needs compassionately, courageously, responsibly, loyally, and so forth. To that degree, they do recognize and respond to moral$_{ai}$ values. That is enough to earn them a place in the moral$_{ad}$ arena and to discredit the claim that only rational beings can occupy that place of honor.

4

People and Persons

THE CONCEPT of "personhood" has become one of the darlings of both moral philosophy and everyday moral practice. It has become especially popular in discussions of moral rights (e.g., the right to life and whether unborn humans have this right). The way these discussions have developed, only persons can have moral rights; this, of course, yields the following common argument against extending moral rights to animals:

A1: Only persons can have moral rights.
A2: Animals are not persons.
A3: Therefore, animals cannot have moral rights.

This argument appears to be as obviously valid as the ones we discussed in Chapter 3. However, it is actually a logical jumble, because the concept of "personhood" is a logical jumble. "Personhood" refers to at least two radically different conditions, and what the relation is between these two conditions is an open question. Once we clear up these conceptual confusions, we will see that argument A either equivocates or begs the question. That recognition should prepare us for a more substantive discussion of the possibility of extending moral rights to animals.

I. Metaphysical vs. Moral Persons

There are many different kinds of concepts and many different ways of distinguishing them. Moral discussions concerning or even just involving personhood commonly employ both moral and metaphysical concepts of personhood. For purposes of this discussion, we can use "moral concept" to refer to evaluative concepts concerned with assigning rights, duties, obligations, and respect but that are not necessarily tied to the legal arena. "Metaphysical concept" will refer to the

47

sorts of things P. F. Strawson discusses in *Individuals*, that is, to concepts that form the basic structure of our experience of the furniture and arrangement of the world.[1] Additionally, it probably bears emphasizing that throughout this discussion, as was the case in the previous chapters, the concepts we are concerned with are those that actually contribute to organizing human behavior. "God" is not the only concept that dies when people do not live by it. Consequently, the relevant test of our analyses remains examples of what people do, rather than quotations from Aristotle, Kant, and other philosophers.

Thus, the moral and the metaphysical concepts of personhood can already be distinguished by their functions, one serving to evaluate, the other to describe. They can be further distinguished by detailing their contents and noting with what other concepts they contrast.

Metaphysically, "person" denotes a kind of thing. (Henceforth, "person$_d$" will stand for this descriptive use of "person.") Things are individuals that endure through space and time and have their own identity, integrity, independence, or self-sufficiency. Roughly but sufficiently for our purposes, "person$_d$" denotes those things that are

> embodied, as opposed to (the possibility of) ghosts, spirits, etc.,
>
> animate, rather than mechanical or otherwise inorganic,
>
> emotive, as opposed to (the possibility of) purely rational beings or machines,
>
> initiators of action, rather than merely reflexive, instinctual, or mechanical respondents to their environment, and
>
> capable of forming ideas about the world, rather than being merely things in the world.

In everyday experience, "person$_d$" is just another name for human beings, and persons$_d$ are commonly distinguished from inanimate objects, machines, plants, animals, and spirits. The first definition of "person" in the seventh edition of *Webster's New Collegiate Dictionary* is simply "a human being"; the second is "a human being as distinguished from an animal or thing." In the first definition of "person" in its second college edition, *The American Heritage Dictionary* combines these into "a human being, esp. as distinguished from an animal or thing."

This distinction is made on the basis of both bodily shape and patterns of behavior, which must have a kind of organic fluidity and unity to them, express some purpose, and appear self-motivated and self-directed. Philosophers have usually emphasized these behavioral traits and the inferences that may be drawn from them concerning consciousness and rationality.[2] However, in everyday experience these traits are not more important than bodily shape for identifying persons$_d$; indeed, they are often less important. For example, the behavior of a normal, adult dog is more organic, intelligent, and self-aware than that of a human infant or a human adult suffering some severe muscular, neurological, or mental disorder; nonetheless, that dog is still not considered a person$_d$, while these humans are. No matter how superior its behavior, a dog can never be a person$_d$, because it does not have a human body, and no matter how inferior the behavior of human infants or handicapped humans, they can still be persons$_d$ if they have reasonably well-formed human bodies. It is the grossly misformed, such as Quasimodo and the Elephant Man, whose humanity we doubt and whom we label "freaks" and "monsters" (using these terms descriptively). Furthermore, even before we had much appreciation of the mentality of apes, there was a tendency to consider them to be, in an extended sense, "little people," because they look like human beings. Again, many discussions of when an abortion ceases to be the termination of an organism and becomes the killing of a person$_d$ focus on when the fetus comes to have human shape. For many people, coming to look human is, apparently, the crucial step in becoming human.

Thus, "person$_d$" does not refer essentially to rational animals, of which human beings are only one kind and just happen to be the only kind we routinely encounter. Having a human body is as essential a part of being a person$_d$ as is being a rational animal. Metaphysically, "person" denotes all and only human beings.

Some readers will certainly object to this conclusion, with Vulcans and other science fiction, nonhuman persons$_d$ in mind. However, such purported counterexamples are insignificant. First, since the creatures that count as persons$_d$ in our science fiction literature are not significantly different from us in appearance, they are human beings, even if not exactly *Homo sapiens*. Common practice is not based on the biological investigations necessary to tell that *Star Trek*'s Mr. Spock is not just a strange-looking man, and where it is obvious that science fiction creatures are not human, for example, space "spiders" and intangible "presences," they are not considered persons$_d$. Second and most important, our concepts have been developed for dealing with ordinary experiences, not with extraordinary ones, which "call for decisions and not for discoveries."[3] It is the study of actual experience and behavior, or of imagined cases patterned closely on the real, lived world, that shows us what our concepts are; science fiction cases can only contribute to inconclusive speculation regarding what our concepts might become.

The same reply applies to theologically based objections, for example, an objection based on the three "persons" of the Trinity. In addition, the religious use of "person" is obviously often metaphorical, as is so much religious language.

These science fiction and religious objections to saying that "person$_d$" refers to all and only human beings are objections to the "only"; some readers would doubtless object to the "all." This objection has been made on the basis of liberal attitudes about abortion and euthanasia and on the basis of references to some humans (e.g., the severely brain-damaged and senile) as "vegetables." However, as noted above, the dictionary indicates that this objection does not reflect the current common usage of "person." Furthermore, we usually say "*human* vegetable," indicating that "vegetable" is being used analogically here. Even if individuals in irreversible comas or terrible, unrelievable pain are coming to be recognized as legitimate candidates for euthanasia, they are still legally and medically persons$_d$, and not some other kind of thing.

Fetuses that do not yet look human constitute the only significant group of *Homo sapiens* widely not considered persons$_d$. However, once again the dictionary indicates that this reform has not yet established itself firmly enough to change common usage. Furthermore, since those who object to calling such fetuses "persons$_d$" also often object to calling them "humans," these fetuses cannot provide clear counterexamples to the thesis that "person$_d$" is just another name for human beings. The confusion between descriptive and evaluative uses not only of "person" but also of "human" and "man" in the abortion debate also insures that usage in that debate cannot provide clear examples for conceptual analysis. Finally, as noted in our discussion of the science fiction cases, the relation between being a *Homo sapiens* and being human is not that of identity. Although having the bodily form characteristic of our species is a necessary condition for being human, having the genes of a *Homo sapiens* is neither sufficient nor necessary for being human. Since genotypes are, as such, not parts of our everyday world, they cannot be among the criteria we employ when assigning our everyday concepts.

Common usage is not monolithic. In addition to definitions, paradigm cases, and standard practices, it is filled with reformed, extended, "to a degree," analogical, and metaphorical usages. This diversity must qualify any assertion about the meaning of everyday concepts. Nevertheless, while acknowledging the existence of speculative, metaphorical, and reformist uses of the term, we can safely assert that in the actual course of our everyday affairs, the primary, descriptive use of "person" is to denote all and only human beings.

Turning to the moral side, we note that "person" denotes a certain status. (Henceforth, "person$_e$" will refer to this evaluative use of "person.") To be a person$_e$ is to be due certain honors and privileges from those whose actions might influence her or his well-being. A person$_e$ is a being whose interests must be respected; when determining what is morally acceptable and preferable, we are morally obligated to take into account what will dignify or demean, benefit or harm, please or pain, aid or thwart, satisfy or dissatisfy, enrich or impoverish, and so forth any being that is a person$_e$ and that is likely to be affected by our actions.

Being a person$_e$ contrasts with being property or a creature of nature. The latter pair may be treated with kindness and be well cared for, but this is not because they are due or owed such treatment. Rather, we look after the needs of property and creatures of nature—for example, by protecting cattle from mountain lions, preserving salmon spawning grounds from pollution, and finding homes for lost pets—because of sentimental attachments to them, out of self-interest in preserving natural resources and useful tools, because they figure in obligations to other persons$_e$, and out of charity. Again, moralists routinely have adamantly

opposed materialism, the theory of evolution, behaviorism, and other attempts to
naturalize humanity, because such theories would deny us the status persons$_e$
have in contrast to creatures of nature: creatures of nature, and those considered
property as well, may be treated as mere means to fulfilling the interests of
persons$_e$, but persons$_e$ are beings whose interests must not be treated and sacrificed as mere means to the fulfillment of the needs of other creatures or persons$_e$.
Although not often focused on in the philosophical literature, which has concen-
trated on the significance of the moral concept of personhood in intrahuman
affairs, this opposition of persons$_e$ to property and creatures of nature is an integral part of the actual, everyday significance of personhood$_e$, just as having
human shape is an integral part of the everyday significance of personhood$_d$.

Another way of saying that persons$_e$ are beings who must be respected is that
persons$_e$ are beings with moral rights. As Michael Tooley puts it, "what is perhaps the most common way of interpreting the term "person" when it is employed
as a purely moral term [is that] to say that X is a person is to say that X has
rights."[4] The most basic of these is the right to life. Beings that are not persons$_e$
may be hunted, "put to sleep," eaten, "sacrificed" in research, and so on when
doing so is useful for satisfying some person$_e$'s interests. Of course, other considerations (e.g., our desires to be humane and to preserve endangered species for
future generations) may qualify the starkness of this, but these are just secondary
qualifications concerning the how, where, and when the lives of nonpersons$_e$ may
be expended. In contrast, a person$_e$'s life must not be dealt with in this way, no
matter how humanely, for he or she has a right to live. Discussions of the morality
of suicide, abortion, capital punishment, war, and euthanasia focus on the issue
of personhood$_e$ because it is recognized that to treat something's life, even if we
are kind about it, as fundamentally a means to some end is to deny that that
being is a person$_e$. (That this is often construed as denying the individual's
"humanity" is a classic example of the confusion between metaphysical and moral
personhood.)

The other moral rights that are part of being a person$_e$ concern those things
that are essential for dignity and a fulfilling life. The rights concerning dignity
include those to freedom, property, a fair wage, civil equality, responsibility, individuality, and procreation. The rights concerning a fulfilling life include those to
society, a family, freedom from pain, security, an education, a vocation, and a fair
share of available goods. To be *fully* a person$_e$ is not only to have a right to life
but also rights to dignity and a fulfilling life. It is these rights that contemporary,
human liberation movements (e.g., women's, gay, and handicapped lib) seek in
order that their members "may look others in the eye and feel in some fundamental way the equal of anyone."[5]

There are various degrees of moral personhood, for example, the moral status
of children and, in many instances, of women, the poor, and outsiders, as contrasted with the honors and privileges of adult male members of society. These

degrees depend on which of these various rights one is accorded and what priority is assigned to respecting them in an emergency or in a conflict of rights. These priorities can be complex and varied. For example, while men long had the vote and could manage property themselves, with women and children being "second-class citizens" in these matters, women and children were extended legal protection against abusive labor practices before men were and in emergencies were supposed to have first call on the lifeboats and other resources to protect their interests. Given the great variety of our interests, the many ways in which we can find ourselves in competition to fulfill those interests, and the multifarious ways in which groups have secured respect for various of their interests, it is not surprising either that there are various degrees of personhood$_e$ or that these degrees seem to form more of a tangled web than a tidy hierarchy.

Thus, personhood$_e$ has much more of a range of "more or less" built into it than does personhood$_d$. Although we speak of "second-class citizens" but not of "second-class persons," we do commonly recognize that children, for example, have rights to life, against exploitation, and so on, even though they are denied rights to property, marriage, and the like and may have others of their rights (e.g., to self-determination) less fully respected than the corresponding rights of adults. Thus, in comparison with human adults, children are not fully persons$_e$. Nonetheless, the rights they do enjoy set them and their moral status off sharply in contrast with the thorough absence of rights that property and creatures of nature must endure. So acknowledging the complication of degrees of personhood$_e$, we can still safely conclude that the evaluative use of "person" is to refer to beings with moral rights.

This distinction between metaphysical and moral personhood can be summarized in the following way:

	"Person$_d$"	"Person$_e$"
Function:	Describes a certain kind of being	Assigns a certain moral status
Content:	Denotes all and only human beings	Denotes beings with moral rights
Contrast:	Separates persons from inanimate objects, machines, plants, animals, and spirits	Separates persons from nature and property

II. The Humanist Principle

Having noted that "person" covers two concepts, one denoting a certain kind of being and the other a certain moral status, the obvious question to ask is, "What is the relation between these two concepts?" The currently dominant humanist, egalitarian morality holds that the relation is one of identity: all and only human beings have moral rights (i.e., rights to life, dignity, and a fulfilling life). (Henceforth, this identity thesis will be referred to as "the humanist principle," and "humanism" will be used to refer to any philosophy that maintains this thesis.)

Interpreting humanism as claiming that *only* human beings have moral rights may seem unjustified. However, again disregarding insignificant science fiction and religious cases, this interpretation can be substantiated by noting, first, that the descriptive use of "person" is to refer to human beings as *distinguished from* things, plants, and animals. Consequently, by employing the concept of personhood$_d$, the humanist principle restricts moral rights to human beings—that is, to *Homo sapiens*, since we are the only human beings we commonly encounter. Second, moral arguments for why all humans merit moral rights invariably presume that the basis for meriting rights is to be found in something, such as a soul, abstract rationality, or self-awareness, that only humans are supposed to possess, something that makes our species stand out from nature and shows us to be particularly estimable in contrast to other creatures. Finally, part of the significance of "person$_e$" is to separate beings with rights from those without rights. Consequently, when moral personhood is identified with metaphysical personhood, persons$_d$ are distinguished as *the* beings with rights. To suggest, as some philosophers have done, that "human rights" refers to rights had by all humans and perhaps by some other beings as well is as morally and linguistically insensitive as to suggest that "white rights" refers to rights had by all whites without commitment as to whether other races have or should have those rights as well. Consequently, it is correct to say that humanism claims that all and only human beings have moral rights.

Given that the humanist principle identifies moral with metaphysical personhood, the next question is, "Just what sort of identity is involved here, and what is the basis of it?" Many humanists, perhaps influenced by the fact that one word, be it "person," "man," or "human," has traditionally been used to label both metaphysical and moral personhood, insist that there is a relation in meaning between being human and having moral rights. For example, prison reformers commonly say things like "prisoners are still human beings," meaning "prisoners are still entitled to respect." However, since the above analysis shows that "person$_d$" and "person$_e$" have different functions, contents, and contrasts, there is no credible theory of meaning that could be employed to support a contention that the two are intentionally identical or even closely related.

Extensional identity seems the only possible identity here. Just as "the winning general at the Battle of Jena" and "the husband of the Empress Josephine" have no relation in meaning but still refer to the same man, so "person$_d$" and "person$_e$" could refer to the same set of beings even though they have different meanings. However, claims of extensional identity are arbitrary unless some explanation or justification can be given of why terms with different meanings nonetheless refer to the same set of beings. Here, a justification is called for and would have to be either

> logico-linguistic, referring to logical or linguistic rules,
>
> phenomenological, referring to intuitions, feelings, or other "psychological" evidence,
>
> transcendental, referring to the necessary conditions for the possibility of morality, or
>
> pragmatic, referring to the morally good consequences that derive from accepting the humanist principle.

However, no such arguments have yet been able to establish the extensional identity of metaphysical and moral personhood, and the reasons for this seem unavoidable. We shall discuss in turn each of these four types of argument and why they all fail.

A. THE LOGICO-LINGUISTIC DEFENSE OF HUMANISM

If there were a logical or linguistic rule relating moral to metaphysical personhood, then we could derive a moral imperative from a description. That someone is a human being is a matter of fact; that someone's life ought to be respected is a moral imperative. Therefore, if the principle that all and only human beings are persons$_e$ were a logical or linguistic rule, like the principle of the excluded middle or "'brother' means 'male sibling,'" we could use it to deduce from the factual premise "Toby is a human being" the conclusion "Toby's life ought to be respected," which is a moral imperative.

Some philosophers have argued that imperatives can be deduced from descriptions.[6] Their most plausible examples of such deductions are drawn from games or based on what are called "institutional facts." For example, Max Black offers the following deduction:

(1) Fischer wants to mate Botwinnik,
(2) The one and only way to mate Botwinnik is for Fischer to move the Queen,
(3) Therefore, Fischer should move the Queen;

and John Searle develops his position by providing the following chain of deductions:

(1) Jones uttered the words, "I hereby promise to pay you, Smith, five dollars,"
(2) Jones promised to pay Smith five dollars,

(3) Jones placed himself under (undertook) an obligation to pay Smith five dollars,

(4) Jones is under an obligation to pay Smith five dollars,

(5) Jones ought to pay Smith five dollars.

While examples like Black's may be of some logical interest, they are morally insignificant, for they work only in the context of a game, that is, in a context where the goals to be obtained and the rules by which those goals may be pursued are clearly defined. Morality, however, does not operate in a context with clearly defined goals and rules. Which of our wants are *appropriate* and which moves are *permissible* for satisfying those wants that are appropriate are often open questions in our everyday lives. Without such evaluative presumptions, an inference from wanting X and Y being the only way to attain X to an imperative to do Y is not justified. Outside the settled context of the game, with all its evaluative presumptions, the following inference is not valid:

(1) Fischer wants to defeat Botwinnik,

(2) Destroying Botwinnik's most prized possession is the one and only way for Fischer to defeat Botwinnik,

(3) Therefore, Fischer ought to destroy Botwinnik's most prized possession.

As for Searle, his argument depends on using so-called "institutional facts" as a bridge between descriptions and imperatives and on claiming that these institutional facts do not themselves contain moral evaluations. Institutional facts are to be contrasted with "natural facts," such as hair color, height, and the number of fingers one has. Institutional facts differ from these other facts in that they depend on cultural traditions or institutions for their existence. Examples of institutional facts are being married, being a judge, and owning property. While we could have ten fingers in a state of nature, we could not get married there; getting married requires a whole network of social customs, ceremonies, offices, declarations, and acknowledgments. The institutional fact at work in Searle's promising argument is that uttering the words "I promise" is one of the ways people place themselves under an obligation in English-speaking countries. This institutional fact appears as the crucial step (1a) in the full-blown formulation of Searle's deduction chain:

(1) Jones uttered the words, "I hereby promise to pay you, Smith, five dollars."

    (1a) Under certain conditions C anyone who utters the words (sentence), "I hereby promise to pay you, Smith, five dollars" promises to pay Smith five dollars.

    (1b) Conditions C obtain.

(2) Jones promised to pay Smith five dollars.

(2a) All promises are acts of placing oneself under (undertaking) an obligation to do the thing promised.

(3) Jones placed himself under (undertook) an obligation to pay Smith five dollars.

(3a) All those who place themselves under an obligation are, other things being equal, under an obligation.

(3b) Other things are equal.

(4) Jones is under an obligation to pay Smith five dollars.

(4a) Other things being equal, one ought to do what he is under an obligation to do.

(4b) Other things are equal.

(5) Jones ought to pay Smith five dollars.

There can be no question that (1a) expresses an institutional fact rather than a natural one, but that is not the decisive issue. The decisive issue is whether such institutional facts (i.e., institutional facts called upon in establishing moral obligations) are not really part of a culture's standard moral principles and practices. If that is what they are, then institutional "facts" are a kind of evaluation, and Searle's deduction fails to show how to derive "ought" from "is."[7]

Searle claims that his deduction rests solely on facts about linguistic practice, because there is nothing "subjective (matter of opinion, not a matter of fact, or a matter of moral decision) in the statement 'He made a promise.'"[8] D. Z. Phillips and H. O. Mounce, who champion the behavioral-paradigm analysis of moral$_{ai}$ value employed in Chapter 2, provide a second supporting reason here. They claim that institutional facts, such as our prohibition against lying, are not moral principles because they cannot, without circularity, be justified in the way moral principles are, that is, by reference to the very institutions in question.[9] However, although they are otherwise suggestive about the complexity of moral value, neither of these reasons is sufficient to establish that the institutional "facts" in question are not really part of our society's moral principles.

As for Phillips's and Mounce's reason, there is no reason to believe that there is only one pattern of moral justification; consequently, that a principle cannot be justified in one manner commonly employed in moral practice does not show that it cannot be justified in any morally relevant manner. There are many different sorts of moral questions, and they call for different modes of resolution. We sometimes question whether an action falls under a specific moral principle, for example, whether telling someone a consoling untruth amounts to lying. At other times, we are concerned about which conflicting moral evaluation has priority over the other, for instance, civic or professional obligations. And on other occasions, we wonder which moral ideology should be followed, for example, whether we should opt for socialized medicine or continue to try to patch up our private enterprise medical system. All these are moral questions and require different patterns of justification, ranging from conceptual clarification and getting the facts straight to trying to imagine what a purported ideal world would feel like. To suggest that a society's basic moral principles are not moral principles because they cannot be justified, without circularity, by reference to those basic moral principles is as mistaken as saying that the basic axioms of Euclidean geometry are not elements of Euclid's geometry because they cannot be justified by being deduced from the axioms of that geometry. All Phillips and Mounce have shown is that the obligations to keep promises and to avoid lying occupy the position of (or analogous to) axioms, rather than that of (or analogous to) theorems, in our society's moral scheme and that, consequently, these obligations cannot be justified in the way the more secondary of our moral principles can be.

Turning to Searle's reasoning, it also suffers from oversimplification. Apparently, Searle's concern in deriving an imperative from a description is really to derive a subjective obligation from a nonsubjective principle. He explains that "the point is merely that when one enters an institutional activity by invoking the rules of the institution, one necessarily commits himself in such and such ways, regardless of whether one approves or disapproves of the institution."[10] He also states that his purpose is to challenge "the theory that every member of this class [evaluations] must be subjective."[11] Of course, our analysis in Chapters 2 and 3 thoroughly confirms Searle's purpose; we have emphasized the various ways in which there are nonsubjective dimensions to our moral values. However, accomplishing his purpose undermines Searle's reason for believing that his institutional "facts" do not contain basic moral principles. If not all evaluations are subjective, then the fact that institutional facts contain nothing "subjective (matter of opinion, not a matter of fact, or a matter of moral decision)" cannot show that they do not contain evaluations.

Furthermore, that certain institutions contain moral principles, and not merely logical and linguistic rules, is indicated by the fact that our obligation to the rules of these institutions, such as keeping our promises and not lying, is a moral obligation quite unlike our conceptual obligation to *modus ponens*, "'bachelor' means 'unmarried male,'" and other logical and linguistic rules. This, in turn, is shown by the fact that while we find someone who regularly breaks logical or linguistic rules by constructing invalid arguments or misusing words, to be irrational or nonsensical, we find someone who regularly lies and breaks his or her promises not to be irrational or nonsensical but unreliable and lacking character. When people cheat at poker, they are still playing poker, and we understand what they are up to and, sometimes, may even admire how cleverly they are going about it, even though we believe that, morally, they ought not to be doing it. Playing by the rules is a moral, not a conceptual, obligation.

Thus, to maintain that there is a logical or linguistic rule relating moral to metaphysical personhood contradicts a traditional logical principle that has withstood the test of many ingenious challenges. Discarding that principle *because* it poses an obstacle to justifying the humanist principle would, of course, leave the project of founding humanism on logic circular and, consequently, still a failure.

B. THE PHENOMENOLOGICAL DEFENSE OF HUMANISM

Turning to phenomenological issues, the idea here is that the humanist principle is rooted in human nature. It is supposed to be a part of our "true selves," which moralists often counsel us to "return to" or "get in touch with" in order to discover and do what is morally right.

A problem that this approach encounters immediately is the fact that there have been and remain long-standing, widely subscribed to moral and religious traditions that do not accept or employ the humanist principle. For example, some tribes consider only tribe members to be persons$_e$; antebellum slave owners and white South Africans consider only members of their own race to be persons$_e$; and Hinduism and other vegetarian traditions consider animals other than human beings to be persons$_e$. Thus, history suggests that denying personhood$_e$ to large segments of the human population is at least as native to human psychology as the humanist principle, and given the great number of adherents to Hinduism and other religions that teach the transmigration of souls and reverence for nonhuman life forms, the humanist principle may not be the second but, at best, only the third most common view of the relation between moral and metaphysical personhood.

It might be objected that people who deny that some persons$_d$ are persons$_e$ or who believe that some nonpersons$_d$ are persons$_e$ are somehow confused or demented and, consequently, do not typify human nature. However, people who deny that certain human beings are persons$_e$ seem quite aware that these beings are human, that is, that they are self-aware, self-motivated, in possession of a language, and capable of making and executing plans. The way these nonhumanists protect themselves against slaves and other tribes, in contrast to the way they deal with animals, indicates this. Consequently, it cannot be said that these nonhumanists hold the humanist principle but fail to recognize that some of the beings they consider nonpersons$_e$ are persons$_d$. Similarly, there is no evidence to suggest that Hindus and other ethical vegetarians believe that cows and other nonhuman beings are human beings. Nor do either those who limit or those who expand the scope of personhood$_e$ beyond the humanist identification seem to be otherwise out of touch with reality or mentally deficient; so their views cannot be dismissed as being unrepresentative of normal human psychology. To respond that, nonetheless, these religious and moral traditions are immature, degradations, distortions, or otherwise divorced from *true* human nature would be to beg the question here, since the reason these expressions of human nature would be considered false is simply that they are at odds with the humanist principle. Consequently, historical and anthropological evidence seems to count not for but against the humanist principle being a native part of human feelings or intuition.

Perhaps the most notable phenomenological evidence that suggests that slave owners, cannibals, Nazis, and so forth do not consider slaves, nontribe members, Jews, and others to be persons$_d$ is the tendency to label slaves, criminals, opposing soldiers, the oppressing class, and the like as "beasts," "animals," "pigs," "vermin," "snakes in the grass," and "insects that prey on the life of the people." It would seem that before we can treat human beings as less than persons$_e$, we have to "psyche ourselves up to it" by denying their personhood$_d$.

While intriguing and suggestive in many ways, this practice does not provide unequivocal support for the humanist principle, since it would appear to be an historical accident consequent upon our society's having already accepted that principle. Having been raised in a culture with a strong humanist tradition, we must convince ourselves that the humanist principle does not apply to our situation before we can comfortably demean, harm, impoverish, and so forth other human beings. Allowing ourselves to be dominated by slogans, symbols, and strong emotions accomplishes this. However, those who have not been raised within such a tradition, for example, Asian warlords, the slave merchants of the pre-Christian Mediterranean, and Indian husbands who kill their wives if dowry payments cannot be made, do not appear to need to psych themselves up in this way before treating some human beings as other than persons$_e$. Once again, to respond that these other social traditions are distortions and not expressive of *true* human nature would be to beg the question. Thus, our tendency to deny the metaphysical personhood of those whom we want to treat as nonpersons$_e$ would appear to be a product of the humanist tradition and cannot, therefore, provide a phenomenological justification for it.

Phenomenologically, then, the diversity of moral traditions developed by otherwise rational people indicates that the humanist principle is not a native part of human feelings or intuition, and that we live in a humanist culture provides a plausible explanation of the phenomenological evidence that seemed to challenge this conclusion. Furthermore and most important, wherever there are disagreements between moral traditions, attempts to resolve these disagreements by reference to human nature are doomed to failure. If a moral value were really a part of human *nature*, normal humans could not feel or believe differently. A few seriously deformed humans, such as Hitler and Manson, could feel differently— the concept of human nature allows for a few exceptions—but traditions of such feelings could not develop if they were contrary to human nature. Consequently and ironically, founding the humanist principle on human nature would discredit the humanism and morality of that principle, since such a foundation would require claiming that all those who do not subscribe to that principle are immature, demented, corrupted by society, or otherwise "not truly human," that is, would require denying their personhood$_d$. Begging the question is the least of the evils contained in such a strategy.

.C. The Transcendental Defense of Humanism

Turning to the transcendental strategy for justifying the humanist principle, we find that arguments in support of a necessary condition relationship between metaphysical and moral personhood generally take the following form:

B1: Rationality is a necessary condition for morality.

B2: Moral respect is due that without which morality could not be.

B3: Therefore, rational beings are due respect.[12]

We have already dealt at length in Chapters 2 and 3 with most of the issues underlying and undermining this argument. So we may here limit ourselves to quickly pointing out two further, serious problems with this argument.

First, in order for argument B to support the humanist principle, it must be shown that all and only human beings are rational. However, infants and the severely retarded, senile, and brain-damaged cannot be labeled "rational" in any of the senses of that term discussed in Chapters 1 and 3. On the other hand, normal adults of many nonhuman species can solve practical problems, communicate their needs and other information, engage in social orders, assume responsibilities, and otherwise lead independent, successful, fulfilling lives; consequently, these animals can meaningfully be called "rational." Therefore, assuming that "rational being" is not defined as yet another name for human beings, argument B does not support the humanist principle, because "rational being" does not meaningfully refer either to all or to only human beings.

Actually, I suspect that "rational being" is merely another name for human beings. Here is an example of why I suspect this: Alan Donagan, commenting on Genesis 1:26, "And God said, Let . . . man . . . have dominion over all the earth," writes, "This is reasonably interpreted as an affirmation that the earth and all that is on it exist for the sake of the rational beings who live on it; *that is,* for the sake of man."[13] If this suspicion is correct, then this first criticism of argument B is incorrect. However, such a stipulative response to this first criticism would only make the second criticism more severe.

Second, as discussed in Chapter 3, the claim in B1 is misleading. Reason (i.e., normal, adult, human intelligence) is not necessary for being any kind of moral being but only for being a fully moral$_{ad}$ agent (i.e., an agent who does good out of her commitment to realizing a moral ideal). As noted, members of many species of animals exhibit moral virtues such as compassion, responsibility, and parental concern, even though they clearly lack normal$_h$ intelligence and cannot, therefore, be fully moral$_{ad}$ agents. Now, whether it is a question of moral$_{ai}$ or moral$_{ad}$

value, it is the virtuousness of kind, courageous, and other virtuous actions, rather than their being parts of an ideal world or being pursued as such, that is the more basic moral value. As Socrates might have admonished Euthyphro, it is the virtuousness of such actions that makes them parts of an ideal world and worthy of pursuit, not *vice versa*. Consequently, pursuing ideals is not the *sine qua non* of moral$_{ad}$ value; rather, to borrow Kant's metaphor, pursuing ideals is part of the superstructure of moral$_{ad}$ value, which is built upon the foundation of virtue. Therefore, following the spirit of argument B, we note that it is the virtuous agent to which we owe respect, and that argument thus covers nonhuman as well as human beings.

As also noted in the previous chapter, the traditional tactic of discounting these animal expressions of moral virtues as merely instinctual or reflexive and, therefore, lacking moral$_{ad}$ significance will not do. We may add here that this tactic can itself be seen and discredited as an expression of ignorance and of species prejudice. Only those who have never lived with and cared for animals can believe that animals are merely bundles of instincts and reflexes lacking individuality, practical reason, and free will. Contemporary ethological studies are starting to confirm what pet owners and other "animal lovers" have long known:

> By close and careful observation, ethologists have learned to recognize the individuals in these groups [of vervet monkeys] and have been able to study the behavior of each one relative to his companions over extended periods. Learning to recognize individual animals under natural conditions, a very important advance in ethology, has led to the discovery of previously unsuspected patterns of behavior that could not be appreciated when the animals were treated as interchangeable units. One discovery has been that not only the ethologist but the animals themselves often recognize their companions as individuals and treat them accordingly.[14]

Much of the evidence of "animal awareness" and "animal thinking" that Griffin and his followers report is not new. Rather, the cognitive significance of well-known observations had gone unrecognized because "scientists" were complacently sure that animals were not aware and could not think. The same, I would suggest, has been true in the area of "animal virtue," especially where it has been presumed that morality was a cognitive activity. It is our complacent assurance that we are morally superior and even unique that has prevented us from acknowledging obvious expressions of animal virtue, from looking for further expressions of animal virtue, and from adjusting our moral concepts and principles to recognize and reward nonhuman, virtuous agents. One is reminded of the complacent assurance of gentlemen from ancient Greece to Victorian England concerning the intellectual and moral inferiority of women and of the embarrassing blindness to which that assurance led otherwise perceptive men.

Thus, there is significant evidence to challenge the claim that normal, adult, human intelligence is a necessary condition for the existence of all kinds of moral value. Furthermore, the traditional refusal to acknowledge this evidence bears the marks of traditional refusals to acknowledge the evidence against similar prejudices (e.g., racism and sexism). Finally, this argument, which is explicitly about the moral significance of rationality, not of humanity, does not exactly fit the humanist principle anyway, since not all and only human beings can be meaningfully called "rational." Therefore, the transcendental argument for the humanist principle fails.

D. THE CONSEQUENTIAL DEFENSE OF HUMANISM

Thus, the logico-linguistic, phenomenological, and transcendental arguments to justify extensionally identifying metaphysical and moral personhood all fail. The only remaining option would seem to be trying to give the humanist principle a pragmatic, moral justification by basing the principle on a judgment of how moral rights should be distributed in order to make the world a morally better place. The proper justificatory question then becomes, "How well does the humanist principle contribute to the progress of morality?"

Trying to formulate such a justification may seem a hopeless task simply because identifying moral progress seems a hopeless task. For example, what seems to be moral progress to the Christian will be a further step into decadence for the Nietzschean, and what is moral progress for the utilitarian will not even be morally relevant for the Kantian. With so many conflicting moral systems, both philosophical and popular, it may seem that any evaluation of moral progress must be arbitrary.

Perhaps the best we can do in response to this difficulty is to continue to acknowledge the diversity of morality and to evaluate the humanist principle against the general goals of the Christian, Kantian, utilitarian tradition in which that principle has arisen. These goals may be roughly characterized as follows:

> developing moral character, so that our actions will be based on compassion, respect, courage, and other moral virtues,
> both reducing the suffering in life and otherwise making life more enjoyable and fulfilling, and
> insuring that opportunities, goods, punishments, and rewards are distributed fairly.

These goals are, of course, platitudinous and must be so, if we are to avoid becoming entangled in sectarian squabbles that are irrelevant to the issue at hand. Nonetheless, they will provide sufficient indicators of the moral value of humanism.

The superior moral value of humanism over feudalism, caste societies, racism, anti-Semitism, sexism, and so on will be accepted here without question. Perhaps having been born and educated into a humanist tradition, we are complacent in our belief that humanism has done more to minimize suffering, develop moral character, and make the world a more enjoyable, fulfilling, and fair place than have these other systems. Be that as it may, we shall not raise such questions here. Rather than contrasting humanism with other established moral systems, we shall consider the general thrust of the humanist principle and of the concept of personhood$_e$ it employs. That is, we shall be concerned with whether that principle and that concept point us unequivocally toward accomplishing our moral goals, or whether they have serious drawbacks in the pursuit of a morally better world.

One such drawback to the humanist principle is indicated by the following example. It follows from that principle that a human thief who robs a blind man merits moral rights, because he is still a human being, while a Seeing Eye dog does not merit moral rights, because it is just a dog. However, if the actions of these two could be described without indicating the agents' species, we would commonsensically say that the thief merits our contempt (*ceteris paribus*), while the Seeing Eye dog deserves our respect. The dog is both a moral$_{ai}$ and a virtuous being, while the thief is neither; consequently, that the thief, but not the dog, enjoys moral rights under the humanist principle certainly does not help make the world a fairer place. Put generally, that outstandingly virtuous and even merely innocent animals may be killed for human pleasure, in food or sport, for human vanity, in furs and cosmetics, for human curiosity, in science, and to bear the burdens of human ills, in medicine, while even the most heinous of human criminals is protected by moral and legal rights against such treatment is as blatant an example of prejudice as is the following infamous exchange between Huckleberry Finn and Aunt Sally:

> "It wasn't the grounding—that didn't keep us back but a little. We blowed out a cylinder-head."
> "Good gracious! anybody hurt?"
> "No'm. Killed a nigger."
> "Well, it's lucky; because sometimes *people* do get hurt." [15]

What has gone morally wrong both in the case of the "nigger" and in that of the thief and the Seeing Eye dog is that the moral status of various individuals is being determined by their metaphysical characteristics (i.e., race and species) without regard to their moral character, to their crimes or contributions to making the world a morally better place, or to accomplishing the goals of morality such as minimizing suffering. According to Meredith Williams, who has written in opposition to extending moral rights to animals, "prejudice essentially involves a failure to treat a group appropriately, a failure based on irrelevant, arbitrary, or trivial grounds." [16] Racism is a prejudice because individuals' race is irrelevant to their ability to benefit from an education, to be informed voters, and otherwise to enjoy and exercise many rights and responsibilities, yet they are denied these rights and responsibilities precisely on the basis of this irrelevant metaphysical condition. Conversely, people born into a royal family will be considered superior persons and will enjoy educational opportunities, the prerogatives of power, and so forth, even though they are dullards, vicious, or otherwise unable to benefit from these opportunities or to exercise authority wisely, compassionately, and fairly. These individuals benefit from their royal birth, another morally irrelevant metaphysical characteristic, in spite of their lack of fitness for those benefits. This is why aristocracies of birth are another form of prejudice. Humanism shares this logic of prejudice with racism and feudalism: it assigns and denies moral rights on the basis of a metaphysical characteristic, being human, rather than basing these assignments and denials on moral character, moral accomplishments, or other evaluative considerations, such as minimizing suffering, relevant to making the world a morally better place.

Metaphysical characteristics can enter without prejudice into the issue of who does and who does not deserve moral rights only where it can be shown that those metaphysical characteristics are necessary for developing some moral virtue, making some moral contribution, or otherwise attaining some moral goal. For example, as discussed in the previous chapter, possessing normal$_h$ intelligence seems to be a morally relevant metaphysical characteristic because it seems necessary for being a fully moral$_{ad}$ agent. Simply being a certain kind of thing can never be sufficient to determine one's moral status, since that status depends on whether one uses what he has (including himself) to make the world a morally better place. Observing this limitation would seem to leave only the following three functions for metaphysical characteristics to perform in determining moral status:

(1) If an individual lacks metaphysical characteristics essential for possessing certain moral virtues, making certain moral contributions, or participating in the attainment of certain moral goals, then that individual cannot be entitled to whatever moral status is peculiar to possessing those virtues, making those contributions, or participating in attaining those goals. For example, individuals lacking normal$_h$ intelligence cannot be entitled to the rights and responsibilities due only fully moral$_{ad}$ agents, and since beings lacking nervous systems apparently cannot suffer pain, they cannot participate, at least directly, in the assignment of moral rights deriving from our efforts to minimize the amount of pain in the world.

(2) If an individual possesses the characteristics necessary for developing a moral virtue or making a moral contribution but does not do so, then that individual may be guilty and may be denied certain moral rights and responsibilities, while an individual who behaves in a similar manner but is not capable of pos-

sessing the virtue or making the contribution in question cannot be guilty in the same way and cannot deserve the same sort of punishment. For example, as discussed in the previous chapter, a dog or a child who digs up the neighbor's tulips or makes off with some candy is not guilty of vandalism or theft and does not merit punishment in the way a normal, adult human who did such things would.

(3) If an individual is a still undeveloped member of a metaphysically identifiable group the normal, fully developed members of which ordinarily possess moral virtues, make moral contributions, or are extended moral rights as part of our efforts to make the world a morally better place, then that individual may merit certain provisional moral rights to protect her interests until she has the opportunity to develop and meet the morally relevant criteria ordinarily met by fully developed members of her group. For example, even though a fetus is not yet sentient, it could still be provisionally extended certain moral protections (e.g., the right to life) on the basis of its being an early stage in the development of a sentient life.

None of these three moral functions of metaphysical considerations can support the humanist principle. That principle would make the metaphysical condition of being human both a necessary and a sufficient condition for meriting moral rights. However, the first of these three functions could only make being human necessary but not sufficient for moral rights. The second function could make being human sufficient only for rendering us liable to losing moral rights, and the third function could make being human sufficient only for a provisional extension of rights. In all three cases, metaphysical considerations like being human are not the decisive factor but only the handmaidens of moral considerations, and that is the way things must be to avoid the logic of prejudice.

Some readers, with the abortion issue in mind, may find the third of these ways of interjecting metaphysics into morality disturbing. However, these worries can be readily allayed by emphasizing that citing this possibility of provisionally extending moral rights certainly does not settle the abortion issue. The fundamental point of detailing the ways in which metaphysical considerations can enter into the unprejudiced assignment and denial of moral rights is to emphasize that metaphysical characteristics cannot by themselves provide an unprejudiced basis for assigning moral rights. While the lack of certain metaphysical characteristics can provide a sufficient basis for denying certain moral rights, the converse does not hold, since it is only insofar as those characteristics figure into actually developing moral character, really making moral contributions, or actually attaining moral goals such as minimizing suffering that possessing them acquires moral significance. There is no reason to believe that the abortion issue is not covered by this thesis. Indeed, it would be strange if the possibility of developing certain metaphysical characteristics (e.g., becoming a person$_d$) were sufficient to gain one a moral right (e.g., the right to life) even provisionally, which the actual possession of those characteristics was not by itself sufficient to procure.

Returning to the humanist principle, we note that it is because it goes far beyond these three legitimate interjections of metaphysical characteristics into moral concerns that that principle expresses a form of prejudice and leads us into moral errors like those cited above, that is, respecting individuals who do not deserve it while failing to respect the interests of individuals who merit respect because of their virtues and contributions to making the world a morally better place. In this way, the humanist principle interferes with, rather than aids, our making the world a fairer place. It also interferes with our efforts at minimizing suffering in the world, since there is a natural tendency to take less seriously the suffering of those whose interests are not considered worthy of protection by moral rights. The low priority given enforcing anticruelty to animals laws and the meager penalties meted out by such laws are examples of this. Consequently, the proper answer to "Should we continue to accept the humanist principle as an effective tool for making the world a morally better place?" is "Yes, if we can do no better, but as fully moral$_{ad}$ agents, we should try to remove even this form of prejudice from our way of life."

The obstacles to such an advance are both biological and epistemological. The biological obstacle is the instinctual pull of species preference and preservation. The physician who killed a baby baboon to transplant its heart into "Baby Fae" responded to animal rights concerns with "I am a member of the human species," and ethologist Donald R. Griffin has noted that "it seems plausible that animals would be more likely to survive and reproduce if their beliefs included confident faith in their own superiority and the assurance that exploiting other species was normal and correct behavior."[17] The epistemological obstacle is the possibility that we cannot evaluate moral virtues, contributions, and goals without reverting to some form of parochialism, that is, without presuming that the tradition of moral virtues, contributions, and goals in which we have been raised is *the* correct one. An example of such parochialism is the habit of narrators on wildlife programs who extol the virtues of animals to include, wherever possible, monogamy among those virtues. Thus, it might seem that both genetics and cultural relativism leave humanism the least evil form of prejudice of which we are capable.

Whether or to what extent we can progress beyond the limits of humanism is not a matter to be settled by philosophical or any other sort of deductive, armchair reflection. It is an empirical matter that will be settled only if we give it a try. The history of moral progress that has led up to humanism shows that we are capable of overcoming long-ingrained prejudices, such as racism and sexism. Furthermore, the immediate epistemic problem concerning animal virtues is not the difficult one of recognizing and appropriately responding to what animals consider virtuous behavior; rather, the immediate challenge is to recognize and make a place in our network of moral concerns and obligations for the many instances among animals of what *we* consider to be virtuous behavior. Thus, the pragmatic justification for resting content with humanism is as scanty as the phenomenological justification proposed for the humanist principle.

The other question of moral justification raised at the beginning of this subsection was whether we should continue to distinguish persons$_e$ from nonpersons$_e$. It is with this question that we shall conclude this section.

The concept of personhood$_e$ has a dual function:

> it helps to protect those considered persons$_e$ against suffering the hurts and indignities that the selfish tendencies of human psychology could inflict on them, and
> it helps to justify treating those creatures not considered persons$_e$ selfishly.

By assigning them moral rights, the concept of personhood$_e$ protects some creatures from being treated merely as means to human satisfaction. By denying them moral rights, the concept of personhood$_e$ opens the door to treating creatures considered property or creatures of nature merely as means to human satisfaction. Is it morally acceptable and preferable to have a concept that functions in these ways?

The moral value of personhood$_e$ is usually determined through a contrast with what the world would be like if there were no moral protection at all against human selfishness. We would then be thrown into Hobbes' "war of every man against every man." In contrast to an amoral world in which no one respects anything, the concept of personhood$_e$ has obvious moral value: a world in which human selfishness is somewhat inhibited is morally better than one in which selfishness reigns unchallenged.

However, if we evaluate personhood$_e$ on the basis of its permissive function, this traditional, positive moral evaluation is thrown into question. By limiting moral rights to a small sphere of beings and actions, namely, to persons$_e$ and to the actions that affect their basic interests, the concept of personhood$_e$ encourages us to think of morality as basically a narrow range of restrictions placed on beings who may otherwise do pretty much as they please, who have a right to have their interests satisfied, and who may treat property and creatures of nature merely as means to that satisfaction. The concept of personhood$_e$, with its sharp separation of rights-bearing persons$_e$, including the lower-class ones, such as children, from rights-deprived creatures of nature and property, suggests that, basically, to be moral one need only observe the obligations due persons$_e$. In all other areas and endeavors, we are basically free to satisfy our needs and desires pretty much in whatever way we please, as long as this does not incidentally intrude upon the rights of other persons$_e$, for example, by destroying their property, interfering with their enjoyment of nature, or offending their sensibilities concerning the suffering of nonpersons$_e$.

Here are two contemporary examples of the consequences of not being a person$_e$. Many proabortion advocates follow Justice Blackman, in his famous *Roe* vs. *Wade* decision, in acknowledging that if an unborn infant is a person$_e$, then it may not be aborted, but if it is not a person$_e$, then one may kill it, they conclude, merely because it will interfere with one's social life or career or otherwise prove inconvenient. If the fetus is not a person$_e$, then it has no moral claim on life at all; consequently, the woman carrying the fetus need not even supply a reason for terminating that life — her simply desiring the abortion is considered the only morally relevant issue. Again, since the end of the Vietnam War, the plight of several hundred thousand displaced Vietnamese has generated a moral obligation, especially in the United States, to undertake extensive and expensive programs to aid these desperate persons$_e$. At the same time, tens of millions of displaced dogs and cats are simply exterminated annually in the United States, because we do not want to be bothered with running orphanages for these animals and feel no moral obligation to undertake such an effort for these displaced and desperate nonpersons$_e$.

Because part of its meaning is to contrast persons$_e$ to property and creatures of nature, the concept of personhood$_e$ contributes to a Philistine conception of morality. Instead of encouraging the development of morality as an all-pervasive, fundamental world outlook — which is what, let us not forget, is supposed to give those of us with normal$_h$ intelligence our special moral value as fully moral$_{ad}$ agents — it suggests restricting moral concern to the observance of a small number of rules, rather like the old joke of religion being something we must endure on Sunday, while the rest of the week, all is permitted. Since one of the goals of morality is to have human actions based on kindness, respect, and the other moral virtues, to the degree that the concept of personhood$_e$ justifies selfish action (i.e., action that shows a lack of compassion or respect for the interests of others), it frustrates the progress of morality.

Admittedly, there are other moral restrictions on doing what we please besides those involved in respecting the moral rights of others. For example, we are supposed to live up to ideals of civility and humaneness that cover the treatment of nonpersons$_e$. However, the point being made here is not that to have any moral standing at all individuals must have moral rights — although in some cases, such as in the abortion debate, that may, indeed, be the case. The point being made here is a pedagogical one concerning the direction for thought and attitude suggested by the concept of personhood$_e$, especially in the sharp contrast it draws and justifies between those with moral rights, on the one hand, and property and creatures of nature, on the other. These other moral considerations are irrelevant to that pedagogical issue. Furthermore, in actual practice, when the welfare of animals is at issue and is not buttressed by some issue concerning the welfare of persons$_e$ (e.g., the rights of future generations), these nonrights restrictions on doing what we please with animals count for very little. The factory farming of animals, the frivolous reasons for which people turn in their unwanted pets to be destroyed, and the many merely curious experiments performed on animals are examples of the very tenuous entry nonpersons$_e$ have into the moral arena.

Once again, it may seem that a protected oasis of respect in a world of selfishness is the best we can do. Since we humans already have great difficulty inhibiting our selfishness toward each other, it may seem to be folly to try to get us to extend moral rights to other beings. However, many people do care about the quality of life of other creatures, and some elements of the environmental protection and the animal welfare/rights movements are directly concerned with and respectful of the needs of creatures of nature and those considered property, instead of seeking protection for them merely as a means to insuring the quality of life of present and future human generations. The existence of these individuals and movements suggests that the distinction of persons$_e$ from nonpersons$_e$ is not a psychologically unavoidable part of morality. If this suggestion is correct, then the pragmatic justification of the concept of personhood$_e$ is no better than that of the humanist principle: both that concept and that principle may have served us well, but they are not free of prejudice, nor is there reason to believe that theirs is a prejudice we cannot overcome in our efforts to make the world a morally better place. Overcoming the humanist prejudice would probably be as great a step forward toward attaining our moral goals as was the triumph of humanism over feudalism, racism, and the like.

III. Conclusion

In conclusion, let us return to argument A. If we reformulate it using the terminology developed during this chapter, it looks like this:

A1′: Only persons$_e$ can have moral rights.
A2′: Animals are not persons$_d$.
A3′: Therefore, animals cannot have moral rights.

It is now clear that the first premise of argument A is a tautology deriving from the moral definition of "personhood" and that the argument equivocates by employing the moral sense of "person" in its first premise but the metaphysical sense of the term in its second premise. To avoid this equivocation by employing person$_e$ in both premises would leave the reconstructed second premise, "Animals are not persons$_e$," begging the question. Employing person$_d$ in both premises would leave the reconstructed first premise, "Only persons$_d$ can have moral rights," begging the question. Consequently, argument A is condemned to being either equivocal or circular.

Thus, argument A and the concept(s) of personhood on which it is based fail to settle the issue of extending moral rights to animals. If animals can and should have moral rights, then they can and should be persons$_e$. Being persons$_e$ is the same thing as having moral rights; therefore, being a person$_e$ cannot be a necessary condition for having those rights, except in the trivial sense that being a bachelor is a necessary condition for being an unmarried male. Nor have we seen any reason so far for believing that being a person$_d$ is a necessary condition for having moral rights. The substantive issues concerning whether or not animals can and should have moral rights must lie elsewhere.

Part II

"Animal Rights"?

WHICH ARE morally considerable beings and which are not has been a concern of moral philosophy ever since Aristotle declared that enslaving men was wrong —if they were Greeks. Through the years, we have observed and then rejected various criteria for meriting respect. We no longer think that slavery is wrong only if the enslaved are Greek, but we did for a considerable time think that slavery was permissible if the enslaved were black. We also treated women and children as property, though we no longer do so, and anti-Semitism, once considered the morally required attitude to take toward "Christ-killers," is now a dirty word. We are far from perfect, but we have produced a "Universal Declaration of the Rights of Man"—oops, let's make that "People"—in which we recognize that all people are entitled to have their basic interests respected.

One would have thought that the "history of freedom," to borrow Hegel's phrase, had run its course with the recognition that all people are entitled to basic freedoms. Now, the job remaining would be just to see that that recognition is translated from words into institutions and practice. But that is not the way history has been developing of late. As shown in Chapter 4, the principle making humans the only holders of basic moral rights is arbitrary, and during the past fifteen years, a new liberation movement has developed, one that claims that we must extend the frontier of freedom or moral respect beyond the human boundary to include animals. Such claims have impressed many as fantastic. Historically, the issue has always been distinguishing those people who were entitled to respect from those who could be enslaved or otherwise exploited. The result of that history has been that no such distinction is justified. But that still left "us," humans, segregated from "them," the animals, not to mention plants, rivers, and nature in general. Even if some among us were not morally unique, at least we, as a whole, have remained unique throughout our history of moral progress. All other Copernican revolutions notwithstanding, we have remained securely at the center of the moral universe. Animal liberation now claims that even this claim to distinction is erroneous. Morally, it is argued, *we* are on all fours with *them*.

Such claims have startled, dismayed, and infuriated many people, including some philosophers. The point of the following two chapters is to show that such reactions are unjustified. Chapter 5 clarifies what I, at least, think is being sought for animals under the rhetoric of "animal liberation" and "animal rights." Key terms like "animal," "liberation," "rights," and "equality" are clarified, and the analogy between animal liberation and other liberation movements is discussed. Chapter 6 shows that even our common morality, which has in practice so far provided so little relief for animals, in principle provides substantial support for liberating them. This defense of animal liberation is conducted along three fronts, the common moral concerns with happiness, fairness, and virtue.

What follows will not conclusively demonstrate that we ought (morally) to liberate animals. Since, as argued in Part I, morality is not the product of reason alone, I doubt that such demonstrations are possible when fundamental moral concerns are at issue and suspect that insisting on such demonstrations is merely an excuse for doing as one pleases, when, as is inevitably the case, no such demonstration can be provided. However, I do think that these chapters establish a presumption in favor of liberating animals, a presumption that will weigh heavier and heavier as we discover, in Part III, that the arguments that have been put forth to justify our continuing to deny moral rights to animals are unsound.

5

What Liberating Animals Is and Isn't About

ALTHOUGH THEY provide catchy labels, "animal liberation" and "animal rights" have occasioned considerable misunderstanding and much pointless debate. In this chapter I want to explicate what I believe is being sought for animals under these labels. This explication should help to undo some of the misunderstandings about liberating animals and extending moral rights to them. After this explication, we will be in a position to address the issue of justifying "liberating" animals and extending moral "rights" to them.

I. The Moral Sense of "Animal"

One of these misunderstandings concerns the use of "animal" in these labels. At most animal liberation presentations there is someone who rises to inquire whether flies, cockroaches, and other vermin are to enjoy rights to life, liberty, and the pursuit of happiness. Is swatting a fly to be murder in the Brave New World of animal rights? This heckler is soon joined, if not preceded, by another who accuses the animal liberationist of discriminating against plants and, consequently, being guilty of "fauna chauvinism." Do the arguments for animal liberation entail plant liberation as well? Of course, these hecklers are not really activists in the mosquito and tomato liberation movements. What they are attempting to do is to dispose of the animal liberation movement through a *reductio ad absurdum* argument (i.e., by showing what silly consequences it would have). As William James noted many years ago, the first response to a revolution is ridicule.

The insect and flora *reductios* will not work, however, because most animal liberationists accept what has come to be called "the interest requirement" for having moral rights. According to this criterion, which was apparently first proposed by Leonard Nelson in *A System of Ethics*, all and only beings with interests can have moral rights.[1] Having interests is to be interpreted as follows: S has an interest in x if and only if x affects (will affect, would affect) S's feelings of well-being. In turn, "feelings of well-being" is to be interpreted as referring to pleasure and pain, feeling fit and feeling ill, elation and depression, feelings of fulfillment and feelings of frustration, and the many other feelings that contribute to or detract from the enjoyment of or satisfaction with life. Now, the "animal" in "animal liberation" and "animal rights" refers to all and only those beings that meet the interest requirement. The phrase "sentient being" or "sentient animal" is sometimes employed to make this reference—and, incidentally, covers those infamous people who cannot feel pain, since pain is only one of the many feelings of well-being. (Other reasons for accepting the interest requirement will be discussed in Chapters 7 and 14.)

Thus, the criterion for being an "animal," in this moral sense, is not the biological criterion that distinguishes fauna from flora. Nor are animal liberationists confused about this, since most of them readily acknowledge that very probably not all biological animals have interests and, consequently, cannot have moral rights. However, since the nonhuman beings that would commonsensically be most readily acknowledged to have interests (e.g., dogs and deer) are commonly called "animals" (and this common term is not the biological term, either), talking about extending moral rights to cover all beings with interests in terms of "animal" liberation and "animal" rights is an understandable, if not entirely happy, convenience. Although employing "interests liberation" and "sentient rights" might allow us to communicate more precisely at a philosophical conference, they would hardly do as slogans for a movement that is at least as much a popular one as a professional philosophical movement.

As for the insects and the plants, all those that can meet the interest requirement must, if animal liberationists are to be consistent, be included in the concerns of this movement. However, to date there has been no serious evidence to show that plants have feelings of well-being—requiring *serious* evidence rules out the infamous "secret life of plants" reports. (Environmental ethics issues concerning plants will be discussed in Chapter 14.) Whether or which insects have interests is a more open question. If, as Donald R. Griffin argues, there is good reason to believe that at least some social insects are conscious, thinking "natural psychologists," then there may be good reason, if we take an unbiased look at the evidence, to believe that at least some insects have feelings of well-being. Griffin states his guiding idea as follows:

> I have mentioned the thought-provoking suggestion of Jolly (1966) and Humphrey (1978) that consciousness may have arisen in human evolution when social groups reached a size and degree of interdependence that made it important for each member to understand his companions' moods, intentions, and thoughts. Humphrey's idea that

socially interdependent primates or early men had to be what he calls "natural psychologists" rests on the assumption that for efficient interaction each group member must be able to understand his companions' frame of mind. . . . Can we extend this idea to other animals that live in social groups, even to the social insects? They are even more dependent on one another than any vertebrate, except perhaps for our own species. It may be even more important for a worker bee or ant to judge her sisters' moods correctly than it is for primates to assess one another as natural psychologists.[2]

It does not follow from this, however, that the insect *reductio* carries the day against animal liberation. If some insects have feelings of well-being, then a morality that attempts to respect all sentient beings will be more complicated than it would be if no insects were sentient. Of course, this sort of consequence is true of all moralities: the more diverse the group owed respect, the more complicated the morality must be. For example, dealing morally with one's "fellows" is more complicated now that women and racial and ethnic minorities are included among the rights-holders who are due respect. To one degree or another, we probably all share a yearning for a simpler life, but that practicing a revolutionary morality would be more complicated than resting content with the status quo does not indicate that that revolutionary morality is ridiculous, wrong, or even less warranted than the status quo.

Furthermore, acknowledging that some insects have moral rights would not by itself resolve the matter of how we are to deal with them, especially in conflict of interests situations. Especially since, as recognized in our analysis of personhood $_e$, to have moral rights is not necessarily to have the same set of rights as or equal priority of rights with other rights-holders, extending moral rights to those who have not enjoyed them before does not settle the matter of how we are to treat them. Rather, it opens the door to questions about how we ought (morally) to treat them that had not previously seemed relevant.[3] For example, the Emancipation Proclamation was not the culmination but the beginning of the civil rights movement, and Kant's *Metaphysics of Morals* is not a series of simple deductions from his *Foundations of the Metaphysics of Morals* but is, rather, much more complicated and entangled than that work. Also, in attempting to answer these new questions about how we ought (morally) to treat animals, if simple applications of ideas of equality, self-determination, and similar concepts commonly associated with liberation and rights would be ridiculous, then we can expect that those simple applications will, *for that very reason*, be rejected. This is what has happened in working out other liberation movements, as exemplified in the recent rejection of the claim that an end to sexual discrimination entails that male workers are entitled to maternity leave. In actual practice, ridiculous consequences do not discredit the basic principles of moral reform; rather, such consequences lead to a more subtle and practical understanding of those principles, an understanding that eliminates the ridiculous consequences. (We shall return, in Chapter 13, to discuss the place, or lack thereof, of *reductio* arguments in ethics.)

Finally, we may note that although these "Where do you draw the line?" questions may be amusing and conceptually intriguing, they are irrelevant to the current, major, practical concerns of the animal liberation movement, such as the (im)morality of factory farming, animal research, hunting, rodeos, and so forth. If any nonhuman animals have interests, then the animals (e.g., pigs, monkeys, bears, horses, etc.) that the animal rights movement is currently seeking to liberate surely do. Once the questions currently being raised concerning how we ought (morally) to treat these animals have been settled, it may be time to wonder whether insects have moral rights, need to be liberated, and what form such an enlightened morality should take. To bring up the question of insects before these current questions have been resolved is merely an attempt to avoid facing the real and clear issues at hand. (Of course, the arguments of this section presume that we are not the only animals with interests; this presumption will be defended in Chapter 7.)

II. Applying the Rhetoric of Liberation to Animals

"Liberation" also requires some explication when applied to animals. Advocates of liberating or extending moral rights to animals view this extension as a revolutionary break with moral tradition, including the anticruelty to animals part of that tradition, and as providing for animals something of great moral importance. However, according to Joel Feinberg, who has expressed sympathy for animal rights, having rights has special moral significance because

> having rights enables us to "stand up like men," to look others in the eye, and to feel in some fundamental way the equal of anyone. To think of oneself as the holder of rights is not to be unduly but properly proud, to have that minimal self-respect that is necessary to be worthy of the love and esteem of others.[4]

Thus, Feinberg locates the special moral importance of having rights in the area of enhancing one's self-respect, and the close connection between rights and dignity found in the goals and rhetoric of human liberation movements supports Feinberg's analysis. But while we can commonsensically acknowledge that cats, cattle, chickens, monkeys, pandas, and so on have interests in avoiding pain, freedom to move about, companionship, and quite a variety of other things, it is not easy to imagine them needing to feel "the equal of anyone" or "properly proud." If enhancing one's self-respect is an essential part of what is supposed to be accomplished by liberating a group and extending moral rights to its members, then animals would seem to be incapable of being liberated or of having moral rights. This would seem to leave us back with the anticruelty tradition as the moral basis for combatting the excesses of factory farming, animal research, hunting, and the like.

However, concluding as some philosophers recently have that the animal liberation movement is "a bizarre exaggeration" of the anticruelty to animals tradition would be a mistake.[5] Although liberating animals and extending moral rights to them cannot, presumably, have the special importance described by Feinberg and found in human liberation movements, what animal liberationists are calling for still differs fundamentally from the anticruelty to animals tradition.

The anticruelty to animals tradition has been a powerful force in shaping our moral and legal codes concerning animals since the early nineteenth century; so we may judge its fundamental principles from our contemporary moral and legal attitudes and practices concerning animals. The predominant attitude regarding animal interests today is that what animals require for an enjoyable, satisfying life (e.g., freedom to roam, freedom from pain, and life itself) may be routinely sacrificed in the pursuit of human happiness, provided the animals are not treated sadistically and are spared suffering that can be conveniently and economically avoided. Discussing the issue of killing animals to satisfy human desires, Bonnie Steinbock expresses this traditional, anticruelty ethic clearly and concisely: "Their [animals'] capacity to suffer provides us with some reason to kill them painlessly, if this can be done without too much sacrifice of human interests."[6] Thus, the anticruelty to animals tradition continues to consider and treat animals as fundamentally resources for human consumption, limiting moral concern to the humane handling and processing of those resources.

On the other hand, "liberating" animals refers to putting an end to the routine sacrifice of animal interests for human benefit, even where the sacrifice is executed humanely. Animal liberationists emphasize respecting the interests of animals themselves, as opposed to being solely or even primarily concerned with the interests that humans have in using animals. For example, Tom Regan seeks to have the logic of what makes it wrong to treat even "marginal" humans (e.g., the severely retarded or brain-damaged) as "means merely" applied to animals as well:

> It would be wrong to treat [marginal] humans merely as a means because it would fail to acknowledge and respect the fact that they are the subjects of a life whose value is logically independent of any other being's taking an interest in it. . . . The subjects of a more or less good life have value that is logically independent of their being valued as a means by anyone else. . . . All those beings (and only those beings) which have inherent value have rights. . . . It is difficult at best to understand how anyone could reasonably deny that there are many, many species of animals whose members satisfy this requirement.[7]

The primary purpose of extending moral rights to animals would be to insure that their interests could be sacrificed for fulfilling the interests of others only in the sorts of situations and according to the sorts of principles that justify sacrificing the interests of some humans to fulfill the interests of others. For example, just as current regulations basically restrict risky medical research on humans to experiments that seem likely not only to benefit the wider community but also to be therapeutic (or otherwise beneficial) for the research subjects themselves, so the extension of moral rights to animals would basically limit risky medical research on animals to experiments that would have a good chance of being therapeutic (or otherwise beneficial) for the animal subjects of that research. Such a restriction would, of course, go far beyond even the most liberal of our current humane regulations concerning the use and sacrifice of animals in medical research, and its adoption would mark a revolutionary step beyond our anticruelty to animals tradition.

Thus, even if talk of "liberating" animals and extending moral "rights" to them cannot plausibly refer to changing animals' attitudes toward themselves, it can and does plausibly refer to changing our attitude toward animals from one that regards them as beings that must be treated humanely but that are, nonetheless, fundamentally resources for fulfilling human interests to an attitude that regards animals as fellow beings whose interest in an enjoyable, satisfying life must be respected and protected in the way basic human interests are respected and protected. In this way, liberating animals would require changing our attitude toward them in basically the same way liberating blacks and women requires changing the attitudes concerning them held by whites and men. Consequently, even if animal liberation lacks the self-consciousness-raising dimension of human liberation movements, applying the rhetoric of "liberation" and "rights" to animals is understandable and appropriately expresses this call for a revolutionary change in our moral tradition.

III. Applying the Concept of Equality to Animals

Another source of misunderstanding lies in the use of the phrase "equal rights" when discussing animal liberation. For example, Ruth Cigman characterizes animal liberationists as claiming that "as women and blacks should have equal rights to those of men and whites, animals should have rights equal to those of persons, because difference of species does not constitute a morally relevant difference."[8] That such a characterization should come to mind is understandable, since "equal rights" is the rallying cry of so many contemporary liberation movements, but how "equal rights" could be meaningfully used to characterize the goals of animal liberation is not easily understood.

As already noted, animal liberationists routinely deny that they are seeking for animals the same set of rights already enjoyed by humans. Recognizing that rights are tied to interests and that animals do not have all the interests we do (e.g., in religion and education), animal liberationists recognize that it would be nonsensical to seek for animals all the rights we require. For example, Roger W. Galvin, the attorney who prosecuted the infamous Taub case, proposes the following rights for animals:

> 1. All sentient beings have a right to live out their lives according to their nature, instincts and intelligence.
> 2. All sentient beings have a right to live in a habitat ecologically sufficient for normal existence.
> 3. All sentient beings have a right to be free from exploitation.[9]

These are sufficiently different from our Bill of Rights and Declaration of the Universal Rights of Man to make clear that animal liberationists are not seeking extensional equality of rights for animals.

It might be thought that what animal liberationists are seeking is equal priority of rights for animals. For example, Bonnie Steinbock suggests that animal liberationists would feel an obligation to show no preference for feeding starving children over feeding starving dogs.[10] However, once again matters are not nearly so simple. Many animal liberationists contend that it is not a violation of the animal liberation ethic to consider some forms of animal (including human) life more valuable than others. For example, Peter Singer writes:

> A rejection of speciesism does not imply that all lives are of equal worth. While self-awareness, intelligence, the capacity for meaningful relations with others, and so on are not relevant to the question of inflicting pain—since pain is pain, whatever other capacities beyond the capacity to feel pain the being may have—these capacities may be relevant to the question of taking life. It is not arbitrary to hold that the life of a self-aware being, capable of abstract thought, of planning for the future, of complex acts of communication, and so on, is more valuable than the life of a being without these capacities.[11]

While Singer's utilitarian separation of pain issues from mortal issues is not commonly accepted by animal liberationists, the idea that some lives are more valuable than others is not uncommon.

Not a few philosophers have criticized this sort of position, contending that the claim that it is not arbitrary, even for an animal liberationist, to consider the life of a highly rational being to be worth more than that of a less rational one amounts to taking back the claim that animals merit equal consideration for their interests with humans.[12] However, this is no more true than would be the claim that someone who believes that women and children should be given priority in an emergency would be taking back her belief that men, women, and children have equal moral status. No one would suggest that if we hold the traditional belief that women and children are entitled to first place in the lifeboats, consistency requires us to conclude that they would be justified in using men as research tools, eating them for dinner, and hunting them for sport. So why should one require such an inference in the case of comparing the moral value of human life with that of animal life?

We cannot infer from the principles used when we are forced to choose the lesser of two evils to the principles of moral status in force when such a hard choice is not required. Such emergency principles are invoked not as extensions of common moral principles but as auxiliaries needed because those common principles do not provide satisfactory guidance in these uncommon situations. Consequently, it is not self-contradictory to say that when we can fulfill both human interests (e.g., in food) and animal interests (e.g., in life), we ought (morally) to do so, but when we cannot fulfill the interests of both, we ought (morally) to give preference, within the bounds of fairness, to fulfilling the interests of those beings capable of the greater range of moral actions. The first part of that conjunction applies to one kind of situation, the second part to a thoroughly different kind of situation; so they cannot contradict.

Furthermore, neither of these imperatives is arbitrarily based on mere sentiment or species prejudice. Both are based on a concern with making the world a morally better place; the second expresses that concern by giving priority to the life of those beings best able to maximize happiness or other moral values. Nor would this second imperative always favor humans. It could command us to sacrifice humans to save animals on occasion; for example, it could (*ceteris paribus*) command us to sacrifice cancerous old men to save healthy young wolves and to sacrifice rapists to save Seeing Eye dogs.[13] Therefore, it is not speciesist, or otherwise morally prejudiced, to hold that although all are entitled to equal consideration of their interests, there may be occasions on which there would be adequate moral justification for sacrificing the interests of some individuals to fulfill the interests of others.

This idea is an extension beyond the limits of our own species of an evaluation that is common even within our humanist, egalitarian tradition. Even if we advocate equal human rights for all, we can still acknowledge that the life of a normal, healthy young adult is (*ceteris paribus*) more valuable than that of a retarded, senile, or brain-damaged person, that of a person suffering from some crippling disease, or that of someone with a progressive, incurable disease. Fortunately, this sort of evaluation ordinarily remains behind the practical scene, becoming relevant only when, as in practicing medicine during time of war, we have to choose which endangered lives to save with scarce resources. Extending moral rights to other animals would work in the same way: the everyday presumption of "equal consideration" for the interests of all sentient beings, to use Peter Singer's phrasing, would not prohibit morally relevant preferences for one life over another in extraordinary, otherwise irresolvable conflict of interests situations.

This common distinction of ordinary from extraordinary cases in morality undercuts the many "burning building," "desert island," "lifeboat," and other supposed *reductios* of the animal liberation position. That Mark and Samantha have equal moral rights in normal situations does not preclude giving Mark priority over Samantha in abnormal situations. For example, Mark and Samantha may enjoy an equal right to vote, but if Mark is an able-bodied soldier, and Samantha is not, then in time of war, Mark may have first claim on scarce rations and medical supplies. Conversely, that animals' lives could justifiably be sacrificed in preference to human lives in certain situations where such a hard choice had to be made does not entail that their lives can (morally) be routinely sacrificed to support our eating habits, clothing preferences, entertainment, reluctance to control the size of our own population, unwillingness to adopt healthier ways of life, desire to avoid certain risks, and so on. Consequently, such "them or us" cases are logically isolated and insignificant for the animal liberation debate, since that debate is primarily concerned with the principles governing our ordinary moral practice.

Thus, animal liberation seeks neither to extend to animals the same set of rights enjoyed by humans nor to deny that normal human life—assuming that we ordinarily have a greater range of capacities for making the world a morally better place and will put these capacities into action—can have a greater moral worth than animal life. Rather, animal liberationists contend that just as it would be immoral to follow Swift's "modest proposal" routinely (and avoidably) to sacrifice some people's interest in life in order to fulfill others' interest in food, so it should be immoral routinely (and avoidably) to sacrifice animals' interest in life for such purposes.[14]

Of course, what is and what is not "avoidable" will always be a slippery issue. The animal liberation literature suggests that, roughly, "avoidable" here means "eliminable without severely compromising the general welfare." For example, it is repeatedly emphasized in the animal liberation literature that a vegetarian diet can be a healthy, appetizing one, that we can both keep warm and be ostentatious without furs, and that we can enjoy the wilderness without hunting. I am unaware of any animal liberationist saying something like, "We must liberate animals, even if that means an end to human civilization!" It should go without saying that issues of what is and what is not avoidable can become quite complex and must (logically) be decided on a case by case basis. What is important to the general animal liberation position is that the burden of proof is to be on those who would sacrifice animal interests for the general welfare, just as it is on those who would sacrifice the interests of some humans to help other humans (e.g., in time of war), and that justification requires demonstrating not merely some marginal increase

in utility through the sacrifice but, rather, requires demonstrating both that prohibiting the sacrifice would severely compromise the general welfare (which is not
to be restricted to human welfare) and that the sacrifice is distributed fairly.

Talk of "equal rights for animals" is probably too misleading and inflamma-
tory to be of much service, either philosophically or practically. Nonetheless,
there is an intelligible place for the concept of equality in "a new ethics for our
treatment of animals," once again to borrow Peter Singer's phrasing: it is in
sharing current legal and moral protections against the routine, avoidable sacrifice
of one's interests that animal liberation seeks "equality" for animals. (How sharing
the protection of the consent requirement in human subjects research would work
will be discussed in Chapter 12.)

IV. Applying the Rhetoric of Rights to Animals

It is often suggested that in seeking reforms of our treatment of animals,
animal liberationists would do better to avoid the concept of rights altogether,
since this concept raises unnecessary complications, such as whether beings who
cannot claim rights can have them. Furthermore, "rights" is a serious contender
for the title of currently most overused and abused moral concept, and, if H. L. A.
Hart is correct, it may not even be a totally coherent concept.[15] Why muddy the
waters with such rhetoric?

It is my impression that in spite of these drawbacks, many animal liberationists place special importance on applying the term "rights" to animals because
it accurately communicates the general and fundamental change they seek in our
attitude toward the moral and legal status of animals. Roger W. Galvin's recent
"working definition" of a "legal right" clearly indicates what animal liberationists
are seeking for animals under the "rights" rhetoric:

1. A legal right is recognized as such by the law and protected thereby from destruction or infringements;
2. The entity holding the right can seek legal protection on its own behalf;
3. The assertion of the right is supposed to protect the entity from injury; and
4. The relief the law provides should directly benefit the holder of the right.[16]

Thus, seeking "rights" for animals refers both to seeking recognition that animals
have interests of their own and to seeking direct, enforceable protection of those
interests. This "modest proposal" contrasts clearly with the current policy of protecting animal interests on the basis of animals' importance for fulfilling human
interests and when such protection can be secured "without too much sacrifice of
human interests."

Some philosophers (e.g., H. L. A. Hart, Stanley I. Benn, Mary Anne Warren, Ruth Cigman, and L. B. Cebik) would doubtless criticize the adequacy of this modest conception of rights.[17] These philosophers set a particularly high premium on claiming or exercising rights, on a link between having rights and being an autonomous agent in the society that recognizes those rights, or on the value for one's self-respect that having rights can have. This leads such philosophers to deny not only that animals can have rights but also that infants, the retarded, and other insufficiently intellectual humans can have rights.

However, at this point the debate becomes a merely verbal one. Most animal liberationists would, I believe, be content to secure for animals the moral and legal status and protections currently enjoyed by human infants and other "marginal humans." Those who deny that these people can be properly described as "rights-holders" are, nevertheless, not advocating that we start routinely sacrificing their interests to satisfy our desires for food, clothing, entertainment, biomedical research subjects, and so on, even though, especially in the area of biomedical research, such use of these people could be highly beneficial for the rest of us. If the status and protections these humans enjoy would be more accurately referred to by some other label than "rights," then let these philosophers develop and deploy that vocabulary so that we can use it to describe more accurately the animal liberation concerns. However, until this more accurate vocabulary is developed, using "rights" in the way the animal liberationists do is both in line with ordinary usage, which does not deny "rights" to infants and marginal humans, and also accurately connotes, at least, the sort of changes in our current moral and legal treatment of animals that the animal liberation movement seeks.

There are, of course, many other detailed questions concerning rights that may be raised when discussing extending moral rights to animals, such as questions about negative vs. positive rights, active vs. passive rights, natural vs. legislated rights, claims rights vs. liberties, whether rights are a kind of property, whether we can have rights if we do not understand the concept of rights or are unable to decide whether and how to exercise our own rights, and so forth. I do not propose to enter into a discussion of these questions here, because for the reasons discussed in the preceding paragraph, I do not think these details are significant for the questions currently at issue in discussions of animal "rights." The currently significant questions concerning animal rights I take to be the following:

> Do animals have interests?
> Can we identify those interests?
> Can we identify how we are impacting those interests?
> Can we stop impacting those interests adversely?
> Can we help animals live better lives?

What would be the cost to us of reducing our reliance on animals and of working to make the world a better place for all sentient beings?

Are we under any sort of moral obligation to undertake that cost?

If we become convinced that the answers to these questions call for us to revise our estimation of the moral status of animals, I am confident that we will be able to deploy the concept, institutions, and practice of rights in the ways needed to implement those answers. It would not be the first time that a change in moral conviction has been able to overcome supposed conceptual barriers to such change. In the meantime, technical questions about whether animals can (logically) have rights are, like the "Where do we draw the line?" questions, merely distractions from the substantive issues at hand. All we need to understand about rights to proceed with these substantive issues is that

> a right is a recognized entitlement or valid claim designed to protect or further its holder's interests,
>
> a moral right is one based on "the principles of an enlightened conscience," to borrow Joel Feinberg's phrase,[18] and
>
> moral rights are sufficiently diverse to allow beings like children and animals who may not be capable of enjoying all of them to enjoy some of them.

V. Is Animal *Liberation* an Affront to Human Liberation?

Apparently, many people are offended when animal liberationists draw analogies between animal liberation and the various human liberation movements. For example, Leslie Francis and Richard Norman assert that "the equation of animal welfare with genuine liberation movements such as black liberation, women's liberation, or gay liberation has the effect of trivializing those real liberation movements,"[19] and Richard A. Watson adds that "Singer's claim that the struggle against the tyranny of human over nonhuman animals is a struggle as important as any of the moral and social issues that have been fought over in recent years is insulting to past and recent victims of moral and social oppression."[20]

Unfortunately, it is not immediately obvious what makes a liberation movement "genuine," "real," or "as important as" other, certified liberation movements. If we were to judge by the number of suffering individuals involved, then the animal liberation movement is clearly more serious than any human liberation movement. We kill approximately five billion mammals and birds annually in the United States alone. That is many times the number of women and people of color in the United States. If we are to judge by how fundamental the interests being violated are, then once again, liberating animals is very serious business, since they are routinely tormented and mutilated in laboratories, are denied any sort of normal, fulfilling life in factory farms, and have their very lives taken from

those feelings have been justified, I think those feelings can be considered expressions of human chauvinism and can be dismissed. (We shall return to Francis and Norman and Watson's objections to animal liberation in Chapter 8.)

VI. Summary

To summarize, in traditional, Western morality, being human has been a necessary condition for having moral rights. At times, being human has not been sufficient to have moral rights; one had to be Greek or Christian or white or male or something else as well. Still, being human was necessary for enjoying this moral status, and those who have not enjoyed this status have been treated as being basically means for satisfying the interests of rights-holders. Animal liberation seeks to eliminate being human as a necessary condition for having moral rights and to substitute sentience, having interests of one's own, or feelings of well-being as not only the necessary condition but also, as long as the individual is innocent of crime, a sufficient condition for having moral rights.

This change in the moral status of animals would not settle questions concerning the priority of rights in conflict of interest situations and would not, presumably, have the self-consciousness-raising dimension that extending rights to minorities and women has had. However, this change would represent a fundamental and pervasive change in our moral attitudes toward animals and in our daily dealings with them, for it would require that they no longer be treated basically as means for satisfying human interests. That would put an end to the routine sacrifice of their interests in favor of ours, which is, I believe, the fundamental objective of the animal liberation movement. So it must be agreed that there are differences between animal liberation and human liberation movements, especially in the significance of autonomy as a goal of liberation. Nevertheless, in seeking for all beings with interests of their own the sort of moral respect for and protections of their interests currently enjoyed only by humans, animal liberation represents a revolutionary break with our traditional humane ethic and resembles human liberation movements sufficiently to make using the rhetoric of "liberation" and "rights" meaningful here.

6

Three Reasons for Liberating Animals

MOST PEOPLE, philosophers included, seem to feel that we are *obviously* justified in sacrificing animals to fulfill human interests and that, consequently, calls for liberating animals *must be* mistaken. This feeling places a heavy burden of proof, if that is the proper term, on those who would liberate animals from the routine sacrifice of their interests for our benefit. Some advocates of animal liberation, such as Tom Regan, in *The Case for Animal Rights,*[1] have tried to shoulder this burden by developing an extensive, impressive, systematic animal liberation ethic. I do not have a novel, systematic animal liberation ethic of my own to offer. Rather, I propose to develop some everyday moral concerns that, if considered impartially, indicate that liberating animals is what we ought (morally) to do. I hope this indication can be made strong enough to remove the burden of proof from the shoulders of the advocates of animal liberation and to place it on the shoulders of those who oppose liberating animals. Richard Rorty has written that "philosophical discussion, by the nature of the subject, is such that the best one can hope for is to put the burden of proof on one's opponent."[2] The analysis of this chapter will not even try to prove Rorty wrong about that.

In Chapter 4, we carried out our pragmatic analysis of the moral value of "personhood$_e$" and of the humanist principle by employing the following three platitudinous goals of morality:

> developing moral character, so that our actions will be based on compassion, respect, courage, and other moral virtues,
>
> both reducing the suffering in life and otherwise making life more enjoyable and fulfilling, and
>
> insuring that goods, opportunities, punishments, and rewards are distributed fairly.

What I propose to do here is to discover the moral value of liberating animals in the same pragmatic manner and by once again employing these three moral goals as our indicators of pragmatic moral value. If liberating animals, rather than continuing routinely to sacrifice their interests for our benefit, would better advance us toward accomplishing these goals, then that would indicate that we ought (morally) to liberate them. That is the modest case to be made here. (Henceforth, "consuming animals" will be used to refer to the many ways in which we routinely sacrifice their interests for our benefit.)

I. Liberating Animals and Developing Moral Character

In Chapter 4, we discovered that one of the shortcomings of "personhood$_c$," and the humanist principle is that rather than suggesting that morality should be treated as a pervasive way of life, they suggest that morality is merely a limited set of restrictions on the actions of beings that are basically free to do pretty much whatever they can and want to do. Liberating animals would help overcome this limitation by extending moral concern and such concepts as "rights" and "justice" into areas from which humanism has excluded them. Decisions about what to eat or wear and what sorts of experiments to conduct, which are currently not considered moral issues, would become, through animal liberation, situations calling for compassion, altruism, respect for the interests and rights of others, a sense of fairness, a willingness to stand up and take risks in defense of those who cannot defend themselves, and so forth. Thus, on the surface of it, it seems clear that liberating animals is one thing we ought to do in order to work toward attaining the goal of developing moral character through treating morality as a pervasive way of life.

It might be objected that this is mere appearance. It could be argued that our traditional humane ethic already directs us to be morally concerned about the treatment of animals. It would then seem to follow that what animal liberation seeks is not an extension of moral concern into new areas but simply different answers in long-established areas of moral concern.

Such a rebuttal would be mistaken for two reasons. First, our traditional, humane ethic has basically limited moral concern about our use of animals to questions concerning the handling and processing of animals. For example, humane concern in agriculture is directed toward the procedures for transporting and slaughtering food animals, not toward whether we ought (morally) to be raising animals for food at all. Again, the Animal Welfare Act, which is the sole federal legislation concerning laboratory animals in the United States, concerns only the housing and veterinary care of these animals, specifically avoiding questions about how or whether animals ought (morally) to be employed as research subjects. In general, our traditional, humane ethic does not raise questions about whether or not we ought (morally) to treat animals basically as resources to be consumed in fulfilling our interests. However, such questions are precisely the ones raised by the animal liberation movement. Consequently, liberating animals would extend our moral concern beyond traditional limits.

Second, we need to make something of an "existential" distinction here between the nonmoral and the conventionally moral. "Nonmoral" refers to those things that, though they can certainly be described as "morally permissible," are not experienced as being morally significant. For example, whether to plant impatiens, fibrous begonias, or nothing at all around the border of one's patio garden is a nonmoral issue. Barring the most extraordinary of circumstances, each alternative is not only as morally acceptable but also as morally innocuous as the others, and anyone questioned about the moral significance of his decision in this matter would be mystified by the question. On the other hand, "conventionally moral" refers to those things that we routinely do with a sense that they are the morally right thing to do. For example, giving time, money, or materials to charity is something many of us routinely do and do with a sense that that is what we ought (morally) to do. Except under the most extraordinary of circumstances, we would not be mystified if asked about the moral significance of what we are doing when we contribute to charity.

We need to make this distinction in order to prevent the nonmoral from becoming a vacuous category and to prevent it from becoming a truism that our morality—indeed, any morality—makes of morality a pervasive way of life. If simply being morally permissible (i.e., not being morally prohibited or otherwise morally negated) were sufficient to make an action a moral action, then any value scheme that indicated what is morally impermissible would be a pervasive moral value scheme. Consequently, even raising questions about restricted moralities vs. pervasive moralities presupposes that we distinguish the nonmoral from the conventionally moral.

Now, if we employ this distinction, it seems uncontroversial to assert that currently, most people would regard the question of whether to have beef, chicken, or vegetables for lunch to be a nonmoral issue, rather than a conventionally moral one. Such a question is, for most of us, ordinarily on a par with the question about which if any bedding plants to put in our garden; it is simply not experienced to be a moral issue. However, the animal liberation movement seeks to make such questions about what to eat into questions of moral concern. The same holds true of many questions concerning what to wear, how to be entertained, how to conduct science, and so forth. Consequently, animal liberation is not merely seeking unconventional answers to questions that already have standard moral answers. Animal liberation is seeking to expand our moral concern to cover issues that are ordinarily experienced to be nonmoral issues.

It might be objected that, nonetheless, liberating animals would not represent a *fundamental* moral improvement here, because animal liberation carries on the "us vs. them," line-drawing attitude toward moral rights that was the fundamental problem we discovered in "personhood$_e$," and humanism. Liberating animals would involve drawing the line further out, so that not only humans but all sentient beings would be protected against human selfishness by moral rights, but it could be argued that the basic "we're in, they're out" mentality remains the same from humanism to animal liberation and that, consequently, all that has been done is to extend a bit that morally protected oasis in the desert of human selfishness.

Once again, this rebuttal is mistaken for two reasons. First, even if this characterization of animal liberation were correct, it would remain the case that liberating animals, rather than continuing to consume them, is what we ought (morally) to do. As Kant argues, even if we are unable to attain the ideal, we can distinguish closer from more distant approximations to it and are morally obligated to prefer those closer approximations to the ideal over the more distant ones.[3] So even if liberating animals represented only a secondary moral change and improvement in our development of moral character through treating morality as a pervasive way of life, it would still be morally preferable to our continuing to consume animals. Consequently, even if this rebuttal points out continued moral shortcomings in animal liberation, it fails as a rebuttal to the contention that this way-of-life criterion of moral worth indicates that liberating animals is morally preferable to continuing to consume them.

Second, it is not clear that an animal liberation ethic would continue the "ins vs. outs" mentality characteristic of humanism and other, even more restrictive moralities. This is because animal liberation does not share humanism's basic tenet, emphasized in its many battles against tribal, religious, racial, and other chauvinisms, that, fundamentally, everyone should be treated the same (i.e., as persons). As Lt. Hunter, a chastised male chauvinist on "Hill Street Blues," sadly concludes after having his consciousness raised, "From now on, Lucy, you're just a person for me." Here, in accordance with the humanist principle, "person" means persons$_d$ who are persons$_e$.

More specifically, humanism treats all holders of moral rights as beings that seek to be autonomous agents leading enjoyable, fulfilling lives in human society. As noted in Chapter 3, traditional ethical theory and everyday morality focus on normal human adults. If it were up to paradigm moral principles and theory, we would all, like Athena, spring forth fully grown and normal, thereby avoiding the conceptual and practical messiness that children and the handicapped can create. In this way, humanism projects the image of moral rights-holders constituting a fundamentally homogeneous group that contrasts starkly with the group of non-persons$_e$. Of course, animals are among those who clearly do not seek to be autonomous agents leading enjoyable, fulfilling lives in human society. Consequently, by extending moral rights to them, we would severely compromise the supposed homogeneity of the group of moral rights-holders. We would also undercut the starkness of the contrast between those beings that possess moral rights and those that still would not (e.g., plants and rivers), since many animals do not live in socially reconstructed environments, as we do, but are more integrated into or a part of nature. In this way, liberating animals would not simply carry on the "us vs. them" attitude embodied in humanism but would, rather, require a more complex, varied moral attitude.

Most if not all wild animals would seem to be quite content without any contact whatsoever with human society. While these animals seek autonomy, in the sense of freedom to pursue their own way of life, they do not seek to be agents in human society. This would have to be taken into account in moral "calculations" of the general welfare and in principles for respecting the rights of others. Bringing wild animals into the moral arena would require giving diversity a much more fundamental place in that arena. Extending moral rights to domesticated animals would lead to the same result. These animals (e.g., dogs and sheep) have been made to be dependent on us; so they cannot share the interest in independence of wild animals. Furthermore, since they are beings who will never attain normal$_h$ intelligence, they cannot share our goal of being autonomous agents in human society. They will always be dependent on us in many of the ways children temporarily are. Consequently, liberating domesticated animals would require recognizing that enjoyable, fulfilling, but nonautonomous lives can be the goal of moral rights-holders and that those in power (i.e., normal human adults) have a permanent obligation of stewardship to insure that the interests of domesticated animals, like those of children, are protected. Thus, in contrast to the basic homogeneity of moral rights-holders envisioned by humanism, liberating both wild and domesticated animals would require recognizing and making moral provisions for the basic diversity of the interests of the group of moral rights-holders.

Finally, if animals were liberated, they would constitute a majority of the moral rights-holders in the world. Those humans (e.g., the disabled) who cannot fully share in the autonomous-social-agent ideal of the good life still constitute a very small fraction of the current population of moral rights-holders. Consequently, they have been regarded basically as atypical cases and more or less accommodated into our standard morality in a patchwork manner. Animals are not atypical humans, nor relatively few in number. Liberating them would force us to think more fundamentally about how we are to respect differing ways of life.

Thus, the number of animals, their permanent dependence in many cases, and their distance from our traditional social goals would seem to require that if animals become holders of moral rights, we would have to move away from a simple "us vs. them" outlook. The diversity of what can make life enjoyable and fulfilling would have to become a more central determinant of moral concern as we incorporated different species into that concern.

Similarly, given the earth's limited resources and the many competing interests among animals, including ourselves, how to establish priority among rights would become a more common problem, if we expanded the domain of moral rights-holders to include animals. For example, it would become important to distinguish not only different interests, such as interests in mating and voting, but also different degrees of interest, such as interests of crucial importance to the quality of life like adequate space to move about, and peripheral interests, such as having a vacation home.[4] Thus, it is likely that working out the details of our moral principles, procedures, and practices following the liberation of animals would require scrapping the "us vs. them" mentality and the emphasis on so-called "differences in kind" characteristic of humanism and developing a "differences of degree"–oriented morality and mentality that would emphasize our membership in a fundamentally diverse community of interests. Consequently, it seems likely that animal liberation does project a fundamental change in our moral attitude away from the line-drawing attitude previously criticized in the case of humanism.

Furthermore, this is a change that would have to be carried out consciously. Liberating animals is not something that would occur *ex nihilo*. Rather, it is something that would develop gradually, against the background of our traditional consumption of animals. It would be an educative process in which we would come to understand that what had previously been considered nonmoral issues must (morally) now be considered moral issues. This process is commonly called "consciousness-raising" today and refers not only to the education of those who have heretofore been subjugated (e.g., blacks and women) but also to the education of those who have been doing the subjugating (e.g., whites and men). Although, as acknowledged in the previous chapter, this first form of consciousness-raising is, presumably, not to be part of animal liberation, the second part is. Liberating animals would require that we come to reflect on our traditional consumption of them and recognize that such consumption is not a nonmoral issue, even when done humanely, but is morally wrong. Thus, liberating animals would involve consciously expanding our arena of moral concern, thereby advancing us toward our goal of developing moral character through treating morality as a pervasive way of life.

However, it might be objected, finally, that we have been wrong in supposing that treating morality as a pervasive way of life is involved with our common goals of morality. After all, it could be argued, there are some issues that, except under the most extraordinary of circumstances, simply are not moral issues, such as deciding which brand of personal computer to buy. Furthermore, it is not always selfish to pursue one's own interests without worrying about the well-being of others. It is not always wrong to indulge in the purchase of a well-tailored suit or a fine wine, even if people somewhere in the world are ill-clothed and hungry. It would not be unreasonable to claim that a world in which all decisions had to be treated as morally serious ones would not be an ideal or even a desirable world. Consequently, it could be argued that treating morality as a pervasive way of life is a gross, undesirable exaggeration of everyday morality's emphasis on developing moral character.

On the other hand, we should remember that pursuing morality as a way of life was discovered, in Chapter 3, to be what characterizes fully moral$_{ad}$ agents and distinguishes (some of) the virtuous deeds of humans from the virtuous deeds of animals. Thus, to borrow Kant's terminology, postulating that morality should be treated as a pervasive way of life in order better to attain our moral goal of developing moral character is not without its practical reason. What the supposed *reductio* counterexamples of the previous paragraph indicate is merely that "morality as a way of life" must be interpreted in a way that

> is compatible with the limited resources of our environment and the diversity within human nature,
>
> recognizes that moral principles are artifacts we create to make life more enjoyable and fulfilling, rather than being hard taskmasters adding to the burdens of life, and
>
> recognizes that we need not be aiming at moral$_{ad}$ sainthood in order to be moral$_{ad}$.

That such an interpretation of morality is possible is indicated by the lives of many decent, ordinary people like Frank Furillo of "Hill Street Blues," Sophie Zawistowsha in *Sophie's Choice*, and Mac Sledge in *Tender Mercies*. These lives indicate that a sense of responsibility and concern for the well-being of others can imbue, structure, and come to identify one's life without becoming obsessions that deprive life of pleasure and a reasonable balance of the self-sacrificing and the dutiful with the self-indulgent and the whimsical. Regarding morality as a pervasive way of life does not require or even project the elimination of the nonmoral; rather, it merely requires having moral concern be one's basic attitude, with nonmoral concerns being pursued within the parameters established by that moral concern. This is the reverse of the restricted conception of morality projected by humanism and criticized in Chapter 4.

Thus, although the issue is not a simple one, it seems fair to conclude that until some argument to the contrary is produced, if ever, the goal of developing moral character through treating morality as a pervasive way of life would be better pursued by liberating animals than by our continuing to consume them. This is the kernel of truth that lies in the popular argument, put forth by Thomas Aquinas and Immanuel Kant among others, that we ought to treat animals decently to avoid developing the habit of insensitivity to the interests of others.[5] Advocates of animal liberation have often and properly objected to the anthropocentric form this argument usually takes: we should treat animals decently, because if we do not, that will incline us not to deal decently with humans, which is where the real moral issue lies. However, from a deontological or "mixed" utilitarian viewpoint, this argument need not be developed in this anthropocentric manner. From these viewpoints, compassion, courage, honesty, dutifulness, and the other moral virtues are as intrinsically valuable as the pleasure and fulfillment, human or otherwise, that they may produce. Consequently, the development of these virtues does not have to be tied to consequences for human enjoyment and fulfillment to be of moral value. It follows that the argument for the moral value of liberating animals based on the development of moral character can be developed, as it has been here, in a nonanthropocentric manner.

II. Liberating Animals and Making the World a Happier Place

The second of our everyday moral goals is the consequential one of reducing the suffering in life and otherwise making life more enjoyable and fulfilling. "Life" here refers not merely to being organically functional but also to being sentient, and it refers to all sentient life forms indiscriminately. That is, of course, not quite the meaning of the term in everyday morality. While "life" does not there refer merely to being organically functional, it does not refer indiscriminately to all sentient beings; rather, in everyday morality, "life" refers primarily, if not exclusively, to human life, with nonhuman animal life being accorded only secondary, humane consideration at most. Such common expressions as "the sanctity of life" and "prolife" clearly refer only to human life. However, there are two reasons for setting aside this anthropocentric use of "life" in this context. First, our moral concern here is not with reducing or increasing things that are uniquely human. Suffering, enjoyment, and fulfillment are things that we share with animals. Second, even though our humane considerations may be secondary, they express some current, common recognition that at least this second of our moral goals concerns other species of sentient beings. Consequently, the anthropocentric use of "life" in everyday morality cannot be interpreted as a conceptual obstacle to the possibility that our ordinary moral concern with reducing suffering in life and otherwise making life more enjoyable and fulfilling may be better served by liberating animals than by continuing to consume them.

Now, it is indisputable that our consuming animals causes them to suffer a great deal. For example, they suffer the confinement of factory farms, the distress of induced diseases in laboratories, the trauma of being caught in leg-hold traps, and the terror of watching those at the front of the line in the abattoir being killed. They also suffer, in the vast majority of cases, the loss of the remainder of lives that would have held more enjoyment and fulfillment than distress and frustration, or at least lives that could have held such a positive result with our assistance or even just without our interference. (Henceforth, "lives worth living" will be used to refer to such lives.) For example, a monkey killed painlessly after being imprisoned for a year in a small laboratory cage could have had a life worth living if we had simply left it in its native jungle. Even if the experiment in which this monkey participated involved no other experiential suffering than the boredom and frustration of its imprisonment, the monkey has still suffered severely, for it has suffered the loss of the longer life worth living it could have had if it had not been interfered with. (Henceforth, when discussing what animals suffer, "frustration" will refer not only to certain unpleasant experiences but also to this sort of loss.)

On the other hand, consuming animals contributes to fulfilling our interests in food, clothing, medical inventions, entertainment, and so forth. Our consumption of animals thereby contributes to the enjoyment and fulfillment in life. Consequently, it may seem that the issue here is whether the benefit we gain from sacrificing animal interests to fulfill our interests outweighs the animal interests sacrificed in the process. But once again, the issue is not nearly so simple.

As utilitarians have long been reminding us, in this consequential area of our moral reasoning, if not throughout, we must (morally)

> consider, as far as possible and practical, the full range of alternative courses of action available to us and
>
> follow that option that seems likely to lead to the greatest excess of enjoyment and fulfillment over distress and frustration (or to the least excess of distress and frustration over enjoyment and fulfillment, if that is the best we can hope to achieve).

Consequently, in addition to estimating the contribution to or subtraction from life's excess of enjoyment and fulfillment made by the routine sacrifice of animal interests for our benefit, we must also estimate the contribution or subtraction that would be made by liberating animals and frustrating those of our interests that have heretofore been fulfilled by the animals' sacrifice. If the latter option would result in a greater excess of enjoyment and fulfillment over distress and frustration than the former, or even just a smaller excess of distress and frustration over enjoyment and fulfillment than the former, then we would be morally obligated, on these consequential grounds, to frustrate ourselves in order to spare them.

For example, the consequential issue concerning consuming veal is not just whether the human benefit from the production of veal outweighs the suffering incurred by the veal calves. We must also consider whether prohibiting the production of veal would benefit the veal calves enough to outweigh the frustration humans would suffer from that prohibition. If that benefit for the calves out-weighed the harm to humans, then prohibiting veal production would strike a more positive balance of enjoyment and fulfillment with distress and frustration than would the continued consumption of veal. It would then follow that pro-ducing veal ought (morally) to be prohibited, even if veal production already produces an excess of enjoyment and fulfillment over distress and frustration.

Even more to the point, we need to consider options involving the substitution of nonanimal procedures and products for our current consumption of animals. Many vegetarians contend that in discussing diet with meat eaters, they often get the impression that the meat eaters think vegetarians simply make do with what is left over when we remove the meat from the traditional meat, potatoes, and vegetable dinner plate. That is certainly not the case, as even a cursory glance through a vegetarian cookbook or at the menu of a vegetarian restaurant will confirm. Similarly, researchers who use animals in ways that harm the animals often suggest that research would come to a halt if they were not allowed to continue to use animals in these ways. However, there are many research prob-lems to be tackled which do not require the use of animals, many alternatives to animal research procedures, and many noninvasive and innocuous animal re-search problems and procedures, and there is also the likelihood that since neces-sity is the mother of invention, researchers unable any longer to harm animals would develop many other procedures to keep themselves employed. Thus, our way of life following the liberation of animals would not be one in which a giant hole had been cut; rather, it would be a way of life in which there would sooner or later be substitutions most everywhere that there had been excisions. It is the consequential value of such a way of life—theirs as well as ours—that must (morally) be compared with the consequential value of our contemporary, animal-consuming way of life to determine the moral superiority here of animal liberation or continued animal consumption.

Of course, it is not possible to give a precise, quantitative response to such a question. Since we have no way of measuring quantities of enjoyment, distress, fulfillment, and frustration and no crystal ball to show us beforehand exactly what life following the liberation of animals—or following any other moral revo-lution—would be like, Bentham's moral calculus must remain a dream at best. Once again, we must proceed in a rough-and-ready manner.

The great number of animals we consume counts heavily here in favor of animal liberation. It is estimated that in the United States alone we annually slaughter four to five billion farm animals. We also annually kill several hundred million animals in hunting and trapping, approximately seventy million animals in our laboratories and testing centers, and roughly twenty million abandoned dogs and cats in our animal "shelters." If fish are sentient beings, then the number of animals consumed annually in the United States quickly jumps to several trillion. Virtually all these animals suffer to one degree or another, both in the sense of having painful or frustrating experiences and of losing the remainder of what would or could have been lives worth living. For our current, animal-consuming way of life to produce an excess of enjoyment and fulfillment over distress and frustration, the benefit we receive from consuming animals must outweigh this massive burden of suffering. Even more to the point, for our animal-consuming way of life to be superior on these grounds to a way of life in which animals have been liberated, the loss that we would incur in shifting from consuming animals to consuming animal substitutes would have to be greater than the benefit that these billions or trillions of animals would realize from this shift.

It is hard to imagine that we would lose more in turning to animal substitutes than the animals could gain by being liberated; so it is hard to imagine that liberating animals would not lead to a morally better balance of enjoyment and fulfillment with distress and frustration in life than would continuing to consume them. There are only about 230 million people in the United States at present. Consequently, for our current practice of animal consumption to produce an excess of enjoyment and fulfillment over distress and frustration, the benefit each of us receives, on average, from the consumption of animals must outweigh the harm suffered by approximately 25 animals annually if fish are not counted, and of over 12,500 animals annually if fish are counted. Furthermore, for animal consumption to be morally preferable, on these grounds, to animal liberation, the loss (assuming there would be a net loss here, which might not be the case) each of us would suffer if we had to shift to animal substitutes would, on average, have to outweigh the benefit that 25 (or 12,500) animals annually could realize from that shift. Although we will never be able to test such equations precisely, we would have to place an extraordinary price on the enjoyment and fulfillment we receive from consuming animals to believe that whatever loss would be involved in switching to animal substitutes would not be more than outweighed by eliminating the distress and frustration of billions (or trillions) of animals annually. This would seem to place the burden of proof squarely on the animal consumers' shoulders.

Perhaps the most ambitious attempt to date to shoulder this burden has been made by R. G. Frey in *Rights, Killing, and Suffering*. In this work, Frey offers us no fewer than fourteen (supposedly) seriously adverse consequences of eliminating meat eating. With some abridgment, here they are:

(1) The collapse of the meat industry would have terrible effects on the livestock and poultry farmers and on the middlemen who deal in these animals, together, of course, with their families.

(2) All those in the food industry generally whose products, services, and jobs depend

upon the meat industry, from those involved in the manufacture of steak and barbecue sauce to those who actually market the products themselves, would be hit.

(3) It is most unlikely that, with the collapse of the meat industry and, therefore, of a major portion of the food industry as a whole, the dairy industry would escape unscathed.

(4) Three major industries in the United States over the last 30 years, and now, increasingly, throughout the world, would be affected: the fast food industry, the pet food industry, the drug/pharmaceutical empire.

(5) Universities would have to shed labour, as departments of veterinary science and other animal-related departments, particularly those involved in research into food and food-animal disease, came under pressure.

(6) The publishing business would suffer. Many firms specialize in books related to all facets of animal farming.

(7) The advertising industry would be seriously affected, as would the revenues of those publications and newspapers that carried meat and meat-related advertisements.

(8) Social life will be seriously affected. The restaurant business and all those connected with the catering industry would suffer loss, probably catastrophically in the short run.

(9) The leather and leather goods industries will collapse, with massive losses.

(10) One must not overlook uses we make of food animals other than eating them and tanning their hides. Consider only one other: the wool industry, and, through it, the clothing industry generally.

(11) Whole economies, and at various levels, would be affected: some small communities depend vitally upon livestock and poultry; the economy of the state of South Dakota is founded not only upon wheat but also upon dairy farms, hogs, and cattle; some countries, such as Argentina, Poland, Australia, and New Zealand, as well as the United States and the European Economic Community as a whole, have a massive stake in the meat trade.

(12) Some countries depend upon meat, less as producers than as consumers, though consumers with a difference; thus, France, the bastion of *haute cuisine*, and Italy, would see one of their glories disappear.

(13) I shall not go into the extensive use made of food animals in religious rites and festivities in general.

(14) Finally, there is the general financial picture to consider. First, loss of tax revenues from all those businesses and industries even indirectly associated with the meat trade will affect local, state, and national budgets and programmes and will almost certainly affect export markets and the financing of imports from other industrialized countries and the Third World. Second, loss of revenues and of earnings by a great many people will increase the need for costly subsidies and social programmes, which in turn seem likely to feed inflationary pressures. Third, the loss of investment capital and of plant; the loss of income, with consequent effect on mortgages, loans, and credit of all kinds; the disruption in community, regional, and national economies; the demise of savings from individuals who would otherwise bank them; all these and a great many other factors are likely in the United States to place some banks, savings

and loan institutions, and loan companies in trouble. This in turn affects confidence. Fourth, loss in confidence will be exacerbated as whole businesses and industries fail or are threatened with going under. Fifth, financial storms of the sort in question are bound to affect the stock market. A massive loss of confidence is likely to be reflected by panic in the market. Sixth, growth in the economy is likely to cease as whole areas come under intense pressure and confidence is so low as to deter investment; besides a great many people will be out of work and out of hope, as whole industries disappear or contract.[6]

Little do advocates of animal liberation realize that they are pushing us down the slippery slope to Armageddon! More seriously, Frey overlooks almost entirely the development of alternatives to animal consumption that would certainly moderate, if not entirely eliminate, the negative consequences he foresees. Indeed, the spectre of these fourteen possibilities would itself provide adequate incentive to develop quickly alternative businesses, industries, occupations, and pleasures to replace the losses occasioned by liberating animals. Furthermore, the liberation of animals would likely take place gradually, perhaps starting with bans on sport hunting, working through eliminating painful, nontherapeutic animal research, and ending with the virtual elimination of meat from the diet. This gradual process would also help to moderate the negative consequences Frey envisages. Finally, the problems Frey outlines are by and large only transitory, albeit extensive, dislocations that we would have to go through to switch from an animal-consuming to a liberated way of life. On the other hand, the relief for animal pain and frustration attained through liberating animals would go on indefinitely. Consequently, as time progressed, the negative impact of these transitory dislocations would become more and more insignificant in comparison with these accumulating benefits.

Thus, while Frey is certainly correct that liberating animals would have pervasive consequences—that is part and parcel of animal liberation being a major liberation movement, as discussed in the previous chapter—he is wrong in thinking that the dislocations that would be involved in accomplishing this revolution constitute a significant objection to the consequential superiority of animal liberation over continued animal consumption. I think that by and large we can safely disregard such supposedly "practical implications" of animal liberation as being in the same family with the questions, discussed in the preceding two chapters, about where we are to draw the line of sentience and how we are to accommodate animal "conceptions" of virtue. They are all basically just distractions.

There is another, more substantive argument against the consequential superiority of animal liberation over continued animal consumption. This argument was called "the logic of the larder" by Henry S. Salt [7] and has more recently come to be known as "the replacement argument." Roughly, this argument contends that our consumption of animals enhances the enjoyment and fulfillment of life, not only of human life or of sentient life in general but also of nonhuman animal life in particular. This is because we bring into the world many more animals than there would be if we were not interested in consuming them. The enjoyment and fulfillment these animals experience would not exist if we were not allowed to consume animals, and there is no loss involved in this consumption, for we replace the animals we consume.

This argument has developed into a complicated nest of issues that go far beyond the commonsensical level we are working at here. Consequently, I propose to delay dealing with it until Chapter 10, where I argue that the argument is sound from only one common moral perspective and that we have no particular reason to adopt that perspective, although we have good reason not to do so. Here, it will suffice to make two quick points. First, even if the replacement argument were sound, it would not justify many of our current practices of animal consumption. This is because most of the animals we bring into the world to satisfy our interests, especially those in factory farms and laboratories, do not lead lives worth living. Consequently, the lives of these animals actually detract from the enjoyment and fulfillment in life, and our continually replacing them insures that this burden continues unrelieved.

Second, since the ironic contention of the logic of the larder is that our consuming animals can actually be in *their* best interest, we should expect that the forms of animal use that could pass this logic would coincide more with the circumscribed uses of animals permitted under animal liberation than with our current, basically uninhibited consumption of animals. For example, raising animals in order to eat their bodies after they have lived enjoyable, fulfilling lives and have died of old age would pass the logic of the larder and would also, *ceteris paribus*, be compatible with liberating animals. As discussed in the previous chapter, liberating animals is not directed toward ending all human use of them. Rather, its goal is to provide for animals the same sort of protection against the routine sacrifice of their interests currently enjoyed only by humans. Consequently, it too aims at having us do what is in the animals' best interest, which may very well include our benefiting from them in certain ways. Just as it is ordinarily in our best interest not to be hermits but to be of benefit to others in certain ways, so it may well be in the best interest of animals to be of benefit to us in certain ways. It follows that if the basic point of the replacement argument is that it can be in the best interest of animals to be of benefit to us, then that argument is not basically an argument against animal liberation. Just which uses of animals are really *mutually* beneficial is, of course, the controversial issue.

The replacement argument raises one further possible objection to what we have said here. It might be contended that our references to the great number of animals that would benefit from animal liberation is mistaken. If we were no

longer permitted to consume animals, we would cease to raise them, and, consequently, many animals would never exist to benefit from being liberated.

Such an objection would suffer from tunnel vision. While it is likely that liberating animals would lead to a substantial reduction in the number of chickens,
hogs, cattle, mink, white mice, and other animals bred for our consumption, it is
also likely that the number of wild animals would increase substantially. That
increase would be due in part to our not needing to farm as much land to support
ourselves on a vegetarian diet as on a meat diet, thereby releasing land for wild
animals to live on. That increase would also result from our recognizing the right
of wild animals to their own homeland, thereby halting our continual expropria-
tion of their habitats for our benefit.[8] Furthermore, given our moral goal of
making life more enjoyable and fulfilling and our ability to care for animals, we
would be obligated (*ceteris paribus*) to act as nature's caretakers in order to
insure the flourishing of sentient life on earth. Consequently, there is no reason to
believe that liberating animals would leave significantly fewer animals to benefit
from that liberation.

Thus, the extensive distress and frustration occasioned by our current consumption of animals constitutes a serious obstacle to accomplishing the moral
goal of reducing suffering in life and otherwise making life more enjoyable and
fulfilling. To paraphrase Winston Churchill, never have so few inflicted so much
on so many. Eliminating that distress and frustration might cause us some frustration and transitory economic, social, and religious dislocation. But it is very
hard to believe that relieving the animals' distress and frustration would not
outweigh our frustrations and dislocations. Consequently, even without considering the other ways in which we, as conscientious stewards of sentient life on earth,
might make life more enjoyable and fulfilling for us all, human and nonhuman, it
is hard not to conclude that liberating animals would be a step forward toward
accomplishing this consequential goal of morality.

III. Liberating Animals and Being Fair

The third of our common moral goals is to insure that available goods, opportunities, rewards, and punishments are distributed fairly. On the face of it, our
animal-consuming way of life seems clearly to detract from, rather than contribute to, making the world a fair place in which to live. For example, in order to
cure our ills, to continue enjoying unhealthy life-styles with impunity, or simply to
pursue our research careers, we take healthy, innocent animals and inflict painful,
debilitating, and mortal diseases and disabilities on them. We also drive animals
out of their homes so that we can enjoy suburban life and crowd them into factory
farms so that we can have abundant, inexpensive meat. In these and many other
ways, we take for ourselves the available goods of the earth with little if any

concern for insuring that animals receive a fair share of these goods, and we destroy (the quality of) their lives in our efforts to satisfy our needs and desires and to protect ourselves, often from ourselves. In the past, we have treated other people in similar ways, for instance, when "conquering the New World" and through the institution of slavery.[9] Today, such treatment of people would be considered grossly unjust, and that we no longer treat people in these ways we consider to be a mark of the moral progress we have made toward making the world a fair place in which to live. It would seem to follow that liberating animals from such discrimination would be yet a further step toward attaining this goal of morality.

Just what is and is not a "fair" distribution has been shown (e.g., through the work of John Rawls) to be a much more complicated issue than we ordinarily believe it to be. Adjusting our principles and procedures of justice to cover animals' interests would probably make questions of fairness even more complicated than they currently are. For example, our concepts of property would have to be expanded to include recognition of animal territories, and something like a public defender's office devoted to the safeguarding and pressing of animals' rights would probably be needed. However, once again, that one moral scheme is more complicated than another does not show that it is mistaken, faulty, or even less preferable than the simpler one. Furthermore, the complications that liberating animals would probably introduce into our principles and procedures of justice could not represent fundamental changes in those principles and procedures. Since animal liberation seeks merely to extend to animals the same sort of protection of interests already enjoyed by humans, the fundamental issues of fairness involved in animal liberation must be included among those involved in treating humans fairly. The differences between human and animal interests and capabilities would call for differences of detail, but these are not matters that need concern us here.

Avoiding the conclusion that liberating animals would be fairer than continuing to consume them requires either showing that the concept of fairness cannot be meaningfully applied to our dealings with animals or finding reasons for believing that it is fair for us routinely to sacrifice animals' interests for our benefit. We shall deal with each of these strategies in turn.

Pursuing the former strategy, we could try to introduce a restricted definition of "fairness" that could not apply to animals, for instance, that "fairness" can be an issue only within some sort of contractual situation. However, such a definition would be artificial. Consider the case of two hungry men in Hobbes's "state of nature" who chance upon some food at the same time. Assume that David is much stronger than Toby and could take all the food for himself with impunity. What should the men do? While it would be difficult to understand how "David *owes* Toby half the food" would be a meaningful answer to that question in this situation, "the fair thing would be for the two men to split the food between them" would not be an unintelligible or even an inappropriate answer. That answer would reflect that neither man has a prior legal or moral claim on the food, that neither man is under a prior obligation to defer to the other, that both are in need of the food, and that they would presumably both benefit (and about equally so) from an equal share of the food.

The same sorts of considerations could be raised in a similar situation, where Toby was not a weaker man but a hungry dog. It follows that even if some of our institutionalized senses of "fairness" may not apply to our dealings with animals, our intuitive sense of fairness can be meaningfully applied here. When animal liberation advocates talk about the unfairness of research animals bearing all the burdens while we reap all the benefits and about our "taking unfair advantage" of the fact that we are so much more powerful than other animals, we understand what they mean, even if we do not agree. Consequently, questions about the fairness of our consuming animals cannot be dismissed as category mistakes.

Turning to the second strategy, since we are simply trying to locate the burden of proof here, we shall restrict this discussion to three commonly proposed justifications for believing that it is fair for us to consume animals. We shall return to the issue of fairness in Chapter 8 and there discuss some of the more philosophically sophisticated justifications that have been proposed for believing that it is fair for us to consume animals.

One of the most common attitudes toward animals is an analog to the logic of the larder: since we brought them into being, they owe their lives to us, and, consequently, it is fair for us to dispose of those lives as we see fit—provided we do so humanely, of course. If we exclude fish, the vast majority of the animals we consume are bred, fed, housed, and otherwise cared for by us; so when we choose to consume them, we are simply exercising our end of the bargain. Being consumed is the only way these animals have of repaying what we have given them, thereby acquiting themselves of the debt they owe us. Thus, there is an interspecies variation of the social contract theory at work in our common attitude toward animals, and this can even extend beyond domesticated animals to wild animals, as when hunters feel something akin to an obligation to help feed starving deer during heavy winters and to protect the marshland homes of ducks and other waterfowl from pollution. Let us label this "the natural contract."

Besides the fact that many wild animals that are hunted, trapped, and displaced by us are not in our debt for anything, so that our consumption of them cannot be defended on these implicit-contract grounds, there is another, pervasive problem with the natural contract: when dealing with people, it does not follow that because we brought them into existence and have fed, housed, and otherwise cared for them, we are entitled to dispose of their lives for our benefit; so it does not seem fair that animals should have to pay with their lives for similar benefits.

Indeed, not only are people not charged that high a price when others bring them into and keep them in existence; it also would be considered morally outrageous even to suggest that people should be held to this natural contract. Many slaves were brought into existence to be slaves and were fed, housed, and so forth by their masters. In that sense, these slaves "owed their lives" to their masters. But we do not conclude from this that these people "owed their lives" in the contractual sense that their masters were entitled, as a return for what they had given these slaves, to dispose of their lives for their (the masters') benefit. We hold that slavery is wrong, whether the slaves were captured or bred for that purpose. It follows by analogy that whether consuming animals is fair or unfair also does not depend on whether the animals were bred and maintained for that purpose.

Today, the group of people to which the logic of the natural contract would obviously apply is children, most of whom were brought into existence intentionally by their parents, who also feed, clothe, house, and otherwise care for them. While we hold that children thereby incur obligations to their parents, we no longer conclude that parents are entitled to dispose of their children's lives, although this conclusion was not uncommon in the past, especially when the children in question were female.[10] Today, children, too, have been liberated from the natural contract, and we regard this as yet another step forward in our moral progress. Consequently, some justification is needed for not liberating animals from the natural contract; so citing that contract cannot provide a justification for our continuing to consume animals.

Another of the most common responses to animal liberation arguments is "But animals eat other animals." This phrase seems to have a double meaning:

> since animals consume other animals, they do not deserve to be treated any better by us, and
>
> since one species consuming another is a standard, even essential part of the natural order, we are merely taking our place in nature and making our contribution to the natural cycle of life on earth when we consume other animals.

We shall call these the "Let them reap what they sow!" and the "It's only natural!" defenses of our consuming animals and shall take up each of them in turn.

Of course, it is immediately amusing when the "Let them reap what they sow!" defense is offered in support of our consuming cattle, sheep, hogs, rabbits, and other herbivorous animals. It is also striking that when animals occasionally turn the tables and prey on us (e.g., shark and bear attacks), we do not resignedly say, "I guess we, too, have to reap what we sow." Rather, we usually brand such animals "renegades," "monsters," or even "murderers" and go after them in a vengeful and punitive manner. Apparently, we feel that if we do the reaping, that balances the books, but if we are the prey, then some punishment is needed to balance those books. This situation is further confused by our often regarding animals as incapable of recognizing and responding to moral obligations. It follows that their predation cannot consistently be considered to be something like a crime for which they can be expected to suffer the just consequences.

Finally, it can be noted that animal predation is usually properly described as "doing what they must in order to survive." So if it is "only fair" for us to treat animals as they treat each other, then we should limit our consumption of them to "doing what we must in order to survive." Given our many frivolous uses of animals and the vast array of alternatives to animal consumption that we already have or could develop, our consumption of animals goes far beyond that limit. Consequently, the "Let them reap what they sow!" justification of why it is fair for us to consume animals is not only a confused but also an insufficient excuse for our continuing to consume animals.

Turning to the "It's only natural!" argument, this defense has often been formulated in terms of a natural hierarchy in which certain life forms are, supposedly, intended for the use of others, for example, plants being intended for animal consumption and animals being intended for human consumption. However, David Hume and Charles Darwin have made it difficult to develop the argument in this way without an embarrassed smile. Perhaps because of this, the offending reference to natural purpose is today usually replaced by a phrase like "the natural order of things": big fish eat little fish, and as the most powerful species on this planet, we are simply carrying on the natural order of things by using other species for our benefit. Two famous American surgeons recently offered explicitly this "king of the jungle" principle to justify painful, lethal research in which healthy animals are sacrificed for human benefit.[11]

However, whether we develop this idea from a teleological or an evolutionary perspective, what we are defending is the practice of the stronger routinely sacrificing the interests of the weaker for their (the stronger's) benefit. Today, such practice is not considered fair in dealings among humans, to put it mildly. This was not always the case, for humans-over-animals is not the only "natural hierarchy" that has been proposed. Aristotle thought that men were naturally superior to women and Greeks naturally superior to other races; Victorians thought white men had to shoulder the burden of being superior to savages; and Nazis thought Aryans were a master race. We have come to reject these and many other supposedly natural hierarchies; the history of what we consider moral progress can be viewed as, in large part, the replacement of hierarchical worldviews with a presumption in favor of forms of egalitarianism. This substitution places the burden of proof on those who would *deny* equal consideration to the interests of all concerned, rather than on those who seek such consideration. Consequently, some reason is needed to justify the fairness of maintaining a hierarchical worldview when we are dealing with animals.

Calling the humans-over-animals hierarchy "natural" will not suffice. The long history of our conquest and enslavement of other humans indicates that it is also "natural" for us to engage in these discriminatory practices with other people. . If its being natural is not sufficient reason morally to justify our conquering and enslaving other people, then its being natural is not sufficient morally to justify our consuming animals.

Furthermore, as John Rawls has noted, one of the primary purposes of principles of justice is to correct "the arbitrariness of this world." [12] "Arbitrariness" here refers, among other things, to the great differences in power that occur naturally among people. To protect the weak against the strong among us is one of the primary reasons we develop principles of justice. But there are also great differences in power between us and animals, differences of which we take advantage in order to consume them. Since "the arbitrariness of this world" is not limited, either conceptually or practically, to the human condition and intrahuman relations, it would seem to follow that since correcting such arbitrariness is a fundamental moral concern, we should develop principles of justice to protect animals from our taking unfair advantage of their weakness. At the very least, since principles of fairness are intended to work against the natural order of the stronger benefiting by sacrificing the weaker, simply intoning, "But it's the natural order of things!" cannot show why morality should not work against the humans-over-animals hierarchy.

It could be objected, following the logic of Rawls's analysis of justice, particularly his proposed "original position," that moral concern with the interests of the weak derives from our self-interest and the possibility that we might become one of the weak. [13] "There, but for the grace of God, go I" is the motive for fairness in this moral scheme. So it could be argued that since we need not fear becoming cattle, rhesus monkeys, and the like, this motive cannot be extended to cover our dealings with other animals.

In response, we may note that, like other proposed egoistic origins for morality, this one fails to distinguish morality from prudence and does not fit with everyday moral psychology. For example, my moral outrage at the injustice of caste systems like that of traditional India does not derive from any concern I have about becoming an untouchable. There is no more chance of that happening than there is of my becoming a rhesus monkey. In my own case, and I do not think that I am unusual in this, it is not any sort of self-interest but something like David Hume's "disinterested sentiment" [14] or a deontological sense of fairness being intrinsically valuable that is the origin of my moral concern about injustices in Asia and other parts of the world remote from my daily life. Thus, self-interest does not set the boundaries of our concern with justice.

Conversely, if, as seems to be presumed in the construction of Rawls's original position, the merely logical possibility that I might have been born an untouchable is somehow of importance for developing the principles of justice that I should respect, then the same sort of merely logical possibility that I might have been born a rhesus monkey or some other animal should suffice to extend these principles of justice to animals. Although the "people" in Rawls's original position are gifted with considerable information and reasoning ability, it does not follow that their principles of justice apply only to the informed and the intelligent. Those principles are to cover even "the least among us," and this opens the door to animals being among the possible incarnations that those in the original position must (logically) be prudentially concerned to have protected against exploitation. It will not do to object that we cannot know "what it is like to be a bat," to use Tom Nagel's famous example,[15] and, therefore, cannot determine exactly what is needed to protect animals' interests against abuse. Even if we cannot directly experience the pleasures of other life forms, we can, if we will make the effort to observe animals closely, come to understand which ways of life provide them more enjoyment and fulfillment, and such commonsensical understanding is all that is required for the protective reflections carried on in the original position.[16] Therefore, Rawls's analysis of the original position does not provide a basis for refusing to extend our moral concern with correcting the arbitrariness of nature to our relations with animals.

Consequently, the egoistic dimension in Rawls's theory of justice does not provide good reason to believe that our moral concern with protecting the weak against the strong and other issues of justice must (logically) be restricted to intrahuman relations. Unless some other, morally significant justification can be provided for respecting the natural order that leaves us the strongest species, that order is no less arbitrary and no less in need of correction by principles of justice than was the "natural" hierarchy Aristotle envisioned that left Greek men free to benefit from the weakness of women and other cultures.

Thus, the apparent unfairness of our consuming animals is not shown to be mere appearance by the natural contract, the natural order, or the idea that animals should reap what they sow. Perhaps what most sharply separates the new animal rights movement from the traditional animal welfare movement is the new movement's insistence that no matter how humanely we do it, our continuing routinely to sacrifice animals' interests for our benefit is unfair. That claim has still to be rebutted, if it can be.

IV. Conclusion

Thus, liberating animals from our routine sacrifice of their interests for our benefit would seem to be the right thing to do in order better to pursue our moral goals of developing moral virtues, reducing suffering, and being fair.

I began this chapter by noting what I believe to be the common feeling underlying opposition to animal liberation. I hope the arguments of this chapter are strong enough at least to indicate that that feeling cannot simply be trusted. I hope these arguments have shown that even though current, common morality does not question our consuming animals—provided the sacrifice is executed humanely—there are fundamental elements of that morality that point in the direction of animal liberation. If that is correct, then there are fundamental reasons for questioning the feeling that we are obviously justified in consuming animals and for requiring that some more substantive justification be offered if we are going to continue to consume animals.

In Part III, we consider several attempts to provide more philosophically sophisticated justifications for continuing to consume animals. I want to close this chapter with a few sentences from William James that I believe nicely summarize the feeling underlying much of the animal rights movement and that clearly express where advocates of animal liberation locate the burden of proof:

> Take any demand, however slight, which any creature, however weak, may make.
> Ought it not, for its own sake, to be satisfied? If not, prove why not.[17]

Part III

Answering Some Objections to Liberating Animals

SINCE HE has no language, he may be killed to make a tasty dish. Since she lacks the capacity to abstract and conceive the future, she may be hunted and killed for amusement. Since they are not capable of forming goals by considering alternatives, they may be used in lethal experiments. Since he lacks an epistemic relation to his interest in life, he may be killed in order that his body may be used for making soap and perfume. Since she lacks a cultural life, she may be trapped and skinned to make a fur coat.

Does this reasoning make sense to you?

It made sense to Descartes: "Please note that I am speaking of thought, and not of life or sensation. I do not deny life to animals, and I do not deny sensation. [But animals' lack of thought] absolves men from the suspicion of crime when they eat or kill animals."[1] Apparently, it continues to make sense to such contemporary philosophers as H. J. McCloskey, Jan Narveson, Bonnie Steinbock, Leslie Francis and Richard Norman, R. G. Frey, Meredith Williams, L. B. Cebik, Ruth Cigman, Charlie Blatz, and Michael A. Fox.[2] These writers all contend that as long as we do not cause animals unnecessary pain and anguish, the fact that humans are, but animals are not, "rational" beings shows that our consuming them is not morally pernicious. For example, Williams writes:

> Our attitudes toward animals as tools for research or as food are not pernicious racism or sexism. There is an important difference between human and animal existence that justifies this difference in attitude. [Human beings stand in an epistemic relationship to their world. . . . Humans can take an interest in their welfare; animals cannot.] But it does not follow that animals warrant no consideration. The fact that they suffer is reason for some but not for equal concern, and I do not deny that causing unnecessary pain and anguish is reprehensible.[3]

111

One of the more interesting innovations in the development of this anthropocentric theme by these recent writers is their claim that there is a fundamental,
morally significant difference between animal and human interests that justifies
our routinely sacrificing their interests in favor of our own. For example, answering the question, "Who or what are logically possible possessors of rights?,"
McCloskey contends that "[Interests] suggest that which is or ought or would be
of *concern* to the person/being. It is partly for this reason that we decline to
speak of the interests of animals and speak rather of their welfare. These considerations exclude animals as possible possessors of rights."[4] Ruth Cigman
makes a similar claim concerning the possibility of suffering the misfortune of
death:

> [Humans have but] animals lack the very capacity which is necessary for the right to
> life: the capacity to have categorical desires [desires which "give point or meaning to
> life"]. This capacity is necessary for a creature to be a possible subject of the misfor-
> tune of death, and *this* possibility is presupposed by the right to life.[5]

We shall spend considerable time in the following four chapters analyzing the
nature, variety, and moral significance of interests.

With the exception of McCloskey, these recent defenders of our continuing to
consume animals have developed their arguments in order to refute Peter Singer's
defense of liberating animals.[6] As Williams puts it, "[Singer claims] that the
principle of equality applies both to humans and animals *on the ground* that the
condition for having interests is the same for animals and humans."[7] My concern
here is not with whether these philosophers have or have not succeeded in re-
futing Singer's argument. What does concern me is whether their analyses of this
"condition for having interests"—which they all tie, in various ways, to human
rationality—justify their conclusion that the interests of animals do not merit the
same sort of moral protection as our own. The underlying theme of the following
four chapters is whether or not the following is a sound inference:

A1: We are rational beings.
A2: They are not.
A3: Therefore, we are morally justified in exploiting them.

To insure that there is no misunderstanding here, I want to emphasize that
the following chapters are *not* about cruelty to animals. The philosophers whose
work is discussed here are unanimous in condemning cruelty to animals, and I
am not suggesting that refusing to liberate animals entails condoning cruelty to
them. What is at issue here is whether the differences between animal and human
rationality morally justify our routinely sacrificing their interests for our benefit.

Chapter 7 discusses the concepts of "having an interest" and "taking an interest" and argues that the former is morally significant and does not require

anything close to human intellectual capacity. This chapter contains an extended critique of R. G. Frey's contention that only rational beings can have interests. Chapter 8 discusses four criteria for having moral rights: recognizing the moral rights of others, being a moral agent, having socioeconomic relations with others, and being the sort of being for which moral rules are created. All four of these criteria have been offered as explanations of why animals cannot have moral rights, but none of them is supported by everyday moral practice. One of the more hotly debated issues even within the animal liberation movement is whether painlessly killing an animal is morally wrong. Chapter 9 discusses this issue, arguing that even in a painless death an animal suffers a morally significant loss. Finally, Chapter 10 deals with the contention that as long as we breed animals for our use, give them happy lives, and replace them with equally happy animals when we kill them, there is no moral wrong in this use. This argument seems to have considerable force against utilitarian defenses of animal liberation such as that of Peter Singer,[8] but it lacks force outside the utilitarian context, and even for utilitarians, the argument loses its force once the goal of utilitarianism is clarified.

Although these four chapters proceed from the more general issue of the moral significance of interests to the more particular moral issues of death and replacement, they do not form a deductive flow from general principles to specific conclusions. Rather, they represent expressions in the diverse contexts established by recent objections to animal liberation of the theme struck in Part II, namely, that everyday moral practice indicates that having interests, not being rational, is what makes a being the sort of being that ought (morally) not to be exploited.

7

Can Animals Have Interests?

I DOUBT that many contemporary philosophers would agree with Thomas Aquinas and Joseph Rickaby that we cannot (logically) be obligated even to be charitable to animals.[1] However, many contemporary philosophers deny that animals can (logically) have moral rights, and this is sometimes done on the grounds that "only those beings with interests" can (logically) have moral rights. This is the "only" half of Leonard Nelson's "interest requirement" for having rights, noted in Chapter 5, where it was also noted that most advocates of animal liberation, perhaps focusing on the "all" more than the "only," accept this requirement. Contemporary opponents of animal liberation turn this requirement against these advocates by emphasizing that "only" and insisting that, for one reason or another, only beings with something very much like normal$_h$ intelligence can (logically) have interests. (Henceforth, unless otherwise noted, "can" and "cannot" will be used for "can [logically]" and "cannot [logically].")

The most extensive development of this argument to date has been put forth by R. G. Frey in *Interests and Rights, The Case Against Animals*.[2] In this chapter, I want, first, to discuss Frey's arguments and, second, to determine in a more general way whether there is a morally significant tie between rationality and interests.

I. Language and Interests

In *Interests and Rights*, Frey apparently believes that he has animal liberation advocates firmly skewered on the horns of a dilemma:

A1: Animal liberation advocates accept the interest requirement that all and only beings that (can) have interests (can) have moral rights.[3]
A2: Interests must (logically) be divided into needs and desires.[4]

A3a: If "interests" in (1) refers to needs, then plants, tractors, cave drawings, and other mere things (can) have interests and, consequently, (can) have moral rights (at least as far as the interest requirement is concerned).

A3b: But this is so counter-intuitive as to be unacceptable, even to animal liberation advocates.[5]

A4a: If "interests" in (1) refers to desires, then animals cannot have them and, consequently, cannot have moral rights.

A4b: Animals cannot have desires because

    (i) having desires requires belief or self-consciousness,

    (ii) both of these require linguistic ability, but

    (iii) animals lack linguistic ability.[6]

Thus, Frey claims that a careful analysis of "interests" shows that the claim that animals (can) have moral rights either leads to absurdity or is false.

Frey is wrong on both counts. If the interest requirement refers to needs, it does not follow that plants, artifacts, and other mere things (can) have moral rights. This is because plants, artifacts, and the like do not have the kinds of needs that generate interests. Consequently, step A3a in our reconstruction of Frey's argument is false. On the other hand, if the interest requirement refers to desires, it does not follow that animals cannot have interests. This is because having desires does not require linguistic ability, since neither belief nor self-consciousness requires this ability. In this half of Frey's dilemma, step A4a is unsubstantiated, because step A4b(ii) is false. We shall discuss needs first and then devote the remainder of this section to an analysis of desires.

A. "HAVING AN INTEREST"

Frey distinguishes "having an interest" in x from "taking an interest" in x, generally using "need" for the former and "desire" for the latter. According to Frey, we "have an interest in" or "need" x if x contributes (will contribute, would contribute) to our good or well-being. We need not care about this relation or even be aware of it for this need to exist. For example, we need vitamin C for good health, whether or not we care about or are even aware of this. Frey then goes on to remind us that plants, artifacts, and other mere things can be intelligibly said to "need" things ("tractors need oil"), to be "harmed" or "benefited" ("the Rembrandt painting would be harmed by exposure to the sun"), to be "good of their kind" ("that's a good example of a night blooming jasmine"), and to have things that are "good for them" ("a sunny corner protected from the wind is a good place to plant this kind of shrub"). He concludes from this that if we interpret the interest requirement as referring to having needs, then plants, artifacts, and other mere things (can) have moral rights.[7]

But would we ordinarily say, as Frey does, that "it is in a tractor's interests to be well oiled"?[8] I think not. While "need," "want," "lack," "harm," "benefit," and "good" are all commonly applied to plants, artifacts, and so on, "interest" is not. "Interest" is commonly reserved for the people and animals who will benefit or be harmed by the needs of the plants, artifacts, and so on being met or unmet. For example, the tractor "needs" oil to run efficiently, but it is "in the farmer's interest," not the tractor's, that the tractor be well oiled. Again, wheat "needs" water to survive and flourish, but it is "in the farmer's interest," not the wheat's, that the wheat be properly watered. Similarly, if the marshland "needs" protection against developers, it is not "in the interest" of the marshland itself but "in the interest" of providing habitat for migrating birds and other animals living there. Thus, the ordinary use of "interest" tells us that plants, artifacts, and other mere things not only take no interest in what benefits or harms them; they also have no interest in these things. So "having a good of one's own," "being capable of being benefited or harmed," or simply "having a need" does not provide an adequate analysis of having an interest. It follows that by basing the *reductio* in his dilemma on interpreting having an interest as having a need, Frey has refuted a straw man.

In Chapter 5, we employed a definition of "having an interest" that provides not only an accurate account of how animal liberationists employ this concept but also a more adequate interpretation of the ordinary use of that concept (setting aside special legal and economic uses, of course). That definition runs as follows:

S has an interest in x if and only if x affects (will affect, would affect) S's feelings of well-being.

It will be remembered that "feelings of well-being" refers to such feelings as pleasure and pain, feeling well and feeling ill, elation and depression, feelings of fulfillment and of frustration, and the many other feelings that contribute to or detract from the enjoyment of or satisfaction with life.

This interpretation of "having an interest" has been criticized in the following way: "The following is unlikely but not inconceivable: by performing operation O on P, we can cut his/her intelligence in half but not affect P's feelings of well-being. According to your analysis of having an interest, performing this operation on P is neither in nor not in P's interest."[9]

This consequence of our analysis of having an interest is supposed to be intuitively unacceptable. But if that is the case, it is because of the world in which our intuitions have developed. If we lived in a Brave New World in which our intelligence could be halved without this reducing our opportunities for enjoyment and fulfillment, without leaving us more vulnerable to abuse and unhappiness, without causing anxiety before the operation and frustration and depression afterward, and so forth, then such an operation would be neither in nor against our interests. But we do not live in such a world. In our world, intelligence is something we both enjoy exercising and find a necessary tool for attaining other enjoyments and fulfillments, which is what makes being intelligent in our interest in our world. What is valuable in our world might not be valuable in a vastly different world. That should not surprise anyone, but it should discourage the practice of trying to refute moral philosophies by developing science fiction counter-examples. Their accuracy and their adequacy for dealing with the problems we encounter in the world in which we actually live is the relevant test of moral principles and of interpretations of morally significant concepts (we shall return to this methodological issue in Chapter 13).

It might still be objected that our interpretation of having an interest is too weak, because "interest" has a prescriptive component that we have not acknowledged. H. J. McCloskey claimed that there is such a component to "interest" in his well-known paper, "Rights,"[10] and Frey defends McCloskey's position (against criticisms by Tom Regan) in chap. II of his book, although he indicates that he does not want to have McCloskey's position identified with or linked to his own.

However, McCloskey has since repudiated this interpretation of "interest," acknowledging that there is greater flexibility in the use of "interest" than he had earlier recognized.[11] Consequently, it seems unnecessary to defend extensively our interpretation of having an interest against an objection based on McCloskey's earlier analysis of "interest." Let me just say that where there is a prescriptive component to "*x* is in *S*'s interest," it can be adequately interpreted in terms of the hypothetical imperative "If he or she can take an interest in *x*, then *S* ought to do so." In cases where that conditional phrase is met, saying that *x* is in *S*'s interest may have direct prescriptive significance. In cases where that conditional phrase is not met, as in some cases concerning infants, animals, and the infirm, the prescriptive component remains subjunctive.

Returning to our interpretation of having an interest, employing it allows us readily to explain why people can unknowingly have an interest in vitamin C, tractors being well oiled, and wheat being properly watered, while plants, artifacts, and other nonfeeling things cannot have an interest in anything. Furthermore, distinguishing affective needs, which generate interests, from nonaffective needs, which do not generate interests, can explain why some people do not even have an interest (and, consequently, justifiably take no interest) in some things they can properly be said to need.

Consider the following example. Suppose that I am definitely overweight and would need to exercise regularly and to go on a diet in order to lose weight. Also, suppose that I do not mind being fat and that my overall enjoyment and fulfillment in life will not be diminished by my being fat. This is because even though my being fat prevents me from engaging in certain activities I would have enjoyed and will shorten my life somewhat, it is also an important contributor to my happiness. My fine tenor voice, which I love and from which I profit handsomely, would not be as fine without the fat. Furthermore, the crowd I go with and whose company I greatly enjoy feels more at ease and jolly with fat people. Finally, exercising and dieting would be highly unpleasant for me and would deprive me of two of my greatest pleasures, eating and drinking with abandon. In this way, remaining fat might give me a somewhat shorter but overall more enjoyable and fulfilling life than would becoming slim.

Now, in this case, although it might be said that I "need" to lose weight or that it would be "good" for me to lose weight (i.e., be "good for my health" or "necessary for good health"), I could properly claim that it is not "in my interest" to spend my time exercising and watching my diet. It is in my interest to spend my time fulfilling those needs that will enhance my enjoyment and fulfillment in life and to neglect those needs that will not. Pursuing good health usually is important for our feelings of well-being, but when that pursuit undermines those feelings, it ceases to be in our interest. Thus, not merely whether we need x but whether x will affect our feelings of well-being seems to be the crucial factor in having an interest in x.

Applying this more adequate interpretation of having an interest to the interest requirement, it follows that all and only those beings that (can) have *affective needs* (can) have moral rights. This certainly excludes plants, artifacts, and other *nonfeeling* things from having moral rights. It also accurately expresses what seems ridiculous in the idea of plants and other "mere" things having rights: a standard purpose of moral rights is to protect the right-holder's condition for his or her own sake, but since their condition cannot matter to nonfeeling things, assigning moral rights to protect them would be like concocting an elaborate Rube Goldberg contraption that can accomplish nothing. It is only when other, feeling beings are affected (will be affected, would be affected) by their condition that protecting plants, artifacts, and other nonfeeling things can serve a moral purpose. (We shall return to this issue in Chapter 14.)

So distinguishing affective from nonaffective needs shows that step (A3a) in Frey's dilemma is false and that, consequently, his purported *reductio* fails. Furthermore, since Frey acknowledges that some animals can at least "suffer unpleasant sensations," [12] it would seem to follow that even he must agree that these animals have affective needs. Consequently, these animals have interests and meet the interest requirement for having moral rights—something plants, artifacts, or other nonfeeling things cannot do, since they do not even suffer unpleasant sensations.

B. LANGUAGE AND DESIRE

Turning to desires, Frey draws a distinction between those that require beliefs such as "I don't have x," "I would be better off if I had x," and "In order to get x, I have to do *y*" and "simple desires," such as wanting food. Simple desires are reflexive and, consequently, cannot involve the mediation of belief, although Frey insists that having any such simple desires requires that at least some of our simple desires involve self-consciousness: "Where the creature in question is alleged to have only unconscious desires, what cash value can the use of the term 'desire' have?" Frey then concludes that animals cannot have desires of either sort, since both belief and self-consciousness require language, and animals are not capable of using language.[13] We shall first consider Frey's contention that belief requires linguistic ability and then his claim that self-consciousness also requires that ability.

1. Language and Belief

Frey offers the following argument to show that only language users can believe:

> Now what is it that I believe? I believe that my collection lacks a Gutenberg Bible; that is, I believe that the sentence 'My collection lacks a Gutenberg Bible' is true. In expressions of the sort 'I believe that . . .', what follows the 'that' is a sentence, and what I believe is that the sentence is true. . . . The essence of this argument is . . . about what is believed. If what is believed is that a certain sentence is true, then no creature which lacks language can have beliefs. . . . I do not see how the cat can be correctly described as believing the laces are tied unless it can, as I do, distinguish between the beliefs that the laces are tied and that the laces are untied and regards one but not the other as true. But what is true or false are not states of affairs which reflect or pertain to these beliefs; states of affairs are not true or false (though sentences describing them are) but either are or are not the case.[14]

Thus, Frey contends that when someone believes something, what he believes is that a certain sentence is true. Frey believes this because

  (a) in belief statements sentences are used to express what is believed and
  (b) what one believes is that something is true (or false), and sentences are the sorts of things that are true (or false).

Both these arguments are seriously faulty; we shall deal with each in turn.

a. The Psychological (In)Significance of Grammar. Which grammatical forms are employed in expressing the objects of intentional verbs is one issue; what those intentional objects are is another; and an answer for the first issue is no more an answer for the second issue than linguistics is a substitute for psychology. The proper conclusion of Frey's analysis of belief *statements* is that in order to understand such statements, one must be able to understand sentences. This conclusion is neither controversial nor relevant to the issue of whether animals can believe; it is relevant only to whether animals can formulate or understand belief statements.

Furthermore, using intentional verbs whose objects are sentences in referring to and describing animals is common practice. We commonly say such things as "The dog thinks that the cat is in the tree," "The bird realizes that one of its chicks is missing," "The cat recognizes that the ice is slippery," "The monkey sees that strangers are invading its territory," "The deer senses that we are closing in on it," "The zebra smells that a leopard is near," and "The horse hears that it is being called." In saying such things, we do not presume that the dog, for example, thinks of the sentence "The cat is in the tree" or that it could assent to that sentence, if asked whether it is true. Nonetheless, we understand the sentences above, know when they do and do not apply, and, in general, use them without problem. Thus, ordinary usage does not support Frey's claim that if an intentional verb takes a sentence for its object, then it properly applies only to those capable of understanding sentences.[15]

Frey might counter that this common usage just shows how pervasive is the pro-animal prejudice. However, such a claim is reminiscent of the band member who claims, "I'm okay; it's the rest of the band that's out of step." If ordinary language philosophy has taught us anything, it has taught us which to choose, when we have to choose between ordinary language being nonsensical and a philosophical analysis being mistaken.

It might be thought that Frey could escape these problems by borrowing a distinction developed by Norman Malcolm in his previously noted article. Malcolm there distinguishes "thinking that," which does not require linguistic ability, from "having the thought that," which does require that ability, since it involves explicitly formulating a thought. It might be thought that Frey could profit from drawing a similar distinction between "believing that" and "having the belief that."

However, acknowledging such a distinction would sink, rather than salvage, Frey's argument. This is because it would follow from deploying such a distinction, while continuing to insist that desiring requires linguistic ability, that we can desire something only when we "have the relevant beliefs" about it. But that is clearly false. For example, I can desire that a long-winded speaker should finish without having such beliefs as "She has not stopped talking" and "I would be happier, if she would stop talking." In order to desire that the speaker cease talking, I need only believe such things (if believing is required at all); I need not actually have (entertain, formulate, express to myself) such beliefs. Consequently, Frey cannot benefit from Malcolm's analysis of ordinary language. On the contrary, he must somehow discredit that analysis, for Malcolm's distinction provides a way of understanding how intentional verbs can be employed in discussing desires without implying that linguistic ability is required for desiring.

Another problem with Frey's argument is that if we were to apply his pattern of analysis to other intentional verbs, we would arrive at the following *reductio* of his position. Just as animals are incapable of belief, so they are incapable of hearing, for when I hear that someone is coming, what I hear is that the sentence "Someone is coming" is true, but animals are incapable of doing this. Again, animals cannot smell, for when I smell that something is burning, what I smell is that the sentence "Something is burning" is true, and animals cannot formulate or understand sentences. Such conclusions seem either to be preposterous or to indicate that stipulative definitions of "hear," "smell," and "believe" are being used. Such abnormal definitions could be based on what Malcolm has described as "the prejudice of philosophers that only propositional thoughts belong to consciousness."[16] Just as we determined in Chapter 2 that moral value is much more varied and complex than many moral philosophers have acknowledged, so we may expect that consciousness is much more varied and complex than many philosophers of mind have acknowledged.

It might be thought that Frey is not really faced with the preceding dilemma, for he does not claim that his analysis applies to all intentional verbs. However, nothing in what Frey says indicates that his analysis is restricted to belief. Since perceptions, like beliefs, can be true or false and since "hear that," "see that," and so on can be parsed like "believe that" to take sentences as their objects, it would be arbitrary to try to escape the problems of the previous paragraph by insisting that Frey's analysis applies only to belief.

Finally, it may be thought that Frey can escape all the preceding objections, since he claims that

> though it may be thought that my analysis of belief requires persons to entertain the concept of a sentence in order to have beliefs, this in fact is not the case. . . . The sentence 'John believes that the window is open' . . . can be plausibly interpreted as 'John would, if asked, assent to some sentence that has for him the meaning that "the window is open" has for us'.[17]

One obvious objection to Frey's contention that being able to formulate sentences is essential for belief is that we often believe things without formulating any sentences about them. For example, if I reach into my pocket for a pencil while listening to a lecture, I believe that I have a pencil in my pocket, but I do not formulate the sentence "I have a pencil in my pocket." Frey formulates the interpretation above to meet this objection.

However, as a response to the objections raised so far in this chapter, this interpretation is simply irrelevant. Since "hear," "see," "recognize," and so forth take sentences as their objects, although we commonly hear, see, recognize, and so forth things without formulating sentences of the form, "I hear *x*," "I see *x*," "I recognize *x*," and the like, they too, presumably, are to be interpreted in terms of what sentences the one who hears, sees, recognizes, and so on would assent to. Consequently, these verbs would still not be applicable to infants, animals, and other nonlanguage users. As long as Frey holds that intentional verbs properly apply only to language users, it is inconsequential whether he maintains that they apply only when we entertain sentences or can apply as well to situations where we would assent to sentences, if asked. Either way, Frey's analysis still runs counter to ordinary usage and is vulnerable to the above *reductio*.

As to whether Frey's interpretation provides an answer to the formidable objection that psychology does not confirm that belief requires linguistic ability, the interpretation does not meet that objection either. First, the interpretation is arbitrary. "John would assent to 'The window is open'" is only one among many candidates to be a conditional interpretation of "John believes that the window is open." (We shall use "John would assent to 'The window is open'" as convenient shorthand for "John would, if asked, assent to some sentence that has for him the meaning that 'The window is open' has for us.") Other possible candidates are "John would close the window, if asked," "John would close the window, if he felt there was a draft," "John, who does not want to break the window, would throw something out the window without first attempting to open it, if he was called upon to throw something out the window," "John would not sit near the window, if he was afraid of sitting near open windows," and so forth.

Frey provides no reason for selecting what John would assent to as the interpretation of "John believes that the window is open," rather than any or all of those other things John would do if he believed that. But without such an argument, it is not obvious that what someone would assent to is even a necessary part of an interpretation, let alone *the* interpretation, of believing. We do not commonly require that an individual assent to or even be willing to assent to *p* in order that we feel we have satisfactory evidence that she believes that *p*. We often just watch what a person does to find out what she believes, and we hold that "actions speak louder than words" in expressing beliefs.

Even if a subjunctive reference to action is a necessary part of an adequate understanding of belief, that reference must be either vague or elaborately disjunctive, for there are many alternative sets of actions that would commonly be considered sufficient to confirm belief. To continue with Frey's example, "John believes that the window is open" might be interpreted as "Depending on what the situation required, John would do those things appropriate to the window being open, rather than to the window being closed" or "Depending on what the situation required, either John would assent to 'The window is open,' or he would close the window, or he would throw something out the window without first attempting to open it, or he would not sit near the window, or . . ." Common experience with beliefs does not indicate that there is one particular form of action, including assenting to sentences, that we must be ready to perform in order to believe something. I would guess that it is Frey's belief that language is necessary for belief that leads him to interpret belief in terms of assenting, but, of course, that belief begs the question.

Furthermore, it is not obvious that "John would assent to 'The window is open'" is properly described as an "interpretation" of "John believes that the window is open." If the former were an interpretation of the latter, then "John believes that the window is open but would not assent to 'The window is open'" would be self-contradictory. But it is not. Rather, it is an instance of the common idea "he or she believes that, but would never admit it." Of course, Frey might try to meet this sort of objection by qualifying his interpretation of "John believes that the window is open" to read something like "John would assent to 'The window is open' in a situation where he felt he had nothing to gain through deception, did not feel like playing a practical joke, felt secure in disclosing what he believed, etc." However, the effect of adding such a *ceteris paribus* clause to Frey's interpretation would be to show just how distant is the relation between belief and willingness to assent. Such a *ceteris paribus* clause appropriately qualifies the relation between something and a sign of it, not the relation between something and its interpretation.

Again, if "John would assent to 'The window is open'" were an interpretation of "John believes that the window is open," then the latter would not be a significant answer to a question as to why John would assent to the sentence, "The window is open." That is, John's believing that the window is open could not *explain* why he would assent to "The window is open." Citing John's belief in response to the query, "Why would John assent to 'The window is open'?" would contain the same category mistake as answering, "Why is John a bachelor?" with "John is a bachelor because he is an unmarried male." However, that John believes that the window is open can provide a significant answer to the question, "Why would John assent to 'The window is open'?" As an explanation of why John would assent to that sentence, John's believing that the window is open is in the same group with the following: John wants to please you and feels that by assenting to that sentence, he will do so; John was told that he will be set free if he assents to that sentence; John figures that he can fool you by assenting to that sentence; John thinks that he can ridicule your research by assenting to that sentence; and many other plausible, common explanations of why someone would assent to a sentence.

That John believes that the window is open may be the explanation for his willingness to assent to "The window is open" that we ordinarily presume to be the correct one. That is why we presume that assenting is ordinarily a reliable sign of belief. However, that priority of place among explanations does not change the relation between belief and willingness to assent into one of interpretation.

The problem with Frey's interpretation of "John believes that p" as "John would assent to 'p' under certain conditions" is that it tries to pass off a subjunctive reference to one thing that belief can lead to as an interpretation of what belief is. But since, for the reasons just developed, believing that p cannot be identified with the fact that one would assent to "p" under certain conditions, Frey has no more succeeded in providing us with an interpretation of belief than Euthyphro succeeded in providing Socrates with an interpretation of piety when he told Socrates that pious men are beloved of the gods (and Euthyphro's mistake would not be corrected by substituting "would be" for "are" in his interpretation of piety).

Thus, Frey's proposed interpretation fails, leaving his contention that belief requires linguistic ability vulnerable to the many counter-examples of believing without using language. Both our experience of our own beliefs and our commonly, significantly applying "believe" and many other intentional verbs to infants, animals, and other nonlanguage users indicate that the fact that these verbs take sentences as their objects does not show that only those capable of recognizing sentences can have these verbs meaningfully applied to them.

b. Language and Truth. Frey maintains that his analysis is correct because we would have to "credit [animals] with language in order for there to be something true or false in belief, [since] sentences are the sorts of things which [are] capable of being true or false, [whereas] states of affairs are not true or false but are or are not the case."[18] If we set aside the issue of whether animals possess sufficient language or something sufficiently like language to satisfy this argument without dispute, Frey's argument here still suffers from the following four problems.

First, validly inferring from beliefs involving truth and falsity to beliefs involving sentences requires the additional premise that *only* sentences can be true or false. This is clearly false. Currency, portraits, friends, omens, impressions, perceptions, examples, tools, and lines are examples that come readily to mind of other things that can be true or false. Thus, Frey's argument rests on a false premise.

It might be contended that this objection equivocates, since the examples above are not all true/false in the same way. However, such a counterargument would just make the objection a bit more complicated. We would have to rephrase it in terms of the following two questions:

> if different kinds of things can be true/false in different ways, then are beliefs true/false in the way sentences are, and
>
> if so, are sentences the only things that are true/false in the way sentences are?

If the answer to either of these questions is "no," then Frey's argument still fails, since his presumption of a very tight relation between sentences and being true/false (in the relevant sense) will be false.

Frey does not seem to have recognized that there is an issue here, for he provides no argument to answer these questions. Furthermore, the answer to the second question seems definitely to be negative; that is, sentences do not seem to be the only things that are true/false in the way sentences are. If we accept a correspondence theory of truth for sentences, then portraits are true/false in the way sentences are. If we adopt a coherence theory of truth for sentences, then omens, impressions, and perceptions are true/false in the way sentences are. If we adopt a pragmatic theory of truth for sentences, then examples, tools, and signs are true/false in the way sentences are. Thus, there would seem to be sets of things that are true/false in the way sentences are, no matter how we interpret the latter. Beliefs may be just another set of things that are true/false in the same way sentences and other things are. So even if beliefs are true/false in the way sentences are, we cannot infer from that that beliefs are about sentences.

The second problem with Frey's truth-based argument is indicated by the fact that if we were told that x and y are both colored or both conduct electricity or are both beautiful or are both complex, it would remain an open question as to just how similar or dissimilar they are and in which sense(s) they are or are not the same kind of thing. In Frey's argument, however, it is presumed that if x and y can both be p, that shows that they are the same sort of thing: Frey argues that since what is believed is that something is true and since sentences can be true, the something that is believed to be true must be a sentence.

But just as one swallow does not make a summer, so having one predicate in common provides only minimal evidence concerning in which way(s) or to what degree those things are or are not the same kind of thing. Frey's argument from having the same kind of predicate to being the same kind of thing runs dangers analogous to those in inferring from similar effects to similar causes; consequently, that argument requires a great deal of confirmation from other arguments. Frey does not provide such confirmation, nor, as the previous objections to his analysis indicate, is there reason to believe that he could find such confirmation.

Third, in the course of developing his argument, Frey provides counter-examples to that argument. He uses such phrases as "the false belief," "true and false beliefs," and "regarding one [belief] but not the other as true." [19] Frey here predicates "true" and "false" of beliefs themselves, rather than predicating these terms of the something that is believed. In making such predications, he follows ordinary usage, since we do commonly talk about true and false beliefs—even more commonly than we talk about what is believed being that something is true or false. However, it would seem to follow from Frey's argument that since beliefs can be true/false, they are sentences, since "sentences are the sorts of things which [are] capable of being true or false." This amounts to another *reductio* of Frey's analysis, since saying that beliefs are sentences clearly confuses the psychological with the linguistic.

It might be countered that Frey could escape this objection by again referring to his interpreting belief in terms of what we would assent to if asked. However, this interpretation would leave us predicating truth and falsity of dispositions, readinesses, or what-one-would-do's. That would be very strange, to say the least. So rather than that interpretation providing an escape from this objection, it would seem that our common practice of predicating truth and falsity of beliefs provides another *reductio* of that interpretation.

Our fourth and final objection to Frey's truth-based argument is that even if we were to try to decide whether what is believed does or does not concern sentences on the basis of how certain predicates are commonly deployed when discussing beliefs, at least as good and probably even a better case can be made for saying that what is believed is that certain states of affairs are (are not) the case than can be made for saying that what is believed is that certain sentences are true (false). We can equally well say either, "What Helen believed is true" or "What Helen believed is the case." Again, in response to a question like, "Does Nathan really believe that?," we can equally well respond, "Yes, he believes that that is true" or "Yes, he believes that that is the case." Additionally, if we were asked, "What makes a belief true?," the common answer would not be, "A belief is true if what is believed is true" but "A belief is true if what is believed is the case." This suggests that what is true/false here are beliefs, with what is believed being that something is or is not the case. And, of course, as Frey himself acknowledges, the sorts of things that are or are not the case are not sentences but states of affairs. Thus, the place of truth or falsity in the analysis of beliefs, belief statements, and statements and questions about beliefs is at least not as clear as and probably other than Frey suggests and his argument requires.

Thus, Frey fails to demonstrate that language is required for belief. Consequently, he fails to demonstrate that animals cannot have belief-mediated desires.

2. Language and Self-Consciousness

Turning to simple desires such as wanting food, Frey presents the following argument to show that the self-consciousness required for having such desires requires linguistic ability:

> I adopt the view that 'P-predicates,' which include such things as thoughts, feelings, memories, and perceptions, can only be ascribed to oneself if they can be ascribed to others and that one can know one has or experiences a particular P-predicate R only if one can know that other people have or experience R. And following Wittgenstein's private language argument, I adopt the view that P-predicate R, for example, 'pain,'

does not (and cannot) have meaning by standing for or naming a sensation to which each of us has access in his own case but rather has meaning in virtue of certain public rules and conventions which can be adhered to and transgressed, where adherence and transgression can be publicly checked. In this way, I come with Hacker to the view that the meaningful ascription of P-predicate R to oneself is only possible . . . within the context and confines of a public language.[20]

The problem with this argument is that it begs the question. Frey infers from Wittgenstein's argument against a private *language* that consciousness requires knowing a public language. However, before Frey's argument that ascribing P-predicates to oneself requires knowing a public language even becomes relevant to whether animals can have simple desires, an argument is needed to show that feeling pain, to use Frey's example, is ascribing the P-predicate "pain" to oneself. That is, an argument is needed to show that self-consciousness is properly interpreted as the linguistic activity of ascribing certain predicates to oneself. Frey provides no such argument.

Psychology does not support a linguistic interpretation of self-consciousness. If I bang my shin on the coffee table, I am conscious of being in pain, but I do not form the thought "I am in pain" or otherwise ascribe the predicate "pain" to myself. Also, interpreting my consciousness of being in pain as the fact that I would, if asked, respond affirmatively to "Are you in pain?" would be blatantly arbitrary. There are many things besides assenting to "I am in pain" that I would naturally (be ready to) do when experiencing pain (e.g., screaming and striking back) if the circumstances permitted.

Additionally, we may note that Frey's argument here would lead to the conclusion that animals are not conscious. Notice that in the quotation above, Frey's analysis of self-consciousness in terms of ascribing P-predicates to oneself is said to apply not only to simple desires but also to "such things as thoughts, feelings, memories, and perceptions." If all such things are beyond the capacities of non-language users, insisting as Frey does[21] that, nonetheless, they are still conscious is devoid of content. How could animals be conscious if they could not perceive, feel, desire, remember, think, or believe?

Furthermore, Frey apparently presumes that to be conscious of *x* involves ascribing predicates to *x* (or being ready to assent to sentences ascribing predicates to *x*). Why else would he presume that being self-conscious involves ascribing P-predicates to oneself? Additionally, Frey's argument concerning linguistic ability and self-consciousness is based on an analysis of the requirements for the meaningful ascription of any sort of predicate, for it is based on an analysis of what makes language in general meaningful. Frey does not give us any reason to believe that being conscious of oneself is essentially tied to linguistic ability while being conscious of other things is not, and on the surface of it, at least, feeling pain does not seem to be intimately tied to language, while seeing colors and hearing noises are not. Consequently, if Frey's argument were sound, only language users could be conscious. Since Frey maintains that animals lack linguistic ability, this would exclude animals from being conscious.

Apparently, Frey is strongly opposed to denying that animals are conscious, since he is adamant in rejecting the suggestion that he is denying consciousness to animals.[22] Therefore, unless Frey can show that being conscious of oneself requires linguistic ability, while being conscious of other things does not, we have a *reductio* of Frey's position here that he would have to accept as discrediting his attempt to deny that animals can have simple desires.

Thus, Frey has not provided us any reason to doubt what we ordinarily believe, namely, that animals can desire food, water, and relief from pain. It follows that Frey has once again failed to show that animals cannot meet the interest requirement for having moral rights. In the cases both of belief-mediated desires and of simple desires, the fundamental flaw in Frey's argument is that he presumes what he claims to be showing, namely, that belief and self-consciousness require linguistic ability.

C. CONCLUSION

In our ordinary dealings with infants, pets, and other nonlanguage-using animals, we successfully deal with them as desiring beings who take an interest in what pleases and pains them and as sentient beings with affective needs, some of which they take an interest in and some of which they merely have an interest in. This places the burden of proof on Frey and others who would deny that animals can have desires or that the interests of animals cannot be significantly distinguished from the needs of plants and other nonfeeling things. Since Frey has failed to shoulder that burden and, to my knowledge, no other proponent of this position has done a better job of defending it, we may continue to rely on ordinary experience and hold that animals have affective needs and that they have mediated and simple desires concerning the fulfillment or frustration of those needs, as well as desires concerning things that are not really in their best interest, such as playing in the street.

It follows that both horns of Frey's dilemma are blunt and harmless. His *reductio* fails, and his attempt to tie desiring to linguistic ability begs the question. Having overcome the most extensive argument to date against animal interests, I would like to conclude this chapter with a somewhat more direct, descriptive analysis of interests and their moral significance.

II. Reason and the Moral Significance of Interests

Contemporary opponents of animal liberation like Frey have fastened on the concept of interests to try to show that we are morally justified in consuming animals. The Cartesian strategy of insisting that animals are machines and, consequently, cannot suffer has lost its credibility; so contemporary humanists have employed the interest requirement in an effort to show that even if animals can suffer unpleasant experiences or loss, that suffering is not sufficiently, morally weighty to merit more than humane concern. They argue that the rational dimension found in humans' taking an interest but lacking in animals' "merely" having interests gives sufficient, extra moral worth to human interests to justify our sacrificing animals' interests to fulfill our own.

Our analysis of Frey's arguments has already shown that attempts to downgrade animals' interests by lumping them with the nonaffective needs of plants and things and attempts to deny that animals can take an interest in things, because they lack linguistic ability, are doomed to failure. What I want to do now in concluding this discussion of interests is, first, to show that taking an interest in something is not necessarily a highly rational activity (i.e., is not always an activity requiring something like normal$_h$ intelligence) and, second, to argue that the ability to take an interest in things does not have the moral significance that humanists would have us believe it has.

A. Being Rational and Having Interests

It will be remembered that we have determined that S "has an interest" in x if and only if S's feelings of well-being are (will be, would be) affected by x. "Taking an interest" in x also requires that x affect (will affect, would affect) our feelings of well-being. To suggest that we could be properly described as "taking an interest" in something about which we are indifferent would ordinarily be self-contradictory. "Sam takes a keen interest in football, although the game leaves him cold" would require considerable explanation and some sort of equivocation on "football" and "the game" to make it intelligible. We may take an interest in something that does not directly affect us (e.g., the plight of starving people in Ethiopia), but that is because we are compassionate beings whose feelings are affected by our awareness of the condition of others. Indirect affect is also involved in our "taking an interest in other people's business" (e.g., our neighbors' divorce), although less laudatory labels such as "meddling" and "sticking our noses in where they don't belong" will likely be employed in these cases. That the affect is produced vicariously does not change the fact that taking an interest, like having an interest, is something that only sentient beings can do. Machines can monitor things, but they cannot take an interest in them.

What taking an interest adds to "merely" having an interest in x is an "epistemic relation" to x. As Meredith Williams puts it, "taking an interest . . . requires the possibility of actively recognizing and understanding that these contingencies affect one's interest."[23] For example, Susan "has an interest" in having certain agricultural pollutants removed from her drinking water, simply because those pollutants are what is making her feel listless. However, she cannot "take an interest" in having these pollutants removed until she gains some understanding of how they are affecting her well-being.

It is this epistemic relation of which animals are incapable according to Frey, Williams, and other opponents of animal liberation. In addition to the sort of linguistic arguments deployed by Frey, humanists generally emphasize four things in their attempts to show that only beings with something like normal$_h$ intelligence can have this epistemic relation to what is in their interest. These four things are temporal awareness, awareness of complex issues, the ability to deliberate, and culture.[24] All four of these claims are mistaken. Although something like normal$_h$ intelligence may be required for achieving certain kinds and degrees of awareness, understanding, and the like, there are under each of these four headings other, less demanding kinds and degrees of awareness, understanding, and so on that are sufficient for those who possess them to be properly described as "taking an interest" in things. We shall discuss each of these four in turn.

It is often emphasized that taking an interest is future-oriented and that, consequently, taking an interest in something is something only rational beings can do.[25] But the future begins immediately, and we may take an interest in things close at hand as well as far off. For instance, in addition to taking an interest in completing college or raising a family, we can also take an interest in seasoning a salad or replacing a broken windowpane. Furthermore, most long-range projects, like raising a family, include many short-term endeavors, such as keeping the youngsters safe while they are at play, and "taking an interest" can properly be predicated of our attitude toward the parts as well as toward the whole.

Since taking an interest requires understanding that something is the cause of something else and since cause precedes effect, taking an interest requires some sense of the future. but this leaves open a wide range of proximate to long-range awareness. It would be arbitrary to say that only awareness of causal chains taking more than five minutes, or two hours, or three days, or whatever "really counts" as future awareness and taking an interest, while nothing less does.

As to the issue of complexity, the contingencies affecting our interests may form a complex causal network, as in the cases of farming and governing a large country. But they may also be simple, as in grooming a lawn or giving a signal to someone to turn on the water. Again, it would be thoroughly arbitrary to say that we do not have an epistemic relation to our interests unless we are aware of at least three causal factors, or ten steps in the process, or whatever.

Since taking an interest requires awareness of contingencies, it requires awareness of relations. But these relations may range from highly complex to simple. For example, a farmer must take into account a vast network of biological, chemical, geological, meteorological, and political relations in order to make a living, but deer seeking a path around a recent avalanche to get to their traditional summer pastures and mice learning to press a bar to get food pellets from a psychologist are also aware of relations, albeit much simpler ones. While taking an interest as the farmer does may require the large capacity for abstraction humanists commonly emphasize when discussing rationality, taking an interest as these deer and mice do does not.

Turning to the issue of deliberation, it enters when taking an interest is characterized in terms of conceiving alternatives, making plans, and other such attentive, reflective activities.[26] However, understanding a situation and knowing how to meet a problem do not require deliberation. When climbing a tree, for example, if I hear something crack and feel the branch I am standing on start to give way, I do not need to (and cannot afford to) deliberate about the problem and the available alternatives for meeting it. By "instinct," "habit," or "common sense" (whatever name you like), I comprehend the situation immediately and just as immediately project what needs to be done in order to protect my interest in avoiding a fall.

Even such an immediate, practical, fallible grasp of relations and what needs to be done in order to fulfill an interest is clearly contrasted—as understanding should be—with mechanical, uncomprehending reactions to simple stimuli such as a chemical path or a sexually exciting odor. The demand for such a contrast, therefore, should not mislead us into confusing understanding with deliberation. Once again, there is a continuum here, ranging from prosaic problems that can be "easily handled," "taken in stride," or "adjusted to automatically" to extraordinary situations and creative innovations that require careful analysis, extensive deliberation, and a soaring imagination. Understanding and an epistemic relation to one's world can be found throughout this continuum. They do not appear only at its creative extreme. This is what evolutionary theory and the survival value of understanding would lead us to expect:

> Environmental conditions vary so much that for an animal's brain to have programmed specifications for optimal behavior in all situations would require an impossibly lengthy instruction book. . . . Providing for all likely contingencies would require a wasteful volume of specific directions. Concepts and generalizations, on the other hand, are compact and efficient. . . . If [an animal] can anticipate probable events, even if only a little way into the future, it can avoid wasted effort. . . . It seems plausible that when an animal faces new and difficult challenges, and when the stakes are high—often literally a matter of life and death—conscious evaluation may have real advantages. . . . It is attractive to suppose that if an animal can consciously anticipate and choose the most promising of various alternatives, it is likely to succeed more often than one that cannot or does not think about what it is doing.[27]

Finally, turning to the importance of having a culture for taking an interest, Meredith Williams contrasts taking an interest with the "gratification of primitive physiological needs" and claims that taking an interest occurs only where one has not only a natural life but also a cultural life.[28] In a similar vein, Ruth Cigman dismisses animals' "acute fear when their lives are threatened" as merely "blindly clinging to life" rather than "valuing life," and Leslie Francis and Richard Norman place great emphasis on the moral significance of a cultural life in arguing that "some animals are more equal than others."[29] But does the fact that I am out to gratify a primitive physiological need and that "the emotional states I experience are tied very directly to concurrent experiences"[30] make it wrong to say that I am "taking an interest" when I am out to seduce someone? Of course not.

If someone responds to sounds, smells, and so on in a blindly reflexive way, that is, without any understanding of what triggered the response or of what the response is a means to or what it is itself accomplishing, then we would be inclined to put the case under the heading of "merely having an interest." For example, humans seem to have a native disposition to seek their spouses outside the group of people that they have been raised with as a family. But we would not be inclined to say that this shows that we "instinctively take an interest" in expanding the gene pool or social relations, for we are not natively aware that this instinct produces such results and that these results are beneficial. On the other hand, we do not hesitate to say that mothers "instinctively take an interest" in the sound, smell, color, and feel of their babies, for we presume that mothers have some native understanding of the significance of what they are responding to.

Once again, understanding may take the form of abstract, innovative reasoning based on cultural tradition, but this is an extreme on a continuum, rather than a necessary condition for understanding. The other end of this continuum is the kind of primitive, practical understanding sufficient for solving many everyday problems of life. This practical understanding is either native or based on simple, personal experience of natural properties, such as hot and cold, solid and weak, sharp and blunt, and so forth. Acquiring a culture expands one's understanding immensely beyond the limitations of such practical understanding. However, it does not mark the advent of understanding, for the ability to recognize and solve many practical problems no more requires the elaborate machinery of language, tradition, and institutions than doing simple arithmetic requires a computer.

One final problem with attempting to require that the interests in which we take an interest be long-range, complex, deliberative, and cultural is that these four properties do not always go together. We can do some complicated things inattentively, as when playing a familiar piece on the piano. Again, some geometry problems are simple and abstract, while some mating and nesting behavior is complicated and natural. Finally, some long-range plans like making monthly deposits in an individual retirement account are much simpler than some immediate interests, such as choosing food and drink for a party. Each of the four continua just discussed represents an independent characterization of interests, and in each case, we can be properly described as taking an interest in something no matter where we are located on the continuum.

B. HAVING INTERESTS AND MORAL STANDING

Meredith Williams indicates that, in the context of a critique of animal liberation, her main concern in contrasting having with taking an interest is to refute "Singer's claim that the basis for animal and human interests is the same."[31] Consequently, having argued that human interests are based on an epistemic relation lacking in animal interests, she feels she has made her point and quickly jumps to the conclusion that since Singer was arguing for animal-human equality and she has refuted him, she has shown that our consuming animals is not pernicious. However, even if we were to grant that animal interests lack the epistemic relation on which (some) human interests are based, how would it follow from this that we are morally justified in consuming animals? What makes *having* an interest something that can (morally) be disregarded (except for humane considerations, of course), while *taking* an interest must (morally) be respected? Williams does not even raise these questions.[32] We shall proceed to remedy this oversight by considering the moral significance of interests from both utilitarian and deontological points of view.

From a utilitarian viewpoint, the moral significance of having an interest seems clear enough: the principle of utility (as traditionally formulated) requires us to maximize happiness; fulfilling or frustrating interests contributes to the happiness or unhappiness in life; consequently, we ought (morally) to fulfill as many and frustrate as few interests as possible. From this classic utilitarian viewpoint, the moral relevance of taking an interest must also be based on its role in creating sources of happiness and unhappiness in life. According to Williams, being able to take an interest in things both expands the range of kinds of interests we can have and adds a further emotional component to the interests we can have. Because taking an interest involves recognizing future possibilities, rational beings can have interests involving "plans and projects" and can experience "dread, anticipation, hope, and grief," neither of which are possibilities for beings incapable of taking an interest in things.[33]

Except that some animals (e.g., dogs) that Williams would consider non-rational and, consequently, incapable of taking an interest in things can obviously anticipate and even hope for the fulfillment of their interests, I think Williams is correct about that: all that taking an interest adds to having an interest here is extending the range of one's feelings and interests. It certainly does not follow on utilitarian grounds that because some individuals have a narrower range of feelings and interests, they may be treated as resources for the gratification of the interests of beings with a wider range of feelings and interests. If that did follow, then Renaissance men could eat peasants and specialists for dinner. All that follows from *P* having a greater range of interests than *Q* is that when doing the moral calculations for actions affecting both *P* and *Q*, *P* will contribute a greater number of the interests that have to be considered than will *Q*.

Humanists would doubtless claim that acknowledging this difference shows that rational and nonrational beings are not to be treated as moral equals.[34] However, such "inequality" is a far cry from the current contrast between the protection accorded human interests and the routine sacrifice of animal interests. Consequently, this difference provides little if anything in the way of a rebuttal to animal liberation. Furthermore, utilitarians have never claimed that treating individuals "equally" requires presuming that they have exactly the same or the same number of interests or that it requires considering only those interests they share. The egalitarianism of utilitarianism requires only that the interests of each individual be given equal consideration in computing the pluses and minuses of the moral calculus. "Each is to count for one and none for more than one" in the sense that it must (morally) not be presumed that because of their different social status, race, sex, and so on, *P*'s interests are more significant than *Q*'s interests. Consequently, from this classical utilitarian viewpoint, the moral significance of the distinction between having an interest and taking an interest is not sufficient to justify our continuing to consume animals.

Would a deontological evaluation of taking an interest justify this consumption? An argument of the following form could be formulated:

B1: Only rational beings are capable of taking an interest in what is morally right and wrong.[35]

B2: Only beings capable of such moral interests merit our respect for their interests.

B3: Therefore, only rational beings merit our respect for their interests.

B4: Animals are not rational beings.

B5: Therefore, animals do not merit our respect for their interests.

This is essentially Kant's argument from the *Foundations of the Metaphysics of Morals*, dressed up in talk of interests.[36] Since we have already dealt with this argument in Chapter 3 and since the switch to interest talk does not significantly alter the argument or affect our earlier, negative evaluation of it, we can safely confine the discussion here to the following brief remarks.

First, insofar as this argument is based on the belief that only humans can take an interest in things, it is clearly unsound for it is clearly false and, in this day and age, even irresponsible to suggest that only humans stand in an epistemic relation to their world and take an interest in things. As already noted several times, animals recognize causal relations and can figure out how to use them to solve practical problems. Even if they are not capable of flights of abstraction, neither are they confined to responding mechanically to simple stimuli and gratifying primitive physiological needs. Anyone still inclined to believe that only humans are sufficiently intelligent to take an interest in things should adopt a dog and get to know it personally. This will quickly give firsthand evidence that the distinction between beings capable of having an epistemic relation to their world and those lacking this ability does not coincide with the distinction between human and nonhuman beings.[37]

Second, the deontological argument above is based on the commonsensical idea that we should reap what we sow. Those who respect the interests of others merit our respect for their interests, while those who do not show respect for the interests of others have not earned the right to claim such respect from us. This meritorian principle is tempered by our idea that one is innocent until proven guilty, so that those with the potentiality or capacity for moral agency (e.g., infants and strangers) are extended moral rights until they demonstrate that they do not deserve our respect. For the same reason, we extend procedural rights like the right to a fair trial even to those we are confident have committed crimes. But even with these modifications, the idea that respect is something that must be earned is part of our common moral lexicon.

Kant believed that only when motivated by pure practical reason could one intentionally and straightforwardly do what is moral, and something like this Kantian position is generally employed by those who wish to deny moral rights to those lacking normal$_h$ intelligence, be they fetuses or animals. However, as discussed in Chapter 3, this extreme position has generally been rejected since it denies moral$_{ad}$ worth to kindhearted people (e.g., saints and loving parents) who do what is morally right out of generous sentiments rather than from a sense of duty. But once kindhearted people are allowed into the moral$_{ad}$ fold, so must many animals be, for they too are virtuous beings. They are intentionally and straightforwardly concerned parents, courageous, compassionate, patient, responsible, temperate, loyal, sympathetic, devoted, self-sacrificing, and so on. So even if we accept the maxim that "rights must be earned," many animals can meet this test and merit our respect—probably many more than we ordinarily think, for we have generally been unwilling to acknowledge that animals may be virtuous beings and have, consequently, generally been unwilling to look for and to attempt to understand their virtues.

I conclude that from a deontological viewpoint, the distinction between having an interest and taking an interest again does not show that our continued consumption of animals is morally justified. From this viewpoint, having vs. taking an interest may have an indirect moral significance. This is because intentionally doing something seems to require the same sort of understanding of relations as taking an interest; consequently, the ability to take an interest may be a reliable indicator of the capacity to be a moral$_{ad}$ agent. However, this capacity is not the highly developed rationality that separates humans from animals. The practical understanding possessed by many animals as well as by humans will do. This is demonstrated by the many cases of taking an interest and of virtuous behavior to be found in the animal kingdom. Consequently, either the above "deontological interests argument" equivocates in its use of "rational" or either the first or fourth step of that argument is false.

Thus, our analysis of the moral significance of the distinction between "merely" having interests and taking an interest in things shows that this distinction does not provide a basis for justifying our continued consumption of animals. Where the moral imperative is to maximize happiness, our epistemic relation, if any, to our interests is not of fundamental importance. From a utilitarian viewpoint, it is the distinction between affective and nonaffective needs that is morally crucial, and animals assuredly have affective needs. From a deontological viewpoint, taking an interest takes on added moral significance. Being able to take an interest in things may well be a reliable indicator of the ability to be a moral$_{ad}$ agent, and deontologists have long maintained that only moral$_{ad}$ agents merit moral rights. But since many animals are moral$_{ad}$ agents, even if virtuous rather than fully moral$_{ad}$ agents, they ought (morally) to be treated as ends in themselves, rather than as mere means for the satisfaction of our interests.

According to Meredith Williams, "any prejudice essentially involves a failure to treat a group appropriately, a failure based on irrelevant, arbitrary, or trivial grounds.[38] Our analysis shows that attempts to discredit animal liberation and to justify our continued consumption of animals on the grounds of the distinction between having and taking an interest fit this definition.

8

Moral Community and Animal Rights

IN THIS chapter we shall discuss four possible justifications for what I believe to be the basic objection to liberating animals: "But they're *just* animals!" This objection remains even after objectors acknowledge that animals have interests and that these interests extend beyond merely avoiding pain. Many people who are well informed about not only the physical but also the psychological and social interests of animals still feel justified in consuming animals. This is because they believe that animals lack that something of fundamental moral worth that calls for respect and not merely for humane handling and slaughter.

It is four interpretations of that morally significant something that I want to consider here. All these interpretations involve the idea that only those who participate in some kind of moral community with us can be entitled to moral rights against us. These four interpretations are the major premises of the following arguments against liberating animals:

A1: Only those who respect the moral rights of others are entitled to moral rights ("the reciprocity requirement").
A2: Animals cannot respect moral rights.
A3: Therefore, animals cannot be entitled to moral rights.[1]

B1: Only moral$_{ad}$ agents are entitled to moral rights ("the agency requirement").
B2: Animals cannot be moral$_{ad}$ agents.
B3: Therefore, animals cannot be entitled to moral rights.[2]

C1: One is entitled to moral rights against others on the basis of his or her (capacity for) familial, personal, political, economic, and so forth relations to them ("the relations requirement").

139

C2: Animals cannot enter into such relations with humans.

C3: Therefore, animals cannot be entitled to moral rights against humans.[3]

D1: Morals develop because
  (i) in order to enjoy a good, human life, we have both to exercise self-control and to live together in society and
  (ii) in order for there to be self-control and for society to exist and flourish, there must be rules of how we may and may not deal with ourselves and with each other.

Moral rights are a part of this network for regulating intra- and inter-human affairs. It follows that only human beings can be entitled to moral rights ("the humanist requirement").

D2: Animals are not human beings.

D3: Therefore, animals cannot be entitled to moral rights.[4]

The strategy underlying each of these arguments is to establish something in addition to the interest requirement (discussed in Chapters 5 and 7) as a necessary condition for meriting moral rights. Of course, this necessary something is supposed to be something that animals cannot possibly possess. We shall take up each of these requirements in turn.

I. The Reciprocity Requirement

The reciprocity requirement is based on one interpretation of the correlation between rights and duties. This interpretation is number (3) on W. D. Ross's famous list of possible interpretations of that correlation:

(3) A right of A against B implies a duty of A to B. . . . What is meant by (3) is that A's having a right to have a certain act done to him by B implies a duty for A to do *another* act to B, which act may be either a similar act (as where the right of having the truth told to one implies the duty of telling the truth) or a different sort of act (as where the right to obedience implies the duty of governing well).[5]

When this correlation is coupled with the common belief that animals are incapable of recognizing and acting on duties, it quickly follows that animals are incapable of having moral rights.

Some people would doubtless object that some animals, especially those with strong social instincts like dogs and wolves, can recognize and respond to (something very much like) moral rights and duties. In Chapter 3, we argued that possessing normal$_h$ intelligence is not a necessary condition for being a moral$_{ad}$ agent; however, recognizing (something very much like) moral rights and duties, especially to members of other species, seems a fairly abstract moral accomplishment, one which might require considerably more intelligence than that possessed by many of the animals whose interests animal liberationists are seeking to protect. For example, birds and rodents do not seem to recognize human rights to property and to enjoying the fruits of our labor. Since what is at issue here is whether animals have moral rights *against humans*, what those pressing this objection to the reciprocity requirement would have to show is that animals recognize and respond to (something very much like) moral duties they have *to humans*. That would, I think, be a very hard case to make.

A much more obvious and defensible response to this argument is that our common practice shows that being able to recognize and act on duties is not a necessary condition for having moral rights. Infants and the severely retarded, brain-damaged, and senile are not regarded as resources for fulfilling the interests of normal humans (even though they could provide outstanding material for biomedical research and product safety testing). In spite of their inability to recognize the rights of others and to act out of respect for the duties correlated with those rights, the interests of these people are protected by moral rights correlated with the duties that we recognize we have to them.

However, while this "argument from marginal cases" strongly suggests that our attachment to our species is stronger than our commitment to the reciprocity requirement, it is neither particularly insightful nor telling against that requirement for having moral rights. It is not telling, because if we make the following revision in our formulation of the reciprocity requirement, then nearly all the marginal cases can be easily and reasonably accommodated:

> A1′: Only those who will be able to, are to at least a threshold degree able to, may again be able to, or did respect the moral rights of others are entitled to moral rights.

The remaining marginal cases, namely, the severely, incurably retarded or psychopathic from birth, constitute a very small, sequestered group. This small, isolated group can plausibly be treated as "honorary rights-holders" out of deference to the feelings of species affinity most all of us share.[6]

This special treatment of these uncommon, isolated cases does not compromise the reciprocity requirement, for that requirement is intended for common cases. As discussed in Chapter 5, giving women and children first place in the lifeboats does not imply that they normally have superior rights to men; similarly, making a few extraordinary people honorary rights-holders does not imply that the reciprocity requirement is not being observed in ordinary cases. Morally special cases are cases in which our common moral principles must be superseded; consequently, we cannot infer from our practice in such special cases to what our common moral principles are. Just as this distinction between ordinary and extraordinary cases and the differing moral principles employed in each of them undercuts "them or us" counter-examples to animal liberation, so it undercuts marginal cases' defenses of animal liberation, once those marginal cases have been seriously reduced in number by qualifications like those employed in A1'.

This argument from marginal cases is also not particularly insightful, because it does not come to grips with the reason why the reciprocity requirement has such intuitive appeal. I think the reason behind this appeal is not species prejudice but a matter of fairness: A's having a right against B is correlated with B's having a duty to A; it would be unfair for B's liberty to be thus restricted without A's liberty also being similarly (or otherwise appropriately) restricted. For example, if Alice has a right to the fruits of her labor, then Bob is obligated (*certeris paribus*) not to go into Alice's field and take her corn. It would be manifestly unfair, then, for Alice not to be obligated to respect Bob's right to the fruits of his labor and to remain free to go into his field and take his corn.

Thus, fairness, coupled with the commonly accepted principle that "a right of A against B implies a duty of B to A" (this is number [1] on Ross's list), requires that we are obligated to respect the moral rights of others only if they are obligated to respect our moral rights. It is this commonsensical argument, and not our treatment of marginal people, that must be analyzed in order seriously to critique the reciprocity requirement.

The Achilles heel of that argument is that it cannot provide a basis for the obligations of the powerful to the powerless. The argument presumes that Alice is powerful enough to interfere with Bob's well-being and that she can inhibit that power in exchange for Bob's inhibiting his power to interfere with her well-being. But what if Alice is blind, sickly, malnourished, timid, squeamish, poor, ignorant, a weakling, kindhearted, or otherwise unable to pose a threat to Bob's well-being? Bob cannot be obligated through exchange to inhibit his power to interfere with Alice's well-being when Alice has no power to interfere with Bob that she can inhibit in return. Thus, if reciprocity were a necessary condition for having moral rights, the weak would be excluded from having moral rights against the strong.

The reciprocity requirement implies that only those strong enough to pose a threat to us can gain moral rights against us. I would suggest that it is also a reference to power, rather than to communicative or legal ability, that underlies the not uncommon contention that only those who can "claim" their rights from us can have moral rights against us. Such a Machiavellian view of moral rights fits ill with our common sense and understanding of morality. First, it confuses morality with prudence, demeaning morality, as the Kantians would insist, by making it merely a cunning, worldly self-interest. (It will be remembered that we confirmed this Kantian position in Chapter 2.) Second, one of the basic purposes of moral rights is to protect the weak against the strong, so that the weak can have a fair chance of fulfilling their interests. To the extent that a theory of moral rights cannot provide a basis for this function of those rights, it is surely inadequate, since we are not discussing a few marginal cases here but a primary, pervasive purpose of moral rights.[7]

We may develop a more adequate theory of the bases for moral rights by noting that just as there is a strong intuitive appeal to the reciprocity requirement, so there is a strong intuitive appeal, again based on fairness, to limiting the application of that requirement by having different requirements for A's having moral rights against those who are roughly as powerful as she is and against those who are decidedly more powerful than she is. If Alice and Bob are equally powerful and if Bob gives up a power that Alice does not reciprocate, then he will be at a disadvantage in the competition for fulfilling interests. Reciprocity is needed here to prevent exploitation and to insure an intuitive sort of equality of opportunity. However, when the weak are dealing with the strong, the situation is reversed. In order to prevent the strong from exploiting the weak and to insure that the weak have a fair chance of fulfilling their interests, what is needed is that the strong inhibit their power over the weak and/or that the weak be given additional power against the strong. The situation is analogous to that in horse racing: when one horse is decidedly stronger than the other, then the stronger horse needs to be handicapped with extra weight to carry or the weaker horse needs to be given a head start in order to insure that the weaker horse has a fair chance of winning the race.

Giving moral rights to the weak, with correlative duties for the strong but without correlative duties for the weak, would help inhibit the strong and/or strengthen the weak, thus helping to make the world a fairer place. For example, if Bob is strong enough to take Alice's territory but Alice poses no threat to Bob, then in order to protect her interest in enjoying her territory and utilizing it to help fulfill her other interests, Alice needs to be given the right to territory, with the correlative duty for Bob to respect her territory. However, Alice need not be placed under an obligation to respect Bob's territory, since she is already too weak to pose a threat to his territory and, consequently, need not be morally inhibited in order to insure Bob's enjoyment and utilization of his territory.

Some might prefer phrasing this conclusion as follows: Alice is under an obligation to Bob, but it does not matter whether she recognizes this, since owing to her weakness, Alice will do what accords with this duty anyway. This formulation would also open the door to animal rights, since, discussing the right to life, we could equally well say that Bob's dog Alex has a duty to respect Bob's life, and it does not matter that Alex cannot recognize this duty, since because of his weakness, Alex will do what accords with this duty anyway. Nonetheless, I prefer the other formulation, which would leave Bob with a duty to respect Alex's life but would leave Alex without a duty to respect Bob's life. This preference stems from my conviction that moral rights and duties should be assigned where they can be of real service in improving the quality of life. They should not be assigned just to balance an abstract formula or to save a philosophical theory. In the examples we have been developing, unless the natural imbalance of power might someday be changed, so that Alice or Alex could come to pose a threat to Bob, talk of Alice's or Alex's duty to respect Bob's territory or life is (directly)[8] pointless—but ethics is supposed to be a practical science. Of course, whatever hope the future might hold for Alice, there is no possibility, except under the most extraordinary of circumstances, that Alex will come to pose a threat to Bob's life.

If this distinction between the logic of moral rights among those of roughly equal power and the logic of the moral rights of the significantly weaker against those stronger than they are is correct and if as a consequence of this, the reciprocity requirement does not apply to dealings between the weaker and the stronger, then the reciprocity requirement generally does not apply to dealings between animals and humans. It follows that the reciprocity requirement generally does not pose an obstacle to extending moral rights to animals. Humans are vastly more powerful than animals. No animal preys on us or ordinarily threatens human lives. No animal ordinarily threatens to imprison us, to take our territory, to destroy our societies, to cause us pain, or otherwise to interfere with our fulfilling our basic interests. On the other hand, we routinely do all these things to animals. So if fairness is the goal, what is needed is not that animals agree to treat us "as well as" we treat them; what is needed is to protect animals from our routinely sacrificing their interests for our benefit. That, of course, is what liberating animals is all about.

It might be objected that some animals do threaten human interests, for instance, shark attacks and coyote raids. But these occasional confrontations cannot (logically) provide the basis for an objection to considering animals as ordinarily too weak to be covered by the requirements for moral rights and obligations among the equally powerful. Marginal case arguments are no more telling against animals than for them, and as discussed in Chapter 5, liberating animals, like other moral reforms, is primarily concerned not with extraordinary cases and the special moral principles that must be invoked to handle them but with our ordinary lives and our everyday moral attitudes and principles. Ordinarily, we have and exercise unchallenged power over other animals.

To summarize, the intuitive appeal of the reciprocity requirement for having moral rights derives from our idea of fairness. However, in relations between the powerful and the powerless, it is not reciprocity but moral rights of the powerless against the powerful, without correlative duties of the powerless to the powerful, that are needed for fairness. Therefore, since animals are vastly weaker than we are, the reciprocity requirement does not apply to human-animal relations. Here, fairness requires that animals have moral rights against us, even if they cannot recognize correlative duties to us.

II. The Agency Requirement

The agency requirement maintains that only moral$_{ad}$ agents are entitled to moral rights. Charlie Blatz has recently offered the following justification of this requirement:

[E1:] Every ethic begins somewhere, saying that the objects of certain aims or certain pursuits themselves are justifiable to realize or engage in and this is not due to some other justifiable aim or pursuit. These are the *beginning points of justification* in the ethic in question. . . . These *ultimate considerations* I call "the seeds of justifiable conduct" in an ethic. Different ethics identify different seeds, classical utilitarianism, for example identifying pleasure and the absence of pain as [its] basis.

[E2:] Once we know what the seeds of an ethic are, we can identify conditions or beings who do (or might) manifest those seeds, and then, these will have standing or be considerable within that ethic.

[E3:] To identify the point of an ethic is to single out what it is about the code that allows it to play a role making some difference to our lives and those of others. . . . The problem is to consider what we would need to count as seeds of an ethic, any ethic, if it is to have any impact at all upon us or others.

[E4:] *If there is any impact that is attributable to the operations of a code of ethics itself, then it is an impact the code has by directing choice and behavior through the application of its norms to the options facing agents.* . . . So, *any ethic [with] point will locate its seeds among the aims of those open to being guided by the justifying reasons it provides.*

[E5:] Thus, the seeds of any ethic with point will be aims and pursuits of humans, as opposed to nonhumans. Since ethical standing belongs to whatever manifests the seeds of justifiable conduct, it is some humans and not other animals that exclusively enjoy such standing.[9]

Thus, Blatz basically attempts to argue from the necessary conditions for an ethic's having a point to the conclusion that animals cannot have moral standing. We can be sure that this argument is unsound, because it is obvious that an ethic whose "ultimate consideration" is to maximize the happiness of all sentient beings likely to be affected by human actions, and that, consequently, extends moral standing to animals, would definitely "make a difference in our lives," presuming, as argued above, that following such an ethic would require that we stop consuming animals. Consequently, that an ethic have a point cannot (logically) entail that animals do not have standing on their own right within that ethic.

The reasons why Blatz's argument is unsound seem to be logical, rather than factual, mistakes and to be two in number. First, his "functionalist perspective" and "rationalist principle," summarized in E3 and E4, entail that any practicable ethic must have as one of its "ultimate considerations" influencing the aims and pursuits of rational agents. This is because these are the only *means* through which an ethic may realize its values. However, an ethic's "ultimate considerations," in another sense of that phrase, are certain of those values or goals (e.g., a happier world for all or the reign of justice) that the ethic aims at realizing. It is these ultimate values or goals, not the necessary means for attaining them, that are the "beginning points" of an ethic in the sense intended in E1, where Blatz explains what he means by "the seeds of justifiable conduct."

Now, one could try to argue from what sorts of means are available to what sorts of values or goals there would be any point in trying to realize. For example, one could argue that since human beings are thoroughly self-interested, the only moral goals that there is any point in trying to realize are goals that humans can be made to believe are in their own interest to realize. However, Blatz does not attempt any such "What sort of goods can we get with the means available?" argument. Rather, he does not seem to have noticed that there are two distinct sorts of "ultimate considerations" at work in his argument: when defining "seeds," he is discussing the consideration of *what*, ultimately, is to be achieved by an ethic, but in E3 and E4, he is discussing the consideration of *how*, ultimately, those values or goals are to be achieved. In this way, one of the logical faults with Blatz's argument can, loosely, be considered equivocation.

Second, Blatz participates in the not uncommon leap from an argument about why human beings should have moral standing to the conclusion that animals cannot have such standing. Notice that in E4, after arguing that any ethic with point must be concerned with influencing the aims and purposes of rational agents, Blatz concludes that "any ethic [with] point will locate its seeds among the aims" of such beings. No quantifier precedes "its seeds," but "all" is certainly to be understood, not just by convention but also because E5 will not follow E4 without that understanding. However, that an ethic with point must locate *all* its ultimate considerations among the aims and purposes of rational agents is not entailed by the fact that an ethic that was not at all concerned with influencing the aims and purposes of such beings would be pointless. That *some* of its concerns be directed toward the aims and purposes of rational agents is all that is entailed here.

Besides Blatz's functionalist requirements, there may be other requirements for an acceptable morality that would lead to assigning ultimate considerations not only among the aims and pursuits of rational agents but elsewhere as well. For example, one could argue that in order to qualify as a set of "moral" principles, those principles must (logically) be concerned with issues of fairness, the well-being of others besides the agent himself, working toward "a better world," and matters of honor. Developing these concerns, as, for example, Peter Singer has developed the second of them,[10] can lead one's ultimate considerations well beyond the restrictions Blatz would place on them. Blatz has provided nothing in the way of an argument to show that ethics that locate their ultimate considera-

tions *only* among the aims and pursuits of humans are the *only* logically acceptable ethics. Consequently, he has provided nothing in the way of argument to
show that animals cannot (logically) manifest the ultimate considerations of an
acceptable ethic and thereby have moral standing. At best (if it were not for the
above equivocation), he could claim to have shown that an ethic's having a point
entails that humans must (logically) have moral standing. But just as Kant's
argument that no rational being should be treated as a means merely does not
show that nonrational beings may be so treated,[11] so Blatz's conclusion that animals are not entitled to moral standing is not justified by his argument that
rational beings must have such standing in a practicable ethic.

Turning to a much less esoteric analysis, in the previous chapter, we noted
that our everyday moral language provides support for a meritorian view of having moral rights. "Having a right to" something is commonly placed in the same
family with being able to claim something "as one's due," being "entitled to" it,
being "owed" it, "meriting" it, "deserving" it, and having "earned" it. These
phrases suggest that in order to have moral rights, we must do something like
pass a test, achieve a certain standing, or attain a plateau to which the appropriate
response is respect. It can then be argued that we can earn the respect embodied
in moral rights only by being (capable of being) moral$_{ad}$ agents. This is because
respect, being the highest of moral acknowledgments, must be reserved for the
highest of values, and as Kant said, "Nothing in the world—indeed, nothing even
beyond the world—can possibly be conceived which could be called good without
qualification except a *good will*."[12]

Kant believed that since animals lack practical reason, they are merely creatures of nature excluded from the community of moral$_{ad}$ agents, or "kingdom of
ends." As a consequence, they may be regarded as mere means to human satisfaction. Others have disagreed. As noted in Chapter 3, Hume thought it so evident
that animals have practical reason that he declared it would be ridiculous to
spend time defending that they do. Darwin thought that animals exhibit a great
variety of virtues, at least some of which contemporary naturalists also believe
they have observed.[13] Even Harry Truman declared, "If you want a true friend in
this life, get a dog!" So, that animals cannot meet the agency requirement has not
been obvious to all. However, since in Chapters 3 and 7 we have already discussed
the ability of animals to meet this requirement, owing to their being virtuous
agents, and since others have also recently discussed the moral agency of animals
at length,[14] I want here to limit our discussion of the agency requirement to
evaluating it from the same perspective from which we have already evaluated
the humanist principle, "personhood$_e$," liberating animals, and the reciprocity
requirement, namely, that of accomplishing the goals of morality.

It will be remembered that in Chapter 4, we identified the following three
common moral goals:

developing moral character, so that our actions will be based on compassion, respect, courage, and other moral virtues,

both reducing the suffering in life and otherwise making life more enjoyable and fulfilling, and

insuring that opportunities, goods, punishments, and rewards are distributed fairly.

How the agency requirement for moral rights impacts these three, common, moral goals will provide us with a substantial indication of its moral worth.

Regarding the development of moral character, the agency requirement functions clearly and directly in promoting and rewarding (the capacity for) virtue: if we employ this requirement, then only the (potentially) virtuous will have their interests protected by moral rights. However, developing moral character does not *require* the agency requirement. Those capable of being moral$_{ad}$ agents, and among moral$_{ad}$ agents, those capable of being fully moral$_{ad}$ agents, can be recognized as being of superior moral worth, even if those who are not capable of being (fully) moral$_{ad}$ agents are accorded moral rights.

As emphasized in Chapter 5, liberating animals would prohibit routinely sacrificing their interests for our benefit, but this would not prohibit giving the interests of (potentially) fully moral$_{ad}$ agents priority over the interests of animals and others incapable of fully moral$_{ad}$ agency in nonroutine situations such as the traditional "them or us" examples (e.g., "Which should be saved from the burning building, the baby or the puppy?"). Recognizing such priority does not require denying that the puppy has moral rights, as shown by the fact that the answer would be the same, *ceteris paribus*, if the question were, "Which should be saved from the burning building, the baby or the cancerous old man?" As discussed in Chapter 4, it is not the case that one simply is or is not a holder of moral rights (i.e., a person$_c$). We can still be persons$_e$, as are children, even though fulfilling our interests is given lower priority than fulfilling those of another in extraordinary, conflict of interests situations. It follows that A can be rewarded for her superior development of moral character and can be acknowledged to be morally more worthy than B while still according moral rights to B as well as to A.

Certainly, giving fully moral$_{ad}$ agents pride of place in our hierarchy of moral values need not involve extending to them something like the divine right of kings, so that they may self-interestedly dispose of those incapable of fully moral$_{ad}$ agency in the way serfs could be disposed of for their master's benefit. But this is the sort of inference being made by those who attempt to use the agency requirement to justify our consumption of animals. Rather, like the rulers in Plato's *Republic*, fully moral$_{ad}$ agents may be entitled to special rights and responsibilities for which their special, moral talents qualify them, but again like those philosopher-kings, they can receive those special rights and responsibilities

without being encouraged or even permitted to be tyrants over those who do not
share their talents. Especially as the presumption of equality continues to replace
principles of hierarchy as our basic moral framework, our being higher on the
moral$_{ad}$ totem pole cannot, either logically or morally, be interpreted as entitling
us routinely to dispose of those of lesser moral$_{ad}$ value for our own benefit.

Thus, while the agency requirement can doubtless function to encourage the
development of moral character, that function of rewarding moral character can
be performed in other ways. Consequently, if employing some of these other ways
of rewarding moral character can do a better job of fulfilling our other two,
common, moral goals than can employing the agency requirement, then this rewarding function of the agency requirement will not be sufficient to warrant
employing it.

Intuitively, it seems clear that reducing the suffering in life and otherwise
making life more enjoyable and fulfilling would be more readily accomplished by
rejecting, rather than employing, obstacles to the impartial consideration of the
interests of all sentient beings. The agency requirement is such an obstacle, since
the purpose for which it is employed is to justify the routine sacrifice of the
interests of those sentient beings that do not meet it. Consequently, it seems clear
that this second of our common, moral goals would be more readily accomplished
by rejecting the agency requirement for having moral rights.

Some philosophers have questioned whether a species-neutral utilitarian calculus would really call for an end to consuming animals.[15] However, as noted in
Chapter 6, several billion birds and mammals—animals that definitely seem to
have interests—are slaughtered annually in the United States alone, and in virtually all cases there are nonanimal alternatives for fulfilling the human interests
for which these animals lose the remainder of their potentially happy lives. These
facts put the burden of proof squarely on those who would counter the intuitive
and contend that utility may be maximized by consuming animals. For the
reasons already discussed, the usual objection to utilitarianism (i.e., that it can
condone the sacrifice of individuals for the general welfare in extraordinary situations) will not serve to meet that burden of proof, and as discussed in Chapter 6,
not even the most extensive development to date of this position has been able to
shoulder that burden. Consequently, we may follow our intuitions and conclude
that the utilitarian component in our common, moral goals would be more effectively pursued without the agency requirement.

Finally, the moral goals of protecting the weak against the strong, giving all a
fair chance at fulfilling their interests, and otherwise insuring that opportunities,
goods, punishments, and rewards are distributed fairly would also be more effectively pursued by extending moral rights to all beings with interests. Since in this
world, the fully moral$_{ad}$ agents, namely, humans, are vastly more powerful than
those lacking this ability, encouraging fully moral$_{ad}$ agents to regard those lacking

this ability as resources exacerbates, rather than corrects, the disparities of power in our world. Unfortunately, having the capacity to be fully moral$_{ad}$ agents does not always translate into acting as fully moral$_{ad}$ agents, and the agency requirement, like the concept of "personhood$_e$," opens the door to our feeling comfortable with being unfair to those it leaves "unworthy" of moral rights. So once again, our common moral goals would be more effectively pursued by rejecting the agency requirement.

It might be countered that our power over animals and our consequent use of them to satisfy our interests do not constitute an unfair advantage needing moral correction. Since we are fully moral$_{ad}$ agents and they are not, we are entitled to have power over them and to exercise that power (humanely, of course) to our advantage.

In response, we may note that it is rather strange, to put it mildly, to say that our ability to judge and act disinterestedly entitles us to disregard with impunity the interests of others. Intuitively, the power that fully moral$_{ad}$ agents ought (morally) to have and exercise is the power to carry out moral judgments and to establish the reign of morality in the world. Once again, it is not the power of the feudal lord to use others (humanely, of course) as he pleased but something like the restricted, counterbalanced power of Plato's philosopher-kings that is the power befitting fully moral$_{ad}$ agents. Only Kant's "holy will," a being that cannot be tempted from or mistaken in the pursuit of the good, is worthy of having and exercising uninhibited power over others. Consequently, it remains arbitrary that other beings with interests are so vastly weaker than we are that they cannot protect their interests from being routinely sacrificed by us. In order to provide these others a fair chance at fulfilling their interests, we need to inhibit, not rationalize, our self-interested exercise of power. The agency requirement for having moral rights is such a rationalization.

Thus, accomplishing our three common moral goals does not require the agency requirement, and two of them would be more readily accomplished without it. The linguistic tradition cited earlier in favor of this requirement is lightweight in comparison with these reasons against it. Similarly, as noted above, while Kant provides a substantive argument for treating fully moral$_{ad}$ agents as ends in themselves, he merely presumes that *only* the interests of fully moral$_{ad}$ agents ought (morally) to be protected against routine sacrifice. To my knowledge, Charlie Blatz is the only philosopher to date even to have attempted to provide a substantive justification of the agency requirement. This may be due to coupling the intuitive appeal of the idea that those who have acted immorally (e.g., burglars and rapists) deserve to have (some of) their rights taken away (at least temporarily) with a failure to distinguish clearly between immoral and nonmoral agents (which is what animals are commonly supposed to be). This coupling leaves the agency requirement looking intuitively acceptable and in need of no further justification. Whatever the reason for this omission, until if ever a substantive justification for the agency requirement is provided, the arguments just developed indicate that being (capable of being) a fully moral$_{ad}$ agent should not (morally) be a requirement for having moral rights.

To summarize, attempts to provide a logical justification of the agency requirement have failed. Furthermore, since common moral goals could be more effectively pursued by extending moral rights to protect the interests of those incapable of fully moral$_{ad}$ agency, the moral propriety of the agency requirement for having moral rights is highly questionable. So even though, as we saw in Chapter 3, many animals can probably meet the agency requirement if the morally more fundamental category of virtuous agency is substituted for the less fundamental one of fully moral$_{ad}$ agency, whether they can meet the agency requirement or not is probably irrelevant. Humans may be entitled to some extra moral consideration because of the wider range of moral agency of which we are capable, but that consideration can be accorded without treating animals as mere means to human satisfaction and would be more appropriately accorded in some such nontyrannical manner. Therefore, our (capacity for) moral$_{ad}$ superiority does not justify our continued consumption of animals.

III. The Relations Requirement

The relations requirement derives from one of the traditional objections to both utilitarianism and Kantianism: the universal egalitarianism that they profess is both unfaithful to common morality and unconvincing as a goal for moral reform. In common morality, we are not under an obligation to give equal consideration to everyone. On the contrary, we are not only permitted but even obligated to give priority to the interests of our families, friends, colleagues, and compatriots. Furthermore, a world from which these nonegalitarian commitments were abolished would not be enhanced but diminished, since it is these special relations to a few others that give life much of its personal, emotional richness and fulfillment. Consequently, a moral theory based on universal impartiality must be artificial and unconvincing. Moral rights and responsibilities are not based on abstract, universal principles but on our living together, entering into familial, personal, political, economic, and other such relations with each other, and in general being involved in each other's lives. It follows that since animals cannot enter into these relations with us, we are not only justified in giving priority to fulfilling human interests but are even obligated to do so.

An obvious response to this argument is that we can have personal, extended-familial, and quasi-economic relations with animals, as in the case of pets and race horses. Consequently, they are part of our community of shared lives and interests. Furthermore, even if the more extensive relations we can have with humans would, according to this theory, justify our giving priority to fulfilling human interests, that does not justify our consuming animals. This is because, as we have already seen, there are ways of giving priority to fulfilling human interests that do not involve or condone our consuming animals. Consequently, more than a justification of giving priority to fulfilling human interests is needed in order to justify withholding moral rights from animals—especially since, as we have also already seen, common moral goals would be more readily attained through liberating animals.

Another more methodological response to the argument for the relations requirement is that it is as mistaken about common morality as is abstract egalitarianism. One of the primary functions of morality, especially of moral rights, is to inhibit favoritism based on familial, personal, and other such relations. To accomplish this, we have developed a "justice is blind" family of moral imperatives: "take a disinterested viewpoint," "give equal consideration to all concerned," "try to universalize your actions," "disregard (as if behind 'a veil of ignorance') individual differences," and so forth. This family of moral imperatives is as much a part of common morality as are the relational priorities noted above. For example, while a father is justified in giving priority to fulfilling the interests of his child, he would not be justified in doing so by taking food from another, needy child, enslaving a stranger, or killing a business competitor. A father can be morally criticized even for using his discretionary income to shower luxuries on his child while contributing nothing to help starving children in other parts of the world.

Thus, in addition to relational rights and responsibilities, common morality also contains egalitarian rights and responsibilities. These latter rights and responsibilities counterbalance the former by restricting the ways in which relational priorities may be pursued. They do this by imposing impartial obligations on us, by requiring us to add a disinterested appraisal to our judgments of what is right, and so forth. Consequently, a strictly relational theory of moral rights and responsibilities would be as unfaithful to common morality as a strictly egalitarian, universalizing theory.

Advocates of the relations requirement seek to meet this objection by incorporating common egalitarian principles into their theory. This they try to do by claiming that these principles are based on the capacity humans have to enter into personal, political, and other such relations with any other human and on the fact that today we do have political and economic relations with people throughout the world. In these two ways, we form a global, human community that, it is claimed, creates the moral rights and responsibilities we have against and to all humans—but, of course, not to animals, since they lack this capacity and are not partners in our global politics and economy.

This analysis simply does not ring true. When I contribute to charities helping starving children in Ethiopia or refuse to purchase products made in South Africa, it is not at all because Ethiopian children or South African blacks are my partners in a global economy. Nor is it because I may come to have personal or political relations with them. I contribute and boycott because I recognize a need I can help meet and an injustice I can help combat. Insofar as there is a sense of community underlying my actions, it is not a political, economic, or linguistic community but, roughly, a sense that we are all vulnerable, suffering beings and ought (morally) to help each other out. If my own experience here is representative of what motivates people to contribute to global charities or to participate in global moral causes, and I have no reason to believe otherwise, then it is not being part of a global community that creates our moral obligations to all humans. Rather, it is feeling that "we're all in the same boat" and morally bound to each other that gives us a sense of being part of a global, moral community.

Thus, at the global level, the relations theory has the relation between morality and community backwards. Here, at least, it is not being part of a community that generates our moral obligations but our sense of moral obligation that generates our community. Consequently, the relations theorists do not succeed in incorporating into their moral theory the common, egalitarian principles that counterbalance our familial, political, and similar priorities.

If our sense of a global, moral community derives from our ability to feel obligated to help relieve the suffering of others, to treat them fairly, and so forth, then that animals are unable to enter fully into familial, economic, and similar relations with us does not preclude their entering into a global, moral community with us and benefiting from having moral rights against us. It would be *our inability* to feel obligated to help relieve the suffering of animals, to treat them fairly, and so on that would prevent the extension of moral rights to animals on the grounds of this sort of community. However, the existence of the animal rights movement shows that we are capable of feeling so obligated. Consequently, the obstacle to developing this sort of community seems to be merely the practical one of educating the animal-consuming majority of people to be as morally, expansively responsive as the animal-liberating minority among us.

Finally, at all levels the fabric of common morality is a weave of contrary forces. Advocates of animal liberation need not deny this nor otherwise attempt to make common morality out to be simpler than it is. This is because, as emphasized in Chapter 5, what is being sought for animals under the banners of "animal liberation" and "animal rights" is the same, basic moral protection against the routine sacrifice of one's interests that is already enjoyed by humans. If equality and priority can interweave, as they have, to form a practicable morality when dealing with interhuman relations, then they can do so when dealing with relations between humans and animals. Perhaps Peter Singer's clarion call for "equal consideration of interests"[16] and loose or strident talk of "equal rights for animals" have caused misunderstanding on this point, as discussed in Chapter 5. However, let us remember that such phrases as "all men are created equal," "equal standing before the law," and "equal opportunity for all" have become parts of our common, moral lexicon without denying that "charity begins at home," that "we have to look after our own, first," and similar, traditional priorities. If we remember that and if we have the good will to allow such misunderstanding about "equal consideration" and "equal rights" for animals simply to fade away, then that is what should come to pass.

To summarize, the relations requirement fails to recognize that some moral rights do not derive from (the capacity for) personal, familial, and other such relations but are intended to counterbalance the priorities that derive from (the capacity for) such relations. Therefore, that animals cannot participate (fully) in such relations with us does not preclude their having those moral rights against us. And once again, common moral goals would be more readily accomplished by not allowing the priority we give to family, friends, and the like to result in the routine sacrifice of animal interests.

IV. The Humanist Requirement

The humanist requirement derives from a classical, naturalist conception of morality: acting morally is required so that we human beings may live with ourselves and with each other contentedly and productively, and that, in turn, is necessary for us to fulfill our peculiarly human potentials and to enjoy the sort of life characteristic of our species. James D. Wallace succinctly states this position in summarizing Aristotle's conception of ethics: "Ethics, for Aristotle, is the study of good human life, and the point of the study is to aid us in ordering our lives, individually and collectively, so that we live as well as possible."[17] Thus, on this view, the direct subject matter of morality is limited to intra- and interhuman affairs, and the purpose of morality is to attain specifically human ends. It follows that nonhuman beings can (logically) enter this moral arena only indirectly, for instance, as property of importance to humans, as objects of human affection, or as providing opportunities for the development of good human character. An example of this third indirect moral significance for animals is the belief, expressed by Aquinas and Kant among others, that being compassionate and even fair to animals is important because it can help us to develop these character traits, which are morally important in our dealings with other people.[18]

Although this indirect moral significance may provide an adequate basis for humane obligations to animals—and, consequently, does not leave animals without any moral protection of their interests whatsoever—if this humanist restriction on the subject matter and purpose of morality is correct, then talk of extending direct moral significance (e.g., moral rights) to animals involves a kind of category mistake. Since moral rights are implements for regulating how we deal with ourselves and with other people, all moral rights must (logically) be possessed by humans. They must be entitlements or claims (or whatever sort of thing rights are) that we have against ourselves or against other people in order to aid us in securing a good, human life. It follows on this humanist view that assigning rights to animals would be as fundamental a misuse of rights as would be attempting to win a football game with a baseball bat.

In response to this limiting conception of morality, we may question its adequacy as an account of the logic of moral concepts and principles. That these concepts and principles are important for attaining a good, human life does not entail, or even suggest, that they are important only where attaining a good, human life is the issue, and there is ample evidence that we can understand how being moral is valuable in contexts where human self-control, the existence or flourishing of human society, and leading a good, human life are not at issue. For example, as discussed in Chapter 3, we can understand that some animals are good parents, courageous, loyal, sympathetic, and so forth with each other. Often, especially since the advent of ethology, we understand the importance of these traits and actions for the existence of the animals' communities and the importance of these communities for the animals living well their own characteristic ways of life. Insofar as the humanist requirement derives from a belief that social existence and moral virtue are something peculiarly human or of importance only for securing the good life characteristic of humans, that requirement derives from a mistake.[19]

Furthermore, we do not find the application of moral terms directly to our dealings with animals to be incomprehensible or merely metaphorical, as is the case with "green ideas," "heavy numbers," "furious sleeping," and other *bona fide* category mistakes. For example, we understand what is meant when we hear that Leibniz, who after inspecting a bug carefully placed it back on a leaf, was "respectful" of the bug and "concerned" that he should do it no harm. We understand what it means to say that some people "care for" animals, are "dedicated" to bettering the condition of animals, show "exceptional compassion" for animals, and are "conscientious" in their treatment of animals. Conversely, we also understand what is meant when it is said that some people are "cruel" to animals, "negligent" in their treatment of animals, "callous" about or "insensitive" to animals, and "selfish" in their dealings with animals. These and many other moral terms are routinely employed without strain or puzzlement in discussing our dealings with animals. And their intelligibility does not derive from some hidden reference to intra- or interhuman concerns or activities. For example, when we say that someone is "compassionate" or "callous" toward animals, we do not mean that he is compassionate or callous toward the people who own or are emotionally attached to animals; we mean that he is compassionate or callous toward the animals themselves. Consequently, the logic of many moral terms does not support the thesis that morality is directly limited to intra- and inter-human affairs.

Finally, certain well-established moral principles are not logically limited to intra- and interhuman affairs. Perhaps the utilitarian side of our everyday morality, with its emphasis on relieving suffering and otherwise making life more enjoyable and fulfilling, provides the most obvious examples of this. Suffering, distress, enjoyment, and fulfillment are not exclusively human conditions; consequently, moral principles that focus on the relief or attainment of these conditions are not logically limited to intra- and interhuman affairs. Similarly, as argued in Chapter 6 and earlier in this chapter, principles of fairness are not logically restricted to interhuman dealings. For example, it is not uncommon to hear complaints of "unfair" when a pet dog or a zoo or park animal is punished for biting someone who has been teasing it. Also, our literature abounds with stories of virtuous animals, like Lassie and Rin Tin Tin, receiving their "just rewards," and especially in connection with endangered species, the idea that animals are "entitled" to habitats in which they can at least survive is current. Again, principles of fairness are intended to protect the weak against the strong—to that extent, at least, correcting "the arbitrariness of this world"[20]—therefore, they are not logically limited to intra- and interhuman affairs, since, as already noted, there are great, morally arbitrary differences in power between us and animals and since many animals are desperately in need of protection against us. Consequently, even if principles of fairness and benevolence are important for human self-control, the existence and flourishing of human society, and our enjoying a good, human life, the logic of these principles does not suggest that moral principles are restricted to regulating intra- or interhuman dealings.

The thesis that morality is necessary for self-control and the existence and flourishing of society and that these are necessary for a good, human life is attractive because it provides the basis both for a tidy answer to the perennial question, "Why be moral?" and for something like an objective, scientific procedure for resolving ethical issues.[21] However, neither common moral practice nor our routine use of moral concepts would support a claim that that thesis identifies the logical limits of morality in general or of moral rights in particular. In spite of the classical credentials of that thesis, even traditional moral philosophy would not support such a claim, since the utilitarian and deontological traditions, the principles of which do not limit moral concern or concepts to intra- and interhuman affairs, are at least as viable schools of contemporary moral philosophy as is the "humanist-eudaemonic" school. Consequently, trying to deny moral rights to animals on the grounds that the moral arena is limited to what is important for attaining the good life for humans would smack of arbitrariness.

V. Conclusion

In conclusion, there is no denying that animals are incapable of entering fully into the community that humans can enjoy with each other. However, that this incapacity justifies our denying moral rights to animals and continuing to consume them is neither self-evident nor established by the arguments for that inference that have been offered to date. The arguments offered here do not demonstrate that that inference could not possibly be justified, but they do strongly reinforce the point emphasized in Chapter 6 that a variety of common, moral concerns with strong intuitive appeal clearly indicate that liberating animals is what we ought (morally) to do. Consequently, until, if ever, serious justification is provided for that inference, it ought (morally) to be rejected.

9

The Misfortune of Death

PHILOSOPHICALLY, THE animal rights movement "took fire" in the mid-1970s with the publication of Peter Singer's *Animal Liberation*.[1] Singer is definitely a Benthamite utilitarian, and his arguments for animal liberation were and remain strictly utilitarian ones, focusing on the pain suffered by animals in our consumption of them. It has been charged that Singer's utilitarian position does not establish that animal life itself is of value or ought (morally) to be protected by something like the right to life currently enjoyed by humans. These charges have been brought not only by critics of animal liberation such as Ruth Cigman.[2] They have also been brought by advocates of animal liberation such as Tom Regan,[3] and there has been considerable discussion within the animal rights movement about whether the utilitarian philosophy on which it has been built can support the respect for animal life itself that most members of the movement seem to feel. Singer's acceptance, in *Practical Ethics*, of the replacement argument seems to support those who claim that it cannot provide that support, since that argument makes animals out to be nothing more than "receptacles" for pleasure that can (morally) be replaced without loss whenever one is "broken," that is, whenever an animal is sacrificed for human consumption.[4]

Since I am neither exclusively a utilitarian nor exclusively a rights theorist, and feel no imperative to swear allegiance to either of these two positions, I do not want to become entangled in this controversy between utilitarian animal liberationists and animal rights theorists. I want to devote this chapter to discussing whether animals can properly be described as having an interest in life and whether they ought (morally) to have something like a right to life that would protect them against even humane slaughter. Furthermore, I want, once again, to discuss whether extending such a right to animals is recommended by everyday, commonsensical moral considerations. Consequently, our focus here

159

will be on criticisms of the idea of an animal right to life, rather than on criticisms of utilitarianism's capacity to establish that there ought to be such a right. Nevertheless, since utilitarian concerns figure prominently among our common moral considerations, as we have repeatedly acknowledged, our discussion here could properly be described as focusing on whether our everyday, "mixed utilitarian" morality indicates that we ought to liberate animals from this ultimate sacrifice for our benefit. (Since Ruth Cigman gives close, careful expression to the contention that animals cannot [logically] have a moral right to life, we shall focus this discussion on her argument.[5])

I. Why (Supposedly) Only Rational Beings Can Have a Right to Life

Cigman's argument against an animal right to life runs as follows:

A right to X entails the right to be protected against certain actions which will result in the misfortune, or possible misfortune, of not-X. A condition for being the subject of a right is therefore the *capacity* to be the subject of the corresponding misfortune. . . . For a creature to be a possible subject of the misfortune of death, life itself must be an object of value for it, and *this* possibility is presupposed by the right to life; otherwise the right to life would be a right to be protected from something which could not conceivably be a misfortune, which does not make sense. . . . The relationship between capacity and desire in this context must be examined. My suggestion is that, when we fill in the concept of desiring not to die in a way which is relevant to the misfortune of death and right to life, we shall have to withhold this from animals.[6]

For convenient reference, we can reduce this argument to the following compact form:

A1: Only beings capable of valuing life itself can suffer the misfortune of death.

A2: Only beings capable of suffering the misfortune of death can have a moral right to life.

A3: Animals are incapable of valuing life itself.

A4: Therefore, animals cannot have a moral right to life.

Each of the premises of this argument is dubious. Even A2, which might seem the safest of the lot, could be challenged, since, as is made explicit in the citation from Cigman's article, it presumes that rights are fundamentally a form of protection. That presumption would provide grounds for a challenge by rights theorists such as H. L. A. Hart, who hold that rights are not essentially protections for our interests but are, rather, basically implements for securing choices.[7] Be this controversy as it may, we shall not pursue this line of criticism here. Whether a careful analysis of rights would reveal that the moral right to life protects our interest in life, secures our choice to remain alive, does something else, or (what I would think most likely) at least both protects and secures, that right seems tied closely enough to death being a misfortune to render A2 reasonable.

A3 would certainly be attacked by many advocates of animal liberation who emphasize "the evolutionary continuity of mental experience"[8] and who would claim that many animals have sufficiently extensive temporal awareness, ample self-consciousness, and enough of any other requisite aspects of rationality to value life itself. We, too, have argued, in Chapters 3 and 7, that animals are more intelligent—and are so in morally significant ways—than humanist philosophers like Cigman acknowledge. It may very well be that many animals besides ourselves are sufficiently intelligent to value life itself. Furthermore, whether (some/many) animals are or are not sufficiently intelligent to value life itself is not a conceptual issue to be settled by philosophical analysis. It is an empirical issue to be resolved by careful, impartial observation. Cigman does not provide significant empirical evidence to support A3.

Nevertheless, since I am not prepared or disposed to enter into a protracted discussion of the empirical evidence against A3 here, I propose to let it stand for the purposes of this analysis of an animal right to life. It would seem reasonable to share Cigman's presumption to the extent of agreeing that at least some of the animals for which animal liberationists are seeking a moral right to life (e.g., chickens) may not be sufficiently intelligent to value life itself and, consequently, would be covered by A3. Furthermore, since animal liberationists generally contend that a being's level of intelligence is not of fundamental moral significance, they would probably contend that even those animals covered by A3 ought (morally) to share in the right to life. Consequently, animal liberationists seem to be committed to finding another weak link in argument A besides A3.

I believe that that other weak link is A1, and since it is the contention that we must value life itself in order to suffer death as a misfortune that defines this line of criticism of an animal right to life, it follows that if A1 is false, then argument A is not just factually mistaken but fundamentally misconceived. I question A1 because in so many other cases, it is not the case that we have to value x itself in order to have a right to x. Consequently, agreeing that if one has a right to x, then not-x must be a misfortune for him or her, it follows that not-x can be a misfortune for an individual, even though she or he does not value x itself.[9]

II. Having vs. Taking an Interest in Life

Cigman's argument is an instance of the following argument form:

B1: Only beings capable of valuing x itself can suffer the misfortune of not-x.

B2: Only beings capable of suffering not-x as a misfortune can have a moral right to x.

B3: S is incapable of valuing x itself.

B4: Therefore, S cannot have a moral right to x.

Reflecting on our current practice of according rights will show that there is something wrong with arguments of this form. Further reflection will show how B1 (and B3) can be revised to yield an acceptable argument form. However, that form will not exclude the possibility of a moral right to life for animals.

Before proceeding with this analysis, we must clarify what "valuing x itself" refers to. It would be obvious that we can have a moral right to x in spite of our not valuing x itself, if "valuing x itself" meant "x has intrinsic value for us, rather than (or in addition to) instrumental value." Whatever "intrinsic value" may mean, it is clear that we have moral rights to things that are of merely instrumental value for us (e.g., an unbiased trial). Nonetheless, Cigman's insistence that misfortunes be tied to desires, her use of the phrase "life itself as an object of value," her rejection of a utilitarian alternative because "it does not justify calling death a misfortune *for the animal who dies*," and her rejection of Thomas Nagel's analysis of the misfortune of death because it does not require that "life is something most of us value and want to experience for as long as possible" all give the impression that some sort of shadowy intrinsic value in life vs. merely instrumental value for life distinction is at work in her argument.[10] Be that as it may, this distinction is incidental to the argument and should not mislead us into dismissing the argument out of hand.

The distinction on which this argument turns is that between having an interest in x and taking an interest in x, and "valuing life itself" should be interpreted as "taking an interest in life." It will be remembered from Chapters 5 and 7 that we can have an interest in something that affects (will affect, would affect) our feelings of well-being but of which we are ignorant. On the other hand, taking an interest in something requires

> that we be aware of the item in question and understand (or, at least, believe that we understand) how it affects (will affect, would affect) us and
> that, as a consequence of this awareness and (believed) understanding, we consciously give a value to the item.

Cigman does not employ this language of interests, but the following passages make clear that she is relying on this distinction:

> Death is not a misfortune merely because it is a bad condition to be in, relative to being alive, healthy, and so on; rather, it is a misfortune because life is something most of us *value* and *want to experience* for as long as possible. . . . I reject the suggestion that a categorical desire, or anything of this nature, is attributable to animals. For

consider what would have to be the case if this were so. First, animals would have to possess essentially the same *conceptions of life and death* as persons do. The subject of a categorical desire must either *understand* death as a condition which closes a possible future forever, and leaves behind one a world in which one has no part as an agent or conscious being of any sort, or he must *grasp, and then reject, this conception* of death, in favor of a *belief* in immortality. Either way, the radical and exclusive nature of the transition from life to death must be *understood*—it must at least be *appreciated* why people think in these terms—so that the full significance of the *idea* that "X is a *reason for living*" may be grasped.[11]

It seems accurate to paraphrase Cigman as claiming that although animals may have an interest in life—since life is a good condition to be in relative to death—they cannot take an interest in life, since they are incapable of understanding the full significance of death. But while this distinction between having and taking an interest in life is real enough, is it relevant to the issue of whether or not it makes sense to say that a certain (kind of) being has a moral right to life? Answering similar questions concerning analogous cases will show that it is not relevant.

III. Having Interests and Having Rights

Is it possible to have a moral right to something that influences (will influence, would influence) our interests but of which we are ignorant? Certainly. People are morally entitled to inheritances they do not know about. Even patients who are unaware of "The Patient's Bill of Rights" have a moral right to see their medical records. Also, people who have never heard of "The Declaration of the Universal Rights of Man" and have grown up in cultures that not only deny them human rights but also have taught them to believe that they are subhuman are still morally entitled to human rights. There is neither conceptual nor moral difficulty with ascribing a moral right to x to someone who is unaware either of x or of the possibility that she could have x or a moral right to x. Therefore, having a moral right to x does not require that we actually know about, desire, or value x itself.

It might be objected that it is not actually understanding (or believing one understands) how x influences (will influence, would influence) one's interests and valuing x itself that is required for having a moral right to x but the *capacity* to so understand and value x itself that is required for having that right. Most fundamental moral principles involve the idea of capacity, for example, the capacity to suffer in utilitarianism and the capacity to reason in Kantianism. Cigman also refers to the capacity to suffer a misfortune. So perhaps the proper question is, is it possible to have a moral right to something that influences (will influence, would influence) our interests but that we are incapable of understanding and valuing?

Again, there are obvious cases of this. Young children are the most numerous example here; they have—and, our enlightened moral conscience tells us, ought to have—legal and human rights that they are incapable of understanding and valuing. They may value the medical care and other benefits that property, social welfare programs, legal procedures, and other things to which they are morally entitled secure for them, but they are incapable of understanding and valuing property, social welfare institutions, legal procedures, human respect, and moral obligation themselves. Children's potential for becoming adults might be raised as an objection here, but while children may have the potential for becoming adults who will have the capacity to understand and value these things, while they are children they are incapable of understanding and valuing many things to which they are, nonetheless, morally entitled. Consequently, current moral practice shows that we can have a moral right to *x* even though we are incapable of understanding and valuing *x* itself.

This conclusion might be criticized for ignoring the fact that "capacity" often involves the idea of what is normal for (fully developed) members of a reference group. Cigman emphasizes what people *normally* value in her discussion of the misfortune of death and in circumventing the possible counter-example to her analysis posed by suicidal people. Similarly, Stanley Benn contends that animal rights arguments referring to the supposed inconsistency in extending moral rights to subrational humans while denying them to more rational animals—the common, so-called "marginal cases" arguments—are fallacious, because moral rights are extended primarily not to individuals but to species, based on the capabilities of normal members of the species.[12] So the proper question may be, is it possible to have a moral right to something that influences (will influence, would influence) one's interests but that even fully developed, normal beings of his or her kind are incapable of understanding and valuing?

Of course, it is impossible for us to refer to any actual cases concerning human beings where this happens. Such examples would require that we understand and value things human beings are incapable of understanding and valuing. However, the following nonhuman example seems plausible enough to show at least that a positive answer to this question would be reasonable.

Like most opponents of an animal right to life, Cigman acknowledges that animals should be spared gratuitous, avoidable suffering. Now, industrial pollution causes many animals gratuitous, avoidable suffering, but animals are incapable of understanding how industrial pollution affects their habitats, undermines their health, and causes them to suffer. It follows that although animals suffer from a polluted environment, they are incapable of understanding and valuing a pollution-free environment. But does it also follow, as Cigman would have to say, that animals whose well-being is destroyed by industrial pollution are not suffering a misfortune in losing their healthy habitat and cannot have a moral right

—call it "the right to a healthful environment"—to be protected against indus-trial pollution?

We do not encounter conceptual difficulty in asserting that people are morally entitled to a healthful environment. Is the fact that adult humans normally can but animals normally cannot understand how industrial pollution causes them to suffer morally significant enough to show that animals cannot conceivably share in this moral right? Since many of the forms of suffering caused by industrial pollution (e.g., blindness, debilitation, cancer, and birth defects) are not diseases of the understanding or otherwise directly related to understanding, and since these forms of suffering are shared by human and nonhuman animals alike, refer-ence to the normal, adult capacity for understanding that differentiates human from nonhuman animals would seem not only to be insufficiently weighty to justify such a claim but also to be so totally beside the point as to be a blatant rationalization of anthropocentric prejudice.

It might be objected that

> C1: Since animals take an interest in enjoyment, gratuitous, avoidable suffering can be a misfortune for them.
> C2: Consequently, animals can, at least as far as Cigman's argument is concerned, have a moral right to a life free of gratuitous, avoidable suffering.
> C3: The moral right to a healthful environment is a part of this right not to suffer, since a healthful environment is essential for a life free of gratui-tous, avoidable suffering.
> C4: Therefore, the example of the moral right to a healthful environment does not show that animals can have moral rights to things that they are incapable of understanding and valuing.

An obvious problem with such an objection is that although a healthful envi-ronment may be "essential for" a life free of gratuitous, avoidable suffering, it is not "a part of" not suffering; so the right to a healthful environment is not accurately described as "a part of" the right to a life free of gratuitous, avoidable suffering. The former right would be more accurately described as "essential for," "derivative from," or "adjunct to" the latter. But while inferring from a moral right to x to a moral right to what is essential for x seems plausible enough, that inference could not be permitted by those who insist that we must (be able to) value what we have a moral right to. That is because it is possible to value something without (being capable of) understanding and valuing what is neces-sary for producing that something. Consequently, the inference from a moral right to x to a moral right to what is essential for x would condone rights to things one does not (cannot) understand and value.

Furthermore, the following argument—which has the same form as C1 through C4 and whose crucial premise, D3, is as much or as little justified as C3—yields the conclusion that animals can have a moral right to life:

D1: Since animals take an interest in suffering, suffering can be a misfortune for them.

D2: Consequently, animals can, at least as far as Cigman's argument is concerned, have a moral right to a life free of gratuitous, avoidable suffering.

D3: The moral right to life is a part of this right not to suffer, since life is essential for a life free of gratuitous, avoidable suffering.

D4: Therefore, animals can, at least as far as Cigman's argument is concerned, have a moral right to life.

Those fond of "negative utilitarianism" might object to argument D that a moral right not to suffer refers just to avoiding suffering, and since this is something one can do by dying, life is not essential for what a moral right not to suffer is about. However, what is ordinarily valued under the label of "avoiding suffering" is not merely the absence of suffering but a life free of gratuitous, avoidable suffering. This is why negative utilitarianism is just a Rube Goldberg creation and does not raise serious moral issues, possibilities, or challenges—either to utilitarianism or to argument D. Furthermore, it is a life free of gratuitous, avoidable suffering, and not merely the absence of suffering, that requires a healthful environment. Consequently, a negative utilitarian response to argument D will not help save argument C, for it will be just as much (or as little) a rebuttal to argument C as to argument D. Thus, the pattern of analysis in argument C cannot be used to support the claim that animals cannot have a moral right to life.

Finally, our common attitude toward cruelty to animals indicates that the inability to understand and value what is causing one to suffer is morally insignificant where gratuitous, avoidable suffering is involved. If asked, "Are you opposed to cruelty to animals?," no one would answer "It depends on the level of understanding of the animals in question." Subjecting animals to gratuitous, avoidable suffering cannot (morally) be excused by referring to the animals' level of understanding and claiming, even accurately, that the animals cannot possibly understand what is causing them the gratuitous, avoidable pain they are suffering. For all these reasons, I conclude that normal understanding is a bogus issue here and that beings can have moral rights to things that normal beings of their kind are incapable of understanding and valuing.

IV. Having an Interest in Life and the Right to Life

These three possibilities—ignorance, individual inability to understand and value, and normal inability to understand and value—seem to cover the field. So

I conclude that taking an interest in or valuing x itself is not a necessary condition for having a moral right to x. Since all the cases just discussed satisfy B3, the problem with the above argument form must lie in B1 or B2. But Cigman's claim that having moral rights entails the vulnerability to corresponding misfortunes (i.e., B2) was conceded. So the failure of this argument form must lie in B1, which is the claim that suffering the misfortune of not-x requires taking an interest in x.

In all the examples above, the individuals who did not or could not take an interest in x nonetheless had an interest in x. This indicates that we can correct argument form B by substituting "having an interest" for "taking an interest" in B1 (and B3). This gives us the following argument form:

E1: Only beings that have an interest in x can suffer the misfortune of not-x.

E2: Only beings capable of suffering not-x as a misfortune can have a moral right to x.

E3: S does not have an interest in x.

E4: Therefore, S cannot have a moral right to x.

This argument form escapes the above counter-examples to argument form B, because it does not deny that there can be moral rights where there already commonly are or reasonably could be such rights. Argument form E also excludes nonsentient animals, plants, stones, works of art, machines, and other inanimate objects from having moral rights. It will be remembered that these nonsentient things cannot have interests, since they have no feelings of well-being. All affective responses to and evaluations of their condition derive from other beings that have or take an interest in them. It would seem that such things ought (logically) to be incapable of having moral rights, if anything is. Consequently, argument form E seems to be putting the line between those logically capable and those logically incapable of having moral rights where it belongs.

It further follows, according to our revised argument form, that no being can have moral rights in areas where its feelings of well-being are not (will not be, would not be) affected. That again seems to be placing the distinction where it belongs and accords perfectly with the animal liberationist's position on the extent of animal rights, as discussed in Chapter 5. This is not surprising, since argument form E is basically a restatement of the necessary condition half of the interest requirement for having moral rights, and as noted in Chapter 5, most advocates of animal liberation accept that requirement.

Acknowledging the possibility of extended rights, such as those of a trustee administering an estate, would require further revisions of argument form E. But such qualifications (e.g., changing E2 to something like "one can have moral rights only in those areas where he or she has an interest or where the individual as whose agent he or she is acting has an interest") would not undermine the present argument. Nor would adding any further caveats concerning capacity and normalcy do more harm than further encumbering the phrasing.

Returning to the specific case of the misfortune of death and the moral right ·to life, the only way to save Cigman's argument would seem to be somehow to show that that misfortune and that right form a special case. One would have to argue that

> even though in all the sorts of cases just discussed, being a possible subject of the misfortune of not-x and of the moral right to x does not require the ability to take an interest in x, in the case of the misfortune of death and the moral right to life, one must be able to value life itself in order to be the subject of that misfortune and of that right. This is because . . .

Cigman does not indicate how that blank is to be filled in, nor do I know how to fill it in. That leaves me with the following speculation and conclusion.

Speculation: We ordinarily consider death a misfortune. So when Cigman claims that the moral right to life presupposes the possibility of suffering the misfortune of death, that seems reasonable enough. However, in developing her argument, she ties "misfortune" to valuing (i.e., to taking an interest). This gives "misfortune" a technical definition that does not quite fit with its common use. For example, a pelican that is born blind will certainly die of its affliction. It would not be more unusual to describe that baby pelican as "unfortunate," as having "suffered a misfortune," or even as "tragic" (since it will certainly die) than it would be to so describe a human infant born blind (who will certainly not be allowed to die). Yet the pelican will never be able to value vision itself. This unnoticed equivocation on "misfortune" (technical use in A1 but common use in A2) is what makes Cigman's argument seem plausible.

Conclusion: A1 is false. One can suffer the misfortune of death even though he or she lacks the intellectual capacity for taking an interest in or valuing life itself. Assuming no afterlife awaits one—the traditional assumption in the case of animals—that is not hard to understand: death is ordinarily a misfortune for an individual (whether he or she knows it or not), because it totally eliminates the possibility of his or her further enjoyment and fulfillment.

For a highly rational, imaginative, self-conscious being with an expansive sense of time and the ability to make long-range projects, the misfortune of death can have additional sources, for instance, the frustration of categorical desires, such as raising a family, which, as Cigman emphasizes, are supposed to "give meaning to life." However, experiencing death as a frustration does not seem to require having long-range plans. If I were to suffer a fatal heart attack while preparing a meal for my family, I might very well experience my death as a frustration of that activity. The same might hold true for a fox shot while taking food home to its young.

Furthermore, projects that give meaning to life can also give meaning to death. Many people who have devoted their lives to their countries, religions, or families have also died for those causes. Without that devotion to a cause, which is a kind of categorical desire, these people might have "held life more dear" and been unwilling to sacrifice it. Consequently, it is not at all clear how, as Cigman claims, categorical desires make "life itself an object of value." [13] It would also seem to follow that since superior rational ability can make possible this sort of commitment "unto death," it can make death *less* of a misfortune for a highly rational being than for a being of lesser intellectual ability. Giving death a purpose, perhaps even a glorious one, can help reduce its sting, as can being able to spend one's last hours remembering past happy days. Assuming, as seems reasonable, that only highly rational beings can imagine and believe in life after death also leads to the conclusion that death can be less, rather than more, of a misfortune for those of greater intellectual capacity. Thus, rationality's role in making death more or less of a misfortune is not obvious or simple and probably cuts both ways.

That cannot be said about the annihilation of the possibility of any further enjoyment or fulfillment for the individual who dies. Nonetheless, we should not be misled by the phrase "*the* misfortune of death" into believing that this misfortune must be a simple matter. Some deaths can be more of a misfortune than others; for example (*ceteris paribus*), the death of a normal, healthy young woman would commonly be considered more of a misfortune than the death of a retarded child, the death of someone who is deaf, dumb, and blind, or the death of an elderly person who has been reduced to more or less trying to enjoy life day by day without any long-range projects. That two deaths are both misfortunes does not preclude one being more of a misfortune than the other. In addition to the misfortune suffered by any sentient being that in dying loses its possibility of any further enjoyment or fulfillment, there may be other sources of or dimensions to the misfortune of death deriving from that which distinguishes a particular (kind of) sentient individual from other (kinds of) sentient individuals (e.g., health, social instincts, and intellectual ability).

Still, whether the more rational or the less rational being suffers the greater loss in death, the annihilation of any further possibility of enjoyment or fulfillment is sufficient by itself to render death a serious enough, morally significant loss to be properly labeled a "misfortune." Therefore, even if animals cannot attend to, understand the full importance of, and value life itself and, because of that, cannot suffer certain dimensions of the misfortune of death that humans can, it does not follow that they cannot suffer the misfortune of death or that it would be nonsensical to extend a moral right to life to them in order to protect them from this misfortune.

V. Suffering a Loss and the Awareness of Loss

One last criticism might be made at this point. It might be objected that for an individual to suffer the misfortune of death, death must be a misfortune *for him* and that this is not accounted for in the analysis above. Cigman writes, "If the most that can be said of the quick and painless death of an animal is that it removes a quantity of pleasurable experience from the world, this does not justify calling that death a misfortune *for the animal who dies*." [14] Weighing this criticism requires that we note that phrases of the form "not-x is a misfortune for S" are ambiguous. They may be equivalent to "not-x is S's misfortune" or to "S considers not-x a misfortune." Even this latter option is ambiguous, since it may be equivalent to "S judges not-x to be a misfortune" or to "S directly experiences not-x to be a misfortune." We shall consider these alternatives in reverse order.

The last alternative is definitely too strong to be part of an acceptable analysis of the misfortune of death. There are two reasons for this. First, there are some forms of death that we cannot directly experience but that we want to be protected against by the moral right to life. Consequently, we want to have those forms of death counted as misfortunes. For example, we cannot directly experience a sudden death while in a deep sleep to be a misfortune.

Second, suffering a loss is not essentially tied to suffering unpleasant feelings at the loss. "He suffered a great loss without even knowing it" is not a self-contradictory statement. It refers to such mundane things as unknowingly putting a rare penny into a gumball machine, setbacks in a politician's investment portfolio when that portfolio has been placed in a blind trust during her tenure in office, and failing to answer a phone call that, if answered, would have earned one a great prize. Failing to recognize this difference between suffering a loss and other kinds of suffering may have misled some philosophers into believing that only those capable of experiencing some feeling of pain, grief, frustration, and the like at (the prospect of) death are capable of suffering the misfortune of death. [15]

Talk of suffering a loss, even though one does not experience adverse feelings at the loss, can be problematic. For example, parents sometimes say things like "Leonard may think he's happy now, but he lost the chance at a really happy life as a renowned physician by marrying so young." Also, moral reformers sometimes say things like "Those women may think they're happy as housewives, but they've lost the chance at really fulfilling lives because of our society's belief that 'a woman's place is in the home.'" Such talk suggests, in the first case, that Leonard's parents are confusing what they wanted from their son to make them happy with what makes the son happy and, in the second case, that the women's liberationist is (mistakenly) presuming that all women are psychologically alike, so that they can achieve "real" happiness only through leading the sort of life that approximates to his or her idea of the good life for women. In both cases, we may justifiably be suspicious that if there is a loss being suffered, it is not the individuals being talked about but the speakers who are suffering the loss.

Such suspicions lift the lid on a Pandora's box of epistemological problems concerning counter-factuals and other minds. This could lead us to attempt to avoid these problems by claiming that "suffering" applies only to cases where the individual who supposedly suffers the loss experiences unpleasant feelings at that loss. However, such a draconian stipulation would not be justified, for the line of criticism directed at Leonard's parents and the women's liberationist cannot be extended to the case we are talking about. When we talk about an individual suffering the loss of the possibility of any further enjoyment or fulfillment, we are not projecting onto him something that we want for him but that he apparently does not care about, as was done by Leonard's parents and by the women's liberationist. In claiming that one who dies without suffering unpleasant feelings at (the prospect of) death can, nonetheless, ordinarily be properly described as "suffering a loss," we are presuming that continued life would have held sufficient enjoyment and fulfillment to have made that life worth living for the individual and that she has, consequently, suffered the loss of something that would have been of value to her. This presumption is not made in spite of evidence to the contrary from the dying individual and is, therefore, significantly different from the parents' and the women's liberationist's presumptions. Our presumption refers to the normal condition of living beings and would be overturned by evidence that the condition of this dying individual was relevantly abnormal, for example, evidence that prolonged agony is all further life held for him or her.

This openness to ordinary patterns of refutation is what basically spares recognizing that the one who dies ordinarily suffers a loss, even if she does not suffer pain, frustration, and so forth at dying, from the problems that have, in other situations, given a bad name to detaching "suffering" from experiencing unpleasant feelings. In this case, at least, claims of the form "S suffered an unfelt loss" are intelligible, verifiable/falsifiable propositions, and any definition of "suffering" that ruled out propositions of that form would thereby prove inadequate.

Turning to the second possible interpretation of "not-x is a misfortune for S" (i.e., "S judges not-x to be a misfortune"), we see that this alternative is too weak. This is because we can judge to be misfortunes things that do not affect our lives and that we consequently do not suffer. For example, I would judge that the members of The People's Temple who suffered a mass death in Guyana several years ago suffered a misfortune, but it certainly does not follow that I have suffered the misfortune of death. Thus, both ways of interpreting "not-x is a misfortune for S" as "S considers not-x a misfortune" fail. These are the two interpretations of that phrase that might have suggested that suffering the misfortune of death requires something like normal$_h$ intelligence. Consequently, we cannot draw from the fact that in order for S to suffer the misfortune of death, death must be a misfortune for S, the conclusion that S must have something like normal$_h$ intelligence to suffer the misfortune of death.

This leaves only the "not-x is S's misfortune" alternative as a suitable interpretation of "death is a misfortune for S." The analysis above of the misfortune of death accounts for this alternative. It is not merely some anonymous "quantity of pleasurable experience" that has been removed "from the world" by S's death. Death is a misfortune *for* S, because it is S's possibility of future enjoyment and fulfillment that is destroyed by S's death. This is true whether S is human or an animal. Consequently, the claim that to suffer the misfortune of death, death must be a misfortune for the one who dies does not constitute an objection to an animal's death being a misfortune.

Common usage confirms our position here. Recently, a young woman was walking along a San Francisco street on a stormy night. As she walked past an old building, a large piece of the building's concrete parapet fell from the sixth floor and struck her on the head. She never knew what hit her; she died instantly. No one would feel any hesitation in saying that this was a misfortune for the young woman—and not just for her family and friends—even though, as we may suppose, she experienced no fear of impending death nor any sense of frustration of her plans for the future. The misfortune is that here was a young woman "cut off in the prime of life," a young woman "with her whole life ahead of her," a young woman who will never have the chance to experience "the joys life would have brought her." These common expressions do not refer to the young woman's philosophy of life, her feelings at dying, or her categorical desires for the future. They refer to the (on-balance) enjoyable, fulfilling life (we presume) she would have had but now never will—and that is very sad.

The same can be said for a karakul lamb killed less than a day out of its mother's womb, a baby seal killed when only a few days old, or a veal calf slaughtered when only a few months old. Their early deaths are misfortunes for them because they, too, were cut off in the prime of life, had their whole lives ahead of them, and will never know the joys (we presume) life would have brought them. These cases, too, are very sad, and if we can set aside our sentimental bias in favor of our own species, we can recognize that we have the same reasons for saying that a misfortune has befallen these animals that we have for saying that a misfortune has befallen the young woman killed by the falling parapet.

It might be countered that, common usage to the contrary not withstanding, Epicurus has shown that death cannot be a misfortune for the one who dies. This is because, according to "Epicurus' dilemma," while we are alive, we cannot suffer death, and when we are dead, we cannot suffer anything. However, there are two reasons why this Epicurean rebuttal would not help save Cigman's argument. First, she believes that death is a misfortune for (normal, adult) humans, owing to their having categorical desires. Epicurus' contention, on the other hand, is that death is not a misfortune for anyone, and he was especially concerned with convincing normal, adult humans that they should not fear death. If he were right about that and if Cigman is right that we cannot have a moral right to be protected against death unless death is a misfortune for us, then normal, adult humans could not have a moral right to life anymore than animals could. That conclusion would not help substantiate the species inequality in which Cigman believes.

Second, the analysis above shows that Epicurus is wrong, for it is the living who suffer the misfortune of death. Consequently, there is a real subject to suffer this misfortune, and this permits our analysis to escape the second half of Epicurus' dilemma. Our analysis blunts the first half of the dilemma by showing that saying that it is the living who suffer the misfortune of death is not self-contradictory. This is because the living suffer this misfortune just when they die. (Of course, some people might be said to "suffer the misfortune of death" long before they die, because they fix on and brood over death. However, it should be clear that we are not talking about such morbidity here; we are referring to the loss the living suffer when they actually die.)

Harry Silverstein has recently written in support of Epicurus, contending that a "deprivation resolution" of Epicurus' dilemma, like ours, will not work. This is because, he claims, it includes a life/death comparison that presupposes that death has a value for the dead person, which is impossible.[16] However, Silverstein here confuses the meaning of "death" that refers to the loss of a possibility (i.e., further life) with the meaning of "death" that refers to the actualization of an alternative possibility (i.e., the state of no longer being alive). The loss is an event; the state is the condition that follows that event. It is the former sense of "death," the one that refers to the loss of further life, that is being employed when we talk about suffering the misfortune of death, and the subject of that loss of life is the living person who dies. Consequently, when we talk about suffering the misfortune of death, we are not comparing the value of life for the living with the value of "death" (i.e., the state of no longer being alive) for the dead.

VI. Summary and Conclusion

To summarize, even if (some) animals cannot take an interest in life, all animals (i.e., all sentient beings) have an interest in life. Furthermore, it is not taking an interest in x but having an interest in x that is essential for being vulnerable to suffering not-*x* as a misfortune. It follows that animals are capable of suffering the misfortune of death and that, consequently, Cigman's "misfortune requirement" for having moral rights is one that animals can meet, even where the issue is the right to life.

Of course, that animals can meet this logical requirement for the moral right to life does not establish that they ought (morally) to be extended that right. However, we have already argued, in Chapter 6, that accomplishing our common moral goals would be more effectively pursued by liberating animals than by continuing to consume them. "Liberating animals," it will be remembered, refers to extending to animals the same sorts of moral protection for their interests that we already enjoy for ours. Consequently, since we hold that we have a moral right to life, once we recognize that animals also have an interest in life, it follows that animals ought (morally) to share in that right. (Such sharing would, of course, include the complications concerning priorities, normal vs. abnormal situations, positive vs. negative obligations, and so on, which already qualify our human right to life.)

This conclusion could be challenged by questioning whether we have a moral right to life. For example, in *Interests and Rights*, R. G. Frey makes clear that he is suspicious about all talk of rights, whether such talk is of animal rights or of human rights.[17] However, this sort of challenge is inconsequential. As discussed in Chapter 5, the goal of animal liberation is not to justify "rights talk"; animal liberation is concerned with extending to animals the same sorts of moral protection currently enjoyed only by humans. If some philosophers prefer to deploy a new moral terminology, one cleansed of all talk of rights, to describe this protection, doing so will in no way compromise the argument we have made or the conclusion we have drawn here.

It might also be objected that since not all humans are extended a moral right to life, some further argument is needed to show that animals ought (morally) to be treated like those humans who are extended this right, rather than like those (e.g., fetuses) who are not. Unlike the previous challenge, this one does make a substantive logical point—provided we presume that there are humans who lack the moral right to life, which is the presumption we shall make here.

However, if we ask whether animals are, in morally significant ways, more like human fetuses or more like humans who are commonly noncontroversially extended the moral right to life—and this includes children, as well as adults—then the answer is clearly that they are more like the humans with that right to life. Animals are not merely beings that potentially have interests; they actually do have interests. While some animals are probably not capable of surviving on their own, many are, and those that are not are dependent on us not in the way a fetus is dependent on its mother but in the way children are dependent on their parents, elderly people are dependent on their children, and the handicapped are dependent on society. Even if animals do not have normal$_h$ intelligence, their intellectual abilities also strongly resemble those of children and are, as we argued in Chapter 3, even superior to those of children in many practical and morally significant ways.

Thus, although the controversy over abortion and a fetal right to life could (logically) give birth to an objection to the argument we have been making for an animal right to life, it does not actually do so. Some philosophical defenses of abortion set the requirements for being a rights-holder so high that it is doubtful that anyone but normal, healthy adults could meet them. However, everyday morality seems little influenced by such extreme arguments. Furthermore, it is highly doubtful that these advocates of abortion would agree to treating children, the elderly, and the handicapped as we now treat animals (e.g., in our laboratories). Consequently, extending to animals the moral protection these nonrights-holding humans would continue to enjoy in the Brave New World of these philosophers would amount to liberating animals.

In conclusion, I think it is worth emphasizing that we have developed this argument for an animal right to life without postulating any special interest that living beings take in life itself or any special value that life itself has. Our argument is based on the fact that life is necessary for enjoyment and fulfillment, that this generates an interest for sentient beings in remaining alive for as long as life holds (the prospect or even just hope of) sufficient enjoyment or fulfillment for them, and that our common moral goals include a concern with insuring that all those capable of enjoyment and fulfillment have a fair chance at achieving an enjoyable, fulfilling life.

This argument may not be strong enough for some, since they see in (certain forms of) sentient life a unique, intrinsic value. However, I must admit that I see no such value and believe that postulating such values raises insuperable difficulties, for example, as to the impartial, verifiable/falsifiable determination of where such value does and does not exist. Consequently, I think that the argument developed here properly evaluates life and provides a stronger, because less controversial, basis for extending a moral right to life to animals than would an argument based on some unique, intrinsic value in (certain forms of) sentient life.

10

The Replacement Argument

WE HAVE several times alluded to an argument against animals sharing in the moral right to life that, when it was put forward in the nineteenth century, Henry Salt called "the logic of the larder" and that has recently reappeared under the title of "the replacement argument." That argument runs as follows:

> It is permissible, *ceteris paribus*, to use an animal and to kill it (for food or research or anything else), provided that the following conditions are met:
> (a) the life of the animal is on balance a life worth living,
> (b) the animal otherwise would have no life at all (would not exist), and
> (c) the animal will be replaced, at or after death, by another animal in the case of which conditions (a) and (b) hold.[1]

(It is to be understood, of course, that if there are differences of degree among lives that are on balance worth living, then the life of the replacement animal must be of at least as high a degree as that of the animal it replaces.)

The basic principle underlying this argument is that if the life of an individual has only instrumental moral value, then we can (morally) dispose of that life without loss, provided that we preserve what that life is valuable for (e.g., experiencing an excess of pleasure over pain). Therefore, those who find morally significant, intrinsic value in the very lives of sentient individuals are immune from the replacement argument. However, as indicated in the preceding chapter, I find that the moral value of sentient life lies in its being essential for enjoyment and fulfillment, the development of moral character, and the realization of moral values such as fairness—our three common moral goals. Consequently, the defense of an animal right to life developed in that chapter is precisely the sort of position the replacement argument seeks to undermine.

As might be expected, I think that this challenge to our argument can be met. At the practical level, it can be argued that the replacement argument has severely limited application. This is because very few of the animals we consume are covered by both conditions (a) and (b). At the theoretical level, it can be shown that the replacement argument does not work from all standard, general moral viewpoints (e.g., Kantian and utilitarian theories), and that since everyday morality contains a mixture of these viewpoints, the replacement argument does not work from the viewpoint of common morality either. This is because even where the lives of sentient individuals are not held to have intrinsic moral value, they are not held to be just alternative ways of attaining things of moral value either. Finally, as previously noted, Peter Singer has come to accept the replacement argument as a valid criticism of an animal right to life from a utilitarian viewpoint —although he continues to maintain that this has little practical significance, for the reason just indicated.[2] I think it can be shown that the argument put forward by Singer, among others, to show that utilitarians must accept the replacement argument is fallacious, and given the prominence of utilitarian concerns both in the animal rights movement and in our everyday morality, I want to devote special attention to analyzing Singer's argument and another concerning replacement and obligations to future generations.

Thus, the point of this response to the replacement argument is not to prove that that argument commits some logical blunder, for it does not. Rather, the main point to be made here is that the moral value the replacement argument would give to the lives of sentient individuals is not confirmed by all standard, general moral theories, including certain forms of utilitarianism. Consequently, even those of us who believe that the lives of sentient individuals are morally valuable only as a necessary condition for other goods can justifiably reject the replacement argument and, for the reasons already given, can continue to maintain that animals ought (morally) to share in the right to life.

I. The (In)Significance of the Replacement Argument

Even those of us who work in the clouds should be aware that about the only current, routine killing of animals that the replacement argument would even be relevant to justifying is that involved in the killing of some animals bred, raised, and more or less released to be game animals. The replacement argument cannot be used to justify the killing of wild animals, because, by and large,

> they would have existed whether or not we had an interest in killing them;
> it is not necessary that the wild animals we kill die in order that the ones that replace them might live; and
> we do not do anything to replace the ones we kill.

Thus, the wild animals we kill are very seldom covered by conditions (b) and (c) of the replacement argument.

Nor can the replacement argument be used to justify the killing of most domesticated animals or animals bred and raised in captivity (e.g., for laboratory use). This is because most of these animals do not lead a life that is, on balance, worth living. Even when not in pain, most animals raised for slaughter or bred for laboratory use lead frustrated, boring lives that fall far short of the quality of life that makes being alive worthwhile.[3] Consequently, they are not covered by condition (a) of the replacement argument.

So although the replacement argument provides an intriguing puzzle for moral philosophers to ponder, it is of little or no consequence as a justification for our consumption of animals.

II. Six Ways of Evaluating Moral Standing

Turning to the puzzle, its solution depends on the way in which the lives of sentient individuals acquire moral value.[4] Our discussion of moral value to this point suggests that there is not a single, correct answer to that question. Since there is a variety of moral values, it is to be expected that there are different ways in which the lives of sentient individuals acquire moral value. Consequently, we will proceed here by considering six more or less standard ways in which the lives of sentient individuals can acquire moral value. After briefly describing each of these six ways, we can determine how well or ill they protect the individual against the replacement argument.

A. DESCRIBING THE SIX WAYS

The first two ways concern autonomy and the belief that autonomous individuals merit the moral right to life. Kant argues that autonomous individuals ought (morally) to be treated as ends in themselves because autonomy is a necessary condition for the possibility of morality.[5] The argument here can be formulated as follows:

A1: Morality is an unqualified good.
A2: Consequently, the source of morality ought to be given the strongest of moral protections (i.e., moral rights).
A3: Autonomous agents are the source of morality—but only, we may presume, while they are alive.
A4: Therefore, autonomous agents ought to have moral rights, including the right to life.

Thus, so long as individuals capable of doing what is morally$_{ad}$ right are innocent of crime, they are morally entitled to live.

We can describe this Kantian position as "the sufficient condition analog" to the agency requirement for having moral rights discussed in Chapter 8. What characterizes this position is the claim that (the capacity for) moral$_{ad}$ agency gives great moral value to the lives of certain individuals, thereby entitling them to the right to life. Kantians would doubtless claim that *only* this capacity gives great moral value to life. However, our analysis of moral value in Part I does not support such a claim. Consequently, we are not including it here. Also, Kant holds that "practical reason" is this capacity, while we have argued at length, in Chapter 3, that one can be a moral$_{ad}$ agent and sufficiently free to be held responsible for his or her actions without possessing Kantian practical reason (i.e., normal$_h$ intelligence). While these differences might lead a card-carrying Kantian to disown the position outlined here, they are not important to the central contention of this position—namely, that (the capacity for) moral$_{ad}$ agency entitles one to the moral right to life—and that contention seems properly labeled as coming from "the Kantian side" of common morality.

The second autonomy-based moral position we will consider here is summarized in the popular slogan, "We don't have the right to force our values onto others." The idea here is that if individuals are capable of valuing things for themselves, then they ought (morally) to be allowed to do so and to pursue their own values (as long as doing so is not unfairly injurious to other independent valuers). This allowance requires that these individuals have their lives protected by the moral right to life, since presumably one cannot pursue his or her values, if he or she is no longer alive.

This independent valuer concept of autonomy resembles but significantly differs from the Kantian conception, which focuses on the ability to recognize *moral* values. Beings may well exist that can value things (i.e., can take an interest in them) but that cannot recognize moral values. Some of the simpler, nonsocial, but still sentient forms of animal life may fit this description. Consequently, this independent valuer conception of autonomy may well encompass more beings than does the Kantian conception. This is so even though, as argued in Chapter 3, members of the human species are not the only animals capable of moral$_{ad}$ agency.

The belief that independent valuers ought to have moral rights has been a fundamental presumption of many natural rights and egoistic moral philosophies. In recent years, it has also become particularly important in work on medical ethics, where it underlies many arguments for patients' rights. In the animal rights movement, this belief has been championed by Tom Regan:

> The suggestion before us, then, is that all but the irreversibly comatose have inherent value because all these humans have a life which is of more or less positive or negative value for them, and this logically independently of whether they (the humans in question) are valued by anyone else. Here, therefore, we have a way of illuminating why it would be wrong to treat these humans merely as a means. This would be wrong be-

cause it would fail to acknowledge and respect the fact that they are the subjects of a life whose value is logically independent of any other being's taking an interest in it. Thus, in treating these humans merely as means one treats them as if their value was logically dependent on their answering to the needs, purposes, etc., of others, when in fact, they, as the subjects of a more or less good life, have value that is logically independent of their being valued as a means by anyone else.[6]

The wide acceptance in current moral philosophy, both professional and popular, of the idea that being an independent valuer entitles one to moral rights, including the right to life, seems beyond question—although most people, philosophers included, seem to apply this idea only to humans.

However, that this idea is justified is not so obviously beyond question. Regan's "illumination" of why it is wrong to treat independent valuers merely as means does not help to justify this idea, for in so treating other such valuers I need not treat them "as if their value was logically dependent on their answering to [my] needs." I can certainly "acknowledge" but fail to (morally) "respect" the value others place on things, including their own lives. For example, if I guard, chain, or cage slaves or animals in order to keep them from escaping my control, that shows that I recognize that they place a different value on their lives and conditions than I do. I could even be said thereby to "respect" their values in the pragmatic way one respects the power of and danger posed by an adversary. However, I do not "respect" their evaluations of their lives and conditions in the moral sense of the term; that is, I do not honor those evaluations, treat them as a basis for rights, consider them to constitute justified claims to something and against me, or feel obligated not to interfere with responsible attempts to fulfill those evaluations. Such lack of moral respect does not commit the faux pas of denying what these individuals in fact are, namely, independent valuers. It merely indicates that I am willing to deny these individuals the satisfaction of their interests in order to satisfy my own. Consequently, Regan's "illumination" does not show why this attitude toward other independent valuers is morally objectionable.

Perhaps the following will suffice to make this second autonomy-based position sufficiently credible for our purposes. We can justify this second conception of the moral respect due autonomy in much the way Kant justifies his position:

B1: The second of our three common, moral goals refers to increasing the enjoyment and fulfillment in life.

B2: This indicates that enjoyment and fulfillment are moral goods.

B3: Therefore, just as these goods merit our moral respect, so those who bring these moral goods into existence merit our moral respect, including rights, such as the right to life, to protect their ability to produce these goods.

B4: It is independent valuers who bring enjoyment and fulfillment into existence, since these are states of experiencing beings.

B5: Therefore, independent valuers are entitled to the moral right to life.

This argument gives a utilitarian twist to Kant's argument, which might make it unacceptable to anti-utilitarians like Regan. However, for those of us who lack that antipathy, the argument seems commonsensical and reasonable enough.

The difference between this and Kant's argument is that this argument does not accept Kant's contention that "Nothing in the world—indeed even beyond the world—can possibly be conceived which could be called good without qualification except a *good will.*"[7] We have already argued extensively, in Part I, against that contention, and our mixed utilitarian, common morality also disputes Kant—perhaps "the common rational knowledge of morals" is not now what it was in eighteenth-century Prussia. Be that as it may, once we recognize that enjoyment and fulfillment are counted among our moral goals, extending moral rights to all independent valuers, whether or not they are (capable of being) fully moral$_{ad}$ agents, would seem to be the form that showing moral respect for the producers of moral value ought (logically) to take. Furthermore, such encompassing moral respect should help to insure that all independent valuers have a fair chance at an enjoyable, fulfilling life, thereby contributing to fulfilling the third of our common, moral goals.

I shall label the first of these autonomy-based moral positions "the moral agency view" and the second variety "the independent valuer view" of what gives moral value to the lives of sentient individuals.

The remaining four views are all forms of utilitarianism. I propose, following Peter Singer here, to divide utilitarianism into enjoyment (Singer's "classical") vs. preference theories and total population (Singer's "total view") vs. prior existence theories.[8]

Enjoyment utilitarianism commands us to do that which will maximize the excess of enjoyment over distress in life (or to minimize the converse), while preference utilitarianism commands us to do that which will accord with the preferences of those to be affected by our actions. These two forms of utilitarianism can lead to significantly different conclusions. Because of ignorance or selfishness, we may not prefer that which would maximize the excess of enjoyment over distress. Also, we can prefer things (e.g., life) the loss of which need not occasion unpleasant feelings.

The total population form of utilitarianism commands us to maximize the amount of utilitarian good in the world, while the prior existence view commands us to maximize that good for the feeling or preferring beings already in the world. The difference between these two forms of utilitarianism is that the former, but not the latter, requires direct concern for the future enjoyment or fulfillment of unborn generations. On the prior existence view, the future interests of the unborn may have to be taken into account, but only insofar as the prospect of their satisfaction or frustration affects the enjoyment or fulfillment of currently existing individuals.

Combining these two distinctions yields four versions of utilitarianism: the preference–total population view, the preference–prior existence view, the enjoyment–prior existence view, and the enjoyment–total population view. On all four of these views, the contribution an individual's life makes to the utilitarian good will, of course, be the measure of that life's moral value.

B. SIX EVALUATIONS OF THE REPLACEMENT ARGUMENT

Now, what is the moral value of the lives of sentient individuals, and especially of animals, from these six perspectives, and is that value capable of protecting the individual against the replacement argument?

On the moral agency view, the paradigm case is that of individuals who have had the opportunity to do wrong but have not done so. This expression of good moral character may be said to have "earned" these individuals moral rights. Just as hard workers have earned their wage, so people of good moral character have earned an enjoyable, fulfilling life, and in this world, at least, moral individuals' interests, and their attempts to fulfill them, must be morally protected if they are to achieve the enjoyment and fulfillment to which they are entitled. Among these interests, as far as we know, is the need to be alive in order to experience enjoyment and fulfillment. So although killing one individual of good moral character and replacing him with another would not reduce the amount of good moral character in the world, it would deprive the slain individual of what he is due on the basis of his good moral character. Giving the replacement individual what the slain individual was due would not, of course, rectify this injustice.

Thus, the moral agency view protects the individual against the replacement argument because, on this view, the individual's life has moral value not only as one among many alternative ways of fulfilling a necessary condition for accomplishing moral$_{ad}$ deeds. It also has moral value as an irreplaceable condition for enjoying the fruits of one's moral labors.

Although bringing in the idea of "the capacity for" moral$_{ad}$ agency as a basis for moral rights strains the analogy with workers who have earned their wage, it is an accommodation this position must make to the fact that we do not spring forth fully grown but, rather, begin as children. Many animals also enjoy the protection of the moral agency view, and with less strain, since even if they cannot be fully moral$_{ad}$ agents, many animals are virtuous agents. Consequently, they have earned moral rights through their virtuous—which is to say, normally decent—lives. Thus, although the moral agency view might not protect all animals against the replacement argument—since it might be that not all animals are capable of being virtuous—it would protect many animals.

Turning to the independent valuer view, we note that it holds that we ought (morally) to respect all individuals capable of forming their own values. As what counts as moral$_{ad}$ agency is a controversial point in applying the moral agency view, so what counts as "valuing" is a controversial point in applying this view. In Chapters 7 and 9, we noted that some philosophers try to make valuing out to be an abstract, conceptual process of which preference behavior does not provide significant evidence:

> To be a possible subject of misfortunes which are not merely unpleasant experiences, one must be able to desire and value certain things. The kind of misfortune which is in question here is death, and to discover whether this is a misfortune for an animal, we must ask whether, or in what sense, animals don't want to die. Of course, in some sense this is true of virtually all animals, which manifest acute fear when their lives are threatened. Yet blindly clinging on to life is not the same as wanting to live because one *values* life. This is the kind of desire for life of which persons are capable. It is this which gives sense to the claim that death is a misfortune, even a tragedy, for a person.[9]

Thus, for these humanist philosophers, normal$_h$ intelligence and linguistic ability are necessary both for being able to make one's own evaluations and for communicating to others that one has this capacity.

We have already argued at length against this sort of position, again in Chapters 7 and 9. So let us here just reaffirm that it is arbitrary to restrict the use of terms like "valuing" to referring to mental processes requiring something like normal$_h$ intelligence. Infants, children, and animals are capable of being happy and clearly want, desire, prefer, grab for, pursue, and "value" that which makes them happy. Similar things could be said about what makes them unhappy. When describing an infant who hugs a doll all day long and resists loudly and aggressively whenever someone tries to take the doll away, it would be strange to say something like "Martha loves the doll, but she does not value it." Yet that is the sort of thing that would follow from restricting "valuing" to intellectual processes of which infants and other nonlanguage users are incapable. Such strained locutions suggest that a technical, uncommon definition is at work.

Also, we can usually tell what infants, children, and animals want, prefer, value, and so on without being told what they want. We need only watch their course of action. In the previous example, we do not need to hear Martha say "I love the doll" in order to recognize that she does. Again, to claim, as these humanist philosophers apparently would, that Martha's behavior shows only that she "wants" the doll, not that she "values" it, would be strange and stipulative.

Thus, possessing normal$_h$ intelligence or having linguistic ability is not necessary for being (and for being recognized as being) an independent valuer. Such intelligence and ability are necessary only for having and communicating certain kinds of desires, wants, preferences, values, and so forth. All that is required for being (and for being recognized as being) an independent valuer is being a sentient agent.

If we employ this conclusion in applying the independent valuer view, it follows that (*ceteris paribus*) we ought (morally) to respect the values and pursuits of all sentient agents. Included among these values will be some reflexive ones, that is, values that would be expressed in the form "I would like to be in condition *x*." Having a warm, dry place during a storm would be such a reflexive value. When caught in a storm, we do not desire merely that there be such places and that they be occupied and enjoyed; we want to occupy and enjoy those places ourselves. It further follows, then, that

> since sentient agents cannot, presumably, pursue their values unless they are alive and
> since another, replacement individual would, at least in the reflexive cases, pursue her own values, rather than those of the individual she replaces,
> it follows that the independent valuer view protects individuals, including animals, against the replacement argument.

Thus, both autonomy-based moral positions deny that replacing a (humanely) slain animal with another, similar individual renders that killing morally permissible. In many cases, either such killing and replacing denies the animal of good moral character the reward it has earned, or it denies the sentient agent the opportunity to continue pursuing its own values. So on both views, animals can merit the moral right to life, and this conclusion follows without our presuming that animals contemplate and directly value their lives and without our postulating that the lives of sentient individuals have a special, intrinsic value.

It does not follow from this conclusion that it is never morally permissible to call upon another, animal or human, to sacrifice his life or to have his life sacrificed. Having to defend the community against clear, present, and severe danger, as in time of war, could make such sacrifices morally permissible—at least as far as the two autonomy-based positions we have developed here are concerned. Neither of these two positions leads to the conclusion that the life of a sentient or moral$_{ad}$ individual cannot (morally) be weighed against other moral goods and cannot (morally) be sacrificed in the pursuit of those goods. Our conclusion here is simply that from both of these autonomy-based views, taking a sentient or moral$_{ad}$ individual's life involves a morally serious loss, even if she is replaced with a similar individual. Consequently, such taking of life is not morally justified by such replacement; the moral justification for taking the life of a sentient or moral$_{ad}$ individual must be sought elsewhere, when it exists at all.

Turning to the utilitarian options, the preference–total population view tells us to do that which will accord with the preferences of those currently alive and the likely preferences of future generations. As valuing has sometimes been made out to be an intellectual activity, so preferring is sometimes made out to be an activity requiring self-contemplation and the projection and analysis of future alternatives. For example, Peter Singer writes:

> A being which cannot see itself as an entity with a future cannot have a preference about its own future existence. This is not to deny that such a being might struggle against a situation in which its life is in danger, as a fish struggles to get free of the barbed hook in its mouth; but this indicates no more than a preference for the cessation of a state of affairs that is perceived as painful or threatening. Struggle against danger and pain does not suggest that the fish is capable of preferring its own future existence to nonexistence.[10]

Immediately, one may wonder how a being that cannot see itself as a being with a future could possibly perceive a state of affairs to be "threatening" or could possibly struggle against "danger." Singer's attempt both to acknowledge some obviously value-expressing behavior of animals and to deny that they have preferences seems to be self-contradictory.

Furthermore, desiring seems to be a paradigm of preferring, and as argued in Chapter 7, desiring requires neither reflective self-consciousness nor great intellectual ability. Of course, we may desire something yet prefer that it not happen, as when our desires conflict with our moral commitments. However, failing such conflicts, to desire x is to prefer that it occur. We would suspect some stipulative definition is at work if we heard someone say something like, "I desire x and feel no conflicting desires or values, yet I do not prefer that x occur."

Again, if a presumption is to be made, it would seem reasonable to presume that no matter how limited their self-consciousness, intellect, and sense of time, all sentient beings have preferences. This is because there would be no evolutionary point to their being sentient if they could not recognize, desire, and pursue those things that give them pleasure and recognize, desire to avoid, and seek to avoid those things that give them pain.[11]

Finally, when it is claimed that animals cannot have a preference for life, it is presumed that to prefer life requires contemplating life and death. But why should "preferring" x require that we contemplate x (i.e., concern ourselves with x) when the question of x is not raised by the environment? Cannot we be properly described as "preferring" x if whenever our environment raises the issue of x, we pursue x (*ceteris paribus*)? It does not seem to do harm to the logic of "preferring" to say that an animal that acts to preserve its life when it is threatened "prefers" to remain alive and is amply demonstrating that preference. Many animals even seem to experience and to cope with the conflict of desires that some philosophers might try to insist is essential to the logic of "preferring." For example, when faced with danger to their young or group, many animals seem both to want to flee and to feel that they must stay and defend their young or group. Perhaps humans are the only animals that are morbid enough to contemplate life and death when that issue is not forced upon them, but preferring life to death does not require such morbid fascination.

It follows that when trying, as preference–total population utilitarians, to figure out what will best accord with the preferences of those who will likely be affected by our actions, we must recognize that many animals must be included. Like children, they are desiring, sentient agents, even if they are not self-contemplative beings. Again as is the case with children, the animals' behavior can make their preferences known to us, and among these preferences will ordinarily be a desire not to be killed, even though the existence of this desire may become obvious only in life-threatening situations.

Also, even if the animal is not aware that its long-term existence is required to fulfill some of its desires (e.g., the raising of its young), its remaining alive for a long period of time may be necessary for fulfilling those preferences. Consequently, doing what accords with those preferences requires morally protecting the animal's life. Furthermore, among the animal's current preferences will ordinarily be a number that are reflexive (e.g., its desire to lie in the sun). Killing the individual will frustrate these preferences, even if she is replaced by another animal with similar preferences. Thus the killing of a nonself-contemplative animal and replacing it with another is a morally significant act on the preference–total population view.

Whether killing and replacing an individual with preferences is morally permissible remains undecided, however—and that is true whether we are dealing with animals or with humans. Self-contemplative beings have an advantage here over the nonself-contemplative, for they can prefer not to worry about being slain and replaced while their demise is still far off, whereas nonself-contemplative beings cannot have such a preference. They can only prefer not to be killed, and that only when the time of their death is close at hand. However, if the possibility of long-range foreknowledge of one's destruction and replacement could be eliminated—merely a technological problem—then the permissibility of killing and replacement would be the same for both humans and animals on the preference–total population view.[12]

An allied but more fundamental issue concerns the fulfilling of long-range preferences, such as raising a family and living out one's natural life-span. If individual A is killed and replaced by B, who has similar short- and long-range preferences and who is then allowed to live out her natural life-span, then (*ceteris paribus*) there would be no loss on preference-total population grounds through this slaughter and replacement. However, if B is killed and replaced by C, who is then killed and replaced by D, and so forth in a process that regularly kills and replaces individuals before their long-range preferences can be fulfilled, then these long-range preferences will never be fulfilled. This will represent a morally significant loss from the option of allowing A to live out her normal life-span, which would give her the option of satisfying both her short- and long-range preferences. In this way, preference-total population utilitarianism would protect the individual against the replacement argument where an indefinite sequence of killings and replacings was contemplated. Since that is precisely what is contemplated where the sacrificing of animals for human benefit in the food industry, laboratories, the fur business, and so forth, preference-total population utilitarianism would seem to condemn these consumptions of animals.

However, counterbalancing this protection is the possibility, perhaps even likelihood, that during the early years of life one has and (ordinarily) has the chance of fulfilling more short-range preferences than during later years. If that is so, then a greater quantity of preferences might be fulfilled by sacrificing the fulfillment of long-range preferences in favor of generating and fulfilling more short-range interests by killing the elderly and replacing them with youngsters. This would, of course, leave individuals vulnerable to the replacement argument. Thus, although preference-total population utilitarianism does offer the individual (animal as well as human) some protection against the replacement argument, that protection is much less secure than is the protection offered by the two autonomy-based moral viewpoints. In the case of nonrepetitive slaughter and replacement, preference-total population utilitarianism offers the individual no protection against the replacement argument whatsoever. And in the case of an indefinite sequence of slaughters and replacements, the protection it seems to offer may be a mirage.

Moving on, we may deal with both the enjoyment-prior existence and the preference-prior existence forms of utilitarianism at one stroke. Both of these views limit direct moral concern to currently existing individuals, thereby unequivocally protecting the individual against the replacement argument. That argument presumes that the future enjoyments or fulfillments of the unborn can be used to compensate for the losses suffered by the slain. By limiting our direct moral obligations to currently existing individuals, prior existence views deny that the future enjoyment or fulfillment of the unborn can be morally equated with the enjoyment or fulfillment of currently existing individuals. So any prior existence view will protect the individual against the replacement argument.

Turning to enjoyment-total population utilitarianism, we see that it requires us to do that which will maximize the excess of enjoyment over distress in life. From this viewpoint, killing, even painlessly, is a morally significant, negative act, for it eliminates the possibility of the future excess enjoyment for the slain (assuming that the future could have held an excess of enjoyment over distress for the slain individual and that death does not lead to a more enjoyable form of existence than continuing life would have). However, if another individual with similar prospects for the future is substituted for the slain individual (and would be brought into existence only if the other were slain), then the balance of enjoyment and distress in life is unaffected. Consequently, enjoyment-total population utilitarianism gives moral significance to sentient life but does not provide any protection for the individual against the replacement argument. Unlike preference-total population utilitarianism, this is true whether or not an indefinite sequence of killing and replacing is involved. The individual is merely a "receptacle" for enjoyment; so as long as there is a ready supply of receptacles to replace the broken ones, nothing important will be lost through the breakage.

Once again, this conclusion applies to humans as well as to animals. If humans are not distressed by foreknowledge of their impending destruction and replacement (because the practice is hidden from them) or if enjoyment is sufficiently less in later years than in earlier years to counterbalance the depression caused by knowing that one is to be killed and replaced by a youngster, then the enjoyment-total population view could not only permit but even require the killing and replacement of humans. Since humans have greater ability to foresee their destruction and replacement than do animals, there would be greater technological problems in applying the replacement argument to humans than to animals. However, humans' extensive foresight provides no more fundamental obstacle to killing and replacement on the enjoyment-total population view than does the limited foresight of animals. The only differences here are the details of implementation.

Once it has been argued, as it was above, that animals have preferences, it can be seen that the difference between enjoyment and preference forms of utilitarianism is not the most crucial one where the question is the permissibility of killing and replacement. Whether one is dealing with humans or animals and with maximizing enjoyment or fulfillment, a more crucial issue is whether a total population view or a prior existence view will be adopted. Prior existence views will definitely protect the individual against the replacement argument, while total population views definitely will not, if maximizing enjoyment is the goal, and only may or may not, if fulfilling preferences is the goal.

III. Total Population vs. Prior Existence Utilitarianism

This conclusion naturally leads to the question, to the degree that we are utilitarians—and the second of our three common moral goals is utilitarian—is there some reason that impels us to be total population rather than prior existence utilitarians?

That total population utilitarianism could, while prior existence utilitarianism could not, justify the killing and replacement of humans would, in the eyes of most people, philosophers included, put a heavy burden of proof on the shoulders of the proponents of the total population view. Also, as Peter Singer points out, total population utilitarianism has the counter-intuitive consequence that it requires us to bring into the world as many individuals enjoying a good utilitarian life as possible. It follows that a couple whose enjoyment or fulfillment would be compromised by a smaller amount than the excess of enjoyment or fulfillment awaiting a child they could have would be under a moral obligation to have that child.[13] Prior existence utilitarianism leads to no such conclusion.

However, Singer also argues that prior existence utilitarianism leads to another, equally counter-intuitive conclusion:

> How do we square prior existence utilitarianism with our intuitions about the case when a couple are considering having a child who, perhaps because it will inherit a genetic defect, would lead a thoroughly miserable life and die before its second birthday? We would think it wrong for a couple knowingly to conceive such a child.[14]

Singer goes on to provide the following resolution for this problem but also indicates that he finds this answer insufficient:

> Perhaps the best one can say—and it is not very good—is that there is nothing *directly* wrong in conceiving a child who will be miserable, but once such a child exists, since its life can contain nothing but misery, we would reduce the amount of pain in the world by an act of euthanasia. But euthanasia is a more harrowing process for the parents and others involved than non-conception. Hence, we have an indirect reason for not conceiving a child bound to have a miserable existence.[15]

I would agree that this indirect answer does not provide an adequate response to the problem Singer has raised for prior existence utilitarianism. However, the following can be added to provide an adequate response to this problem.

Regarding the matter of our intuitions concerning this case, I doubt that we have any, for this is an utterly fantastic case. Cases somewhat like it do occur, but they are cases where there is a statistically significant chance that a couple's infant will inherit a debilitating defect—and, of course, a statistically significant chance that it will not. I do not find that there is a well-established intuition that it would be wrong for a couple to consider conceiving a child under such circumstances, especially if they are prepared to abort a fetus discovered to have inherited the debilitating defect. Similarly, we encounter cases of people whose children will certainly, as far as we can know of such things, inherit their defects (e.g., retardation or blindness), and will consequently be condemned to leading a life that those accustomed to life without the defect might not find sufficiently enjoyable or fulfilling. However, those people may find that life sufficiently enjoyable or fulfilling and, consequently, may feel that they are not bringing misery into the world by having children. Again, it is not intuitively obvious that they are wrong.

In contrast to such real cases, Singer's case verges on being inconceivable. Singer's couple must be so desperate to conceive their own child that they would bring a monstrosity into the world and care for it, knowing with virtual certainty that it will live in misery for two years and then die.[16] The couple must prefer to go through all this and put the child through all this, instead of adopting a healthy child. I doubt that such people exist, and consequently I doubt that this case has moral import.

But if such people did exist, they would have a perverted idea of reproducing and parenting and would show, by keeping the child alive for its two miserable years, their willingness to use others merely as means to their own satisfaction. Consequently, this whole project of parenting would express a kind of demented character that would give the project a strong immoral value. I think that this bad-character evaluation accounts for one idea that, I presume, Singer intended to suggest with this case, namely, that there would be something demented, perverse, selfish, or severely morally insensitive involved in bringing a miserable child into the world—or even in just seriously contemplating doing so. Prior existence utilitarianism can account for this intuition, since this is an evaluation of character, and prior existence utilitarianism no more precludes making character evaluations than does the total population view.

A second weakness in Singer's analysis is that he runs together three stages in the process of bringing a miserable child into the world that are importantly different in their moral value:

    (i) intending to conceive such a child,
    (ii) conceiving such a child, and
    (iii) keeping such a child alive.

If we clearly separate our common moral evaluations of these stages, we shall see that Singer's argument against the prior existence view disappears.

As just discussed, (i) is a bizarre project and expresses bad moral character if the prospective parents intend to keep the child alive. If, however, they intend to abort the potentially miserable child before it develops sufficiently to suffer, then their intention is to satisfy their bizarre compulsion to conceive in a way that does no direct harm from any utilitarian viewpoint. Far from being wrong, such a project would be morally praiseworthy;

    it shows tolerance for unusual psychological needs;

    it expresses, in the parents' willingness to abort the presentient fetus, a commitment to the idea that it is not species membership but the capacity for enjoyment or fulfillment that makes a being morally significant; and it responsibly projects a course of action that will satisfy the bizarre needs of the couple without (directly) causing harm to or frustrating the preferences of anyone else.

Thus, on utilitarian grounds, "considering having a miserable child" is not obviously wrong, and the prior existence view can accommodate the character evaluations that are involved in morally evaluating stage (i).

As for stage (ii), if we set aside the enjoyment or fulfillment that is ordinarily immediately involved and presume that rape, incest, and the like are not at issue, it is morally neutral. There is nothing directly either morally right or wrong with conceiving a child that, if it is allowed to develop, will lead a thoroughly miserable life. Conceiving such a child could be wrong for the indirect reason Singer notes, namely, that aborting the presentient fetus could be more disturbing for the couple (and for others, too, perhaps) than not conceiving at all. But conceiving such a child could also be morally justifiable if the suffering associated with abortion were less than the frustration of not conceiving, or if, as suggested in note 16, the production of such a fetus were important for medical progress.

Conceiving a potentially miserable child can be considered analogous to the moderate use of alcohol or other potentially debilitating drugs. By itself, it is either morally innocuous or morally positive because of the immediate enjoyment or fulfillment it provides. It becomes morally objectionable only if it is allowed to lead to consequences whose disvalue outweighs that immediate good. As long as one takes steps to insure that these adverse consequences will not occur, there is nothing directly wrong with such indulgences in the potentially harmful.

Finally, allowing a thoroughly and incurably miserable child to continue to suffer would, under ordinary conditions, clearly be immoral. Only the possibility of thereby making a great contribution to easing the suffering of others could justify keeping such a child alive. Satisfying the compulsion of the parents to have a living product of their own loins pales by comparison with the misery of such an infant. However, prior existence utilitarianism has no problem accounting for this common evaluation of stage (iii), for at this stage, the suffering child is an existing, sentient being. So at the stage where we intuitively feel that a serious wrong is clearly being done to the suffering child, prior existence utilitarianism also finds that, *ceteris paribus*, having (i.e., keeping) such a child is wrong.

Thus, Singer's case seems to pose a problem for prior existence utilitarianism only if we illicitly transfer the intuitively negative moral evaluation of keeping an incurably miserable child alive back to the consideration of having such a child and the conceiving of it. If we clearly distinguish these three stages, we can see that considering having a child who will be miserable if it is allowed to live and even conceiving such a child do not bring misery into the world. Misery is brought into the world only when that child has developed to the point where it can suffer and when it is allowed to continue to live and suffer. "Bringing a miserable life into the world" refers to actualizing (or allowing to start operating) the capacity to suffer of an already existing individual. Consequently, the difference between "bringing a miserable life into the world" and "bringing misery into a life" is limited to the fact that in the latter case the individual's capacity to feel enjoyment and distress (or to have fulfilled or frustrated preferences) has already been operating for a while, while in the former case we are considering its initial actualization. Since in both cases the individual already exists, this difference cannot provide grounds for criticizing prior existence utilitarianism.

Finally, Singer maintains that in order to be an acceptable moral theory, prior existence utilitarianism must be able to explain the following asymmetry:

> If the pleasure a possible child will have is not a reason *for* bringing it into the world, why is the pain a possible child will experience a reason *against* bringing it into the world? The prior existence view must explain the asymmetry between cases of possible children who are likely to have pleasant lives, and possible children who are likely to have miserable lives.[17]

However, there is no need for such an explanation, for there is no asymmetry here. The possible happy life of a normal child and the possible miserable life of a deformed child become reasons for having (i.e., keeping) the normal child and not having (i.e., aborting) the deformed child only when the child is already in existence and its capacity for happiness or misery is ready to be actualized. At that stage, the obligation to keep the normal child is as strong (on either enjoyment or preference views) as is the obligation to abort the deformed child. Similarly, seriously considering conceiving and keeping an assuredly miserable child is ordinarily an expression of bad moral character, while seriously considering conceiving and keeping a normal child is ordinarily an expression of good (i.e., responsible, generous, or loving) character.[18] The actual conceiving of either child is, of course, in itself just enjoyable or fulfilling (*ceteris paribus*).

So at each of our three stages, there is symmetry in our evaluations concerning parenting a normal child and parenting a miserable one. I would guess that Singer believes there is an asymmetry here because he is comparing our obligation (given current liberal intuitions) to abort an already existing, though not yet sentient, seriously deformed child with our lack of obligation (again, given current liberal intuitions) to conceive normal children. But once again, if we clearly distinguish intention, conception, and maintenance, the supposed obstacle to accepting prior existence utilitarianism disappears.

To summarize this discussion of Singer's objection to prior existence utilitarianism, first, that objection is based on a fantastic case, and the fate of moral theories does not hang on their ability to handle the fantastic. Second, what would be demented or perverse in the project of parenting Singer describes is the character of the prospective parents, and prior existence utilitarianism has no more difficulty making character evaluations than does the total population view. Third, if we clearly distinguish the three stages of the project—considering having a miserable child, conceiving such a child, and keeping the child alive—it becomes clear that there is a definite, direct, moral wrong only at the third stage. However, since the child already exists at that stage, prior existence utilitarianism has no difficulty accounting for that wrong. Finally, the prior existence view does not require an asymmetry in the criteria employed in determining our obligations concerning having or not having normal or miserable children. Thus, Singer's challenge to prior existence utilitarianism has been met. (And the strategy employed here does not suggest that a similar response to his challenge to total population utilitarianism could be made—here there is an asymmetry.)

IV. Prior Existence Utilitarianism and Obligations to Future Generations

There is another objection to prior existence utilitarianism, but not to the total population view, which might be raised here: the prior existence view would seem to rule out direct obligations to future generations. We could, of course, have obligations to respect how currently existing people (and animals?) feel about the life prospects of future generations. But since they do not yet exist, it would seem that we could not have obligations to future generations themselves.

This might seem a serious problem, for the idea of our obligations to future generations is a fairly common one in environmental ethics. Nonetheless, concluding that we do not have obligations to future generations would not pose an obstacle for the development of an effective environmental ethic. On any given day, our obligation to do that which will maximize the long-range enjoyment or fulfillment of those currently alive commits us to looking seventy-five to one hundred years into the future.[19] I doubt that we are capable of making significant projections of use patterns, preferences, technological developments, and other important matters concerning the quality of life more than seventy-five to one hundred years into the future. Consequently, if we insure that our environmentally significant practices will not lead us (humans and animals) to be dissatisfied with the quality of life available to us seventy-five to one hundred years hence, we will be doing the best we can.

Also, every time a decision must be made about maintaining, altering, or abandoning a program, that decision would have to be based on a consideration of what would be best for the seventy-five to one hundred years stretching into the future from that date. It follows that the future a prior existence utilitarian would have to consider is continually rolling forward. Consequently, forgoing the idea of direct obligations to future generations would not cripple environmental ethics.

Still, it may not be necessary for prior existence utilitarians to forgo this popular concept. Although the future existence of some individual (e.g., "the son I some day hope to have") is decidely tenuous, the future existence of generations of sentient beings is assured, unless we suffer some global, natural or human-made catastrophe. Consequently, it would not be inappropriate to require that prior existence utilitarians include among their moral deliberations a concern with the likely effects of their actions on the enjoyment or fulfillment of future generations. Since those generations are (*ceteris paribus*) definitely going to exist, it could reasonably be claimed that, for utilitarian purposes, they already do have a sort of existence and must be included in our moral deliberations.

This sort of extension of the concept of existence and of prior existence utilitarianism would go far toward reducing the difference between the prior existence and the total population views. Consequently, it might be thought that this extension would eliminate the protection that the prior existence view provides the individual against the replacement argument but that the total population view does not.

However, where the replacement argument is concerned, these two forms of utilitarianism would remain significantly different. This is because the replacement argument concerns individuals who will come into being at our behest and only on the condition that they are bred to be replacements for those we kill. Consequently, replacement individuals cannot be numbered among those generations that will (*ceteris paribus*) naturally, assuredly come to be. It follows that even if prior existence utilitarianism is understood in a way that includes obligations to naturally assured future generations, it would still not permit us to justify killing certain individuals by replacing them with equally well-off individuals. "Extended prior existence utilitarianism" could justify compromising the enjoyment or fulfillment of the currently existing population in order better to assure (as far as we could tell) the enjoyment or fulfillment of naturally assured future generations, but such generations are not the subject of the replacement argument.

V. Summary

To summarize our discussion of the replacement argument, four of the six moral theories we have considered extend moral value to life in a way that definitely protects individual humans and animals from the replacement argument. The only moral theories considered here that do not definitely provide such protection are the two forms of total population utilitarianism, and preference-total population utilitarianism may also provide such protection. However, the total population view could justify the killing and replacement of humans, as well as of animals, and would obligate us to have as many children and to breed as many animals as the earth can support without diminishing the overall utilitarian good in the world. The other four moral theories considered here do not encounter these difficulties.

So if these other theories do not fall prey to other, more serious difficulties—and we have seen that some proposed objections to prior existence utilitarianism fail—there is ample, animal-independent reason for us to reject the total population view and to adopt the extended prior existence view in interpreting the utilitarian component in our common morality. Even those like Peter Singer who seem to be intent on being just utilitarians are free to be extended prior existence utilitarians. Either way, this completely undercuts the replacement argument. Consequently, from a theoretical, as well as from a practical, perspective, the replacement argument does not pose a serious obstacle to recognizing that animals ought (morally) to share in the right to life.

Part IV

A Few Consequences

ANIMALS ARE the most extensively and thoroughly exploited group on earth. Consequently, liberating animals would have the largest impact on our lives of any moral reform movement to date. It would require significant changes in our diet, in our apparel, including cosmetics, in our entertainment, in our product testing, research, and educational techniques, in our stock of available chemicals, in our land development and use, and in our laws, governmental agencies, and priorities of law enforcement. Just what the details of these changes would be is not obvious.

For example, it is not obvious that liberating animals would entail veganism (complete abstinence from animal products) or even lacto-ovo vegetarianism. It is easy enough to come up with examples of ways of producing wool and eggs that would provide sheep and hens with a good quality of life in exchange for those products. As we shall see in Chapter 11, these examples can be extended to nonexploitive, nonmisery-generating ways of producing meat. On the other hand, eating meat might, once we have liberated animals, be as repugnant to us as eating human flesh is today. Exactly where liberating animals would lead us is something we can discover only as we go along.

Consequently, the following chapters will not be devoted to developing detailed proposals for carrying out the liberation of animals. Chapter 11 briefly details the dietary consequences of liberating animals—although not explicitly discussed, the consequences for using other animal products like wool and leather follow the same pattern developed in this chapter. It is argued that even though the animal liberation position developed above does not entail either veganism or vegetarianism, what it does entail, or is likely psychologically to produce, is only vanishingly different from vegetarianism. Chapter 12 draws some general conclusions about the extent and conduct of research that would be permitted with liberated animals. It includes a discussion of whether or not animals can consent

197

to being research subjects, and the moral (in)significance of this, and of the common presumptions that human life is morally worth more than animal life and that this justifies our sacrificing animals in research for human benefit. Chapter 13 deals with a popular attempt to show the absurdity of liberating animals: wouldn't we have to become nature's cops, trying to protect prey from predators? That such a conclusion is either absurd or entailed by animal liberation is questioned here, and general strategies for dealing with such attempts to laugh away calls for moral reform are developed. Chapter 14 deals with the relation between liberating animals and environmental ethics. Many people, philosophers included, seem to regard the animal rights and the environmental ethics movements as affiliated concerns, and some advocates of liberating animals have endeavored to portray animal liberation as a part of an enlightened environmental ethic.[1] However, such endeavors have often been rebuffed by environmental ethicists, and the relation between the two movements remains controversial.[2] Tom Regan's and J. Baird Callicott's conceptions of this relation are criticized and an alternative analysis, based on the animal liberation position developed above, is offered.

11

Vegetarianism

THE USE of animals for food probably represents the greatest exploitation of them at present. Several billion animals are "factory farmed" yearly in the United States alone, and probably trillions of fish are also harvested annually, to die, apparently in great distress, from suffocation. Such practices constitute a continuing, massive, uncompensated sacrifice of their interests for our benefit. One of the most striking differences between our traditional, "be kind to animals" morality and the contemporary animal liberation movement is that between the concern with humane slaughter but general indifference to meat-eating of the former and the common advocacy of vegetarianism and even of veganism (i.e., complete abstinence from the use of animal products) in the latter. Is vegetarianism or veganism entailed by the interpretation and defense of animal liberation developed above? At its simplest, the answer is "No," but explicating that simple answer will bring it very close to a "Yes."

I. The Simple Answer

The simple answer is "No," because vegetarianism, when understood as referring to not eating the flesh of animals, commonly employs the term "animal" in the biological sense that designates one of the two great organic kingdoms, "animal" vs. "vegetable." As emphasized in Chapter 5, animal liberation is not directly concerned with "animals" in that biological sense but with "animals" in the morally significant sense of sentient beings, that is, beings capable of feeling pleasure and pain, fulfillment and frustration, and so forth. There is no guarantee that the biological and moral terms designate precisely the same group of beings, and, indeed, there is reason to believe on behavioral and physiological grounds that the class of moral "animals" is smaller than that of biological "animals." For example, Peter Singer writes:

199

In my earlier discussion of the evidence we have that nonhuman animals are capable
of suffering, I suggested two indicators of this capacity: the behavior of the being,
whether it writhes, utters cries, attempts to escape from the source of pain, and so on;
and the similarity of the nervous system of the being to our own. . . . Most mollusks,
[oysters, clams, mussels, scallops, and the like], are such rudimentary beings that it is
difficult to imagine them feeling pain, or having other mental states. Those who want
to be absolutely certain that they are not causing suffering will not eat mollusks either;
but somewhere between a shrimp and an oyster seems as good a place to draw the line
as any, and better than most.[1]

It follows that arguments for deducing vegetarianism from animal liberation
that take the following form are invalid because they rest on an equivocation:

> A1: Animal liberation requires us to put an end to the exploiting of animals.
>
> A2: Animals are exploited when we consume them for food.
>
> A3: Therefore, animal liberation requires that we not consume animals for
> food, that is, requires that we become vegetarians.

In A1, "animals" clearly refers only to sentient beings. The same is true, although
perhaps not as obviously so, of "animals" in A2, since it would not make sense to
talk about (morally) "exploiting" nonsentient beings (see Chapter 14 for a discussion of this). However, in A3, "animals" must refer to all members of the animal
kingdom, since vegetarianism employs that sense of the term.

This equivocation is not a serious matter, however. It can be eliminated simply by stipulating that the term "animals" used in A3 is to be understood in the
same moral sense employed in A1 and A2. It will follow from this, of course, that
"vegetarianism" must also be understood in a morally relevant sense, namely, as
"not eating the flesh of sentient beings." This would definitely represent a change
in the meaning of the term, and some people would surely be perplexed by the
sight of a staunch animal liberation "vegetarian" eating a bowl of clam chowder.
However, some people have also thought it inconsistent for "vegetarians" to eat
eggs or dairy products, although many do. The term "vegetarian" long ago slipped
its etymological mooring of referring only to those who eat only vegetables and
has for at least a century and a half covered a range of those who avoid eating
animal flesh.[2] So further modifying the term to give it a clearly morally relevant
reference could be considered but a further stage in its evolution.

An alternative to this revision of ordinary language would be to remove the
equivocation by substituting "sentient beings" for "animals" throughout the argument and eliminating the reference to vegetarianism altogether. This would yield
the following, less ambiguous argument:

> A1′: Animal liberation requires us to put an end to the exploiting of sen-
> tient beings.

A2': Sentient beings are exploited when we consume them for food.

A3': Therefore, animal liberation requires that we not consume sentient beings for food.

The drawback to this formulation, from the animal liberationist's viewpoint, is that the term "sentient being" is not a common one, and, consequently, arguments employing it will commonly not be understood. For example, if we follow the suggestion in the quotation above from Peter Singer and conclude that liberating animals would permit eating only those (biological) animals that are neurologically as simple as or simpler than oysters, then animal liberation would require a diet very similar to that of a vegetarian—especially if factory farmed eggs and dairy products were also avoided—yet many, perhaps most, people seeing this argument would not realize this. This problem is another example of why, as discussed in Chapter 5, animal liberationists prefer using the word "animal."

Again, the source of the difficulty here is that animal liberation employs "animal" in a moral sense, while "vegetarianism" is ordinarily defined using the biological sense of that term. Consequently, unless and until it is shown that these two senses of "animal" designate the same group of beings, detailing the relation between animal liberation and vegetarianism is going to require juggling terms a bit. Fortunately, this is merely a verbal issue and consequently need not detain us further. Which of the alternatives above to choose is a question of convenience.

II. Exploiting, Slaughtering, and Harvesting

There is another, not merely verbal difficulty with the argument above in either of its formulations: Is A2 (A2') correct, or are there nonexploitive ways of using animals (sentient beings) for food? (Throughout the remainder of this discussion, "animal" will be used in its moral sense, and "A2" will be used to refer to both A2 and A2'.) Interpreted as an immediately practical question (i.e., "Are there readily available, nonexploitive ways of producing large supplies of inexpensive meat for our large, predominantly urban population?"), I think that the answer is almost certainly "No." It follows, if I am right about that, that in the context of immediate, practical concerns, A2 is correct. But let us set aside such concerns and ask the broader question, "Is the use of animals for food inherently exploitive?" The answer to that question is also "No," but from that negative response it follows that the bald assertion in A2 is *in*correct.

The possibility that is usually raised as a counter-example to the claim that meat production is inherently exploitive is that of providing animals with a pleasant life and painless slaughter. A common response to this counter-example is that painless slaughter would be so extraordinarily difficult to accomplish, especially as a routine procedure, as to make it very nearly a merely logical possibility. In the discussion of the suffering of food animals, "pain" is used to cover not only the intensely unpleasant sensations caused by a knife, bullet, or other implement slicing through one's body but also the anticipatory fear of being taken to slaughter, the distress of helplessness that an animal may experience in being sedated or anesthetized for it knows not what reason, and the distress that the individual likely feels as life ebbs away. It follows that truly painless slaughter would have to be totally unanticipated and instantaneous, and it is doubtful that any process for the routine killing of animals could meet these requirements.

Furthermore, even if some process for truly painless slaughter could be devised, that process would not necessarily constitute a counter-example to A2. This is because an animal so killed would still suffer the loss of the rest of its life, and, as argued in Chapter 9, assuming the remainder of the animal's life could have been of sufficient quality to make it worth living, that is a morally significant loss. Unless the animal could be fairly compensated for that loss, it would be exploited, even though painlessly killed. Consequently, even if painless slaughter were possible, A2 might still be correct, and, of course, even if painless slaughter is impossible, there might be other counter-examples to A2. Thus, the question of the correctness or incorrectness of A2 cannot be answered simply by determining the (im)possibility of painless slaughter.

Though inconclusive, the discussion of painless slaughter did raise the crucial question of whether or not animals that are consumed for food can be treated fairly. I think they can be, and egg production can serve as a useful model of what must be done and avoided to accomplish this. Currently, most eggs consumed in the United States are produced through factory farming, which condemns the hens that lay these eggs to miserable lives and premature deaths. However, eggs need not be produced in this way, and, indeed, even today a few eggs are produced by hens that lead a life of seemingly sufficient quality to make it worth living for them. Such hens are allowed to roam about, dust bathe, socialize, and do most of the other things that chickens naturally like to do. Building on this example, we will presume that we are dealing with hens that are fed, housed, and protected against predators, bad weather, and disease by the humans who gather their eggs and that these hens are allowed to live out their normal life-spans, even after they have ceased to lay eggs. Furthermore, to insure that the hens are the only animals at issue in our example, let us also presume either that these eggs are unfertilized or that, if fertilized, the egg contents are not sentient at the time the eggs are harvested and are never allowed to become sentient. Though such fortunate hens may be very few and far between at present, that they should exist is not a merely logical or science fiction possibility. Their existence is well within the possibilities of the world we know.

To complete our example, we need add only one further bit of information: hens do not seem greatly, if at all, distressed by their eggs being taken from them.[3]

Consequently, it seems correct to say that these hens suffer little or no loss in exchange for what they are given. And as a consequence of that, it seems reasonable to say that these hens are not being exploited but, rather, are receiving a fair exchange for their eggs. If that is correct, then animal liberation does not entail veganism, at least as a matter of principle. Actually finding eggs produced by hens enjoying this quality of life and fair treatment is, of course, extremely difficult, and attempting to mass produce inexpensive eggs for our large, predominantly urban population under these conditions might be impractical. Consequently, within the context of the options currently open to us, especially to those of us living in large cities, eliminating eggs and all other animal products from our diet may be the only option entirely consistent with animal liberation. But if such immediately practical concerns are set aside, this example shows that employing animals to produce items for human consumption is not inherently exploitive.

Now, is it possible to produce meat under similar, nonexploitive conditions? We could certainly feed, house, protect, and otherwise provide food animals a good quality of life for their natural life-spans. Also, to my knowledge, there is no evidence that cattle, sheep, and other food animals are concerned about what happens to their bodies after death; so the prospect of our harvesting and consuming their flesh after they die of old age (if they could anticipate this) would probably not distress them. If that is correct, then animals raised for meat under these conditions would, like the above laying hens, not be exploited but given a fair exchange for their eventual use as human food. They would consequently provide a counter-example to A2. It follows that even if "vegetarianism" is redefined as "not eating the flesh of sentient beings," animal liberation does not entail vegetarianism.

Of course, the practical reservations that apply in the egg case also apply here, so that once again, within the context of the options currently open to most of us, not eating animals may be the only option consistent with animal liberation. Furthermore, in the case of meat production, the conditions of nonexploitive production seem much more impractical, even idyllic, than in the case of nonexploitive egg production. This is because, with few exceptions such as wool and dung gathering, these meat animals would have to be cared for for many years before there would be any return for this expense and because it is questionable whether the flesh of animals that "died of old age" (a phrase covering a wide range of conditions) would be a plentiful, safe, attractive food for humans. Thus, even within a practical context much wider than that of immediately available options, not eating animals may still be the only live option consistent with animal liberation.

Recent developments in biology suggest that one way people who are in favor of liberating animals but who enjoy eating meat might try to deal with these practical issues is to develop, through genetic engineering, food animals with naturally short life-spans. The possibility of this kind of genetic engineering project has already occasioned considerable debate within the animal rights movement.[4] It follows from the position developed in response to the replacement argument (Chapter 10) that animal liberation need not (*ceteris paribus*) oppose such projects. Cows that, as a result of genetic engineering, are born with a life expectancy of only three years are not animals that preexisted in some bovine staging area "waiting to be born" and that would have been given longer life-spans if we had not genetically interfered with them. Consequently, these animals have not suffered a loss or been otherwise victimized in being born with short life-spans. Since their interests have not been compromised here, they cannot have been exploited through this genetic engineering. Nor, according to the extended prior existence form of utilitarianism defended in Chapter 10, would utilitarian concerns be compromised by breeding, raising, and harvesting the flesh of these animals under the conditions described in the example above. However, those conditions do require that shortening the life expectancy of food animals be accomplished without rendering these animals incapable of leading a life worth living, and that may pose yet another serious, practical obstacle to nonexploitive meat production. For example, weakening their circulatory system would likely not only lead to shorter life-spans but also to poor quality lives for these animals.

It might be claimed that even if practical, nonexploitive of the animals directly involved, and acceptable on utilitarian grounds, such genetic engineering projects would inspire people to continue viewing animals as a resource for our consumption and that these projects would thereby contribute to a morally bad dimension of human character and tradition. Psychologically, this point seems well taken. That people could treat animals as well-cared-for pets are treated yet simultaneously genetically manipulate and raise them for food is certainly questionable. That is why those who see these food animal genetic engineering projects as insidious, high-tech expressions and extensions of the same old exploitive attitude toward animals are not entirely mistaken. However, if someone did fit the example above (i.e., was opposed to exploiting any food animal once it existed but sought to manipulate the genetic makeup of future food animals for human benefit), he would (*ceteris paribus*) not be inconsistent, hypocritical, or of bad moral character. He would be pursuing human interests within the boundaries of a species-blind fairness and concern for making the world a happier, more fulfilling place for those living in it, human as well as nonhuman.

It might be objected that if this use of animals really were morally acceptable, then we should be willing to use human corpses as food, but the idea of so using humans is morally repugnant, so there must also be something morally wrong with such use of animals. Such an objection presumes that rejecting species prejudice and treating animals fairly requires treating them in the same ways we treat humans. However, as discussed in Chapter 5, the "equality" sought for animals through liberating them from human exploitation is not that of identical treatment with humans but of equal protection for their interests. Since animal interests may differ from human interests, our nonexploitive treatment of animals may differ from our nonexploitive treatment of humans. In the present case, we humans seem to have a deep psychological interest in what happens to our bodies after we die. As already mentioned, I am unaware of any evidence that food animals share this interest. Consequently, since our and their interests differ in this regard, our treatment of animals and of humans regarding the use of their and our corpses for food can differ without prejudice.

Another possible response runs as follows: instead of waiting for an animal to die of old age, would it not be fair to feed, house, and otherwise insure that it has a good quality of life for half of its natural life-span in exchange for humanely slaughtering it at that time, when its flesh would likely be more plentiful, safer, and more appealing for humans? This would deprive the animal of the remaining half of its life, of course, but in exchange for this, it will have been provided an equal number of high-quality years of life.

In response, we can note that even if this procedure were fair, it would run afoul of another crucial issue in the moral evaluation of meat production, namely, the utilitarian dimension of everyday morality discussed in Chapters 6 and 10. Depriving food animals of half of their lives would represent a massive loss of happiness or fulfillment in comparison with the alternative of keeping these animals alive and happy or fulfilled until they die of old age. It is highly doubtful that the gain in happiness or fulfillment for humans from more, safer, and more appealing meat could outweigh this loss, especially since safe, abundant, pleasing substitutes for meat in the human diet are available. On the other hand, the use of animal carcasses for food after the animals have died of old age could represent a gain in human happiness or fulfillment without any loss to animals. It would, therefore, clearly meet our utilitarian moral concerns, while the possibility of animals sacrificing the second half of their lives in exchange for our caring for them during the first half almost certainly would not meet those concerns. Consequently, from this moral point of view, there is little analogy between the "wait till they die of old age" and the "keep them until their prime but cut them down then" possibilities.

It could be responded that even if this "in their prime" possibility is morally unacceptable, there must (logically) be some point in the animals' lives at which the loss of the remainder of their lives would be more than outweighed by the extra benefit to humans of killing the animals before they die of old age. Consequently, there will be some point at which the humane slaughter of these animals would be acceptable on utilitarian grounds. This may or may not be so; it depends on the pattern of flesh loss of animals in old age, the quality of life of older animals, how much, if any, greater happiness or fulfillment humans find in a diet that includes meat, and other complex and elusive variables. Since there is a definite possibility of abuse and of loss of utility involved in slaughtering animals that there is not with letting them die of old age, the burden of proof is on those who would justify the slaughter alternative. As discussed in our previous analyses of supposed utilitarian justifications of animal exploitation (in Chapters 6 and 10), it is highly doubtful that utility is susceptible of the precise identification and measurement that shouldering that burden would require. Consequently, utilitarian concerns weigh on the side of the "wait till they die of old age" alternative. Thus, while eating animals may not be incompatible with liberating them, slaughtering them almost certainly is incompatible with liberating them.

III. Exploiting, Killing, and Scavenging

So far we have dealt only with domestic animals and producing meat through animal husbandry. We should add a few words about obtaining meat from wildlife. Fishing, hunting, and trapping animals for food (or fur) is (*ceteris paribus*) clearly incompatible with liberating animals for the same reasons that slaughtering animals is; that is, these practices are unfair to animals and destructive of the general welfare, when the interests of animals, as well as of people, are included in our utilitarian considerations.[5] On the other hand, scavenging for meat would seem to be compatible with animal liberation in the same way that using the carcasses of domestic animals that have died of old age is. For example, while catching salmon for food is (*ceteris paribus*) incompatible with animal liberation, scooping up their bodies after they have returned to their native streams, spawned, and died would not be. Scavenging would not be a matter of fair exchange, of course, unless we provided these wild animals some service — currently, about the only service we provide wild animals is mildly inhibiting our destruction of them — but we could not be unfair to them in taking for our use something in which they have no interest, namely, their carcasses. The only question of fairness involved in this activity would seem to be that of not becoming so greedy about it that we deprive other scavengers of a fair chance at a decent quality of life. Within those limits, scavenging would appear to be another example of using animals in a way that might increase our happiness or fulfillment without sacrificing their interests.

Nonetheless, even if not morally objectionable, the prospect of our becoming scavengers in order to satisfy our lust for meat strikes me, at least, as bizarre. The prospect of our raising cattle, sheep, hogs, and other animals until they die of old age to satisfy that same lust seems almost equally bizarre. I know of no one who has become convinced of the moral obligation to liberate animals from human exploitation who has also retained such a craving for meat that he or she has resorted to or even seriously contemplated either of these two activities. Perhaps, as Cora Diamond's analysis of the difference between eating meat and eating people suggests,[6] even where animal liberation principles may tolerate continuing to regard animals as resources for human consumption, the actual experience of living with animals as fellow members of a moral community, as beings with whom we sympathize, whose interests must (morally) be respected, and with whom we must (morally) deal fairly makes it psychologically very difficult, if not impossible, to continue to regard animals in this way. If that is so, then except for the eating of (biological) animals that the eater feels confident are not sentient, vegetarianism is a consequence of animal liberation.

IV. Starvation

That conclusion concerns the routine practice of one's life. However, discussions of animal rights and vegetarianism usually include emergency cases, for example, whether or not killing animals to prevent human starvation in situations where that was the only way to prevent starvation would be compatible with animal liberation. In response to such cases, I think that it is sufficient to reiterate what was emphasized in Chapter 5: such extraordinary cases are inconsequential for the animal rights debate. This is because they concern situations where our ordinary moral principles are superseded, while the animal rights debate concerns those ordinary principles and the routine practices they govern. Consequently, even if it is compatible with animal liberation that starving people kill animals (as humanely as possible, of course) when there is no other way for them to survive, that cannot (logically) justify our killing animals for food when doing so is not necessary for survival. Since these emergency cases are thus insignificant, there seems no point in discussing them here beyond (again repeating what was said in Chapter 5) noting that what is morally acceptable will vary with the details of the situation, including the histories, condition, capabilities, and subsequent opportunities of the people and animals involved, and that when evaluated on the basis of moral concerns, like those discussed above, which do not give overwhelming importance to species membership, some situations may, of course, not favor the people over the animals involved.

12

Whither Animal Research?

IN THE controversy concerning animal research, the following arguments are sometimes voiced, more often presumed:

The Pro-animal Argument

A1: Animals cannot freely and with understanding give or withhold consent to participate in experiments.

A2: Experiments can (morally) be performed only on those who freely and with understanding consent to participate in them.

A3: Therefore, experiments cannot (morally) be performed on animals.

The Pro-researcher Argument

B1: Human life is a higher form of life than animal life.

B2: Experiments ought (morally) to be performed to preserve or enhance the (quality of) life of the higher life forms, even if this involves sacrificing the lives or quality of life of lower life forms.

B3: Therefore, experiments on animals to preserve or enhance the (quality of) human life ought (morally) to be performed, even if this involves sacrificing the animals' lives or quality of life.

The pro-animal argument is at least part of what distinguishes "animal rights" concerns with research from "animal welfare" concerns with research. Animal welfarists do not object to animal research as long as it is conducted humanely and seems likely to contribute to preserving or enhancing human or animal life. The Animal Welfare Act and The National Institutes of Health *Guide for the Use and Care of Laboratory Animals* are expressions of this animal welfare ethic. On the other hand, as discussed in Chapter 5, the animal *rights* movement seeks to go beyond this ethic of humane consumption to providing animals with the same sort of moral protection for their interests that we humans currently enjoy for ours. In the area of research, the principle that experiments can be performed only on those who freely and with understanding consent to participate in them is one of the most important of those moral protections. Consequently, the pro-animal argument expresses at least an important part of the animal rights attack on the morality of animal research.

For morally concerned people who are informed about contemporary animal research, the pro-researcher argument is crucial to supporting most of that research with a clear conscience. Most contemporary animal research procedures involve destroying the quality of life and taking the lives of animals, and hundreds of millions of animals are consumed annually in this research. If such destruction can be morally justified, it is only because it is "necessary for attaining some greater good," and that is the commonly offered justification for it. Now, the number of animals used in research to benefit other animals is very small; the good (supposedly) to be obtained from most animal research is the preservation and enhancement of human life. Since so many animals are consumed in research, it cannot be convincingly argued that a few of them are being sacrificed, so that many of us may lead better lives or continue to live at all. Consequently, human (quality of) life must be of greater value than animal (quality of) life if this destructive research is going to have even a chance of producing a *greater* good. Thus, without the pro-researcher argument to justify it, most contemporary animal research would be as obviously immoral as performing that research on refugees.[1]

Each of these arguments forms a tight little syllogism of which even Aristotle could be proud. But are the premises correct? That is where the issue lies in this dispute. We shall question each premise in turn.

I. Can Animals Consent to Research?

Is it true that animals cannot freely and with understanding give or withhold consent to participate in experiments?

A1 would probably be considered the least controversial of the four claims made in these arguments. Nonetheless, it is not obvious that (all) animals lack the intellectual ability needed to give or withhold informed consent to participate in research. In many cases, they clearly indicate their willingness or unwillingness to participate in experiments to anyone willing to notice. Consider the following two examples.

Professor Barnes wishes to determine whether monkeys can combine various objects in their environment to form a useful tool. He puts some bananas inside a large cage but far enough away from the bars so that the monkeys outside cannot reach them. He then scatters several short sticks that can be fitted together to form one long stick on the ground outside the cage and watches to see whether the monkeys, after realizing they cannot reach the bananas either with just their arms or with just one stick, will put the sticks together to form a stick long enough to reach the bananas. The monkeys native to the region have long since become accustomed to Barnes's research station, wander into the compound each morning in search of food and entertainment, and this morning are soon engaged in trying to get the bananas so alluringly out of reach inside the big cage.

Professor Jacobs is engaged in a series of sleep-deprivation experiments involving cats. These experiments require that electrodes be placed into the cats' brains, that the cats be placed in a restraining apparatus, and that they be hooked up to a monitoring device that delivers painful shocks to them whenever they start to fall asleep. When Professor Jacobs comes to the animal storage room to get one of the cats for an experiment, the cats all crawl into the far corners of their cages and cower. When the professor opens one of the cages, that cat hisses and strikes out at him, which is why Professor Jacobs has taken to wearing long, protective gloves when handling these cats. On the way to the laboratory, the cats continually attempt to escape.

Do the monkeys that try to get Professor Barnes's bananas consent to participate in that experiment? Do the cats that try to escape from Professor Jacobs withhold consent?

It is clear in the second case that the cats, by their behavior, indicate their desire not to be placed in a situation where they will be painfully shocked whenever they start to fall asleep. Given the chance, they would "vote with their feet" and leave the good professor behind. But can this contrary behavior be sensibly interpreted as the cats withholding their consent to participate in the experiments? Applying the standard requirements for informed consent when dealing with paradigm human research subjects, some might insist that the answer to that question must be "No." Since the cats cannot understand the experiments in which they are to participate, they cannot formulate informed judgments to participate or not to participate in the research.

That inference is mistaken. The cats do not understand the experiments in the way Professor Jacobs does or even in the way a nonscientist with normal$_h$ intelligence could. However, it does not follow from that that the cats do not understand the experiments at all or that they do not understand them in the way required to give or withhold informed consent. Understanding an experiment is not an all-or-nothing condition; once again, there are different varieties and degrees of understanding.

Professor Jacobs's cats must understand the experiments in some way. If they did not understand the experiments at all, they would not cower when the professor enters the animal room, hiss and strike at him when he removes them from their cages, and try to escape on the way to the laboratory. Cats are naturally inquisitive creatures, and like other animals used in laboratories, cats used in research are chosen for their tractability. Consequently, the behavior of Professor Jacobs's cats is a reliable indicator that they have some understanding of the sleep deprivation experiments.

Furthermore, in order to be capable of giving or withholding informed consent, all that is required is that one be sane and understand how the experiment will (likely) affect his or her interests. To be "informed" about an experiment does not require having detailed, scientific knowledge about it, because the point of being informed about an experiment in which one may participate is not to increase one's scientific education. The point of being informed here is to be aware of what is going to happen to the research subject in the experiment, so that one can determine whether he or she is willing to have that happen to him or her. Cats seeking to escape from the torments of sleep deprivation research would seem to be expressing a sane, reasonable understanding of how these experiments affect them. Indeed, if the cats did not behave in this way in this situation, we would be inclined to say that "they don't know what's going to happen to them" or that they had entered a state of enervating depression (something that does happen to research animals). Consequently, it makes sense to say that Professor Jacobs's cats, through their contrary behavior, are withholding consent to participate in his research.

What about Professor Barnes's monkeys? They are free to roam in and out of the compound, and we may presume that they have not been starved nor are otherwise desperate for food. So they have not been coerced into participating in the experiment. Furthermore, the monkeys understand what the situation holds for them, namely, bananas, if they can figure out how to get them, or disappointment if they cannot. As was the case with Professor Jacobs, Professor Barnes has a more expansive understanding of the situation, including the contribution the experiment could make to science and to his career. But once again, these extra dimensions of the situation do not affect how the experiment will impact the research subjects' well-being. Consequently, these extra dimensions of understanding, of which the monkeys are presumably incapable, do not affect the monkeys' ability to act as sane, reasonably self-interested agents in consenting or withholding consent to participate in the experiment. As long as the monkeys are aware of what is happening to them during the experiment (i.e., are aware of how what is happening affects their feelings of well-being) and as long as they are free to withdraw from the experiment whenever they do not like what is happening to them, it would be reasonable to say that their participation in the experiment is an expression of consent to participate.

The prospect of animals having to sign consent forms is sometimes raised by animal research advocates as a *reductio ad absurdum* of the contention that research animals should enjoy the same sorts of protection as human research subjects. However, what is overlooked in this joke is that we have long recognized that consent can be given or withheld through other behaviors than signing or refusing to sign a form. For example, our interpretation of "consenting through freely participating" in an experiment is analogous to Socrates' oft-repeated claim that merely by living in a free society, we consent to the social contract.[2]

Of course, one could attempt to interpret "consenting" in a way that would make of it something that only those with (something like) normal$_h$ intelligence could do. This would be the same sort of project we have already seen humanist philosophers engage in with "moral agency," "interests," "valuing," "preferring," and so on. However, such a project would be as arbitrary as those others. We consent to x whenever we indicate that we are willing to have x happen to us, and we withhold consent to x whenever we indicate that we are not willing to have x happen to us. As long as that indication is made with sufficient clarity and distinctness to be recognized for what it is, just how the indication is made is a secondary issue.

Thus, to claim that animals can give or withhold consent to participate in an experiment is not absurd. On the contrary, it is something animals commonly do, something that is easily recognized, and something that is often properly informed and reasonable, *from the animals' point of view, which, where consent is the issue, is the viewpoint that counts.* It follows that A1 is false. The problem with applying the requirement for free, informed consent to animal research is not that the animals are incapable of giving or withholding consent or of communicating to us their interests and desires. The problem in applying the consent requirement to animal research lies in us: we do not want to be frustrated by animals refusing to participate in experiments from which we believe we may benefit.

II. Should Research Be Done Only with Those Who Consent?

Can (morally) experiments be performed only on those who freely and with understanding consent to participate in them?

A2 involves a dual claim:

(i) current ethical regulations governing human research restrict such research to experiments to which the research subjects have freely and with understanding consented, and

(ii) common moral principles require that research be limited to experiments in which the research subjects have freely and with understanding consented.

Both of these claims are mistaken.

There are two reasons why the consent requirement has become, over the past few decades, a standard part of the ethics governing research with human subjects. One is the many horrible experiments that scientists have inflicted on defenseless or unwitting research subjects. Not only Nazi experiments but also experiments performed in this country on prisoners, the retarded or mentally ill, racial minorities, and the poor have outraged the public and shown the need to protect people against callous, unscrupulous, and overzealous researchers.[3] The consent requirement is an important part of that protection.

The other reason for the consent requirement is our belief that, *ceteris paribus*, individuals ought (morally) to be free to direct their lives according to their own values. This is the independent valuer view discussed in Chapter 10. According to this view, people's lives should not be controlled by others who think that they know best, since what looks the best to them may not be the best for someone who has different values. For example, to a physician committed to preserving life at all costs, remaining alive on a dialysis machine may "obviously" be the best thing for someone suffering from kidney failure. But the person actually having to live such a life may not find it of sufficient quality to be worth the trouble. The old-fashioned, "Doctor knows best" paternalism would have left the decision to the doctor. Our new respect for self-determination has fostered the consent requirement to counterbalance paternalism and to insure that, *ceteris paribus*, we all have the opportunity to pursue our lives according to our own values. This motive for the consent requirement becomes ever more important as our medical technology progresses in providing us with lives that many of us feel are not worth living.

We hope the consent requirement is helping to reduce the abuse of human research subjects. However, it does not entirely prohibit doing research with humans who have not consented to participate in the experiment. If a person has a legal guardian, that guardian can consent to his ward's participating in research. The guardian's consent can even override the contrary behavior of the ward, as when a frightened child resists submitting to a treatment. Proxy consent is accepted when a person is judged to have lost contact with reality, as in mental illness, to be unable to make a decision, as when one is comatose, to be unable to weigh the long-range benefits of the research for herself, as with children, and when the individual does not yet have his own values, as with infants. In such cases, "paternalism" is not a dirty word. As long as the guardian does what he believes his ward would want or, where that cannot be determined, does what would ordinarily be considered to be in the ward's best interest, such compromises of the independent valuer view are necessary to provide the individual the help needed in order to attain or return to a condition where he can take control of his own life.[4]

It follows that A2 is not an accurate statement of current research ethics concerning human subjects. Nonconsenting humans can be research subjects if they are unable to understand and evaluate the burdens and benefits for them of participating in the research and if they have a guardian who decides that participating in the research will be in their best interest (or will, at least, cause them no harm). Just as this exemption opens the door for *therapeutic or innocuous* research on humans without their consent, so it would leave open the door for *therapeutic or innocuous* research on animals.

That is the way things ought (morally) to be. The reason for insisting on free, informed consent is to protect individuals against abuse. It would be an abuse of that concern to make of the consent requirement an unbending principle that prevents those incapable of assessing the possible long-range benefits *for them* of a procedure from benefiting from research. For example, if the only hope of restoring a heart patient to decent health involves implanting an experimental mechanism, it would be morally wrong to deny this individual that chance just because she cannot sufficiently understand the experiment and its possible benefits for her, since she is an infant or an animal. It follows that A2 would not (*ceteris paribus*) be a desirable, moral reform of our current research codes.

Implementing such exemptions to a principle of personal consent by research subjects can require greater vigilance to avoid paternalistic abuses than would a blanket insistence on such consent. However, undertaking that vigilance in order to make those exemptions is part of insuring that all will have a fair chance at benefiting from research and is consequently part of working toward attaining one of our common, moral goals. On the other hand, focusing on the possibility of paternalistic abuse and, as a consequence, opting for a blanket insistence on personal consent by research subjects would deprive some of the opportunity to benefit from research, thereby insuring their suffering or death. Viewed in this light, I think a blanket insistence on personal consent loses much of the moral luster that seems to motivate some advocates of it. Such an unbending principle would not represent the attainment of a moral ideal of autonomy. It would be a defensive policy, rather like Plato's and Aristotle's embracing democracy as the lesser evil because they believe that we are incapable of attaining the greater good.[5] If such a defensive consent policy is the best we can do, that would be an especially sad commentary on our moral (in)capacities. I like to think that we can implement a "mixed self-determination" policy in a way that will produce less abuse than a defensive policy would guarantee.

Thus, our conclusion must be that neither of the premises of the pro-animal argument is correct and, consequently, the argument is unsound. Nevertheless, we can note that honoring the reasons why A1 and A2 are incorrect would put an end to virtually all animal research. This is because animals that rebel against research are virtually never resisting something that is for their own long-term benefit. Usually, what they fear and seek to escape is all that participating in the research holds for them, namely, frustration, distress, and death. No sane, comprehending individual would consent to participate in most animal research, and no responsible guardian would agree to allow a ward to participate in that research. So while it is true that

> (some) animals can give or withhold consent to participate in (some) experiments and
> where participating in the experiment would be either innocuous to them or in their own best interest, but they cannot understand this, guardians can (morally) give consent for the animals to participate,

it is also true that modifying the pro-animal argument to accommodate these conclusions and then applying the consent requirement to animals would, under ordinary conditions, permit only research with animals that is innocuous to or beneficial for the animals participating in the experiments.

III. Are Humans a Superior Form of Life?

Turning to the pro-researcher argument, we ask is human life a higher form of life than animal life?

While acknowledging that animals have talents we lack (e.g., the bat's sensitivity to sound and the acute vision of many birds), we still consider ourselves to be a superior life form because of our "rationality." Specifically, as noted in Chapter 3, it has been our ability to employ reason to control our lives and surroundings that has been heralded in our traditional moral literature, both philosophical and religious, as the mark of human superiority. This ability has even been called "the image of God," the Creator and controller of the universe, in us. But while it is true that humans are ordinarily capable of flights of reason of which animals are not, it does not immediately follow either that we are *morally* superior to animals or that we are morally justified in sacrificing the interests of less rational beings for our benefit.

For example, if we think of reason in terms of the traditional analogy between human reason and God the Creator, it seems that what we are talking about when we talk about "human superiority" is our great ability to dominate and control. Citing that ability as our morally crucial superiority to animals suggests that the pro-researcher argument rests on the belief that those who are strong enough to exploit others are *for that very reason* morally justified in doing so. If that is what is being argued here—and it was noted in Chapter 6 that two prominent medical researchers recently advocated this "king of the jungle" position— then the pro-researcher argument is an instance of the "might makes right" philosophy. Given our common moral principles and belief that we have made moral progress by abolishing feudalism, slavery, and other forms of subjugation, citing the great power our reason can create and command as justification for our employing that power to dominate those weaker than ourselves and to force them to bear our burdens cannot (logically) be a morally credible argument.

Of course, as discussed in Chapter 3, there is another, more credible interpretation of the moral significance of superior reasoning ability. According to the Kantian side of our common morality, a moral$_{ad}$ agent is supposed to be one who acts out of respect for impersonal laws, and it supposedly requires something like normal$_h$ intelligence to be able to recognize such laws, to counterbalance selfish feelings, and to do the morally right thing consistently.

However, while this Kantian view of the moral significance of reason is morally superior to the previous, Machiavellian account, it is exaggerated. As argued at length in Part I, the Kantian claim that acting from a sense of duty is the *only* moral motive is mistaken. Generous sentiments are commonly considered to be at least as morally$_{ad}$ admirable as motivation through moral reasoning. Our sense of duty is not uncommonly considered to have only the value of something that we must fall back on when our generous sentiments fail us. For example, loving parents are morally$_{ad}$ admirable; indeed, they are morally$_{ad}$ more admirable than "dutiful parents." To use that phrase is to damn with faint praise.

But again summarizing Part I, once we allow sentiment to enter the moral$_{ad}$ arena, instinctual and conditioned actions that are intentional and straightforward responses to the needs of others must (logically) count as moral$_{ad}$ actions and those who do them as moral$_{ad}$ agents. For example, a mother bird that feigns a broken wing and risks her life to distract a fox from her nest is a moral$_{ad}$ agent, even though she is not motivated by judging her maxim to be one she could will as a universal law but acts on "maternal instinct" instead. The same is true of a human mother who instinctively rushes into a burning house to save her baby. Whether bird or human, being a devoted mother is a moral virtue, and this is an evaluation based on the mother's self-sacrificing devotion to her youngsters. A mother's capacity for abstract, practical reasoning is not what is at issue when she is being morally$_{ad}$ evaluated as a mother. As argued in Chapter 2, that ability becomes morally$_{ad}$ crucial only in a limited family of situations, for instance, those requiring the balancing of conflicting claims.

Consequently, we cannot so blithely dismiss loyal dogs, courageous lions, responsible wolves, industrious beavers, self-sacrificing parents of a wide variety of species, and the like, as not being moral$_{ad}$ agents because they are "merely creatures of instinct." Seeing virtue in other animals is not anthropomorphizing, unless we presume that they do their virtuous deeds as a result of the same reasoning process that we have to employ when our own generous sentiments, maternal or paternal instincts, social instincts, moral training, and the like fail us and we have to combat our lesser, selfish selves in order to do what we ought (morally) to do. However, just as there is no reason to suppose that other animals (routinely) go through this process, so there is no moral need for making such a presumption. What makes an action an expression of moral$_{ad}$ agency is not that agents had to put their internal house in order in order to overcome temptation and do what is right. An action is an expression of moral$_{ad}$ agency if it is done intentionally and straightforwardly in response to what agents perceive to be the need of others. The actions of many animals appear to be such expressions, which is why it is anthropocentric to insist that animals cannot (logically) be moral$_{ad}$ agents.

Consequently, if we are morally$_{ad}$ superior to animals, it must be a question of degree. Given our particularly bloody, destructive, exploitive habits and history, that question must be considered open at best.[6] Furthermore, how we would even go about trying to answer that question is itself a staggering question. As long as we think that, on conceptual grounds, animals cannot be moral$_{ad}$ agents at all, we do not have a methodological problem here. But once we recognize that animals are moral$_{ad}$ agents, we encounter severe methodological problems in trying to determine which species is/are morally$_{ad}$ superior. For example, do we evaluate capacity for doing what is right or moral$_{ad}$ deeds actually performed? If we evaluate deeds actually performed, do we just count them, or do we try to evaluate them against the capacity available to be actualized, so that although P has done fewer moral$_{ad}$ deeds than Q, P might still be considered superior to Q, since P has actualized a greater part of his capacity to do such deeds than has Q? What allowance do we make for the different living conditions and traditions of different species? Are certain kinds of moral$_{ad}$ capacities or deeds to be weighted over others (e.g., reflective dutifulness over spontaneous kindness) and if so, on what basis? What is the unit of measurement to be? Answering such fundamental, methodological questions would seem to be impossible. Consequently, even if animals do not possess all the capacities of fully moral$_{ad}$ agents, answering questions about which species is/are morally$_{ad}$ superior would seem to be impossible, once we acknowledge that we are not the only moral$_{ad}$ agents around.

The utilitarian side of our common morality provides another family of interpretations of the moral significance of our superior intelligence. It is often claimed that humans can experience enjoyment, fulfillment, distress, and frustration of a greater variety and subtlety than can animals. The animals' range of experience is (supposedly) limited by their limited intelligence to matters of sensation, digestion, and reproduction, while, thanks to our superior intellect, we are capable of appreciating fine art, conceptual matters, moral fulfillment, flights of imagination, remembrance and anticipation, and so on in addition to what animals can experience. Since one of our common moral goals is to maximize the excess of enjoyment and fulfillment over distress and frustration in life, it can then be argued that our greater sensitivity makes human life a superior form of life in a morally significant way and, consequently, that we are morally justified in sacrificing less sensitive beings (i.e., animals) in order to benefit ourselves. (Henceforth, "feelings" will be used in place of "enjoyment, fulfillment, distress, and frustration.")

In response to this, we could note that empirical studies of animal psychology indicate that animals are capable of a much wider variety of feelings than philosophers have traditionally believed.[7] Noting that the difference between us here is once again a matter of degree once again takes some of the moral luster off this difference and renders its moral implications questionable. For example, while our common morality could support individual sacrifices for massive group benefit (e.g., in time of war) it would not, as W. D. Ross has pointed out, support basing life and death choices on marginal increases in utility.[8] Nonetheless, it still seems beyond question that we can experience some things (e.g., the satisfaction of solving a symbolic logic problem) that animals cannot. However, it does not follow from that that our feelings are superior to those of animals.

We cannot enjoy the life of a dog, a bird, a bat, or a dolphin. Consequently, we cannot appreciate the subtleties of smell, sight, sound, and touch that these animals can apparently appreciate. Here, we are the boors. Of course, they in turn apparently cannot appreciate Michelangelo and Mozart (an insensitivity not limited to members of other species). Here, they are the boors. This would seem to leave us roughly even—except that we go on to claim that the sensitivities of which we alone seem to be capable are "qualitatively superior" to their sensitivities. "Better to be Socrates dissatisfied than a pig satisfied!" However, as John Stuart Mill himself acknowledges, the only way to determine which are the qualitatively superior feelings is to find someone who can appreciate the lot and ask that person which ones he or she prefers.[9] That is impossible here. Even the multitalented John Stuart could not experience the enjoyments of the gull and the fulfillments of the dolphin. Consequently, although we can experience things that animals cannot and although we (or at least some of us) place an especially high value on the things that only those with something like normal$_h$ intelligence can experience, we cannot (logically) justify a claim that our feelings are qualitatively superior to those of other species.

Other utilitarians of a more Benthamite stripe, such as Peter Singer, claim that humans are capable of a greater quantity of feeling, especially of fulfillment, than are animals. This is because we are capable of projecting the future and remembering the past to a vastly greater extent than are animals. These abilities make it possible for us to experience feelings of hope and regret, while animals, with their restricted temporal capacities, cannot experience such feelings.[10]

However, even if this is true—and we have argued in Chapter 7 that there is, once again, more of a continuum than a dichotomy between our and their temporal abilities—it may also be true, for the same reason, that the feelings of animals are more intense than ours. This is because their feelings are not diluted by recollections of the (far) past or hopes for the (far) future.[11] For example, the distress and frustration experienced by a human prisoner of war can be alleviated by recollections of past freedom and hope for future release, while a dog trapped in a laboratory cage (supposedly) has no such recollection or hope to ease its distress and frustration. Similarly, humans are notorious for not getting full enjoyment from present pleasures because they have fixated on past sorrows or are fretting about future difficulties, while animals, like dogs playing on the beach, do not seem to have their present enjoyment thus diluted. Now, if animal feelings are more intense than ours, then this extra intensity could counterbalance the extra feelings our extensive temporal capacity provides us. Thus, on Benthamite grounds, our superior temporal capacity can be as much of a moral liability as an asset; it could even be the case that our more dispersed way of life is morally less valuable than animals' more intense way of life.

Of course, once again, there is no way to tell whether the feelings of animals are more intense than ours and, if so, whether that greater intensity is sufficient to counterbalance or even to outweigh the greater extent of our feelings. Consequently, this Benthamite version of human moral superiority encounters the same sort of problem as the Millian version and must suffer the same fate: since they cannot (logically) be justified, they are not significant claims and cannot (logically) contribute to a justification of our continued consumption of animals, in research or elsewhere.

In listening to utilitarian discussions of feelings, one can get the impression that feelings are like jelly beans in a jar, the jar being an individual life, and that we can evaluate the individual's life by seeing how many and what sort of mix of beans he has in his jar. Human lives are supposed to be more valuable because they have a quantity and variety of beans not found in animal lives.

But feelings are not like jelly beans, and they are not related to the one who has them as beans are to their receptacle. Feelings cannot exist by themselves, and they are what the one who has them makes of them. When it comes to feelings, "To be is to be perceived," as Berkeley says.[12] That is why we cannot simply survey a life to decide its utilitarian value; the one who lives that life must show us what its value is for him or her. A life that looks as if it would be a hard and dull one for us to lead (e.g., the life of a beaver) may be experienced by the one who lives it to be enjoyable and fulfilling. And it is the value that life has for the one who lives it that counts in the utilitarian calculus, since it is only by living it that it exists and actually comes to have value. The value others place on S's life enters into the utilitarian calculus only insofar as S's life impacts their lives, for example, through S's cutting down their trees or providing them entertainment. The value they place on S's life through imagining what it would be like for them to live S's life is merely imaginary and, consequently, is irrelevant to the value S's life really has.

It follows that if we consider the lives of a dog and a human, for example, which are very different lives but which, let us presume, are both experienced by those living them to be enjoyable and fulfilling, it is impossible to determine which life has the greater utilitarian value. The human life may have greater variety to it, and the human might feel frustrated if she or he were given the dog's life to lead. But that is irrelevant to the question of whether its life is more or less enjoyable and fulfilling for the dog than the human's life is enjoyable and fulfilling for the human. Since we cannot feel what the animal feels, we cannot determine whether a human gets more or less enjoyment and fulfillment from his enjoyable and fulfilling life than an animal gets from its enjoyable and fulfilling life.

Since we cannot make such comparisons, utilitarian evaluations must (logically) be limited to determining whether way of life x is more or less enjoyable and fulfilling than way of life y for a particular subject or type of subject that could actually live x or y, for instance, whether hogs prefer to live in factory farms or to be free-roaming. Utilitarian evaluations must (logically) not involve comparing way of life x for P with way of life y for Q, for example, comparing an enjoyable, fulfilling way of life for a hog with an enjoyable, fulfilling way of life for a human. It further follows that our efforts to fulfill our utilitarian goals ought (logically) to be directed at improving the quality of life by finding better lives for sentient beings (e.g., by developing more enjoyable, healthful diets for people) rather than by substituting supposedly superior subjects for supposedly inferior ones (e.g., by killing baby baboons to save the lives of human infants).

A third utilitarian argument for the moral superiority of human life would emphasize that our reasoning ability makes it possible for us to combat distress and frustration effectively and otherwise to increase the enjoyment and fulfillment in life. Our greater intelligence allows us to do far more than other animals to fight diseases, produce food, construct shelter, and develop technologies that otherwise prolong and enhance the quality of life. While the Millian and Benthamite arguments above focus on the ability to experience utilitarian goods, this argument focuses on the ability to produce those goods and sees human moral superiority in our superior ability to be utilitarian agents.

This moral agency argument encounters the same methodological difficulties as its Kantian cousin discussed above. Furthermore, when the effects of our technology on animals are taken seriously, it is doubtful that we are producing more enjoyment and fulfillment than distress and frustration. As noted above, we consume hundreds of millions of laboratory animals every year. It is hard to imagine that our testing and research produces utilitarian goods sufficient to outweigh that massive, annual evil. In the areas of factory farming, fishing, hunting, and trapping, the number of animals consumed annually is even greater, and consequently it is even harder in these areas to imagine that we are producing a better utilitarian world. This is especially true when we remember, as emphasized in

Chapter 6, that utilitarian reasoning requires that we compare what we are doing not only against what things would be like if we did nothing but also against nonanimal-consuming alternatives we could pursue.

So applying this utilitarian agency test to human history and "accomplishments," we might have to conclude that to date our willingness to pursue our own interests at the expense of others has dominated our ability to produce a better world for all and has made of us utilitarian liabilities rather than assets. Like promising young men and women, we cannot continue to be valued for our potential forever; eventually, we must prove our mettle by performing, and to date we have not, as a species, performed as superior, impartial, utilitarian agents.

There could, of course, be other suggestions for how our superior reasoning ability makes us a morally superior form of life. However, we shall not examine any further candidates here. The Kantian and utilitarian arguments we have examined are the ones suggested by our philosophical tradition and common morality. If they cannot justify B1, then it is doubtful that it can be morally justified, and consequently it is reasonable to conclude that B1 ought (logically) to be rejected until, if ever, it is provided a moral justification.

IV. Should Superiors Exploit Their Inferiors?

Is it the case that experiments ought (morally) to be performed to preserve or enhance the (quality of) life of the higher life forms, even if this involves sacrificing the lives or quality of life of lower life forms?

For the purposes of argument, let us presume to be true what we just determined there is not good reason to believe, namely, that humans (ordinarily) are "superior beings" in a morally significant sense. Many people, philosophers included, presume that if we are superior beings, it immediately follows that we are morally justified in disposing of lesser beings for our benefit, even if that involves sacrificing the interests of those inferior beings. However, as it stands, the following is clearly not a valid argument:

C1: *P* is superior to *Q* in a morally significant way.
C3: Therefore, *P* is morally justified in disposing of *Q* for his own benefit, even if this involves sacrificing *Q*'s interests.

There is a missing premise here that must be something like:

C2: Those who are morally superior to others are morally justified in disposing of those others for their own benefit, even if this involves sacrificing the interests of those morally inferior beings.

This general principle is not obviously correct. Morally superior beings sometimes have extensive obligations to and only circumscribed privileges over their inferiors, as in the case of human adults dealing with young children. Similarly, matters of life and death are morally more important than matters of convenience, but as Judith Jarvis Thompson has argued, it does not follow that Isaac is entitled to sacrifice Susan's convenience in order to save his life.[13] Just what follows from P being morally superior to Q is an open question. Consequently, C2 needs to find support in some general moral position if it is to be morally acceptable. Can it do so?

From a Kantian perspective, what would make us a morally superior life form is our (supposedly) greater ability to set aside self-interest and to make disinterested appraisals of what ought to be done. However, as discussed in Chapter 8, it would be at least a cruel irony to cite this ability as justification for our disregarding the interests of weaker, (supposedly) morally$_{ad}$ inferior animals and exploiting them as mere means to our ends. Just as Plato's philosopher-kings would not be justified in consuming those whom their superiority entitled them to govern, so our (supposedly) greater ability to act impartially does not provide a basis for our acting selfishly in our dealings with those of (supposedly) lesser moral$_{ad}$ ability. Indeed, to the extent that we exploit those weaker than ourselves, forcing them to bear our burdens and not providing them a fair return for the services they render us, we bring into disrepute our claim to moral$_{ad}$ superiority. Doing experiments on animals that we would not be willing to do on ourselves and for which we have never been concerned to provide fair compensation for the animals, even where that would be possible, is a clear example of such discrediting exploitation. Therefore, Kantianism does not support C2 and, consequently, does not support B2 either.

The utilitarian concern in research as elsewhere is (i) to maximize the excess of enjoyment and fulfillment over distress and frustration and (ii) to do so without prejudice, that is, without favoring the interests of one group over those of another. This second utilitarian concern is sometimes overlooked, but it was his antipathy to aristocratic privilege that motivated Jeremy Bentham to inaugurate utilitarianism. Replacing a hierarchical worldview, where the interests of "the better classes" are considered more worthy of fulfillment than those of their "inferiors," with a presumption in favor of equal consideration and opportunity for all has always been a fundamental part of utilitarianism.

Now, C2 is an expression of such a hierarchical worldview and is, therefore, not supported by the principle of utility. That principle does support preferring a life capable of a greater utilitarian good over another when we are forced to choose between them (e.g., when we must choose between using scarce medical supplies to save an older or a younger person). However, the principle of utility does not support viewing the world in terms of classes of "superior" and "inferior" beings, with the latter being routinely sacrificed as a resource for pursuing the interests of the former. That is, of course, exactly what C2 proposes.

Consequently, from a utilitarian perspective, we ought (morally) to structure experiments in a way that will involve the greatest excess of benefit over harm *for all concerned*, with "each to count for one and none for more than one."[14] This utilitarian imperative poses a serious moral obstacle to current animal research procedures, since they involve annually destroying the quality of life and taking the lives of hundreds of millions of healthy animals. This destruction adds greatly to the amount of distress and frustration in the world, and when these animals are finally killed, the possibility of hundreds of millions of happy lives is eliminated from the positive side of the utilitarian ledger. As previously noted, it is hard to believe that enough people (and animals) benefit sufficiently from this research to counterbalance this massive, continually repeated suffering and loss. It is even harder to believe that a greater excess of enjoyment and fulfillment over distress and frustration *for all concerned* could not be attained by structuring research in ways that would not introduce this massive, negative component into the utilitarian equation.

Intuitively, the precept that would best meet the two utilitarian concerns listed above is not that research should be governed by a principle like B2 but that research should be restricted to

   (i) experiments that do not require distress, frustration, or the destruction of healthy, sentient life,
   (ii) experiments conducted on those who already suffer from the malady in question and for whom the current, standard remedies, if any, promise significantly less relief than does the experimental procedure,
   (iii) experiments that are compensated with a return for the research subjects that significantly outweighs the burden that they must bear as participants in the experiment, and
   (iv) experiments that require individual sacrifices as the only known way for attaining *clear and present, massive, desperately needed* benefits for others (e.g., developing a vaccine to fight a severe epidemic), where these benefits greatly outweigh the required sacrifices, and where the sacrifices are designed to cause the least possible suffering or loss and are fairly distributed among those likely to benefit from the research (e.g., by sacrificing older individuals in preference to younger ones and by choosing the research subjects randomly from among those likely to benefit from the research).

Structuring research in these ways would hold out the prospect of alleviating distress and frustration in ways that do not create additional suffering or loss, unless they are necessary for and greatly outweighed by some clear and present, massive, desperately needed good. While this would permit sacrificing animals in research under extraordinary circumstances, it would also justify sacrificing humans under similar circumstances, for example, using irreversibly comatose or terminally ill humans to develop vaccines to combat raging epidemics. In this way, these restrictions are neither absolutely rigid in opposing individual sacrifices nor speciesistic in determining where those sacrifices will be made, on the rare occasions when they are morally justified.

Thus, from both Kantian and utilitarian perspectives, designing experiments to sacrifice supposedly lower life forms in order to benefit supposedly higher life forms (i.e., ourselves) is morally disreputable. Experiments ought (morally) to be designed in ways that do not detract from but contribute to attaining the second and third of our common, moral goals, that is, to minimizing suffering and otherwise maximizing well-being and to insuring fairness. (Insofar as doing research contributes to or detracts from developing good moral character, experiments should, of course, be designed to contribute to attaining that moral goal as well.) Securing our own well-being by annually destroying the quality of life and taking the lives of hundreds of millions of healthy animals is neither designed to nor likely to help us attain our moral goals. Rather, it increases the distress and frustration in life and insures that these evils are distributed unfairly. Thus, B2 runs counter to two of our primary moral concerns, and with those two strikes against it, it is doubtful that B2 could ever be morally justified.

V. Summary and Conclusion

So our conclusion is that the pro-animal argument, which would prohibit all research with animals, is unsound, but so is the pro-researcher argument, which would permit all research with animals that might benefit humans. However, our conclusion is only superficially the same in both cases.

We have found that the pro-researcher argument is flawed fundamentally. B1 cannot (logically) be justified, and B2 looks like it cannot (morally) be justified. The pro-researcher argument and the contemporary animal research practices it would justify are expressions of an aristocratic worldview in which we humans, the "better class" in this hierarchy, are entitled to treat those of (supposedly) inferior status as resources for the preservation and enhancement of our "superior way of life." Of course, we ought (morally) to be kind in our use of these inferiors —noblesse oblige!—but this humane obligation remains secondary to and circumscribed by the presumption and exercise of aristocratic privilege. For example, our traditional, humane ethic prohibits randomly tormenting animals but is overruled when it comes to performing painful and lethal experiments on animals if those experiments could prove beneficial for us.

Such aristocratic worldviews have been the target of what we commonly consider to be moral progress. Our rejection of slavery, feudalism, aristocracies of birth, sexual and racial exploitation, and the like all have in common the discrediting of supposed "natural hierarchies" in favor of a presumption of equal consideration and opportunity for all. Consequently, it is not inappropriate to see the pro-researcher argument and contemporary animal research practices as vestiges of feudal mentality on the contemporary scene and as prime candidates for rejection as the next step forward in making progress toward attaining our moral goals.

On the other hand, we have not found the pro-animal argument to be mistaken in its fundamental thrust, namely, that research with animals ought (morally) to be governed by the same ethical concerns and principles as research with human subjects. The pro-animal argument merely mistakes how those principles work. This is a superficial error, one that can be corrected to yield the following, sound version of the pro-animal argument:

D1: Sometimes animals can and sometimes they cannot freely and with understanding give or withhold consent to participate in experiments.

D2: Experiments can (morally) be performed only

    (i) on those who freely and with understanding consent to participate in them,

    (ii) when, in situations beyond the subjects' ability to understand how participating in the experiment will (likely) affect their interests, a guardian determines that participating in the experiment would (likely) be either innocuous to or beneficial for the research subjects and freely and with understanding consents for them, or

    (iii) when conducting this research on these subjects is the only available way to attain a clear and present, massive, desperately needed good that greatly outweights the sacrifice involved in the experiment and where such sacrifice is minimized and fairly distributed among those likely to benefit from the research.

D3: Therefore, experiments can (morally) be performed on animals only when condition (i), (ii), or (iii) in D2 obtains.

To adhere to D3 would be to apply to animals employed in research the same sort of moral protection currently enjoyed by human research subjects. Consequently, adhering to D3 is at least a part of what liberating research animals would involve.

Concretely, what would follow from D3? Returning to Professors Barnes and Jacobs, Professor Barnes's research satisfies D3. By voluntarily participating in his experiment, the monkeys give their free, sufficiently informed consent to participate in the research. Here, condition (i) of D2 is met.

On the other hand, Professor Jacobs's cats, by their contrary behavior, withhold consent. If the cats were given a responsible guardian, it might be possible to structure the sleep deprivation studies in a way that provided the cats fair compensation for participating in the research. If that were done, then the guardian could override the cats' contrary behavior and give consent for them. Condition (ii) of D2 would then be met. Of course, the chance of that happening is currently on a par with the chances of the proverbial snowball in hell. Consequently, it is reasonable to presume that condition (ii) of D2 has not been met in Professor Jacobs's research. Finally, sleep deprivation studies like those here ascribed to Professor Jacobs cannot be justified under condition (iii) of D2. They are not the only way to proceed in trying to relieve sleep apnea and other sleep disorders and do not distribute sacrifices fairly, since the animals on which the research is being carried out, considered either individually or as a species, are not in need of the research. Consequently, sleep deprivation studies such as those ascribed to Professor Jacobs ought (morally) to be stopped, until, if ever, they are structured in a way that meets condition (ii) of D2.

Consider another case much in the news of late, research directed toward using animals as organ donors for humans. It might be thought that this research could be justified under heading (iii) of D2, where the sacrifice of individuals in research is permitted. However, that is not the case, for the following three reasons:

(a) The burdens of this research are not distributed fairly among those likely to benefit from the research. Since it is not contemplated that heart, liver, or other organ transplants will be used to save animals' lives, animals as a group have nothing to gain from this research. And since the individual animals employed in this research are healthy and will be killed in the research, they have nothing to gain here. Since they bear all the burdens and receive none of the benefits, this research clearly exploits animals.

(b) The good to be obtained through this research does not outweigh the evil it generates. Many animals will be killed in this research, and if the transplant techniques prove successful, then the number of animals killed to provide donor organs will be approximately the same as the number of human recipients of these organs. Perhaps some animals will be killed to donate more than one organ, but some people will need to receive more than one donation. Consequently, such research is not directed toward minimizing suffering; it aims merely at shifting that burden, from "us" to "them."

(c) It has not been shown that this research is the only way to attack the problems at hand or that it is even likely to be the most effective way of dealing with defective or diseased organs. Mechanical substitutes, genetic engineering, corrective surgery, and preventive medicine all are alternative ways of dealing with these problems. It is standard medical practice to undertake more destructive, irreversible procedures only after less destructive, reversible procedures have proven ineffective. Condition (iii) of D2 involves applying that principle to animal research and would, therefore, prohibit current organ donor research on animals.

Other forms of animal research, such as mother deprivation studies and psychosexual studies, are even more obviously incapable of meeting the moral standards we have put forward here, that is, the moral standards currently employed in research with human subjects. So although liberating animals would not entail stopping all animal research—any more than respecting human rights entails stopping all research with human subjects—if we were to apply our common moral principles impartially to animal research, virtually all of that research would have to be radically restructured or terminated.

13

Saving the Rabbit from the Fox

IN DISCUSSIONS of animal rights, the issue of predation is usually raised either as a rationalization for our killing animals or as the basis for a *reductio ad absurdum* ("showing what foolishness it would lead to") objection to the claim that we are morally obligated to alleviate avoidable, unjustified animal suffering. That rationalization takes the form, "Since they prey on each other, we are morally justified in preying on them." This "Let them reap what they sow!" response to animal rights was dealt with in Chapter 6. The *reductio*, which will be the subject of this chapter, takes the following form:

The Predation *Reductio*
A1: Suppose that humans were morally obligated to alleviate avoidable, unjustified animal suffering.
A2: Innocent animals suffer when they are preyed upon by other animals.
A3: It would follow that humans are morally obligated to prevent predation.
A4: But an obligation to prevent predation would be absurd.
A5: Therefore, contrary to hypothesis, humans are not morally obligated to alleviate avoidable, unjustified animal suffering.

There are three ways in which this argument may be successfully countered:

I. Challenging the evaluation in A4.
II. Challenging that A3 follows from A1 and A2.
III. Challenging that A5 follows from A1 through A4.

We shall develop each of these response strategies in turn. But before doing so, I want to spend a moment discussing and dismissing some common but faulty responses to the predation *reductio*.

One such response runs as follows:

Moral obligations are directed toward rational agents, who can inhibit or extend their activity in recognition of those obligations. But animals are not rational agents, or at least they are not sufficiently rational to recognize and respond to moral obligations. Therefore, a moral obligation for humans to alleviate avoidable, unjustified animal suffering cannot entail a moral obligation for animals not to be predatory.

This response attempts to follow the second strategy noted above. That is, it challenges the inference from A1 and A2 to A3 in the predation *reductio*.

The problem with this response is that it misinterprets A3. The conclusion reached in A3 is not that *animals* are morally obligated to stop being predators. A3 asserts that *we* (i.e., humans) are morally obligated to prevent predation. Consequently, the inference from A1 and A2 to A3 does not even raise the issue of a moral obligation had by predatory animals that they should somehow recognize and observe. So this first response to the predation *reductio* is simply irrelevant to that argument.

It might be countered that it does not make sense to conclude that we have a moral obligation to prevent animals from being predators unless they are morally obligated not to be predators. It would then follow that even if the inference from A1 and A2 to A3 does not involve an explicit claim that animals are subjects of moral obligation, it presumes that they are.

Such a counterargument would be mistaken. There is no conceptual problem with the idea that we, as moral$_{ad}$ agents, are obligated to prevent others, who (supposedly) are not moral$_{ad}$ agents, from doing harm. We routinely apply this idea when we hold parents responsible for preventing their premoral$_{ad}$ children from doing harm. That a young child "doesn't know any better" does not prevent us from being morally obligated to stop him from tormenting the cat. So that the cat does not know any better cannot prevent us from being morally obligated to stop it from killing birds. Consequently, this attempt to defeat the inference from A1 and A2 to A3 fails.

A second faulty response to the predation *reductio* runs something like this:

Since animals cannot be morally obligated not to be predators, there is nothing wrong with their being predators. But we cannot be morally obligated to prevent predation, if there is nothing wrong with it.

This objection again follows the second of the response strategies above. Here, the specific strategy is to challenge the moral significance of A2 in the predation *reductio*. The animal suffering caused by predation is here denied moral significance by presuming that the moral value of an action derives entirely from the agent's responding or not responding to moral rules, that is, derives entirely from whether or not he or she has acted as a moral$_{ad}$ agent.

As argued at length in Chapters 2 and 3, that presumption is mistaken. Consider once again the example of a young child tormenting a cat. The child may be too young to recognize and respond to humane, moral obligations. However, while this may influence our evaluation of his character and responsibility for his actions, it does not lead us to conclude that there is nothing morally wrong with his tormenting the cat. Tormenting cats remains a moral wrong, whether it is done by someone who "ought to know better" or by someone who "can't tell right from wrong." To take another example, if we determine that someone is criminally insane (i.e., is incapable of distinguishing right from wrong), this affects our evaluation of his responsibility for his actions and of whether he deserves punishment for them. However, it does not lead us to conclude that there was nothing wrong with those actions. That they were committed by the criminally insane does not make cases of unjustified homicide and forced sexual intercourse morally neutral. They are still cases of murder and of rape.

Being unable to distinguish right from wrong may leave agents "innocent" in the sense of "not culpable," but it does not leave their actions "innocent" in the sense of "being neither morally right nor morally wrong." Those actions may still be morally right or wrong; it is just that the agent cannot recognize this. While Kantians are correct when they emphasize that actions done for different reasons may have different moral values, they are not correct when they conclude that the entire moral value of an action derives from the agent's will. There are agent-independent dimensions to our moral evaluations, such as those concerning the consequences of actions, as well as agent-dependent dimensions. Consequently, there could be a moral wrong for us to right in predation, even if that wrong cannot be the animals' failure to fulfill their moral obligations. It may be a moral$_{ai}$ wrong deriving from the utilitarian side of our common morality. So this second response to the predation *reductio* also fails.

The last of the common but faulty responses we will consider runs as follows:

> In being predators, animals are just following their nature. We ought (morally) to respect the natural needs and impulses of others. Therefore, we ought (morally) not to interfere with predation.

This response again implements the second of the response strategies above by challenging the moral significance of A2 in the predation *reductio*. This response presumes that respecting nature has a higher priority among our moral values than does alleviating avoidable, unjustified animal suffering. If correct, that presumption would morally justify the animal suffering caused by predation by making it a lesser evil than would be the disrespect for nature involved in attempting to prevent predation. This response may also be seen as an "environmental ethics analog" to the independent valuer principle, discussed in Chapter 10, that "we don't have a right to force our values onto others." Here, those "others" are predatory animals.

Everyday morality indicates that that presumption is mistaken. One of the fundamental and pervasive functions of moral rules and education is to delimit and inhibit the ways in which native needs can (morally) be fulfilled and natural impulses can (morally) be pursued. Especially when some of our "doing what comes naturally" results in the suffering or death of others, the standard moral response is that here is an aspect or expression of human nature that does not merit our moral respect. Examples of this would be our lack of moral respect for and many efforts to inhibit our tendencies to aggression and dominance. I know of no reason why extrahuman nature should be entitled to moral respect that human nature is not due. We may also note that we simply do not accept this third response to the predation *reductio* when our pets or children are the intended victims of predators, as occasionally happens when we venture into their territory or when, through destroying their habitats, we leave them no other survival option than to venture into our communities in search of prey. When it comes to our loved ones, we clearly give higher priority to preventing suffering than to respecting nature.

The same may be said, if we think of this third response as an analog to the independent valuer principle. The moral respect due others' pursuit of their own values is conditional, at least, on that pursuit's not denying others the opportunity to pursue their values. For example, we are not morally obligated to respect slave owners' desire to dominate and their ideal of a world in which they command vast armies of slaves. Similarly, since predators obviously deny their prey the opportunity to pursue their values, we are not morally obligated by the independent valuer principle to respect predatory pursuits.

Thus, this third response to the predation *reductio* assigns a priority to the natural and to respecting individual values that is not confirmed by common moral practice. While this does not invalidate the argument, it does show that such an argument has a heavy burden of proof to meet before it poses a serious challenge to the predation *reductio*. It also suggests that this third response is disingenuous, as are so many other "It's only natural!" references in moral discussions. Where our interests or the interests of those we care for will be sacrificed, we do not recognize a moral obligation to "let nature take its course." But when we do not want to be bothered with an obligation, "That's just the way the world works" provides a handy excuse.

We shall now develop in turn each of the three response strategies noted at the beginning of this chapter. Each of these strategies provides an answer sufficient to defuse the predation *reductio*. The second and third strategies are not being developed here because of any doubts I have about the adequacy of the first strategy. The reason for taking time to deal with all three of them is that in addition to dealing with the predation issue, they provide opportunities for reflecting on general questions concerning the logic of moral reasoning. Each of these responses raises, and resolves in a different way, the question of the practical significance of *reductio ad absurdum* arguments in moral reasoning, where they are a much used and, I think, abused tactic.

I. The Variety of Absurdity

Would a moral obligation to prevent predation be absurd?

Conjuring up pictures of militant animal rightists fanning out across land and sea to protect mice from snakes and owls, rabbits from hawks and foxes, fish from bears and sharks, and otherwise making the world safe for the small and the herbivorous can easily make a moral obligation to prevent predation appear absurd. But appearances can be deceiving. What is commonly lost in the laugh of the predation *reductio* is that there are several different ways in which something can be absurd and that the legitimacy of the evaluation in A4 cannot be ascertained until we know just which of these forms of absurdity is being asserted.

When philosophers (perhaps others, too) think of absurdity, the first thing that comes to mind is logical absurdity. The classic form of the *reductio ad absurdum* argument requires that the conclusion entailed by the hypothesis in question be inconsistent with some basic principle of reasoning like the laws of geometry, arithmetic, or logic. However, logical absurdity cannot be the sense of "absurdity" employed in A4. That humans ought (morally) to prevent predation is simply not in a class with attempting to square the circle, to make two plus two equal five, or to have a sentence be both true and false at the same time and place and in the same way. Since a moral obligation for humans to prevent predation would not violate the formal laws of reasoning, A3 cannot be logically absurd.

A more modern form of the *reductio* is the use of hypothetical-deductive reasoning to falsify scientific hypotheses. In this sort of *reductio*, the conclusion entailed by the hypothesis must be inconsistent with what is observed as fact. But A3 does not contain a factual claim, for example, about the existence of a legal statute obligating us to prevent predation. Rather, A3 contains an imperative directing us to undertake such prevention. Since A3 does not contain a factual claim, it cannot be inconsistent with some observed matter of fact. Consequently, A3 cannot be "factually absurd" either.

Another way in which A3 might be absurd could be labeled "contextual absurdity." A conclusion is contextually absurd if it is inconsistent with (the spirit of) one or more of its premises. It might be argued that what is absurd about A3 is that in attempting to prevent predation, we would occasion much more suf-

fering than we would prevent. Most obviously, we would have to frustrate predators and perhaps even drive many of them to extinction (in the wild). Furthermore, we would have to control the population explosion among the former prey
that our prevention of predation would occasion. This would require frustrating
many of these animals, too, and would probably necessitate subjecting some of
them to the trauma of surgery in order to sterilize them. Finally, eliminating
predation would be such a massive, onerous task that seriously attempting it
might also seriously compromise the quality of our lives.

As to just how bleak the indirect consequences of eliminating predation might
be, I will not quibble. This sort of objection is easily and reasonably met by
reformulating A3 as follows:

> A3′: It would follow that humans are morally obligated to prevent preda-
> tion whenever doing so would not occasion as much or more suffering
> than it would prevent.

A3′ does not represent a retreat from the moral stance being advocated in A1.
A3′ merely makes explicit how A3 must be interpreted, since A3 is to be a
consequence of A1. A1 refers to *alleviating* animal suffering, and this would not
be accomplished if preventing the suffering caused by predation led to animals'
(and humans charged with preventing predation) enduring even greater suffering.
Hence, only if A3 is interpreted as (something like) A3′ does it validly follow
from A1 and A2.

It might be countered that while A3′ meets the contextual objection, it does
so by postulating a vacuous obligation, since there are no cases of predation that
would fall under it. However, that is not true. A3′ would immediately obligate us
to prevent our pets from being predators. It would also obligate us to begin
exploring other ways in which we could reduce the suffering caused by predation
without occasioning as much or more suffering, for instance, in zoos, wildlife
preserves, and other areas where we are already managing animals.

Thus, A3′ contains a substantive obligation that is in the spirit of our moral
obligation to alleviate avoidable, unjustified animal suffering. Consequently, if
contextual absurdity is the charge in A4, then A4 is unjustified, and we can make
this immediately clear by substituting A3′ for A3.

Recent studies of the use of paradigms in science suggest yet another way in
which a *reductio* may work. The proposed conclusion may be inconsistent with
some well-supported, thoroughly accepted theory, the principles of which seem
much less questionable than the hypothesis from which the offending conclusion
derives. Then, forced to choose between the well-supported, thoroughly accepted
theory and the more questionable hypothesis, we would be justified in rejecting
that hypothesis on the grounds that what it entails is "theoretically absurd." For
example, if the conclusions of one's cosmological theorizing were inconsistent

with contemporary quantum mechanics, those conclusions could (logically) be considered unworthy of serious consideration and the bases for them dismissed. This sort of absurdity is like logical absurdity, the difference being that here the principles with which the offending conclusion is inconsistent are substantive ones, while in the case of logical absurdity, those principles were strictly formal ones.

In the case at hand, environmental ethicists who hold that "a thing is right when it tends to preserve the integrity, stability, and beauty of the biotic community, [and] it is wrong when it tends otherwise"[1] would doubtless find a moral obligation to prevent predation to be theoretically absurd. However, such an evaluation could not be sustained, since the environmental principle above does not enjoy anything like the wide acceptance that the basis for an evaluation of theoretical absurdity must possess. Indeed, that environmental principle is so contrary to paradigm ethical principles (e.g., in giving intrinsic moral value to inanimate objects) that it is much more likely to be the object of a theoretical *reductio* than the basis for one.

A libertarian principle to the effect that we have only "negative obligations" to others (i.e., obligations to respect their liberty and property) and consequently cannot have "positive obligations" to help others out, be they humans or animals, could also be put forward here as the basis for a charge of theoretical absurdity. However, once again libertarianism is simply not itself sufficiently well established to bear the weight of that contention. Moral obligations to contribute to charity, to support social welfare programs, to help defend the weak against the strong, and to engage in other Good Samaritan activities have long been and still are too prominent a part of our common morality for libertarianism to be considered well-supported and thoroughly accepted. The same holds true for any theory that would attempt to restrict our moral obligations to fulfilling contracts we have made. The people who listened but did nothing while Kitty Genovese was being beaten to death on the streets of New York a few years ago did not violate any contract, but they have commonly been held to have shirked their minimal moral duty by not even calling the police to help her. If libertarianism or some sort of contractarianism someday supplants our traditional, everyday morality, then when that happens, they can provide a basis for a charge that A3′ is theoretically absurd. But until that harsh, sad day dawns, if it ever does, they are not in a position to provide that basis.

Of course, we shall not even try to make a complete survey of other possible bases for finding a moral obligation to prevent predation (when we can do so without occasioning as much or more suffering than would be prevented thereby) to be theoretically absurd. Instead, noting the following is sufficient to indicate that that obligation is not theoretically absurd. First, that obligation is not inconsistent with or even an obstacle to attaining the three common, moral goals we have dealt with throughout this study, namely, developing moral character, minimizing suffering and otherwise maximizing well-being, and insuring fairness. In the moral arena, it is such platitudinous principles that form the basis on which a charge of theoretical absurdity would have to be supported. Consequently, unless we have left something out—and I think we have been sufficiently eclectic in our account of everyday morality not to have to fear any serious omissions here—a moral obligation to prevent predation cannot, at least for the present, be theoretically absurd.

Second, the humane principle in A1 is very widely accepted today, even if just what follows from that principle is still a matter of considerable controversy. Usually, it is not the obligation in A1 but interpretations of "avoidable" and "suffering" within that obligation and questions about whether there are rights correlated with this obligation that are at issue. For example, even many hunters would accept A1, contending that in being careful to take only "clear shots" and to track down any wounded animals and quickly "put them out of their misery," they were fulfilling their obligation to prevent "avoidable, unjustified animal suffering." Consequently, it is highly doubtful that there are moral principles that are so much more thoroughly accepted than our obligation to alleviate avoidable, unjustified animal suffering that they could serve as the basis for discrediting that humane obligation on the grounds that A3′ is inconsistent with them and is, therefore, theoretically absurd. Rather, if there are such conflicting moral principles, we would (initially, at least) be left in a condition of moral perplexity, with widely accepted principles entailing inconsistent obligations. So even if A3′ were inconsistent with some moral principles, it would not follow that it could properly be characterized as "theoretically absurd." Principles of humane morality are probably too widely accepted nowadays to permit a theoretical *reductio* of them.

Yet another way in which A3′ might be considered absurd is suggested by the widely accepted principle that "ought implies can." The purpose of morality is to make the world a better place through directing the actions of moral agents to that end. Consequently, a moral obligation to do something we cannot do would contradict the very purpose of morality. It follows that what we can do provides a criterion of whether proposed moral obligations make sense or are absurd. Let us say that an obligation is "practically absurd" if it commands us to do something that we cannot do. Now, it really does seem inconceivable that we will ever be able to eliminate predation. Eliminating carnivorous and omnivorous wildlife entirely is not an acceptable solution to the predation problem, since our commitment to minimizing suffering derives from our common, moral commitment to maximizing the excess of enjoyment and fulfillment in life. But if we do not entirely eliminate carnivorous and omnivorous wildlife, how are we to stop predators from catching rodents in the highland valleys of the Rockies and big fish

from eating little fish in the ocean depths? Only God can see—and could prevent
—each sparrow's fall.

As was the case with contextual absurdity, this objection is not as serious as it
appears to be. That a condition is one that we cannot attain does not disqualify it
from being a useful moral ideal for us. For example, standard Christian ethics
instructs us to follow Christ's example, even though we can never be as good as
Christ, since he was divine, and we are not. Similarly, as noted in Chapter 3,
Kant asserts that the ultimate obligation in morality is to become a holy will,
which is something that we can never do, since we are not purely rational beings
but have a sensuous nature in addition to our rational side. Kant makes this
situation practical by interpreting that ultimate moral obligation as an obligation
for us to strive to approximate ever more closely to the unattainable ideal of
being holy.[2]

Such examples indicate that what is required of a practical moral ideal is not
that it be attainable but merely that it be something that we can work toward. As
noted in the discussion of contextual absurdity, this is a condition that the obligation to prevent predation can meet. There are things that we can do right now,
such as belling our cats, and studies that we can undertake to discover further
things we can do to help alleviate the suffering caused by predation. So even if we
cannot foresee ourselves being able to stop predation entirely, the obligation to
prevent predation can still function as a moral ideal guiding what we can do.
Consequently, it is not practically absurd.

This would seem to leave only the idea that A3′ is absurd because it would
direct humans to overstep their "proper place in nature." It might be claimed that
in even pursuing A3′ as a moral ideal, we would be working toward attaining
Godlike control over nature, something that is not merely impractical but a false
ideal for our moral endeavors.

Basically, this sort of objection is nothing more than purple prose. Appeals to
what is "natural and proper" have routinely been pressed as objections to every
moral innovation from the Emancipation Proclamation through women's suffrage
to birth control. These past appeals to the naturally proper have proven to be
nothing more than excuses for maintaining the status quo or for promoting personal preferences. There is no reason to believe that such appeals are anything
but excuses in the discussion of our moral obligations to animals either.

Furthermore, working toward preventing predation would merely be an extension of a common human activity that is not ordinarily regarded as unnatural
or as an expression of the sin of pride. We routinely interfere with nature in order
to protect ourselves (and animals, too) from such threats to (the quality of) life as
flooding rivers, storms, avalanches, erosion, pestilence, diseases, birth defects,
infections, and decay. Interfering with nature in an attempt to make the world a

less dangerous, more enjoyable and fulfilling place to live is a part of being human and of pursuing one of our common, moral goals. Admittedly, we have not always pursued this project successfully or even wisely, as evidenced by the great expanses of water we have poisoned and the many diseases we have created or exacerbated in our efforts to improve (the quality of) life. But particular failures and stupidities do not demonstrate that the project itself is somehow unnatural, an offense against God, or an attempt to overstep "our assigned place" in the world (allowing, for the purpose of argument, that it even makes sense to use such a phrase).

Finally, since this sort of objection is often expressed in at least quasi-religious terms and probably makes sense only in some sort of religious context, an appeal to religious authority would seem to be the most likely way of trying to support it. However, if we turn to Judeo-Christian scripture, specifically Genesis 1:26, we find that God gave humans dominion over the earth and all that live upon it. No matter how we interpret "dominion," from absolute power to stewardship, it follows that God has, at the very least, given us permission to manage nature. Furthermore, since that same verse tells us that God is a creator and that humans have been created in His image, it follows that in exercising our dominion over the earth, we can be expected to re-create it to some degree—and that re-creation is not limited by a commandment stating, "Thou shalt not interfere with predation!" Thus, Judeo-Christian tradition does not support the contention that it would be improper for us to attempt to prevent predation.

Of course, there are other scriptures besides the Bible. However, if there are conflicting religious teachings on this issue, that fact, along with the notorious difficulties involved in trying to find rational grounds for choosing among competing religious traditions, is sufficient to blunt the force of this objection to our having a moral obligation to prevent predation. Consequently, it seems fair to conclude that the charge that A3' is "unnaturally absurd" is merely rhetorical, does not fit with common practice and draws unjustified conclusions from our past failures in attempting to improve (the quality of) life, or is unjustified by the religious context needed to make it at all sensible. Whichever the option, when interpreted as a charge of unnatural absurdity, A4 is left unjustified.

Thus, we have noted that A4 might be claiming any one of six different things in charging that an obligation to prevent predation would be "absurd." Surveying these six, we have determined that:

> two, logical and factual absurdity, are clearly irrelevant,
> one, contextual absurdity, is irrelevant, once we have clarified A3, as we did in formulating A3',
> two, theoretical and unnatural absurdity, cannot be justified, given our current, common moral practice, and

one, practical absurdity, is defused by acknowledging that preventing predation may be an unattainable but approachable moral ideal, rather than an
attainable moral goal.

It follows that A4 is unjustified and that, consequently, the predation *reductio* of
our moral obligation to alleviate avoidable, unjustified animal suffering fails.

Of the reasons just offered for this failure, perhaps the one with the greatest
general import is that although something may be impractical as an attainable
goal of our moral endeavors, that does not disqualify it from being a useful moral
ideal guiding what we can accomplish. The specter of gross impracticality seems
to be what underlies the feeling that there is something absurd in the idea of
humans being morally obligated to prevent predation. Recognizing that an unattainable condition can still serve as a useful guiding ideal for what is attainable
disperses this specter by giving practical import to the unattainable and by showing that an obligation is not absurd just because it commands us to pursue what
we cannot attain.

II. Ought Implies Can

Would a moral obligation to prevent avoidable, unjustified animal suffering
entail a moral obligation to prevent predation?

Through the years, moral philosophers have agreed with Aristotle that ethics
is "a practical science," but just what is involved in a science's being practical
is not well established. A classical ideal, exemplified in Plato's *Republic* and
Spinoza's *Ethics*, is that reason functions in fundamentally the same way in all
the sciences. Only the subject matters and the conclusions are supposed to be
different, the conclusion of theoretical reasoning being knowledge, while the conclusion of practical reasoning is action. On the other hand, contemporary, noncognitivist meta-ethical theories point toward fundamental differences in the
operations of reason in practical and theoretical endeavors. For example, according to such theories, while theoretical reasoning aims at discovering what is true,
practical reasoning aims at determining what is "acceptable" or "warranted."[3]

I find the noncognitivist analysis more credible than the classical ideal, and
what I want to suggest here is that there is a rule for practical reasoning that
renders one kind of *reductio* invalid in practical contexts, even though that kind
of argument does not violate the general rules of logic. The effect of this rule will
be to render a certain critical strategy fallacious in practical contexts like ethics.

This rule is suggested by a recent response to one of the critical strategies
traditionally employed against utilitarianism. Such criticisms of utilitarianism
take the form of imagining some Brave New World that seems to fulfill the principle of utility but is intuitively unacceptable. This is supposed to provide a

reductio of utilitarianism (presumably, it is supposed to be a theoretical *reductio*). For example, environmental ethicists have criticized utilitarianism on the grounds that if we were capable of replacing nature with a plastic environment that would give as much happiness as the natural one to all sentient beings involved (something we are not even near being able to do), then the principle of utility could not generate an obligation for us to favor the natural environment over the plastic one. From this they conclude that utilitarianism does not provide an adequate foundation for environmental ethics. For example, Tom Regan writes, "Hedonistic utilitarianism fails to qualify as an ethic of the environment. Its shortcomings are highlighted by asking, 'Why not plastic trees? Why not lawns of astro-turf, or mountains of papier-mache suitably coated with vinyl to withstand harsh weather?'"[4]

A recent line of response to this sort of criticism has been to deny the relevance of such imaginary constructions by arguing that since moral philosophies, such as utilitarianism, are designed for working with the problems of the world in which we actually live, they must (logically) be evaluated on the basis of how they instruct us to deal with real, not imaginary, problems, endeavors, and possibilities.[5] Thus, this defense of utilitarianism undercuts a line of criticism by emphasizing the practicality of ethics, and this takes the form of confining the domain of inference from the principle of utility to matters of contemporary concern and possible response.

I find this defense of utilitarianism thoroughly appropriate, since I find science fiction and "worst conceivable case" criticisms of ethical principles to miss the point of doing ethics, a *practical* science, altogether. Now, what I want to do here is to propose a Kantian analog to this defense of utilitarianism. What I propose is that "ought implies can" be interpreted as a principle of practical reasoning. In that capacity, it specifies a rule of inference for practical reasoning that can be formulated as follows:

> R1: An argument of the form "P1, P2, P3, . . . , Pn/Therefore, *S* ought to *z*" is valid only if "*S* can *z*" is true (where "can" means actually or theoretically but not merely logically possible).

I am not suggesting that R1 is an adequate logical translation of "ought implies can." Indeed, I suspect that logically specifying "ought implies can" as a principle of practical reasoning would require elaborating a whole family of rules for practical reasoning. For example, in addition to the inference rule above, there must also be a selection rule (e.g., for underived moral principles) that could be formulated in the following way:

> R2: "*S* ought to *z*" is an acceptable principle only if "*S* can (actually or theoretically but not just logically) *z*" is true.

Fortunately, it is not necessary to produce the entire family in order to deal with the predation *reductio*. So we will be concentrating here on the implications of adopting R1.

We discussed above several different kinds of *reductios*, differentiating them on the basis of the way in which the proposed conclusion is supposed to be absurd. Although R1 will occasionally rule out theoretical *reductios* on practical grounds, as in the case of the supposed environmental *reductio* of utilitarianism just discussed, it does not essentially affect most of those kinds of *reductios*. However, it does essentially affect those of the form

B1: If *P* were accepted, then *S* would be obligated to do something, *z*, that she cannot do.

B2: But since "*S* can *z*" is false, "*S* ought to *z*" is absurd.

B3: Therefore, *P* is unacceptable.

According to R1, this practical *reductio* does not discredit *P*. Rather, the inference, contained in B1, from *P*'s being accepted to *S*'s being obligated to do *z* is invalid precisely because *S* cannot do *z*. That is, in a practical science (i.e., one that, among other things, adopts R1), the practical *reductio* is not an available line of criticism. This is because in a practical science, it is not the case that inferences to impractical obligations are valid but unsound, as they would have to be for a legitimate *reductio*. Rather, here such inferences are simply invalid. (Since it is doubtful that a *practical reductio* would be of any use in a nonpractical context, it follows that the practical *reductio* is probably an altogether worthless form of criticism.)

To make this a bit more concrete, consider the following example:

C1: We ought to make the world a happier place in which to live.

C2: Inventing a perpetual motion machine would make the world a happier place in which to live.

C3: Therefore, we ought to invent a perpetual motion machine.

C4: But we cannot invent a perpetual motion machine.

C5: Therefore, we are not obligated to make the world a happier place in which to live.

Employing only the standard principles for valid syllogistic reasoning (e.g., having the right number of terms and distributions of terms in the argument), the inference from C1 to C3 is a valid argument. But as indicated in C4, C3 is not an acceptable conclusion, since it would obligate us to do something we cannot do. Consequently, the inference from C1 to C3 must be unsound, and presuming that C2 is not in dispute, C1 must be unacceptable. (Soundness usually concerns whether statements in the premises are true, but in a practical syllogism, some of the premises are imperatives, not statements, so the concept of soundness must be expanded a bit to include the acceptability of imperative premises.) Now, following the proposal above, since C1 to C3 is a bit of practical reasoning, we will add R1 to our arsenal of rules for valid reasoning. With R1 in place, that "We can invent a perpetual motion machine" is false now shows that the inference from C1 to C3 is not merely unsound but *invalid*. It follows that the *reductio* of C1 based on that inference is unsound, since C1 no longer entails the unacceptable conclusion, C3. Thus, if we employ R1, the information supplied in C4 no longer functions logically to show that C3 is unacceptable; rather, its logical import is now to show that the inference from C1 to C3 is invalid.

Of course, this conclusion depends on R1 (or something very much like it) being acceptable, and while having special rules of inference for limited domains of reasoning is unproblematic, it might be objected that a rule of reasoning which bases the validity of an inference on something's being true confuses logical with factual issues. However, while such a criticism might be well taken from the viewpoint of theoretical reasoning, if one's concern is practical, then keeping inferences in touch with the problems, endeavors, and possibilities of the world in which we actually live is not confusion but reasonableness. Limiting our concern to real problems, endeavors, and possibilities is at least an important part of what it means to be "practical," and what R1 does is to make a formal contribution to specifying that practical attitude. (R2 and further members of this family would further that contribution.) Consequently, it would be a category mistake to criticize R1 for not employing the distinction between logical and factual issues employed in admittedly nonpractical contexts.

We may also note that basing the validity of inferences on factual considerations is not unheard of, even in the theoretical sciences. The most obvious example of this is the "existential hypothesis" found in syllogistic logic. When employing this logic to draw conclusions about S, we are to presume that there are some Ss. This presumption is necessary, for example, for the immediate inference from "All dogs are animals" to "Some dogs are animals" to be valid. Perhaps Aristotle's presumption of the existential hypothesis is a testimony to his belief that even logic should be practical. While the logician in us may be intrigued by empty sets and their logical peculiarities—for example, if there are no mermaids then "All mermaids are compassionate" and "No mermaids are compassionate," which would otherwise be contrary, are both true—it is difficult, perhaps impossible, to think of cases where we attempt to resolve real, nonlogical problems by making inferences from statements predicating properties of things that (we believe) do not exist. Consequently, something like Aristotle's existential hypothesis could be another rule for reasoning in a *practical* science.

The following objection has also been raised, by Evelyn Pluhar, against R1:

Technically valid but impractical ethical arguments seem easy enough to construct. For example, consider the argument that "We all ought to bring the dead back to life. S's mother is dead; so, he ought to bring her back to life." Wouldn't a practical *reductio* be very appropriate here? Surely the *premise* of this argument, not just its conclusion, is unacceptable.[6]

The point of this criticism seems to be that the practical *reductio* is an "appropriate" way of keeping "our *premises* in touch [with the facts]," as Pluhar goes on to say.

What is and what is not "appropriate" is a difficult issue to get a firm grip on. We can note that adopting R1 certainly would not render "We all ought to bring the dead back to life" acceptable. Nor would it leave us unable to show that that imperative is unacceptable. Since "We all can bring the dead back to life" is false, that imperative would be ruled out by the selection rule R2, mentioned above, if it were put forward as an underived principle, and it would be ruled out by R1, if it were being derived from other principles. Consequently, adopting R1 and, thereby, eliminating the practical *reductio* from our critical arsenal, would not make it impossible for us to criticize impractical premises. Nor do R1 and R2 seem cumbersome, unintuitive, or otherwise less "appropriate" than a practical *reductio* for accomplishing such criticism.

Pluhar's dissatisfaction with R1 is only a particular expression of her general dissatisfaction with the concept of practical reasoning we have been developing in this section. Following the comments above, she adds:

> Certainly, ethical theories are meant to guide us in "the real world," but they do so by grounding our moral obligations in principles of moral considerability and significance. These basic principles can only be tested clearly if relevant factors are isolated, as they can be (and sometimes only) in imaginary cases. For example, quantitative hedonistic utilitarianism implies that if we could keep an otherwise normal human in a permanent state of euphoria through drugs or direct brain stimulation without shortening his life or decreasing the happiness of others, we should do so. To object that we cannot do this *now* is beside the point. The question is whether our only basic obligation is to increase the quantity of happiness in the world. This is what our case is meant to test.

In response, we may note that we do not have to imagine something like Pluhar's Brave New World in order to determine "whether our only basic obligation is to increase the quantity of happiness in the world." Indeed, we do not at all *discover* the inadequacy of quantitative hedonistic utilitarianism through constructing Brave New Worlds like Pluhar's. Rather, the construction of such *reductio* worlds is guided by the conviction we already have that theories like quantitative hedonistic utilitarianism are inadequate. This is a conviction that we have gained through (reflecting on) our common moral experience and that, because it rests on that real, substantial foundation, could not be overturned by any merely imaginary, so-called "test" case.

The sort of important conceptual work of clarification, testing, and refinement of moral principles that Pluhar has in mind can certainly be done through a process of imaginative variation. But I find that this work provides significant answers only when those cases are imagined variations of real situations, rather than imaginary extensions beyond the realm of current problems, endeavors, and possibilities. The discussion of the bank robbery in Chapter 2 is an example of such imaginative variation of a real possibility. Nothing said in this chapter about limiting practical reasoning to the currently "real world" would preclude that sort of imaginative analysis.

What that restriction would prohibit are fanciful extensions, like Pluhar's case and the "plastic environment" objection to utilitarianism noted earlier. Such cases are unnecessary for accomplishing ethical analyses and seem to do little if anything besides emotionally reinforce what we already believe, thereby forestalling serious objections to those beliefs. For example, phrases like "plastic environment" and "plastic trees" are supposed to make it *obvious* that something has gone wrong. For many of us, to say that something is made of plastic is still to say something derogatory about it—metal, wood, and glass are what substantial, honest, dependable, quality things are made of. Also, the phrase "plastic trees" refers to artificial trees planted along some Los Angeles freeways because "real trees" could not grow in the fouled air there. Thus, the phrase reminds us that we would certainly never want to live in a world composed of Los Angeles freeways.

But if we fight our way through these connotations and associations, things are not really so obvious. If we really could manufacture an environment that, for as far into the future as we could see, would have a greater excess of enjoyment and fulfillment over distress and frustration than would the natural environment for all sentient beings involved, what would be wrong with preferring that manufactured environment over the natural one? Would it not be merely an expression of some sort of misanthropic prejudice to object, "But it wouldn't be natural!"? The environmental *reductio* of utilitarianism is not intended to provide a serious test for such questions; rather, by focusing our attention on "ticky-tacky plastic" and Los Angeles's fouled air, it is intended to forestall the asking of such questions.

Pluhar says that "we need some powerful reasons to accept [R1 as] an inference rule in moral contexts." I agree. And I think that the fact that R1, along with R2 and other members of their family, can eliminate without loss strategies that are not only unnecessary for doing moral philosophy but that also confuse emotional reinforcement with conceptual testing, thereby forestalling serious discussion, is a sufficiently powerful reason for adopting "ought implies can" as a principle of practical reasoning.

Returning to the predation *reductio*, the analysis of the previous section indicates that if A3′ is absurd, it is because it contains an obligation that we cannot fulfill. Consequently, if the predation *reductio* is to succeed, it must be as a practical *reductio*, rather than as a logical *reductio*, factual *reductio*, and so forth. But since this is a moral issue, the rules of practical reasoning apply, including R1, the prohibition against impractical inferences. Consequently, if A3′ is impractical, A1 and A2 do not entail A3′. That is, if we cannot prevent predation (without occasioning as much or more suffering than we would prevent), then R1 tells us that our moral obligation to alleviate avoidable, unjustified animal suffering cannot entail a moral obligation to prevent predation. Thus, the predation *reductio* is fallacious. The very thing that was supposed to render A3′ absurd actually renders the inference from A1 and A2 to A3′ invalid.

Of course, the analysis of the previous section indicates that a moral obligation to prevent predation would not be impractical, even though completely eliminating predation might be impossible. So R1 is not necessary to save our moral obligation to alleviate avoidable, unjustified animal suffering from the predation *reductio*. Nonetheless, I think that the analysis of this section is especially important, because R1 expresses the proper role for practical absurdity in ethics: impractical inferences do not discredit ethical principles; rather, such inferences help mark the boundaries of ethical concern. We shall develop this idea further in the next section.

III. "Avoidable" Suffering

If a moral obligation to alleviate avoidable, unjustified animal suffering entailed a moral obligation to prevent predation and if the latter obligation would be absurd, would it follow that we are not morally obligated to alleviate avoidable, unjustified animal suffering?

When we find that a hypothesis leads to a false or otherwise unacceptable conclusion, we need not simply infer that the hypothesis is also unacceptable. Rather, the conclusion may be used as a guide for discovering what is wrong with the hypothesis, how we should interpret the hypothesis, how we might revise the hypothesis, or what is and what is not covered by that hypothesis. If in spite of the analyses of the previous sections, we accept A1 through A4 in the predation *reductio*, that argument falls under the last of these options. That is, rather than discrediting A1, the predation *reductio* helps show us what is and what is not covered by our moral obligation to alleviate avoidable, unjustified animal suffering. As noted in our discussion of theoretical absurdity, even many hunters would accept that humane obligation. What is at issue is how that obligation is to be interpreted, and the predation *reductio* actually helps to establish how that humane obligation ought (logically) to be interpreted. It does not show that that humane obligation is unacceptable.

In the first section, we noted that A4 is ambiguous, and the only substantive interpretation we discovered for it would be more clearly formulated as follows:

A4′: That we ought (morally) to prevent predation would be an impractical obligation.

A4′ clearly indicates that what is (supposedly) absurd about the obligation in A3′ is that it is beyond our power to fulfill that obligation. But if we cannot prevent predation, it follows that the suffering of animals preyed upon by other animals is not *avoidable* suffering and, therefore, is not covered by our moral obligation to alleviate avoidable, unjustified animal suffering. This is because in A1 "avoidable" does not mean "not necessitated by logic" or "not necessitated by the (known) laws of physics" or anything of that sort. Here, "avoidable" means "preventable by human beings." Therefore, the conclusion to be drawn from A1 through A4′ is not A5 but the following:

A5′: Therefore, animal suffering due to predation is not included among the cases of animal suffering that humans are morally obligated to alleviate.

Now, saying that predation is "unavoidable" may strike some as being as simplistic and self-serving as saying that eating meat is "necessary" for human health and happiness. However, while predation that is avoidable (e.g., predation by our pets) escapes the argument of the preceding paragraph, it will not help salvage the predation *reductio*. Any predation that is avoidable in the sense at issue here (i.e., preventable by humans) is not something it would be practically absurd for us to be morally obligated to prevent. Therefore, predation covered by A1 is not covered by A4′. So in every case, either the predation is not covered by A1, or it is not covered by A4′. Consequently, in no case can A1 through A4′ justify A5.

In line with the discussion of contextual absurdity in section I, it might be claimed that "avoidable" in A1 should be interpreted as "preventable by humans without occasioning as much or more suffering than is prevented." This interpretation would support the point being made here just as well as the shorter interpretation just discussed. Using the expanded interpretation of "avoidable" would require that we interpret A4 as follows:

A4″: That we ought (morally) to prevent predation would be an obligation to occasion as much or more suffering as we would prevent.

It follows that any case of predation covered by A1 would not be covered by A4″ and *vice versa*. So A1 through A4″ could not support A5 any more than can A1 through A4′.

Of course, the point still remains that not all predation is beyond our power to prevent or even to prevent without occasioning as much or more suffering than is caused by predation. But we now know the practical conclusion to be drawn from this:

Where we can prevent predation without occasioning as much or more suffering than we would prevent, we are morally obligated to do so by the principle that we are morally obligated to alleviate avoidable, unjustified animal suffering. Where we cannot prevent predation or cannot do so without occasioning as much or more suffering than we would prevent, that principle does not morally obligate us to attempt to prevent predation. Indeed, in cases where our interfering with predation would occasion significantly more suffering than the predation would create, we would (*ceteris paribus*) be morally obligated not to interfere with predation, although the humane principle in A1 does morally obligate us to try to discover ways in which we could reduce the number of such regrettable cases, while still working to sustain or improve (the quality of) life and to insure fairness.

IV. Conclusion

The analyses of this chapter allow us to trade in the discredited predation *reductio* for the following inference about our moral obligations concerning predation:

D1: We are morally obligated to alleviate unjustified animal suffering that it is in our power to prevent without occasioning as much or more unjustified suffering.

D2: Innocent animals suffer when they are preyed upon by other animals.

D3: Therefore, we are morally obligated to prevent predation whenever we can do so without occasioning as much or more unjustified suffering than the predation would create, and we are also morally obligated to attempt to expand the number of such cases.

Once this obligation to prevent predation is acknowledged, further issues must be considered in determining how much and what sort of effort ought (morally) to be devoted to fulfilling it. Among these issues is whether we will do more good by attempting to fulfill this obligation or by seeking to alleviate other forms of avoidable, unjustified animal suffering. Now, other than by preventing predation by animals under our control (e.g., pets), it seems likely that for the foreseeable future, animal rights activists will do better by directing their organized efforts on behalf of animals toward alleviating the unjustified suffering humans cause animals than by attempting to prevent predation among animals. Perhaps this question of where one can do the most good is the most substantive question concerning the practicality of a moral obligation to prevent predation.

While that is the specific moral of this story, the general moral that runs through all the analyses above is that although a concern with practicality is definitely relevant in ethical disputations, exactly how the issue of practicality figures into ethical deliberations is not immediately obvious and is in need of careful reflection and clarification. Such clarification may involve carefully differentiating the ways in which different elements of our morality work, for example, differentiating unattainable but approachable moral ideals from attainable moral goals, as was done in section I. Or it may involve recognizing that there are rules for practical reasoning not found in theoretical reasoning, such as the rules discussed in section II. Or it may involve clarifying ambiguities in key terms related to practicality, as was done with "avoidable" in section III. Whichever of these procedures is followed, the issue of practicality will be treated as a guide for moral concern, rather than as an occasion for ridiculing that concern.

14

Plants and Things

THE ANIMAL rights movement has grown dramatically and achieved considerable public and philosophical attention since the early 1970's. During this same time span, the environmental ethics movement has run a parallel course. Many people, philosophers included, believe that these two movements naturally go together. Some animal rights philosophers, most notably Tom Regan, have even tried systematically to extend their animal rights position to develop a non-anthropocentric ethic for the environment.[1] On the other hand, some environmental ethicists, such as J. Baird Callicott, have emphasized fundamental, theoretical and practical differences between animal rights ethics and environmental ethics, finding, of course, the latter to be superior to the former.[2] I agree with Callicott that there are fundamental differences between animal liberation ethics, like the one developed above, and the sort of environmental ethics he espouses, that is, ecological "holism," deriving from the writings of Aldo Leopold.[3] However, I find that these differences favor animal liberation, both logically and morally, over ecological holism.

In this chapter, we first review Tom Regan's attempt to develop an environmental ethic from his animal rights position and the problems besetting that attempt. Next, we critique Callicott's ecological holism and his criticisms of animal liberation. Finally, we sketch the environmental ethic that follows from the animal liberation ethic developed in the preceding chapters.

I. Environmental Ethics and Inherent Value

Regan's conception of environmental ethics seems to be guided by the desire for a firm foundation from which we could morally condemn not only individuals but also cultures and humanity in general, when they do not care about preserving natural entities, including plants, rivers, and other nonconscious things.

He recognizes that arguing for the preservation of nature—by which he means unmanufactured environments[4]—on utilitarian grounds cannot (logically) fulfill that purpose. This is because preserving natural entities may not always be what is best for sentient beings. Similarly, arguing for the preservation of nature, as does Mark Sagoff,[5] on the grounds that natural entities embody important cultural values (e.g., the way a wild river expresses freedom) will not fulfill this purpose, since values vary from one culture to another and change through time within a culture. Consequently, Regan rejects both of these otherwise promising bases for environmental ethics.

The inadequacy, for Regan's purpose, of these two bases for environmental ethics is not the consequence of superficial errors made in formulating them. It is a consequence of the logic of such ethics that arguing for the preservation of nature on anthropocentric, sentient-centric, or conscious-centric grounds cannot provide Regan the critical foundation he wants. This is because it cannot (logically) be guaranteed that preserving natural entities will always be what is best for people, sentient beings, or conscious beings. Regan seems to have concluded —rightly, I think—that the only way to secure an unvarying moral foundation for preserving natural entities would be to establish that they have a morally significant good of their own. This would be a good "inherent" in them, to use Regan's terminology, that is, a good independent of their effects on or value for human, sentient, or conscious beings.

Regan does not attempt such an argument in "The Nature and Possibility of an Environmental Ethic," which is his main contribution to date to the field of environmental ethics. Nor does he attempt such an argument in the others of his writings to which he refers in that essay. Rather, he limits his case to showing that the proposition that (some) nonconscious, natural entities are inherently good

(a) is not incoherent, and
(b) must be true, if the development of environmental ethics is to be possible.[6]

The argument for (b) is intended to show the imperative, practical need for ascribing inherent goodness to (some) natural, nonconscious entities, while the argument for (a) is supposed to overcome conceptual obstacles to doing so. We shall first consider his argument for (b), then devote the remainder of this section to arguments concerning (a).

A. ENVIRONMENTAL CRISIS AND THE (SUPPOSED) NECESSITY OF INHERENT VALUE

The basic problem with Regan's attempt to demonstrate that (some) natural, nonconscious entities must be inherently good, if the development of environmental ethics is to be possible, is that it begs the question. Regan's argument here consists of considering four other possible bases for environmental ethics, showing that they cannot "reasonably account for our duties regarding the environment,"[7] and concluding that in the absence of any other viable alternative, environmental ethics must be based on accepting that (some) natural, nonconscious entities are inherently good. Among these four alternatives are the two mentioned above, a utilitarian environmental ethic, which would preserve the natural environment because doing so is important for the well-being of sentient beings, and an "embodiment" environmental ethic, which would preserve nature because it expresses or symbolizes important (trans-?)cultural values, for example, tenacity, grandeur, freedom, endurance, and power.

As noted above, Regan finds these two promising alternatives inadequate, because they would not commit us to preserving nature in situations where doing so would not benefit sentient beings or where the environment does not embody the current cultural values of those intending to destroy that environment. However, the issue now is not whether these alternatives can (logically) provide Regan what he wants from an environmental ethic but whether they can "reasonably account for our duties regarding the environment." That is, these limitations on the commitment to preserving nature do not constitute objections to utilitarian and embodiment environmental ethics, unless we presume that among our duties regarding the environment are duties to preserve nature in situations where doing so would not be better than replacing it for the sentient beings that might be affected by our preserving or replacing that natural environment.

It is not obvious that we have such duties, and Regan does not even attempt to establish that we do. For example, if there are desert or arctic areas in which no sentient beings have or take an interest, except as a storehouse of natural resources, are we morally obligated to preserve these areas against oil exploration? Regan must (logically) demonstrate that we actually have such duties before his criticisms of these alternative environmental ethics can take on practical significance.

Another weakness in Regan's argument against a utilitarian environmental ethic can be found in his claim that such an ethic would be susceptible to the environmental *reductio* noted in the preceding chapter:

A1: Suppose that we were able to manufacture an environment that would be significantly better for sentient beings than is the natural environment.

A2: Also suppose that there was no more beneficial (for sentient beings) way for us to employ our energies and resources and that the benefits from this manufactured environment would be distributed fairly, including appropriate consideration for future generations.

A3: It would follow that we ought, on utilitarian grounds, to replace the natural environment with this manufactured one.

A4: But A3 is an unacceptable conclusion.

A5: Therefore, a utilitarian environmental ethic is unacceptable.[8]

Now, is the utilitarian conclusion in A3 really unacceptable? Given our current, limited capacity for manufacturing beneficial environments, can (logically) that conclusion be detrimental to developing a coherent, effective ethic for dealing with our contemporary environmental problems? Or, as suggested in Chapter 13, is this *reductio* merely a case of emotionally reinforcing beliefs dogmatically held? Some argument is needed to show that there really is a problem with a utilitarian environmental ethic here. But once again, Regan does not even attempt to provide the needed argument.

Rather, he moves on to claim that "in the world as it actually is, there are grounds for thinking that environmental protection efforts favor the interests of a powerful elite rather than maximizing the pleasure of all."[9] This is supposed to show that even under current conditions, utilitarianism cannot justify preserving nature.

However, this "argument" is merely rhetorical flourish. First, the fact that "rising property values in protected areas drive the poor out" does not even suggest what Regan claims utilitarians would have to infer from it, namely, that the most effective way to maximize the general welfare, or even just the welfare of the poor, would be to replace natural environments with "parking lots, condominiums, and plastic trees."[10] How to deal with this problem of rising property values in order to insure that all who want to enjoy protected wilderness areas have a fair chance to do so is not indicated by simply stating the problem. Perhaps rent control, subsidized housing, or other government programs for the general welfare in these areas are needed. Regan does not pause to indicate why these or other possible solutions to this problem would not be viable options for a utilitarian environmental ethic. Consequently, he has once again failed to provide the argument needed to support his criticism of utilitarianism.

Second, a practicable utilitarian ethic will include provisions for minority opportunities—even for the elite! This is because there is no reason to believe that the general welfare will be maximized by forcing all of us to live the way only most of us want to. So utilitarianism would not undermine attempts to preserve some natural environments, even if the majority did prefer manufactured environments.

Third, utilitarianism requires considering the well-being of animals, as well as of humans, and indirect contributions to (the quality of) sentient life, such as providing oxygen, enriching the soil, and making other vital contributions to the biosphere. Parking lots, condominiums, and plastic trees hold no promise of making such contributions or of fulfilling the needs of animals. Consequently, careful argument is needed to show that they will be favored by utilitarianism, but, of course, Regan provides no such argument.

Finally, there is no reason why a utilitarian environmental ethic cannot recognize the benefit obtained through having natural expressions of (trans-)cultural values like power and freedom. Utilitarianism can incorporate the embodiment environmental ethic and thereby dispel the impression that the only value utilitarianism can give to nature is that it is a resource to be harvested, processed, and consumed. It follows from all four of these considerations that the current prospects for the well-being of sentient beings do not support Regan's claim that a utilitarian environmental ethic could not justify current preservation efforts.

To conclude this discussion of Regan's claim that the development of environmental ethics requires that (some) natural, nonconscious entities have inherent goodness, it is trivially true that no principle for determining our duties regarding the environment that bases that determination on something other than the inherent goodness of the environment will be able to show that we have duties regarding the environment independent of the well-being of other beings or things than the environment. That is, it is trivially true that any such principle will be unable to support Regan's conception of an environmental ethic and the duties that follow from such an ethic. However, since Regan does not even attempt to demonstrate that his conception of environmental ethics correctly expresses the sorts of duties we have (or commonly recognize we have) regarding the environment, his conclusion here should (logically) be limited to saying that utilitarianism, embodiment, and other conscious-centric ethics do not provide adequate bases for the kind of environmental ethics *he wants*. Before he can (logically) move on to concluding that what he wants does, and the other theories do not, reasonably account for our duties regarding the environment, he must provide credible arguments in favor not just of the logical possibility of his theory but also of its adequacy and accuracy. As it stands, he has given us no reason to believe that we must postulate the inherent goodness of (some) nonconscious entities in order to account for our duties regarding the environment.

B. The Variety of Goodness and the (Supposed) Necessity of Inherent Value

As to Regan's other claim, that it is logically possible for nonconscious entities to be inherently good, his arguments for this proposition are limited to showing that some arguments against it contain premises, interpretations, and presumptions that are not "self-evident and stand in need of rational defense, something not provided by the argument itself."[11]

Once again, this objection is merely rhetorical flourish, since no argument justifies the definitions, presumptions, or premises it employs. Still, Regan's claim is probably irrefutable. If a conception like G. E. Moore's[12] of goodness as a simple, nonnatural property is coherent, then it will be impossible to prove that nonconscious entities cannot (logically) be inherently good. As Moore's famous critique of naturalism amply demonstrates, a simple, nonnatural property could (logically) be associated with anything. Regan does not explicitly subscribe to Moore's interpretation of goodness—although it is hard to imagine any other interpretation that could accommodate the claims he makes for his "logically possible I-know-not-what." However, even if Regan did not have Moore's position in mind when formulating his theory of inherent goodness, the logical possibility of such an interpretation, in conjunction with Regan's never explaining what makes something inherently good, explains why he can so easily refute attempts to prove that nonconscious entities cannot (logically) be inherently good.

It also explains why this defense of his position is insignificant. Intuitionism has long since proven a dead end, and the merely logical possibility of resurrecting it provides little if any evidence to show that there is "something worth thinking about"[13] in Regan's conception of an environmental ethic. To show that his environmental ethic holds the promise of significantly advancing our understanding, Regan needs to demonstrate that his conception of inherent goodness can help us to understand cases or aspects of goodness that other interpretations, such as those based on happiness or interests (the two alternatives Regan criticizes), cannot help us to understand. This time, Regan has attempted to meet the challenge.

In another article to which he here refers several times,[14] Regan argues that

   (a) something (e.g., a gardenia bush) can be good of its kind independent of its relation to any conscious being and
   (b) since something (e.g., a car) can be good but not valued, there is a distinction between being valued, which is what requires consciousness, and being good, which is something the object is in its own right.

Thus, being good of its kind and being good even though unvalued are supposed to be cases of goodness that happiness- and interest-based interpretations of goodness cannot help us to understand and that indicate that we need to acknowledge that nonconscious entities can be good independent of their (possible) effects on or value for conscious beings if we are to develop a comprehensive understanding of "goodness." We shall discuss both of these two cases in turn.

Regan has come to reject the concept of being good of its kind as a basis for environmental ethics. This is because such goodness need not be morally significant, that is, need not call for "admiring respect."[15] For example, some thieves may be highly accomplished at thievery, but that goodness of their kind does not command our moral respect. Since Regan considers calling for admiring respect to be a defining characteristic of inherent goodness,[16] being good of its kind cannot, strictly speaking, be a form of what he calls "inherent goodness." However, Regan apparently still considers being good of its kind to be an objective goodness that (some) nonconscious entities have independent of conscious beings.

Consequently, it is still supposed to provide evidence of the inadequacy of happiness- and interest-based interpretations of goodness and to point in the direction of what we may call "objective goodness" ("goodness$_o$," for short), meaning "the goodness of things which is independent of their (possible) effects on or value for human, sentient, or conscious beings." Being good of its kind, which may or may not be morally significant, and being inherently good, which is by definition morally significant, would be two ways of being good$_o$—if anything is good$_o$.

But is it the case that an interest-based interpretation of goodness cannot help us to understand how things come to be *good* of their kind? A plant's being good of its kind clearly does not depend on anyone's direct interest in it: weeds are often healthy, flourishing paradigms of their species. However, this does not show that plants are good independent of conscious beings, for a possible, plausible explanation of how even weeds can be good of their kind is that they express or symbolize the values of conscious beings, for instance, health, tenacity, fulfilling one's potential, and survival. Thus, understanding how nonconscious entities can be good of their kind is not beyond the reach of interpretations of goodness that tie it to the (possible) interests of conscious beings.

Furthermore, Regan acknowledges that the goodness of nonconscious entities that is supposed to be goodness$_o$ is a supervenient property of those entities.[17] Now, if we adopt the embodiment position and interpret the noninstrumental, nonaesthetic goodness of (some) nonconscious entities as the expressive or symbolic value they have (can have, normally have, or would have if observed) for conscious beings, then we can readily understand how this evaluative characteristic arises and why it is not a defining property of the object but is supervenient on those properties. (Henceforth, "goodness$_n$," will be used to refer to the noninstrumental, nonaesthetic goodness of nonconscious things. That some nonconscious things are good$_n$ is not in dispute here; whether things that are good$_n$ must at least sometimes be interpreted as being good$_o$ is what is at issue.)

For example, Mt. Rainier can be good$_n$ because it symbolizes grandeur and power for us, and it can have this symbolic value for us because of what it is. Thus, the superveniency of the goodness$_n$ of (some) nonconscious entities does not pose an obstacle to accepting the embodiment interpretation of that goodness.

Indeed, it seems especially clear in the case of rivers, cliffs, and other inorganic entities that the goodness$_n$ of (some) nonconscious entities must (logically) be interpreted in terms of the expressive or symbolic value they (can) have for conscious beings. Consider the case of the unimpeded flowing of the Colorado River vs. the river as it currently is, with several major dams impeding its flow. If we do not allow references to the instrumental, aesthetic, expressive, or symbolic value either of these conditions can have for conscious beings, then what can be cited to show that one condition is good, bad, or better or worse than the other? The water would move differently, the cliffs be formed differently, and the mud be deposited differently if the river's flow were not impeded, but when the impact of these differences on the (possible) interests of conscious beings is not involved, there would seem to be nothing in either pattern of movement, erosion, and sedimentation to make it good, bad, or better or worse than the other. The burden of proof is definitely on those who claim that there is an inherent goodness in the unimpeded flowing of the river and in the undisturbed condition of other natural, inorganic entities to substantiate those claims and to do so without surreptitiously referring to the (possible) interests of conscious beings. Until, if ever, such demonstrations have been provided, that inorganic entities can be $good_n$ does not pose a challenge to the adequacy of interest-based value theories such as utilitarian and embodiment environmental ethics.

Finally, the embodiment theory can also account for the fact that sometimes the $goodness_n$ of nonconscious entities can be morally significant. According to the embodiment theory, these entities acquire this significance because some of the values they express are moral values like freedom and endurance. For example, a pine tree growing from a crack in the sheer face of a granite cliff may be of no instrumental use to us nor be aesthetically attractive, but it can come to symbolize tenacity and the will to survive, thereby coming to serve as an inspiration for us not to lose hope and to try harder in trying circumstances. In this way, that clinging pine takes on moral significance and becomes an object of our "admiring respect." Consequently, the embodiment interpretation of the $goodness_n$ of (some) nonconscious entities does not have difficulty accounting for the fact that some of these things have acquired moral significance.

To summarize, the embodiment of (trans-)cultural values interpretation of the $goodness_n$ of (some) nonconscious, natural entities can explain how the goodness of these entities can be

> dependent on the objective properties of the nonconscious entity,
> supervenient,
> not limited to that of resources to be harvested, processed, and consumed,
> independent of direct desires concerning the survival or flourishing of the thing, and
> morally, yet noninstrumentally, significant, in some cases.

Of course, this does not show that there cannot be another, equally successful interpretation of this goodness, for example, by postulating the $goodness_o$ of (some) nonconscious entities. However, it does show that being good of its kind and being good in a morally significant but noninstrumental and nonaesthetic way are not kinds of goodness that can be accounted for only by postulating $goodness_o$.

Turning to Regan's other point in his contra-Feinberg essay (i.e., the distinction between being valued, which requires consciousness, and being good, which does not), we note that this distinction can also be understood without postulating goodness$_o$.

An unvalued car, to use Regan's example, can be good in the same way that an unseen apple can be red. "The unseen apple is red" can be understood to mean that its physical properties are such that if a being relevantly like us were to see the apple under normal lighting conditions, the color that being would see is what we call "red." That is, the objective redness of the apple is its capacity to influence certain beings in a certain way. It has this capacity whether or not it ever affects such a being in this way. Similarly, "The unvalued car is good" can be understood to mean that its physical properties are such that if a being relevantly like us wanted reliable (or fast or ostentatious or state-of-the-art or . . .) transportation, knew how to use a car, had the materials necessary for using a car, and came across this car, then she would (*ceteris paribus*) value it. This capacity is something the car has whether or not any being ever actually values the car. So the car can be good in this way even though never valued, and this is a supervenient goodness of the car itself. But this goodness retains an essential reference to the possible desires, beliefs, understandings, and other capabilities of conscious beings.

Given these plausible, alternative interpretations of being good of its kind and of being good though unvalued, Regan's arguments in his contra-Feinberg essay fail to give us any reason to believe that nonconscious entities are good$_o$. Furthermore, since the embodiment theory can also account for the noninstrumental moral significance of some nonconscious entities and since it is apparently this moral significance that has led Regan from his position in that essay to his conception of "inherent goodness," it follows that we still have not found cases or aspects of goodness that interest-based value theories cannot help us to understand and that we have to postulate inherent goodness in order to understand.

Regan makes one other attempt at providing such cases. In the "Nature and Possibility" essay, as well as in the contra-Feinberg essay, he insists that "having an interest in X" may mean either "being interested in X" or "X will contribute to the individual's good, well-being, or welfare."[18] He then argues that only being interested in X requires consciousness and concludes from this that it is possible for nonconscious entities to have interests and, consequently, a good of their own.

Regan is certainly correct in stating that one can have an interest in something in which she is not interested (e.g., her diet). But as discussed at length in Chapter 7, this is ordinarily because that something will affect what she does care about (e.g., her health), even though she does not realize it. Consider the following example: suppose that I have a strawberry birthmark on my shoulder, that I do not know about the new laser treatments that now make it possible to remove such blemishes (nor have any indirect, for instance, financial, interest in these treatments), and that I do not care (even subconsciously) about having this birth mark or about any of the consequences of having it. Could it be said that nevertheless, unbeknown to me, I have an interest in those treatments? That would be a strange thing to say, and the only way to make common sense of such a claim is in terms of people normally not wanting to have such skin blemishes and the possibility that in spite of what I currently think and feel, I will be happier if I have my birthmark removed. However, this saving interpretation does not suggest that nonconscious entities can have interests, since it makes reference to normal feelings.

Of course, it is possible to stipulate that "*P* has an interest in *x*" may refer to situations in which *P* cannot have any feelings about what will be produced by what he/she/it has an interest in. However, such a stipulative definition would not help support Regan's argument, since he claims to be relying on our common distinction between taking and merely having an interest in something. But our common understanding of "*P* has an interest in *x*, even though *P* takes no interest in *x*" strongly suggests that the kinds of good, well-being, or welfare to which things one has an interest in but takes no interest in can contribute are limited to the feelings of well-being discussed in Chapter 7, that is, feelings of pleasure or pain, the fulfillment or frustration of wants and desires, and other such conscious, sentient goods and evils.

It seems fair to conclude that Regan has begged the question and been insensitive to the meaning of "having an interest" by presuming that the kinds of good, well-being, or welfare to which the things in which one merely has an interest can (logically) contribute do not themselves essentially involve a reference to feelings, desires, and other things that only conscious beings can (logically) have. Thus, having an interest in things in which one takes no interest does not indicate that interpretations of goodness that tie it to wants, desires, cares, hopes, enjoyment, fulfillment, and so on have left something out, something that requires postulating a goodness that nonconscious entities can have independent of (the possibility of) conscious beings. Consequently, just as Regan fails to show that there is a practical need for postulating the inherent goodness of nonconscious, natural entities, so he has not shown that there is a conceptual need for doing so either.

C. CONCLUSION

To conclude, in discussions of the moral status of animals, Regan's conception of "inherent goodness" can be given the same sort of foundation we suggested for the independent valuer view discussed in Chapter 10. Since sentient beings are the source of values in the world, each sentient individual is valuable in itself, whether or not it is the object of evaluations by other valuers. Furthermore, each sentient individual enjoying life is also valuable for itself, whether or not it reflects on its condition, since, as noted in Chapter 7, feelings of well-being are a form of evaluative self-consciousness. However, that foundation is not available when Regan attempts to ascribe inherent goodness to nonconscious entities.

These ascriptions of inherent goodness to nonconscious entities are not only unfounded but also unmotivated and strategically questionable. They are unmotivated, because Regan has not provided us with good arguments showing that there are either conceptual or environmental ethical problems needing such ascriptions for their resolution. They are strategically questionable, since they involve basing one's ethics on a merely logically possible I-know-not-what and point in the direction of mysterious, objective value properties, conflicts among moral goods that are in principle incapable of rational adjudication,[19] and a long-discredited, intuitionist account of goodness. While being unfounded, unmotivated, and strategically questionable is not necessarily to be wrong, it certainly suggests that this attempt to fuse animal rights and environmental ethics is not going to succeed.

II. Environmental Ethics and Ecological Holism

In contrast to Regan's attempt at harmony, J. Baird Callicott writes that the impression of unity deriving from the opposition to humanist ethics that animal liberation and environmental ethics share may be "rather superficial and conceal substrata of thought and value which are not at all similar."[20] He goes on to conclude that

> humane moralism has located moral value in individuals, [centering] its attention on the competing criteria for moral standing and rights holding, while environmental ethics locates ultimate value in the "biotic community" and assigns differential moral value to the constitutive individuals relatively to that standard. . . . Allied to this difference are many others. One of the more conspicuous is that in environmental ethics, plants are included within the parameters of the ethical theory as well as animals. Indeed, inanimate entities such as oceans and lakes, mountains, forests, and wetlands are assigned a greater value than individual animals. . . . There are intractable practical differences between environmental ethics and the animal liberation movement. The animal liberation/animal rights movement is in the final analysis utterly unpracticable. An imagined society in which all animals capable of sensibility received equal consideration or held rights to equal consideration would be so ludicrous that it might be more appropriately and effectively treated in a satire than in philosophical discussion. The land ethic, by contrast, is eminently practicable.[21]

Thus, Callicott sees animal liberation and environmental ethics differing over holism vs. individualism, extending "*direct* ethical considerability"[22] to nonsentient entities, and certain practical matters, such as the morality of hunting, and he believes that because of these differences, environmental ethics is at least closer to providing an acceptable ethic than is animal liberation. He also considers the holism vs. individualism issue to be "perhaps the most fundamental theoretical difference between environmental ethics and the ethics of animal liberation."[23]

We shall discuss in turn the two theoretical differences Callicott notes. Perhaps taking his own advice to heart, Callicott has chosen not to discuss seriously the practical consequences of animal liberation but to satirize them. Consequently, we can be excused for not taking seriously his "practical" fantasies, for example, animal liberation leading to "most feed cattle and sheep starving or freezing as soon as winter settled in" or to animal liberationists destroying wildlife in their zeal to care for "institutionalized animal incompetents."[24] Our critique of the replacement argument in Chapter 10 and the strategies for dealing with the predation *reductio* developed in the preceding chapter implicitly provide sufficient responses to Callicott's supposed *reductios*.

A. THE BIOTIC "COMMUNITY" VS. ANIMAL LIBERATION

Callicott claims that "ecology has made it possible to apprehend the landscape as an articulate unity" and that "land is integrated as a human community is integrated."[25] The moral significance of this ecological discovery is that "the good of the community as a whole serves as a standard for the assessment of the relative value and relative ordering of its constitutive parts and therefore provides a means of adjudicating the often mutually contradictory demands of the parts considered separately for equal consideration."[26] He goes on to claim that Plato proposes a similar holistic view in his *Republic*,[27] and ostensively defining "environmental ethics" by reference to Aldo Leopold's "land ethic," he identifies its basic principle as Leopold's claim that "A thing is right when it tends to preserve the integrity, stability, and beauty of the biotic community. It is wrong when it tends otherwise."[28] Finally, Callicott concludes that by adopting this environmental holism,

> we human beings could reaffirm our participation in nature by accepting life as it is given without a sugar coating. Instead of imposing artificial legalities, rights, and so on on nature, we might take the opposite course and accept and affirm natural biological laws, principles, and limitations in the human personal and social spheres. Such appears to have been the posture toward life of tribal peoples in the past.[29]

This reaffirmation he takes to be the opposite of the "world-denying," "life-loathing" philosophy of the animal liberation movement.[30]

This account of environmental holism and its supposed moral consequences raises numerous questions, of which we shall consider the following three:

    (a) Is holism, as Callicott portrays it, an acceptable moral position?
    (b) Is Leopold's principle an acceptable moral principle?
    (c) Is animal liberation a "life-loathing" morality?

1. The Arbitrariness of Total Holism

Both mainstream moral philosophies and everyday Western morality have long had a holistic dimension to them. Moral philosophers as different as Hobbes, Jefferson, Kant, and Mill agree that

> a part of an individual's value lies in his or her role in a community,
>
> the good of the community can (morally) sometimes be cited in adjudicating conflicts, and
>
> individuals can (morally) sometimes be called on to make sacrifices for their community.

Let us call any moral philosophy or everyday morality that incorporates these three principles "partially holistic." Judaism and contemporary English socialism are examples of current common moralities that are partially holistic.

The animal liberation ethic proposed here is also partially holistic. The same is true of the animal liberation ethics proposed by Peter Singer and Bernard Rollin.[31] The strong utilitarian strain in the animal liberation movement that has developed since the early 1970s entails taking such a partial holistic view, and some animal rights philosophers like Tom Regan have even criticized such utilitarian animal liberationists as Singer for going too far in this holistic direction.[32] Consequently, it misrepresents animal liberation to locate it on one side of a simplistic individualism vs. holism dichotomy.

However, it does not misrepresent animal liberation, or mainstream moral philosophy and practice, to oppose them to what Callicott is proposing. The possible extreme that disturbs Regan about utilitarian versions of animal liberation is apparently just the extreme that Callicott is advocating, for he would have us believe that an individual's moral value should be *totally* determined by his or her role in a community. Callicott says things like the following in discussing (his version of) environmental holism:

> The land ethic is holistic in the sense that the integrity, stability, and beauty of the biotic community is its *summum bonum*. . . . The good of the biotic *community* is the ultimate measure of the moral value, the rightness or wrongness, of actions. . . . In every case the effect upon ecological systems is the decisive factor in the determination of the ethical quality of actions. . . . Modern ethical theory has consistently located moral value in individuals, and humane moralism remains firmly within this modern convention, while environmental ethics locates ultimate value in the "biotic community" and assigns differential moral value to the constitutive individuals relatively to this standard.[33]

While such statements do not explicitly state that individuals have moral value *only* through their contributions to a community (specifically, the so-called "biotic community"), they do strongly suggest that that is what Callicott understands by "holism."

It is this view of the moral role to be played by holism that I shall be referring to as "total holism" and be discussing here. Anything less than this total view would not represent the "fundamental theoretical" break with standard moral philosophy and practice that Callicott sees in (his version of) environmental holism, since standard moral philosophy and practice are partially holistic. Consequently, it seems not only more interesting but also fair to interpret Callicott's holism as total holism.[34] Now, has Callicott provided us with good reasons to move from partial to total holism?

"The body of empirical experience and theory which is summed up in the term *ecology*," and which Callicott identifies as "the philosophical context of the land ethic and its conceptual foundation"[35] cannot (logically) entail that we ought (morally) to take such a step. If all forms of life on earth, including the human form, in some sense "depend on" each other for their survival, it could follow that our role in the biotic "community" is our "ultimate" significance, in the ironic way that, as Camus says, suicide is the "fundamental" philosophical question.[36] That is, it could be that unless we pay attention to the biotic significance of our actions, we will not be around to appreciate aesthetic, moral, or other values. However, that these values would cease to exist if we destroy the balance of nature does not entail or even suggest that our moral value is limited to or in any other than this ironic sense "derives from" the value we have for maintaining that balance.

Similarly, Plato's moral philosophy does not propose or even suggest total holism. The guiding concern of Socrates' thought experiment in the *Republic* is not "the integrity, stability, and beauty" of the state. Rather, that guiding concern is what will produce the best life for human beings:

> Socrates: My notion is that a state comes into existence because no individual is self-sufficient; we all have many needs. . . . Having all these needs, we call in one another's help to satisfy our various requirements; and when we have collected a number of helpers and associates to live together in one place, we call that settlement a state.[37]

Thus, the individuals in Plato's ideal state are valued not only as contributors to the state but also as the ends for which it exists. Furthermore, Callicott says that "from the vantage point of ecological biology, pain and pleasure seem to have nothing at all to do with good and evil."[38] Plato, however, is a eudaemonist. Beginning with a minimal community, he adds to it in order to enhance the quality of life of its members, and he concludes by arguing that the value of justice, both in the state and in the individual, lies in the happiness it provides.[39] Thus, the ultimate goal of Plato's ethics is not the structure and maintenance of a community but the quality of life of individuals, the structuring and maintenance of the community being ordered to that end. So total holism cannot find respectability through association with Plato's *Republic*.

As noted above, another reason Callicott gives for valuing total holism is that it provides a way of adjudicating conflicts of interests. However, as a logical claim, that much can be said for all moral principles, for example, the principle of utility, the categorical imperative, the principles of fairness elaborated in *A Theory of Justice*,[40] and so on. This is because one of the functions of moral principles is to provide guidance in resolving conflicts of interests. Consequently, there is nothing logically unique about total holism here.

As a practical claim, it is to say the least not obvious, nor has it been shown, that total holism would be a more practicable guide for adjudicating conflicts of interests than contemporary morality is or than other ethical theories would be. Any theory that, like total holism, advocates a single goal for action will be tidy. However, total holism is not the only moral theory that rests on only one ultimate principle. Utilitarianism and Kantianism are similarly single-minded moral theories. Consequently, total holism does not have a practical advantage on this score. We may also note that single-principled moral theories have repeatedly proven unacceptable. As discussed in Chapter 2, everyday morality does not follow any such simplifying philosophy. It seems unlikely that a principle that proposes making the *summum bonum* something that is indifferent to individual well-being will be able to reverse that trend. Therefore, the simplicity Callicott seems to admire in total holism may actually be more of a vice than a virtue. Thus, on both logical and practical grounds, total holism's suggested ability to adjudicate conflicts of interests does not indicate that it is preferable to partial holism.

Finally, there is no moral reason for adopting total holism. The common moral goal of reducing the suffering in life and otherwise making life more enjoyable and fulfilling would not obviously be more effectively pursued by valuing individuals only as contributors to a community. Indeed, since it is individuals, not communities, that experience enjoyment, fulfillment, distress, and frustration, and since total holism proposes regarding individuals as disposable items in the pursuit of the integrity, stability, and beauty of the community, it seems reasonable to conclude that total holism would not provide as likely a path to this moral goal as our current, mixed morality, which directly values individuals and their quality of life. Certainly, considerable argument would have to be provided to warrant believing otherwise. Similarly, there is no reason to believe that total holism would provide a better way of developing moral character. Certain traditional moral virtues like compassion, tolerance, love, and other emotional attachments to specific individuals, individual initiative, and self-respect could actually be discouraged by various forms of total holism, including Callicott's. Finally, total holism need not contribute to insuring fairness. Insofar as a wilderness area in which "one being lives at the expense of others"[41] is an example of a total holistic order, insuring fairness seems irrelevant to total holism.

Thus, it seems fair to conclude that total holism is not obviously a superior or even an acceptable moral outlook and that it would take considerable argument to demonstrate that it is—if such arguments could be found. Callicott does not provide that argument, and nothing he says suggests how such an argument could be developed. (I have not found that other environmental holists provide compelling or coherent arguments for total holism, either.)

2. Environmental Ethics vs. Personal Preferences

Turning to Leopold's claim that whether something is right or wrong is determined by whether or not it contributes to the integrity, stability, and beauty of the biotic "community," is this an acceptable moral principle? Once again, there are both practical and logical questions here. This time, we shall consider the practical issues first.

Callicott is clearly opposed to the utilitarian elements in contemporary morality, which he identifies as "a prophylactic ethic of maximizing rewards (pleasure) and minimizing unwelcome information (pain)," [42] and he sees Leopold's principle as pointing us toward a more strenuous way of life. He seems to regret that "it is impossible today to return to the symbiotic relationship of Stone Age man to the natural environment" and to favor all of the following: simple diet and vigorous exercise, a renaissance of tribal cultural experience, cultivating a tolerance for pain, optimizing population by sexual continence, abortion, infanticide, and stylized warfare, regarding sickness as a worse evil than death, eating only what one can hunt, gather, or grow for oneself or barter from one's neighbors and friends, and leaving people who are injured in wilderness areas to get out on their own or "die in the attempt." [43] These are the "practical" consequences of the ethic Callicott describes as "eminently practicable."

As these consequences indicate, (Callicott's interpretation of) Leopold's principle is fundamentally out of touch with contemporary morality, which emphasizes compassion for the injured, the sick, and the handicapped, tolerance for diverse ways of life, concern to expand the diversity of opportunities and experiences available to people, protecting the weak against the strong, and hope for progress. Callicott doubtless regards this being out of touch as a mark of the holistic environmentalists' willingness "to undertake creative ethical reflection, exploration, [and] reexamination of historical ethical theory." [44] However, since "morality" is a common concept, rather than a technical term that experts can stipulatively define, its meaning is established through our common moral practice. Consequently, to the extent that a proposed "ethic," meaning merely "a code for conducting one's life," is fundamentally out of touch with our common moral practice, to that extent it is questionable whether that proposed code is a morality at all.

Significant *moral* criticism of common, moral practice cannot (logically) be based solely on the findings of a science, such as ecology, remote from the history and practice of morality. Significant moral criticism must (logically) be based, at least in part, on currently accepted moral principles or values. Even Immanuel Kant, perhaps the most abstract of moral philosophers, acknowledges this, beginning his *Foundations of the Metaphysics of Morals* with a section on the "Common Rational Knowledge of Morals" and confirming his ultimate moral principle by showing that it yields the same answers as everyday morality in four clear cases.[45] Similarly, in this work, we have criticized contemporary humanist morality by showing how common moral concerns point toward liberating animals. This requirement that significant moral criticism keep in touch with moral history and practice is presumably why Callicott attempts to draw an analogy between his environmental holism and Plato's moral philosophy. However, that analogy fails. This leaves it highly doubtful that environmental holism provides a basis for moral criticism of moral practice or moral philosophies such as animal liberation, and equally doubtful whether environmental holism is itself a moral philosophy at all.

The terms of Leopold's principle reinforce this doubt. Leopold mentions three specific values in his principle: integrity, stability, and beauty. The last of these is, directly, an aesthetic value. It can take on moral significance only by being tied to some moral value, for example, through the principle that "Goodness, truth, and beauty are one and the same" or the argument that "Beauty is something people enjoy; so, since the principle of utility instructs us to maximize happiness, we ought (morally) to consider the aesthetic consequences of our actions when determining what we ought (morally) to do." Leopold and Callicott have not provided principles or arguments to establish the moral significance of the beauty of the biotic community. Since Leopold's principle is supposed to be the fundamental principle of the land ethic, stating its *summum bonum* and ultimate measure of moral value, the logic of this total environmental holism would seem to preclude such a principle or argument. Consequently, it is at least highly doubtful that the beauty of the biotic community can have moral significance here.[46]

The first of Leopold's value terms, "integrity," can refer to a moral value, but the term does not here have its moral meaning. It does not mean "probity," "rectitude," or "firm adherence to a code of values." Talk of "the probity of the biotic community" would be nonsense. Rather, "integrity" here means "unity" and "completeness," referring to the condition of not having been dismembered or otherwise reduced to a truncated version of its fully functional form. Thus, "integrity" here denotes biological or ecological conditions. Once again, some principle or argument tying these conditions to moral values is needed to give them moral significance, and once again, neither Leopold nor Callicott provides, nor likely could provide, such a principle or argument.

Finally, the second of Leopold's three value terms, "stability," also refers to a physical condition—and it definitely is startling to see this condition offered as an ultimate value for a "biologically enlightened" value theory in a post-Darwinian era. Once again, we are given no reason to believe that the stability of the current state of nature has moral significance.

Thus, there is nothing in Leopold's principle that identifies it as a moral principle. Labeling something an "ethic" in the sense of being a code for conducting oneself, such as "the hunting ethic," does not establish that it is a code of moral values or even that it has moral significance. The moral value of hunting remains an open question, even though hunting has long had an "ethic."[47] Considerable argument is needed to show that a principle referring to an aesthetic value and ecological conditions has moral value, let alone expresses an acceptable, ultimate moral principle. Until such argument is provided, if it can be provided, the so-called "land ethic" would less misleadingly be renamed "the land aesthetic" or "the ecologist's code."

Beyond his mistaken analogy to Plato's *Republic*, the only suggestion Callicott offers for why we should regard (his interpretation of) Leopold's environmental principle as a moral principle is that "the representation of the natural environment as, in Leopold's terms, 'one humming community' brings into play, whether rationally or not, those stirrings of conscience which we feel in relation to delicately complex, functioning social and organic systems."[48] However, this suggestion begs the question, for it is far from obvious that the environment can properly be described as a "community" in a morally significant sense. Ecologically, "community" means merely "a group of plants and animals living in a specific region under relatively similar conditions" or "the region in which they live."[49] There is nothing here of the *feeling* of community, including being cooperative, mutual care and respect, sharing of burdens and responsibilities, emotional and moral attachments, intentionally formed alliances, a sense of obligations to, responsibilities for, or rights against other members of the group, and identifying with, feeling one can rely on, and feeling one is making a contribution to the group—all of which contribute to making communities morally significant. Lacking all of these dimensions, a merely ecological "community" lacks moral significance. That plants and animals, including ourselves, need each other and other inorganic things like unpolluted water and air to survive does not make us a "community" in a morally significant sense, and to try to stir moral feelings by employing that term in discussing ecological issues is to equivocate and to substitute rhetoric for argument.

Until further argument is supplied to show, if it can be shown, that Leopold's principle is a moral principle, it seems fair to regard his land "ethic" as the statement of the way of life he personally preferred, rather than as a moral principle. Some people like cities and luxury; others prefer the country and austerity —in terms of the substance of Leopold's principle, the significance of the land "ethic" is that it provides a guide for the latter group.

Finally, Leopold's principle could be given moral significance if it provided useful guidance for accomplishing our common moral goals. However, it is doubtful that it can play that role. As already indicated, it would not, at least as interpreted by Callicott, encourage the development of some morally highly prized character traits such as compassion. Also, it would not help to insure fairness, since it would apparently counsel against defending the weak against the strong. Finally, in directing us to cultivate a tolerance for pain, to leave injured people to die, to destroy animals in order to save plants, and so forth, it seems unlikely that it would provide us much guidance in reducing suffering and otherwise making life more enjoyable and fulfilling. Consequently, Leopold's principle is not likely to be of service in attaining our common moral goals.

It seems fair to conclude that for all the reasons above, Leopold's principle is not an acceptable moral principle. (This is not to say, of course, that ecology cannot provide important information for making enlightened moral decisions.)

3. Morality and the Affirmation of Life

Finally, let us briefly turn to Callicott's charge that animal liberation is "world-denying" and "life-loathing." As discussed in Chapter 3, morality involves inhibiting and redirecting native desires and tendencies. It also involves, in its fully developed form, projecting "better worlds" for us to work toward. It follows that concerns, values, principles, codes, guides for action, and the like cannot be restricted to merely "accepting life as it is given" and "accepting and affirming natural biological laws, principles, and limitations," if they are to constitute a morality. Consequently, taken at face value, Callicott's supposedly "life-affirming," "world-accepting" environmental holism cannot (logically) be a morality.

Such advice can take on moral significance only if it is understood as encouraging us to do something that is not currently being done and that would make for a better world. Since Callicott proposes the land "ethic" as an alternative not only to animal liberation but also to contemporary, civilized life, he apparently does understand it in this way. However, when so understood, the phrase "life as it is given" cannot (logically) refer to life as it actually is being led by us. Thus, Callicott is not really proposing that we "accept life as it is given." Rather, behind that misleading rhetoric, he is rejecting life as it currently is and advocating that we follow a way of life as he would like it to be. Furthermore, suggesting that as far as possible, we foresake thousands of years of evolution and history and return to the way of life of Stone Age tribes marks Callicott's "ethic" as a particularly "world-denying" vision. Consequently, when interpreted in the way that makes it logically possible for Callicott's "ethic" to be a morality, it is neither life-affirming nor world-accepting.

On the other hand, refusing to accept and affirm avoidable suffering, unfair distribution of goods, uninhibited aggression, and so forth are refusals that have long been and continue to be part of everyday morality. As such, they are a well-established part of life as it is. Animal liberation extends such concerns, which have traditionally been focused on the human world and on human life, to include equal consideration for animals. In this way, animal liberation is simply carrying on the business of everyday moral practice. Therefore, it does not loathe or deny life as it is. Rather, unlike Callicott's proposed retreat to the wilderness, animal liberation is participating in life and, we hope, in its continuing moral evolution.

4. Summary

Thus, Callicott's total environmental holism and his criticism of animal liberation have little if anything to recommend them as moral theory and criticism. First, Callicott has not provided any reason for believing that holism should be more than a part of morality. Second, the specific holistic principle Callicott advances—Leopold's so-called "land ethic"—has not been shown to be a moral principle at all nor to be of particular use in attaining our common moral goals. Finally, Callicott's criticisms of animal liberation are incoherent. Consequently, total holistic, environmental "ethicists" will have to marshall a great deal more argument, if that can be done, to show that their principles and criticisms are morally significant.

B. The Good of Nonsentient Things

One of the clear and striking differences between the land "ethic" and animal liberation is that the former ascribes while the latter denies "direct ethical considerability" to nonsentient things like plants, rivers, and ecosystems. As noted in Chapter 5, animal liberationists tend to accept the interest requirement for having direct moral status, and as argued in Chapter 7, only sentient beings can have interests, since having interests requires having feelings of well-being. Land "ethicists," on the other hand, want to deny that nonsentient entities have value only as instruments for sentient beings and to affirm that such entities have goods or interests of their own that we ought (morally) to respect. It is doubtful that this affirmation can (logically) be defended.

Callicott acknowledges that "there can be no value apart from an evaluator" and seems to accept that nonsentient things cannot be evaluators. He goes on to note that things can be "valued for themselves as well as for the contribution they might make to the realization of someone's interests" and cites the value many people place on their children and pets as examples of this.[50] Apparently, this is supposed to show how nonsentient entities can have direct moral status even though their having value depends on (the possibility of?) there being a sentient being to evaluate them.

However, while Callicott is certainly correct that things can be valued for themselves, that is irrelevant to whether they can have "direct" moral status, which, at least in the arguments over human and animal rights and in discussions of "inherent value," refers to their having value whether or not some other being values them (or could value them) in any way at all. For example, that I (can) value a painting not (only) as an instrument for profit or prestige but (also) simply because I "delight" in it, to use Callicott's term, does not show that the painting would have value even if no sentient being valued it (or could value it). Although they are often valued for themselves, paintings have long been paradigm examples of things that lack direct moral status. By way of contrast, consider the case of a dog: even if no *other* sentient being values it (or could value it), the dog can still have feelings of well-being about itself and its condition and can, therefore, still be of value for itself. Thus, the dog can be valued not only by another, either as an instrument or for itself; the dog can also be valued by itself, and it is that latter possibility, and the moral significance of it, that is at issue in the debate over animal rights and that is completely lacking in the case of nonsentient entities.

As long as one acknowledges that values require (the possibility of) evaluators, that nonsentient entities cannot (logically) be evaluators, and that ecosystems, rivers, plants, and so on are not sentient, then plants and things cannot have direct moral status in the sense in which human and animal liberation movements seek direct moral status for humans and animals. It follows that someone who grants those three conditions, as Callicott does, but who goes on to maintain that nonsentient entities have direct moral status, as Callicott also does, is inconsistent.

We should emphasize that, contrary to what Callicott seems to think, it does not follow from denying them direct moral status that plants and things can have only crudely "instrumental" values that we "selfishly" place on them.[51] As noted in our discussion of Tom Regan's environmental ethic, nonsentient entities can have aesthetic, expressive, and symbolic significance, and judging from the benefit that many of us receive from "getting away" to the country, they can also have what we may call "psychological renewal" value for us. Furthermore, liberating animals would involve giving equal consideration to their environmental needs. Consequently, an environmental ethic based on animal liberation could not be anthropocentric. Thus, acknowledging the many different sorts of value nonsentient entities can have for us and for animals provides a basis for deploring the pervasive human destruction of nature and for arguing (morally) for an end to that destruction. Carrying on the work of environmental protection and reform does not require ascribing direct moral status to nonsentient entities.

Finally, it might be countered that Callicott was mistaken in conceding that values require an evaluator. It might be claimed that plants, rivers, and so forth have goods of their own and that giving plants and things direct moral status would involve respecting these independent goods. For example, life can sensibly be said to be "flourishing" in a certain locale without reference to sentient interest in the ecosystem.

Such a rejoinder would amount to embracing a total holistic version of Tom Regan's inherent value theory. The criticisms of that theory raised in the preceding section apply to this holistic version of it as well. Furthermore, as discussed in Chapter 9, sensible talk of "S's good" requires that a condition be a "good for" or a "good of" S itself. It is difficult if not impossible to think of how a condition could be a good for or of a nonsentient entity.

For example, how is containing a wide variety of life-forms—the ecological value Callicott repeatedly employs—a good for or of an ecosystem? Presumably, a more diverse system is more likely to survive than a less diverse one; so it has greater "stability" through its diversity. But the ecosystem—which is not to be confused with the sentient beings in the system—(logically) cannot care whether it survives or not, cannot feel fulfilled by or proud of surviving, and cannot be afraid of or frustrated by (the prospect or even just the possibility of) not surviving. Since it is not sentient, the ecosystem cannot (logically) even unknowingly have an interest in surviving. With all these elements missing, statements like "Surviving is a good of the ecosystem itself" and "Given the sorry state into which it has declined, it would be a blessing in disguise for this ecosystem if it were to cease to exist" are nonsensical. Consequently, talk of "the good of" an ecosystem or of "what is good for" an ecosystem cannot (logically) refer only to what the ecosystem requires to survive. It also refers to the interests of those sentient beings that (could) have or take an interest in the ecosystem's survival. Indeed, those interests—which need not be limited to crudely instrumental interests—are where the goodness of the ecosystem's survival has its source. Without those interests, the survival or replacement of an ecosystem is merely the value-neutral continuation of one physical condition or its replacement by another.

Thus, rather than being one of its great achievements, extending direct moral status to nonsentient entities is likely the chief conceptual failing of the land "ethic." In contrast, by accepting the interest requirement and acknowledging that interests are tied to feelings, animal liberationists avoid this logical blunder.[52]

III. The Environmental Ethics of Animal Liberation

Turning from criticism to construction, we ask what sort of environmental ethical conclusions follow from the animal liberation ethic we have developed in this study? They can be summarized as follows:

(1) Only sentient beings can have moral rights. Since an essential function of moral rights is to protect and further interests and since having interests requires having feelings of well-being, nonsentient entities cannot have moral rights.

However, this is not to say that nonsentient entities have value only as "natural resources," that is, as things to be harvested, processed, and consumed. They can also be "valued for themselves," insofar as simply experiencing them or just "knowing they're there" is valued by sentient beings. That trees, for example, cannot have moral rights does not entail that they can be valued only as building material. They can still have aesthetic, expressive, symbolic, and psychological renewal value, in addition to their value as natural resources. These other values, along with the value of the environment for animals to be noted in the following paragraph, can be expected often to be weighty enough to indicate that we ought (morally) to preserve these values and to forgo the natural resource value of nonsentient natural entities.

(2) The morally significant value of the environment is not limited to its value for human beings. Equal consideration must (morally) be given to the value of the environment for animals. Insuring that animals receive a fair share of environmental goods would call for a massive change in our attitude toward and interactions with nature. For example, we could (morally) no longer presume that human uses of the land (e.g., for subdivisions or farming) have priority over animal uses of the land (e.g., for their homes and food). We would be morally obligated to seek ways in which our use of land, water, and other parts of nature allowed animals also to benefit from and to enjoy the environment.

(3) Insofar as we are able to interfere with the present structure of nature in ways that enhance the general welfare, including equal consideration for animals, or that can help to establish a more equitable order, we are (*ceteris paribus*) morally justified and even obligated to do so. For example, efforts to control or even to eradicate diseases, to nurse sick or injured people and animals back to health, to domesticate, provide good homes for, or otherwise enter into mutually rewarding relationships with animals, and to drain marshes, control underbrush, or otherwise rearrange the environment could be morally justified, if doing so would contribute to attaining our common moral goals, for example, by reducing the suffering in life or by helping to insure a more equitable distribution of available goods. On evolutionary grounds, we must (logically) presume that the natural order ordinarily provides sentient beings with a quality of life sufficient to make life worth living. However, this does not preclude the possibility that that quality of life can be improved and that this improvement can be accomplished through our understanding, concern, and initiative. We should be cautious about interfering with the present natural order, but there is no moral imperative against doing so.

These conclusions fit Tom Regan's description of an ethic that is "on the way to becoming" an "ethic of the environment," as opposed to being merely "an ethic *for the use* of the environment." Although these conclusions "hold that there are nonhuman beings which have moral standing," they would, according to Regan, "fail to qualify as a genuine environmental ethic," because they do not "hold that the class of beings which have moral standing is larger than the class of conscious beings."[53] However, the criticisms above of both Regan's and Callicott's attempts to ascribe "direct ethical considerability" to nonsentient entities indicate that stopping short of Regan's (and Callicott's) conception of a "genuine" environmental ethic is a virtue rather than a vice. It follows that animal liberation is not accurately categorized as a stage in the development of a "genuine" environmental ethic. Rather, liberating animals would eliminate anthropocentric prejudice from morality, thereby providing the foundation for nonanthropocentric deliberations concerning how we ought (morally) to interact with nature. In this way, the above environmental ethical conclusions deriving from the animal liberation ethic we have developed provide the foundation for a complete, coherent, practicable environmental ethic.

Notes

PART I

Chapter 1

1. Jean-Jacques Rousseau, *Emile* (1762) and Herbert Marcuse, *Eros and Civilization* (New York: Random House, 1955).

2. Paul Feyerabend, *Against Method* (London: Verso, 1975).

Chapter 2

1. Such an analysis of moral action is presented by D. Z. Phillips and H. O. Mounce in *Moral Practices* (New York: Schocken Books, 1970).

2. According to Aristotle, "It is not merely the state in accordance with the right rule, but the state that implies the *presence* of the right rule that is virtue." *Nicomachean Ethics* 1144b 26–28, trans. W. D. Ross. According to Kant, "The pre-eminent good can consist only in the conception of the law in itself so far as this conception is the determining ground of the will. This pre-eminent good we call moral. *Foundations of the Metaphysics of Morals*, trans. Lewis White Beck (Indianapolis: Bobbs-Merrill, 1959), 17.

3. R. M. Hare, *Freedom and Reason* (Oxford: Oxford University Press, 1963), chap. 9.

4. See Joel Feinberg, "The Nature and Value of Rights," *The Journal of Value Inquiry* 4 (1971): 243–257.

5. All unqualified references to "utilitarianism" in this study refer to classical act-utilitarianism. Other varieties of utilitarianism, especially forms of "mixed utilitarianism," which recognize other basic moral principles besides the principle of the greatest happiness, may provide more adequate analyses of the various dimensions of moral value. It is not my purpose to criticize utilitarianism; indeed, I would hope that the analyses presented here could contribute to the refinement of utilitarianism. However, simple, classical act-utilitarianism provides a useful foil for pointing out the directions these refinements need take, and it is as such that I will use it, unless otherwise specified.

6. Whether the agent would have done the right thing even if he had not had ulterior motives for doing so, whether he intends to benefit from the fact that his action seems

273

to express moral character, whether he is aware of how others will evaluate his action, whether he is personally committed to the value he believes others will interpret his action as expressing—all these issues contribute to the complex question of moral motivation and can yield varying degrees of falling short of this value.

7. Peter Singer, *Practical Ethics* (Cambridge: Cambridge University Press, 1979), 9–10.

Chapter 3

1. Charles Darwin, "Comparison of the Moral Powers of Man and the Lower Animals," in *Animal Rights and Human Obligations*, edited by Tom Regan and Peter Singer (Englewood Cliffs, N.J.: Prentice-Hall, 1976), 74.

2. Mary Midgley, *Beast and Man* (Ithaca: Cornell University Press, 1978), 25–26.

3. David Hume, *A Treatise of Human Nature*, edited by L. A. Selby-Bigge (Oxford: Clarendon Press, 1888), 176.

4. Richard A. Watson, "Self-Consciousness and the Rights of Nonhuman Animals and Nature," *Environmental Ethics* 1 (1979): 127–128. Watson goes on to offer the following suggestive speculation: "My guess is that the worry about anthropomorphizing animals often stems from a desire to keep them out of the moral milieu, much as Descartes refuses them self-consciousness in part because he does not think they have Christian souls" (p. 128).

5. Jan Narveson, "Animal Rights," *Canadian Journal of Philosophy* 7 (1977): 161.

6. Darwin in *Animal Rights*, 75.

7. See, for example, the discussions of instinct, conditioning, and reason in Maurice Merleau-Ponty, *The Structure of Behavior* (Boston: Beacon Press, 1963), Mary Midgley, *Beast and Man*, Donald R. Griffin, *The Question of Animal Awareness* (New York: Rockefeller University Press, 1981) and *Animal Thinking* (Cambridge: Harvard University Press, 1984), and Stephen Walker, *Animal Thought* (London: Routledge & Kegan Paul, 1983).

8. See Antony Alpers, *Dolphins: The Myth and the Mammal* (Boston: Houghton Mifflin, 1960) and Robert Stenuit, *The Dolphin, Cousin to Man* (London: J. M. Dent & Sons, 1968). For some examples of native, virtuous behavior among elephants, baboons, and wild dogs, as well as dolphins, see Richard Leakey and Roger Lewis, *Origins* (New York: E. P. Dutton, 1977), 76, 155–157.

9. Watson, "Self-Consciousness and the Rights," 128. See also Stephen R. L. Clark, *The Nature of the Beast* (Oxford: Oxford University Press, 1982) and Lawrence E. Johnson, "Can Animals Be Moral Agents?," *Ethics & Animals* 4 (1983): 50–61.

10. St. Thomas Aquinas, *Summa Contra Gentiles*, Third Book, Part 2, chap. 113.

11. Immanuel Kant, *Foundations of the Metaphysics of Morals*, trans. Lewis White Beck (Indianapolis: Bobbs-Merrill, 1959), 70–71.

12. Immanuel Kant, *Critique of Practical Reason*, trans. Lewis White Beck (Indianapolis: Bobbs-Merrill, 1956), 126–127.

13. This sort of argument is developed by Harry Frankfurt in "Freedom of the Will

and the Concept of a Person," *Journal of Philosophy* 68 (1971): 5–20, Stanley I. Benn in "Freedom, Autonomy, and the Concept of a Person," *Proceedings of the Aristotelian Society* n.s. 76 (1976): 109–130, and David A. J. Richards in "Rights and Autonomy," *Ethics* 92 (1981): 3–20. These writers emphasize the human "capacity for second-order, rationally self-critical evaluations and wants and plans" (Richards, 13) in the development of "the human rights perspective" and the interpretation of "personhood," "autonomy," and "free will." Frankfurt even goes so far as to label those who are not self-critical "wantons," which, however, is certainly unjustified, since the nonself-critical can still be virtuous.

14. Immanuel Kant, *Foundations*, 30–31.

15. Ibid., 14–15.

Chapter 4

1. P. F. Strawson, *Individuals* (London: Methuen, 1959), 9–11.

2. For some recent examples of this, see Harry Frankfurt, "Freedom of the Will and the Concept of a Person," *Journal of Philosophy* 68 (1971): 5–20, Stanley I. Benn, "Freedom, Autonomy, and the Concept of a Person," *Proceedings of the Aristotelian Society* n.s. 76 (1976): 109–130, and David A. J. Richards, "Rights and Autonomy," *Ethics* 92 (1981): 3–20.

3. Hillary Putnam, "Robots: Mechanisms or Artificially Created Life?," *Journal of Philosophy* 61 (1964): 691.

4. Michael Tooley, "Abortion and Infanticide," *Philosophy and Public Affairs* 2 (1972): 401.

5. Joel Feinberg, "The Nature and Value of Rights," in *Rights*, edited by David Lyons (Belmont: Wadsworth, 1979), 82.

6. See Max Black, "The Gap Between 'Is' and 'Should,'" *The Philosophical Review* 73 (1964): 165–191, and John R. Searle, "How to Derive 'Ought' from 'Is,'" ibid., 48–58. These two and other classic pro and con essays in this debate have been collected by W. D. Hudson in *The Is/Ought Question* (New York: St. Martin's Press, 1969).

7. R. M. Hare convincingly develops this case against Searle in "The Promising Game," *Revue Internationale de Philosophie* 70 (1964): 398–412.

8. John Searle, *Speech Acts* (Cambridge: Cambridge University Press, 1969), 194.

9. D. Z. Phillips and H. O. Mounce, *Moral Practices* (New York: Schocken, 1970), 4–9.

10. Searle, *Speech Acts*, 189.

11. Ibid., 196.

12. Kant puts forward this argument in his *Foundations of the Metaphysics of Morals*, trans. Lewis White Beck (Indianapolis: Bobbs-Merrill, 1959), 46–47.

13. Alan Donagan, *The Theory of Morality* (Chicago: University of Chicago Press, 1977), 96 (emphasis in original).

14. Donald R. Griffin, *Animal Thinking* (Cambridge: Harvard University Press, 1984), 165.

15. Mark Twain, *The Adventures of Huckleberry Finn* (New York: Washington Square Press), chap. 32 (emphasis added).

16. Meredith Williams, "Rights, Interests, and Moral Equality," *Environmental Ethics* 2 (1980): 150.

17. Donald R. Griffin, *The Question of Animal Awareness* (New York: Rockefeller University Press, 1981), 88.

PART II

Chapter 5

1. Leonard Nelson, *A System of Ethics* (New Haven: Yale University Press, 1956), 136–144.

2. Donald R. Griffin, *Animal Thinking* (Cambridge: Harvard University Press, 1984), 186.

3. Arthur L. Caplan has emphasized this point in his writings on the ethics of animal research, for example, "Beastly Conduct: Ethical Issues in Animal Experimentation," *New York Annals of Science* 75 (1983): 159–169.

4. Joel Feinberg, "The Nature and Value of Rights," *The Journal of Value Inquiry* 4 (1970): 252.

5. Leslie Francis and Richard Norman, "Some Animals Are More Equal than Others," *Philosophy* 53 (1978): 527. Also, see Christine Pierce, "Can Animals be Liberated?," *Philosophical Studies* 36 (1979): 69–75.

6. Bonnie Steinbock, "Speciesism and the Idea of Equality," *Philosophy* 53 (1978): 253.

7. Tom Regan, "An Examination and Defense of One Argument Concerning Animal Rights," *Inquiry* 22 (1979): 208–209, 212.

8. Ruth Cigman, "Death, Misfortune, and Species Equality," *Philosophy and Public Affairs* 10 (1981): 47.

9. Roger W. Galvin, "What Rights for Animals? A Modest Proposal," *Agenda, Newsmagazine of the Animal Rights Network* 4 (Nov./Dec., 1984): 28.

10. Steinbock, "Speciesism and the Idea of Equality," 251.

11. Peter Singer, *Animal Liberation* (New York: Avon Books, 1975): 21–22. See also Tom Regan, *The Case for Animal Rights* (Berkeley: University of California Press, 1983), 324–325.

12. See Steinbock, "Speciesism and the Idea of Equality," 254; Francis and Norman, "Some Animals Are More Equal than Others," 515; Richard Watson, "Self-Consciousness and the Rights of Nonhuman Animals and Nature," *Environmental Ethics* 1 (1979): 116–117; and Meredith Williams, "Rights, Interests, and Moral Equality," *Environmental Ethics* 2 (1980): 156.

13. Bernard Rollin discusses some similar cases in *Animal Rights and Human Morality* (Buffalo: Prometheus Books, 1981): 58–62.

14. Swift proposed that the Irish problem, too many people and too little money, be solved by selling Irish infants for English roasts. Jonathan Swift, "A Modest Proposal for

Preventing the Children of Poor Parents from Being a Burthen to Their Parents or Country, and for Making Them Beneficial to the People" (1729); reprinted in *Animal Rights and Human Obligations*, edited by Tom Regan and Peter Singer (Englewood Cliffs, N.J.: Prentice-Hall, 1976), 234–237.

15. See the concluding section of his "Bentham on Legal Rights," in *Rights*, edited by David Lyons (Belmont: Wadsworth, 1979): 147–148.

16. Galvin, "What Rights for Animals?"

17. H. L. A. Hart, "Are There Any Natural Rights?," *The Philosophical Review* 64 (1955): 175–191; S. I. Benn, "Abortion, Infanticide, and Respect for Persons," in *The Problem of Abortion*, edited by Joel Feinberg (Belmont: Wadsworth, 1973), 92–104; Mary Anne Warren, "On the Moral and Legal Status of Abortion," *The Monist* 57 (1973): 43–61; Ruth Cigman, "Death, Misfortune, and Species Equality," 47–64; and L. B. Cebik, "Can Animals Have Rights? No and Yes," *The Philosophical Forum* 12 (1981): 251–268.

18. Joel Feinberg, "The Rights of Animals and Unborn Generations," in *Philosophy and Environmental Crisis*, edited by William T. Blackstone (Athens: University of Georgia Press, 1974): 43–44.

19. Francis and Norman, "Some Animals Are More Equal than Others," 527.

20. Watson, "Self-Consciousness and the Rights," 119.

Chapter 6

1. Tom Regan, *The Case for Animal Rights* (Berkeley: University of California Press, 1983).

2. Richard Rorty, *The Linguistic Turn* (Chicago: University of Chicago Press, 1967), 33.

3. Immanuel Kant, *Critique of Practical Reason*, trans. Lewis White Beck (Indianapolis: Bobbs-Merrill, 1956), 126–127.

4. Donald VanDeVeer has taken some interesting steps toward working out the details of a "degrees" ethics in "Interspecific Justice," *Inquiry* 22 (1979): 55–80.

5. St. Thomas Aquinas, "On Killing Living Things and the Duty to Love Irrational Creatures," and Immanuel Kant, "Duties to Animals," in *Animal Rights and Human Obligations*, edited by Tom Regan and Peter Singer (Englewood Cliffs, N.J.: Prentice-Hall, 1976), 118–123.

6. R. G. Frey, *Rights, Killing, and Suffering* (Oxford: Blackwell, 1983), 197–203.

7. Henry S. Salt, "Logic of the Larder, in *Animal Rights and Human Obligations*, 185–189.

8. See Peter Wenz, "An Ecological Argument for Vegetarianism," *Ethics & Animals* 5 (1984): 2–9.

9. In the film *Mandingo*, which is supposed to provide an accurate portrayal of slavery in the antebellum South, his doctor tells the plantation owner that if he will rest his feet on the back of a slave boy, the gout will pass from his feet into the boy's body. One shudders to think what life would be like if slavery had not been abolished before our contemporary research and medical technology developed.

10. Bernard Rollin makes a similar point in *Animal Rights and Human Morality* (Buffalo: Prometheus Books, 1981), 49.

11. Dr. A. K. Ommaya of George Washington University, on the spring 1984 "Frontline" program (PBS Television) devoted to animal research, and Dr. Norman Schumway of Stanford University, on the fall 1984 segment of "60 Minutes" (CBS Television) devoted to the same topic.

12. John Rawls, *A Theory of Justice* (Cambridge: Harvard University Press, 1971), 141.

13. Ibid., 118–122. Just what role the original position plays in Rawls's theory of justice is a matter of controversy with which we have no need to become entangled. We will try to make common sense of Rawls here, and will return to a more philosophically sophisticated Rawlsian position in Chapter 8.

14. David Hume, *A Treatise of Human Nature*, edited by L. A. Selby-Bigge (Oxford: Clarendon Press, 1888), 470–476.

15. Tom Nagel, "What Is It Like to Be a Bat?," *The Philosophical Review* 83 (1974): 435–450.

16. For a fine survey of the ways of discovering what makes animals suffer, see M. S. Dawkins, *Animal Suffering* (New York: Chapman and Hall, 1980).

17. William James, *Essays in Pragmatism*, edited by A. Castell (New York: Hafner, 1948), 73.

PART III

Introduction

1. René Descartes, "Animals Are Machines," in *Animal Rights and Human Obligations*, edited by Tom Regan and Peter Singer (Englewood Cliffs, N.J.: Prentice-Hall, 1976), 66.

2. H. J. McCloskey, "Rights," *Philosophical Quarterly* 15 (1965): 115–127; Jan Narveson, "Animal Rights," *Canadian Journal of Philosophy* 7 (1977): 161–178; Bonnie Steinbock, "Speciesism and the Idea of Equality," *Philosophy* 53 (1978): 247–256; Leslie Francis and Richard Norman, "Some Animals Are More Equal than Others," *Philosophy* 53 (1978): 507–537; R. G. Frey, *Rights and Interests* (Oxford: Clarendon Press, 1980); Meredith Williams, "Rights, Interests, and Moral Equality," *Environmental Ethics* 2 (1980): 149–161; L. B. Cebik, "Can Animals Have Rights? No and Yes," *The Philosophical Forum* 12 (1981): 251–268; Ruth Cigman, "Death, Misfortune, and Species Inequality," *Philosophy and Public Affairs* 10 (1981): 47–64; Charlie Blatz, "Why (Most) Humans Are More Important than Other Animals: Reflections on the Foundations of Ethics," *Between the Species* 1, no. 4 (1985): 8–16; and Michael A. Fox, *The Case for Animal Experimentation* (Berkeley: University of California Press, 1986).

3. Williams, "Rights, Interests," 153, 161.

4. McCloskey, "Rights," 126.

5. Cigman, "Death, Misfortune," 59.

6. Peter Singer, *Animal Liberation* (New York: Avon Books, 1975).

7. Williams, "Rights, Interests," 151.

8. As mentioned in the Preface, Singer actually accepts this argument in principle, although he denies that it covers many animals, since few of the animals we breed for our use lead happy lives. See chap. 4 of his *Practical Ethics* (Cambridge: Cambridge University Press, 1979).

Chapter 7

1. St. Thomas Aquinas, "On Killing Living Things and the Duty to Love Irrational Creatures," and Joseph Rickaby, "Of the So-called Rights of Animals," in *Animal Rights and Human Obligations*, edited by Tom Regan and Peter Singer (Englewood Cliffs, N.J.: Prentice-Hall, 1976), 118–121 and 179–180.

2. R. G. Frey, *Interests and Rights: The Case Against Animals* (Oxford: Clarendon Press, 1980).

3. Ibid., 5.

4. Ibid., 78–79.

5. Ibid., 79–82. Since Frey's book appeared, Tom Regan, the animal liberationist Frey is primarily addressing at this point in his argument, has embraced the idea that nonsentient beings like trees and rivers (can) have moral rights; see Regan's "The Nature and Possibility of an Environmental Ethic," *Environmental Ethics* 3 (1981): 19–34. I do not find this way of disarming Frey's dilemma either necessary or attractive; we shall return to this issue in Chapter 14.

6. Ibid., 83–110.

7. Ibid., 78–83.

8. Ibid., 80.

9. This objection was made by one of the referees for my article "Interests and Animals, Needs and Language," which is one of the articles from which this chapter derives.

10. H. J. McCloskey, "Rights," *Philosophical Quarterly* 15 (1965): 115–127.

11. See McCloskey's "Moral Rights and Animals," *Inquiry* 22 (1979): 23–54.

12. Frey, *Interests and Rights*, 100.

13. Ibid., chaps. VII and VIII.

14. Ibid., 87, 88, 89–90.

15. The argument of this paragraph is developed at length by Norman Malcolm in "Thoughtless Brutes," *Proceedings and Addresses of the American Philosophical Association* 46 (1972–1973): 5–20.

16. Ibid., 20.

17. Frey, *Interests and Rights*, 88.

18. Ibid., 89–90.

19. Ibid.

20. Ibid., 105–106.

21. Ibid., 109.

22. Ibid.

23. Meredith William, "Rights, Interests, and Moral Equality," *Environmental Ethics* 2 (1980): 152–153.

24. See Leslie Francis and Richard Norman, "Some Animals Are More Equal than

Others," *Philosophy* 53 (1978): part 2; Ruth Cigman, "Death, Misfortune, and Species Inequality," *Philosophy and Public Affairs* 10 (1981): 57–59; and Williams, ibid., 154.

25. Williams, "Rights, Interest," Francis and Norman, "Some Animals," and Cigman, "Death, Misfortune," all argue emphatically that human temporal awareness is the basis for our interest in and moral right to life.

26. Williams, "Rights, Interests," 153–154.

27. Donald R. Griffin, *Animal Thinking* (Cambridge: Harvard University Press, 1984): 49–51.

28. Ibid., 153, 155.

29. Cigman, "Death, Misfortune," 59, and Francis and Norman, "Some Animals Are More Equal," part 2.

30. Williams, "Rights, Interests," 153.

31. Ibid., 153.

32. Bonnie Steinbock, "Speciesism and the Idea of Equality," *Philosophy* 53 (1978): 252–255, and Charlie Blatz, "Why (Most) Humans Are More Important than Other Animals: Reflections on the Foundations of Ethics," *Between the Species* 1, no. 4 (1985): 8–16, are critics of animal liberation who recognize and respond to these issues. Their position, that the intelligence necessary for taking an interest is also necessary for being a moral agent, will be discussed below, when considering the deontological significance of the variety of interests, and in Chapter 8, when discussing the agency requirement for having moral rights.

33. Williams, "Rights, Interests," 153.

34. Ibid., 157.

35. Perhaps this is what the following sentence, which appears unannounced on page 158 of Meredith Williams's article, "Rights, Interests," refers to: "Only in a cultural life can one make sense of having interests *informed by morality*" (emphasis added).

36. Immanuel Kant, *Foundations of the Metaphysics of Morals*, trans. Lewis White Beck (Indianapolis: Bobbs-Merrill, 1959), 46–47. Similar arguments are developed by Bonnie Steinbock, "Speciesism," 254–255, Richard A. Watson, "Self-Consciousness and the Rights of Nonhuman Animals and Nature," *Environmental Ethics* 1 (1979): 99–129, and Charlie Blatz, "Why (Most) Humans," 8–12.

37. See Donald R. Griffin, *The Question of Animal Awareness* (New York: Rockefeller University Press, 1981) and *Animal Thinking*, for myriad examples of animal rationality.

38. Williams, "Rights, Interests," 150.

Chapter 8

1. See Richard A. Watson, "Self-Consciousness and the Rights of Nonhuman Animals and Nature," *Environmental Ethics* 1 (1979): 88–129; L. B. Cebik, "Can Animals Have Rights? No and Yes," *The Philosophical Forum* 12 (1981): 251–268; and Michael A. Fox, *The Case for Animal Experimentation* (Berkeley: University of California Press, 1986), 56–57.

2. See Bonnie Steinbock, "Speciesism and the Idea of Equality," *Philosophy* 53 (1978):

249–256; Charlie Blatz, "Why (Most) Humans Are More Important than Other Animals: Reflections on the Foundations of Ethics," *Between the Species* 1, no. 4 (1985): 8–16; and Michael A. Fox, *The Case for Animal Experimentation,* 49–56. John Rawls suggests an agency requirement for being "entitled to equal justice" in section 77, "The Basis of Equality," of *A Theory of Justice* (Cambridge: Harvard University Press, 1971).

3. See Cora Diamond, "Eating Meat and Eating People," *Philosophy* 53 (1978): 465–479, and Leslie Francis and Richard Norman, "Some Animals Are More Equal than Others," *Philosophy* 53 (1978): 507–537.

4. This conception of morality is advocated by Aristotle and, at least as regards virtues, by James D. Wallace, in *Virtues and Vices* (Ithaca: Cornell University Press, 1978), chap. 1.

5. W. D. Ross, *The Right and the Good* (Oxford: Clarendon Press, 1930), 48.

6. Michael Wreen, "In Defense of Speciesism," *Ethics & Animals* 5 (1984): 47–60, and James A. Nelson, "The Tragedy of Marginal Cases," delivered to the American Philosophical Association, March 1985, have both recently criticized the argument from marginal cases on the grounds of "our ability to *identify* with human nonpersons" and the idea that "fairness requires us to ascribe basic rights to human nonpersons" who have been deprived of personhood$_d$ through "chance occurrences" (Wreen, 50, 52). Wreen's provocatively titled article might suggest to some readers that his criticism of the argument from marginal cases amounts to a criticism of extending moral rights to animals. However, Wreen does not even attempt to show that the concept of fairness cannot be employed, as it has been employed here, to extend moral rights not only to marginal humans but to animals as well. Consequently, his arguments could not support such a conclusion.

7. It may be in part to avoid this problem that contract theories of obligation and justice, such as those of Hobbes and Rawls, begin with imaginary situations in which there are no great disparities of power. However, imaginary "original positions" are only imaginary solutions to this problem if individuals are really supposed to meet the reciprocity requirement in order to have moral rights.

8. Actually, there might be some benefit to Alice in recognizing that Bob is entitled to his territory, rather than just being strong enough to hold it against her: she might take some comfort in the belief that things are as they ought (morally) to be. (I owe this insight to James Nelson.) However, when dealing with those (e.g., young children and animals) who do not recognize obligations because they are incapable of doing so, this indirect benefit of holding that the weak have duties to the strong cannot (logically) be an issue. Consequently, this indirect benefit can be disregarded when discussing the legitimacy of and drawing analogies to animal rights, as we are doing here.

9. Blatz, "Why (Most) Humans Are More Important than Other Animals," 8–12.

10. Peter Singer, *Animal Liberation* (New York: Avon Books, 1975), chap. 1.

11. Immanuel Kant, *Foundations of the Metaphysics of Morals,* trans. Lewis White Beck (Indianapolis: Bobbs-Merrill, 1959), 46–47.

Michael A. Fox has also recently addressed the question, "Why do only autonomous beings have rights?" His answer runs as follows:

(1) Autonomous beings are capable of free (self-determining, voluntary), deliberative, responsible action and have the sort of awareness necessary to see this kind of action

as essential to their nature, well-being, and development as individuals. (2) Autonomous beings are capable of recognizing autonomy in others and of full participation in the moral community. (*The Case for Animal Experimentation*, 56.)

These two reasons are not even relevant to showing why "it is not arbitrary to hold that all *and only* such beings qualify for the possession of rights" (ibid., emphasis added). Fox concludes the paragraph beginning with the above question by referring to an "I won't interfere with you, if you won't interfere with me" principle (ibid., 57), thereby, apparently, offering the reciprocity requirement as warrant for his version of the agency requirement. Since we have already demonstrated the inadequacy of the reciprocity requirement, we may safely conclude that Fox's restriction of rights to autonomous agents is unwarranted. Apparently, Fox has come to agree; in a letter published in *The Scientist*, December 15, 1986, Fox says that he is now "profoundly dissatisfied" with the argument developed in his book.

12. Immanuel Kant, *Foundations*, 9.

13. See chaps. 3 and 4 of Darwin's *The Descent of Man* and the ethological studies cited in Mary Midgley's *Beast and Man* (Ithaca: Cornell University Press, 1978).

14. See Mary Midgley, *Beast and Man*, Stephen R. L. Clark, *The Nature of the Beast* (Oxford: Oxford University Press, 1982), and Lawrence E. Johnson, "Can Animals Be Moral Agents?," *Ethics & Animals* 4 (1983): 50–61.

15. See Philip E. Devine, "The Moral Basis of Vegetarianism," *Philosophy* 53 (1978): 481–505; Meredith Williams, "Rights, Interests, and Moral Equality," *Environmental Ethics* 2 (1980): 149–162; Tom Regan, "Utilitarianism, Vegetarianism, and Animal Rights," *Philosophy and Public Affairs* 9 (1980): 305–337; and R. G. Frey, *Rights, Killing, and Suffering* (Oxford: Blackwell, 1983), 197–203.

16. Singer, *Animal Liberation*.

17. Wallace, *Virtues and Vices*, 26.

18. See the selections by Aquinas and Kant on human obligations to other animals in *Animal Rights and Human Obligations*, edited by Tom Regan and Peter Singer (Englewood Cliffs, N.J.: Prentice-Hall, 1976), 118–124.

19. Wallace's comments about convention suggest that he holds such a mistaken position:

The most striking difference between human life and all other kinds is that human life is characterized by activities that are possible only in a community with elaborate conventions. Language, knowledge (which is transmitted and therefore cumulative), commerce, art, morality, and politics are some important areas of characteristically human activities. (Ibid., 34.)

20. John Rawls, *A Theory of Justice* (Cambridge: Harvard University Press, 1971), 141.

21. Wallace discusses the second of these at length in chap. 1 of *Virtues and Vices*, where he also portrays it as a particular virtue of his, and Aristotle's, naturalist approach to ethics.

Chapter 9

1. Peter Singer, *Animal Liberation* (New York: Avon Books, 1975).

2. Ruth Cigman, "Death, Misfortune, and Species Inequality," *Philosophy and Public Affairs* 10 (1981): 47–54.

3. Tom Regan, *The Case for Animal Rights* (Berkeley: University of California Press, 1983).

4. Peter Singer, *Practical Ethics* (Cambridge: Cambridge University Press, 1979), chaps. 4 and 5.

5. The following all employ similar lines of argument: H. J. McCloskey, "Rights," *Philosophical Quarterly* 15 (1965): 115–127; Jan Narveson, "Animal Rights," *Canadian Journal of Philosophy* 7 (1977): 161–178; Bonnie Steinbock, "Speciesism and the Idea of Equality," *Philosophy* 53 (1978): 247–256; Leslie Francis and Richard Norman, "Some Animals Are More Equal than Others," *Philosophy* 53 (1978): 507–537; R. G. Frey, *Interests and Rights* (Oxford: The Clarendon Press, 1980); Meredith Williams, "Rights, Interests, and Moral Equality," *Environmental Ethics* 2 (1980): 149–161; and Michael A. Fox, *The Case for Animal Experimentation* (Berkeley: University of California Press, 1986), 22–24.

6. Cigman, "Death, Misfortune," 48–50, 58.

Michael A. Fox is another humanist philosopher who presumes that things can be of value only for intellectually sophisticated beings and then concludes from this that animals derive whatever value they have from the valuations of them by such sophisticated beings (i.e., by human beings). In *The Case for Animal Experimentation* (Berkeley: University of California Press, 1986), Fox sets us a kind of dilemma concerning the origin of values: apparently he believes that either we must agree with him that "if there were no sophisticated minds like our own in the world or in the universe, then nothing would be of value," or else we must suppose that "values would remain in nature if we subtracted valuing beings from the picture" (pp. 22, 24). Of course, this latter supposition can be discredited without difficulty, thereby leading to Fox's conclusion that "animals cannot have value in themselves, though they can and do have value if conscious beings capable of valuing can perceive and interact with them" (p. 25). The following will undercut this dilemma, thereby exposing the presumptive, groundless nature of Fox's critique of animal rights, by demonstrating that things can be of value for sentient beings who do not have "sophisticated minds like ours." (Perhaps this problem is another part of the reason why Fox no longer subscribes to the argument in *The Case for Animal Experimentation*; see *The Scientist*, December 15, 1986.)

7. H. L. A. Hart, "Bentham on Legal Rights," in *Oxford Essays in Jurisprudence* (second series), edited by A. W. B. Simpson (Oxford: Clarendon Press, 1973).

8. This is the subtitle of Donald R. Griffin's *The Question of Animal Awareness* (New York: Rockefeller University Press, 1976). Even as severe a critic of Peter Singer's position as Richard A. Watson would seem ready to dispute A3; see his "Self-Consciousness and the Rights of Nonhuman Animals and Nature," *Environmental Ethics* 1 (1979): 99–129.

9. Readers who may be concerned that I am now talking about "valuing," while A1 talks about being "capable of valuing," need not worry. After establishing the meaning of

"valuing" something, I intend to discuss the moral (in)significance both of valuing life itself and of the capacity for valuing life itself.

10. Cigman, "Death, Misfortune," 54, 56–57, 59.

11. Ibid., 56, 58–59 (emphasis added).

12. Stanley I. Benn, "Egalitarianism and Equal Consideration of Others," in *Nomos IX: Equality*, edited by J. Roland Pennock and John W. Chapman (New York: Atherton, 1967), 62 ff. The relevant passages can also be found on pp. 160–161 of Peter Singer's "All Animals Are Equal," in *Animal Rights and Human Obligations*, edited by Tom Regan and Peter Singer (Englewood Cliffs, N.J.: Prentice-Hall, 1976).

13. Cigman, "Death, Misfortune," 57–58.

14. Ibid., 54.

15. Ibid., 57–58, and Francis and Norman, "Some Animals Are More Equal," 515.

16. Harry Silverstein, "The Evil of Death," *The Journal of Philosophy* 77 (1980): 401–424.

17. Frey, *Interests and Rights*, chap. 1 and postscript.

Chapter 10

1. This is the formulation of the argument found in *Ethics & Animals* 3 (1982): 1.

2. Peter Singer, *Practical Ethics* (Cambridge: Cambridge University Press, 1979), chap. 4.

3. See, for example, Richard Ryder, *Victims of Science* (London: David-Poynter, 1975), and Jim Mason and Peter Singer, *Animal Factories* (New York: Crown, 1980).

4. By "individual," I do not mean anything having to do with the quality, nature, or complexity of different personalities or characters. I am referring only to the quantitative distinction of one being from another.

5. Immanuel Kant, *Foundations of the Metaphysics of Morals*, trans. Lewis White Beck (Indianapolis: Bobbs-Merrill, 1959), 46–47.

6. Tom Regan, "An Examination and Defense of One Argument Concerning Animal Rights," *Inquiry* 22 (1979): 208–209. T. L. S. Spriggs also uses this argument to advocate animal rights in his essay, "Metaphysics, Physicalism, and Animal Rights," ibid., 101–143.

7. Kant, *Foundations*, 9.

8. Singer, *Practical Ethics*, 79–80, 86–87.

9. Ruth Cigman, "Death, Misfortune, and Species Inequality," *Philosophy and Public Affairs* 10 (1981): 57.

10. Singer, *Practical Ethics*, 81.

11. See Donald R. Griffin, *The Question of Animal Awareness* (New York: Rockefeller University Press, 1981), and *Animal Thinking* (Cambridge: Harvard University Press, 1984).

12. Michael Lockwood in "Singer on Killing and the Preference for Life," *Inquiry* 22 (1979): 157–170, also questions whether preference utilitarianism draws a significant distinction between humans and animals in regard to the morality of killing and replacing them.

13. Singer, *Practical Ethics*, 86–87.

14. Ibid., 87.

15. Ibid., 87–88.

16. If the fetus is not allowed to develop to the point where it will experience pain or other miseries, then there is no harm. However, it is even harder to conceive of people who are so desperate to conceive a child that they would do so knowing full well that the fetus will be aborted before the end of the first trimester. The only faintly realistic possibility of this I can imagine is where the aborted fetus would be crucial for research toward curing some debilitating disease or defect. However, in this case, far from doing wrong, the couple could be considered self-sacrificing, even heroic.

17. Singer, *Practical Ethics*, 87.

18. This is not to say that not considering or considering not having normal children is ordinarily an expression of bad moral character—although, contrary to Singer's intuitions, that would be a fairly traditional evaluation.

19. The seventy-five-year figure is close to correct if we use average human life expectancy as our basis. The one-hundred-year figure is correct if we use the normal maximum human life expectancy as our basis, since every human generation seems to produce some centenarians. What the correct figures would be if we included animals, as we should, in figuring the average or normal maximum life expectancy, I do not know.

PART IV

Introduction

1. Perhaps the most notable example of this is Tom Regan's "The Nature and Possibility of an Environmental Ethic," *Environmental Ethics* 3 (1981): 19–34.

2. For example, see John Rodman, "The Liberation of Nature?," *Inquiry* 20 (1977): 83–145, and J. Baird Callicott, "Animal Liberation: A Triangular Affair," *Environmental Ethics* 2 (1980): 311–338.

Chapter 11

1. Peter Singer, *Animal Liberation* (New York: Avon Books, 1975), 176, 178–179.

2. According to Peter Singer, "the term 'vegetarian' came into general use as a result of the formation of the Vegetarian Society in England in 1847," and "the rules of the society permit the use of eggs and milk" (ibid., 179).

3. Ibid., 180.

4. For example, see Evelyn Pluhar, "On the Genetic Manipulation of Animals," *Between the Species* 1, no. 3 (1985): 13–19, the response to it by Michael W. Fox, *Between the Species* 2 (1986): 51–52, the response to Fox by Bernard Rollin, *Between the Species* 2 (1986): 88–89, and the rebuttal by Pluhar, *Between the Species* 2 (1986): 136–138. Rollin raises the further, morally cleaner possibility of developing cows, sheep, and the like that are not sentient. The raising and slaughtering of such (biological) animals for food

would, in itself, be no more an issue for animal liberation than is the raising and harvesting of carrots, though the extended questions occasioned by the large amount of feed, land, and other resources required to produce meat and the possibility that these resources might be used more fairly and efficiently for the general welfare, including that of non-human, sentient beings, would still arise.

5. Hunters often claim that hunting contributes to the welfare of wild animals by controlling disease, preventing starvation, and so forth. That hunting accomplishes these goods is questionable, but even if it does, it seems obvious that there are other, more selective, less destructive ways of enhancing the welfare of wild animals. Consequently, besides being disingenuous, such proposed utilitarian justifications of hunting (and trapping) involve the false dilemma of restricting our options to hunting or doing nothing.

6. Cora Diamond, "Eating Meat and Eating People," *Philosophy* 53 (1978): 465–479.

Chapter 12

1. A recent variation on the pro-researcher argument is the contention that because of our extensive, elaborate economic, political, and similar relations with other people, relations that we (supposedly) cannot have with animals, we are morally justified, even obligated to put human interests ahead of animal interests. Leslie Francis and Richard Norman in "Some Animals Are More Equal than Others," (*Philosophy* 53 [1978]: 507–537), and Arthur Caplan (comments made during "Frontline" program on animal research, PBS Television, spring 1984) have put forward such a claim. However, as discussed in Chapter 8, it does not follow from our having obligations to P that we do not have to Q that we would be morally justified in destroying Q in order to secure P's interests. Something like the pro-researcher argument must be added to our having special obligations to humans in order to infer from our having those obligations to B3, especially since, it is safe to presume, these philosophers intend to rule out such practices as destroying strangers to further the interests of loved ones. Consequently, the "special obligations" position is not an alternative to the "superior worth" defense of animal research—or of other forms of our continued consumption of animals.

2. "You have undertaken, in deed if not in word, to live your life as a citizen." Plato, *Crito*, 52d (Tredennick translation).

3. For examples, see Paul A. Freund, *Experimentation with Human Subjects* (New York: Braziller, 1970), Jay Katz et al., *Experimentation with Human Beings* (New York: Russell Sage Foundation, 1972), and Jessica Mitford, *Kind and Unusual Punishment: The Prison Business* (New York: Knopf, 1972).

4. See Alan Donagan, "Informed Consent to Experimentation," in *Ethical Issues in Modern Medicine*, 2nd ed., edited by John Arras and Robert Hunt (Palo Alto: Mayfield Publishing Co., 1983), 300–306.

5. Plato, *The Statesman*, 303a, and Aristotle, *Politics*, 1288a.

6. Robert Ardrey argues in *The Territorial Imperative* (New York: Dell, 1966), perhaps with too much enthusiasm but with considerable weight, that humans may have a great deal to learn from the "biological morality" of animals.

7. See, for example, Mary Midgley, *Beast and Man* (Ithaca: Cornell University Press, 1978), and the many psychological and ethological studies listed in her bibliography.

8. W. D. Ross, *The Right and the Good* (Oxford: Clarendon Press, 1930), chap. 2.

9. John Stuart Mill, *Utilitarianism*, edited by Oskar Piest (Indianapolis: Bobbs-Merrill, 1957), 12.

10. Peter Singer, *Practical Ethics* (Cambridge: Cambridge University Press, 1979), chap. 4. -

11. Bernard Rollin raises this possibility in *Animal Rights and Human Morality* (Buffalo: Prometheus Books, 1981), 33.

12. George Berkeley, *A Treatise Concerning the Principles of Human Knowledge* (1710).

13. Judith Jarvis Thompson, "A Defense of Abortion," *Philosophy and Public Affairs* 1 (1971): 47–66.

14. Jeremy Bentham, *Introduction to the Principles of Morals and Legislation* (1780).

Chapter 13

1. Aldo Leopold, *A Sand County Almanac* (Oxford: Oxford University Press, 1949), 224–225.

2. Immanuel Kant, *Critique of Practical Reason*, Book 2, chap. 2, part 4.

3. See, for example, Charles L. Stevenson, *Ethics and Language* (New Haven: Yale University Press, 1944), and Robert J. Fogelin, *Evidence and Meaning* (London: Routledge & Kegan Paul, 1967).

4. Tom Regan, "The Nature and Possibility of an Environmental Ethic," *Environmental Ethics* 3 (1981): 26.

5. R. M. Hare develops this sort of defense of utilitarianism in "Ethical Theory and Utilitarianism," in *Contemporary British Philosophy*, vol. 4, edited by H. D. Lewis (London: Allen and Unwin, 1976).

6. Professor Pluher put forward this and the following objection in her commentary on my paper "Predation," delivered at the December, 1984, meeting of The Society for the Study of Ethics and Animals.

Chapter 14

1. Tom Regan, "The Nature and Possibility of an Environmental Ethic," *Environmental Ethics* 3 (1981): 19–34, and reprinted in *All That Dwell Therein* (Berkeley: University of California Press, 1982).

2. J. Baird Callicott, "Animal Liberation: A Triangular Affair," *Environmental Ethics* 2 (1980): 311–338.

3. Aldo Leopold, "The Land Ethic," in his *A Sand County Almanac* (Oxford: Oxford University Press, 1949), 201–226.

4. Regan, "The Nature and Possibility," 28.

5. Mark Sagoff, "On Preferring the Natural Environment," *Yale Law Journal* 84 (1977): 205–267.

6. Regan, "The Nature and Possibility," 19.

7. Ibid., 30.

8. Ibid., 27. Regan's brief statement of this *reductio* does not include the qualifications in A2, but not to accept them would be to misrepresent utilitarianism and to refute a straw man.

9. Ibid.

10. Ibid.

11. Ibid., 23.

12. G. E. Moore, *Principia Ethica* (Cambridge: Cambridge University Press, 1903), especially chaps. 1 and 2.

13. Regan, "The Nature and Possibility," 19.

14. Tom Regan, "Feinberg on What Sorts of Beings Can Have Rights," *The Southern Journal of Philosophy* 14 (1976): 485–498, and also reprinted in *All That Dwell Therein* under the title, "What Sorts of Beings Can Have Rights?"

15. Regan, "The Nature and Possibility," 33.

16. Ibid., 31.

17. Ibid.

18. Ibid., 20.

19. Ibid., 21.

20. Callicott, "Animal Liberation: A Triangular Affair," 315.

21. Ibid., 337–338.

22. Ibid., 312.

23. Ibid., 337.

24. Ibid., 331.

25. Ibid., 321–322.

26. Ibid., 324–325.

27. Ibid., 327–329.

28. Ibid., 311, 320.

29. Ibid., 334.

30. Ibid., 333.

31. Peter Singer, *Animal Liberation* (New York: Avon Books, 1975), chap. 1, and Bernard Rollin, *Animal Rights and Human Morality* (Buffalo: Prometheus Books, 1981), part 1.

32. Tom Regan, "Utilitarianism, Vegetarianism, and Animal Rights," *Philosophy and Public Affairs* 9 (1980), 305–324.

33. Callicott, "Animal Liberation," 311, 320, 337.

34. Evelyn Pluhar also interprets Callicott's position in this way, in "Two Conceptions of an Environmental Ethic and Their Implications," *Ethics & Animals* 4 (1983): 120–123, and Ernest Partridge, another noted environmental ethicist, at least does not object to this interpretation of Callicott's position, in "Three Wrong Leads in a Search for an Environmental Ethic: Tom Regan on Animal Rights, Inherent Values, and 'Deep Ecology,'" *Ethics & Animals* 5 (1984): 73, note 18.

35. Callicott, "Animal Liberation," 321.

36. Albert Camus, *The Myth of Sisyphus* (New York: Vintage Books, 1955), 3.

37. Plato, *Republic*, 2, 369b–c (Cornford translation).

38. Callicott, "Animal Liberation," 332.

39. Plato, *Republic*, 2, 367e–374e; 9, 576b–592b; and 10, 612a–621d.

40. John Rawls, *A Theory of Justice* (Cambridge: Harvard University Press, 1971).

41. Callicott, "Animal Liberation," 333.

42. Ibid., 333. Callicott treats pain as if it were merely an organic monitoring system putting messages on a mental display screen, for example, "Your ankle is broken." He simply passes over the fact that in addition to delivering unwelcome information, pain hurts.

43. Ibid., 327, 334, 336, 338.

44. Ibid., 319.

45. Immanuel Kant, *Foundations of the Metaphysics of Morals*, trans. Lewis White Beck (Indianapolis: Bobbs-Merrill, 1959), 9–22, 30–41.

46. While this is clearly a criticism of Callicott's conception of environmental ethics, it is not entirely clear that it is an objection to Leopold's position. This is because it is not clear that he regarded his principle as *just* an ethical principle. He introduces that principle in *A Sand County Almanac*, 224, with the following remarks: "Quit thinking about decent land-use as solely an economic problem. Examine each question in terms of what is ethically *and* esthetically right, as well as what is economically expedient" [emphasis added]. Consequently, it may be that Leopold intended "beauty" to have only aesthetic significance in his principle. Callicott, however, does not even suggest splitting Leopold's principle into aesthetic and (supposedly) ethical components.

We may also note that, as this quotation indicates, Leopold offers his principle as *the* curative for the problems caused by adopting an exclusively economic, anthropocentric evaluation of the environment. Consequently, his arguments for his principle fall prey to the same objections raised against Tom Regan's claim that ascribing inherent value to nonconscious things is necessary for the possibility of an environmental ethic that regards the environment as more than a storehouse of natural resources for human consumption.

47. Robert W. Loftin makes this point in "The Morality of Hunting," *Environmental Ethics* 6 (1984): 241–250.

48. Callicott, "Animal Liberation," 322.

49. *American Heritage Dictionary* (2nd college ed., 1982).

50. Callicott, "Animal Liberation," 325.

51. Ibid.

52. A portion of the above critique of "Animal Liberation: A Triangular Affair" was published in *Ethics & Animals* 5 (1984): 113–121, which did not appear until August, 1985. The same issue of *Ethics & Animals* contains a reply from Callicott (pp. 135–139), indicating that he now "eschews total holism" (p. 136). He explains that his earlier advocacy of total holism was just a ploy to gain attention and that his considered philosophy accommodates "the primacy of human interests" (p. 138). However, in conversation he has indicated, if I understood him correctly, that total holism is still considered an attractive option by many philosophers in the "deep ecology" movement. Consequently, the above critique of total holism still has point.

In his reply, Callicott again claims that animal liberation is "life-loathing" and theoretically "timid" in comparison to the "much more creative" environmental ethics and does so on the basis of the same sorts of arguments offered in the earlier article. Consequently, the criticisms just offered of these contentions in his earlier article retain their relevance regarding (what appear to be) his current views on the relative merits of animal liberation and environmental ethics. Beyond denying that he was "personally advocating a philosophy of any sort" in the "Triangular Affair" article (p. 136; see also pp. 136–137)—a claim that readers of that article must find incredible—Callicott's primary response to the above criticism of "his" version of environmental ethics as a *moral* philosophy is to attack what he (apparently) believes I believe to be the scope of moral philosophy. Unfortunately, his comments here so thoroughly misrepresent and fail to come to grips with the above critique that discussing them would be a waste of time. Finally, in his reply, Callicott offers two quotations from Plato (*Republic* 420b and 519e) that are supposed to support his claim that Plato is a total holist. However, both of these quotations express Plato's eudaemonism, clearly indicating that it is not the integrity, stability, and beauty of the state but human happiness that is the goal of his moral philosophy. Furthermore, neither of these quotations is even about total holism, that is, about whether individuals have moral value only through their contributions to a community. Rather, both of these quotations are about "the law [being] concerned [not] with the special happiness of any class in the state but [with] producing this condition in the whole" (519e). Consequently, whatever Callicott really does or does not believe about total holism, he has still failed to give it respectability by showing that Plato advocates total holism.

53. Regan, "The Nature and Possibility," 19–20. Also, see Callicott, "Animal Liberation," 312–313.

Bibliography

Ardrey, Robert. *The Territorial Imperative*. New York: Dell, 1966.

Aristotle. *Nichomachean Ethics*.

Benn, S. I. "Abortion, Infanticide, and Respect for Life." In *The Problem of Abortion*, edited by Joel Feinberg. Belmont, Calif.: Wadsworth, 1973.

Bentham, Jeremy. *Introduction to the Principles of Morals and Legislation* (1780).

Bishop, John. "More Thought on Thought and Talk." *Mind* 79 (1980): 1–16.

Black, Max. "The Gap Between 'Is' and 'Should'." *Philosophical Review* 73 (1964): 165–181.

Blatz, Charlie. "Why (Most) Humans Are More Important than Other Animals: Reflections on the Foundations of Ethics." *Between the Species* 1, no. 4 (1985): 8–16, 24.

Callicott, J. Baird. "Animal Liberation: A Triangular Affair." *Environmental Ethics* 2 (1980): 311–338.

———. "Reply to Sapontzis." *Ethics & Animals* 5 (1984): 135–137.

Caplan, Arthur L. "Beastly Conduct: Ethical Issues in Animal Experimentation." *New York Annals of Science* 75 (1983): 159–169.

Cave, George P. "On the Irreplaceability of Animal Life." *Ethics & Animals* 3 (1982): 106–117.

Cebik, L. B. "Can Animals Have Rights? No and Yes." *The Philosophical Forum* 12 (1981): 251–268.

Cigman, Ruth. "Death, Misfortune, and Species Inequality." *Philosophy and Public Affairs* 10 (1981): 47–64.

Clark, Stephen R. L. *The Nature of the Beast*. Oxford: Oxford University Press, 1982.

Darwin, Charles. "Comparison of the Mental Powers of Man and the Lower Animals." In *Animal Rights and Human Obligations*, edited by Tom Regan and Peter Singer. Englewood Cliffs, N.J.: Prentice-Hall, 1976.

Dawkins, Marian Stamp. *Animal Suffering*. New York: Chapman and Hall, 1980.

Descartes, René. "Animals Are Machines." In *Animal Rights and Human Obligations*, edited by Tom Regan and Peter Singer. Englewood Cliffs, N.J.: Prentice-Hall, 1976.

Devine, Philip E. "The Moral Basis of Vegetarianism." *Philosophy* 53 (1978): 481–505.

Diamond, Cora. "Eating Meat and Eating People." *Philosophy* 53 (1978): 465–479.

Donagan, Alan. *The Theory of Morality*. Chicago: University of Chicago Press, 1977.

————. "Informed Consent to Experimentation." In *Ethical Issues in Modern Medicine*, 2nd ed., edited by John Arras and Robert Hunt. Palo Alto: Mayfield, 1983.

Feinberg, Joel. "The Nature and Value of Rights." *The Journal of Value Inquiry* 4 (1970): 243–257.

————. "The Rights of Animals and Unborn Generations." In *Philosophy and Environmental Crisis*, edited by William T. Blackstone. Athens: University of Georgia Press, 1974.

Feyerabend, Paul. *Against Method*. London: Verso, 1975.

Fogelin, Robert J. *Evidence and Meaning*. London: Routledge & Kegan Paul, 1967.

Fox, Michael Allen. *The Case for Animal Experimentation*. Berkeley: University of California Press, 1986.

Fox, Michael W. "On the Genetic Manipulation of Animals: A Response to Evelyn Pluhar." *Between the Species* 2 (1986): 51–52.

Francis, Leslie, and Richard Norman. "Some Animals Are More Equal than Others." *Philosophy* 53 (1978): 507–537.

Freund, Paul A. *Experimentation with Human Subjects*. New York: Braziller, 1970.

Frey, R. G. *Interests and Rights*. Oxford: Clarendon Press, 1980.

————. *Rights, Killing, and Suffering*. Oxford: Blackwell, 1983.

Galvin, Roger W. "What Rights for Animals?" *Agenda, Newsmagazine of the Animal Rights Network* 4 (Nov./Dec. 1984): 28.

Griffin, Donald R. *The Question of Animal Awareness*. New York: Rockefeller University Press, 1981.

————. *Animal Thinking*. Cambridge: Harvard University Press, 1984.

Hare, R. M. *Freedom and Reason*. Oxford: Oxford University Press, 1963.

————. "The Promising Game." *Revue Internationale de Philosophie* 70 (1964): 398–412.

————. "Ethical Theory and Utilitarianism." In *Contemporary British Philosophy*, vol. 4, edited by H. D. Lewis. London: Allen and Unwin, 1976.

Hart, H. L. A. "Are There Any Natural Rights?" *Philosophical Review* 64 (1955): 175–191.

————. "Bentham on Legal Rights." In *Oxford Essays in Jurisprudence (second series)*, edited by W. B. Simpson. Oxford: Clarendon Press, 1973.

Hume, David. *A Treatise of Human Nature*, edited by L. A. Selby-Bigge. Oxford: Clarendon Press, 1888.

James, William. *Essays in Pragmatism*, edited by A. Castell. New York: Hafner, 1948.

Johnson, Lawrence E. "Can Animals Be Moral Agents?" *Ethics & Animals* 4 (1983): 50–61.

Kant, Immanuel. *Critique of Practical Reason*, translated by Lewis White Beck. Indianapolis: Bobbs-Merrill, 1956.

————. *Foundations of the Metaphysics of Morals*, translated by Lewis White Beck. Indianapolis: Bobbs-Merrill, 1959.

Katz, Jay, et al. *Experimentation with Human Beings*. New York: Russell Sage Foundation, 1972.

Leakey, Richard, and Roger Lewis. *Origins*. New York: Dutton, 1977.

Leopold, Aldo. *A Sand County Almanac.* Oxford: Oxford University Press, 1949.

Lockwood, Michael. "Singer on Killing and the Preference for Life." *Inquiry* 22 (1979): 157–170.

Loftin, Robert W. "The Morality of Hunting." *Environmental Ethics* 6 (1984): 241–250.

Malcolm, Norman. "Thoughtless Brutes." *Proceedings and Addresses of the American Philosophical Association* 46 (1972–1973): 5–20.

Marcuse, Herbert. *Eros and Civilization.* New York: Random House, 1955.

Mason, Jim, and Peter Singer. *Animal Factories.* New York: Crown, 1980.

McCloskey, H. J. "Rights." *Philosophical Quarterly* 15 (1965): 115–127.

———. "Moral Rights and Animals." *Inquiry* 22 (1979): 23–54.

Merleau-Ponty, Maurice. *The Structure of Behavior*, translated by Alden L. Fisher. Boston: Beacon Press, 1963.

Midgley, Mary. *Beast and Man.* Ithaca: Cornell University Press, 1978.

Mill, John Stuart. *Utilitarianism*, edited by Oskar Piest. Indianapolis: Bobbs-Merrill, 1957, 12.

Mitford, Jessica. *Kind and Unusual Punishment: The Prison Business.* New York: Knopf, 1972.

Nagel, Tom. "What Is It Like to Be a Bat?" *The Philosophical Review* 83 (1974): 435–450.

Narveson, Jan. "Animal Rights." *Canadian Journal of Philosophy* 7 (1977): 161–178.

Nelson, James A. "The Tragedy of Marginal Cases." Delivered to the American Philosophical Association, March 1985.

Nelson, Leonard. *A System of Ethics.* New Haven: Yale University Press, 1956.

Partridge, Ernest. "Three Wrong Leads in a Search for an Environmental Ethic: Tom Regan on Animal Rights, Inherent Values, and 'Deep Ecology.'" *Ethics & Animals* 5 (1984): 61–74.

Phillips, D. Z., and H. O. Mounce. *Moral Practices.* New York: Schocken Books, 1970.

Pierce, Christine. "Can Animals Be Liberated?" *Philosophical Studies* 36 (1979): 69–75.

Plato. *Crito.*

———. *Republic.*

———. *The Statesman.*

Pluhar, Evelyn. "On the Irreplaceability of Animal Life." *Ethics & Animals* 3 (1982): 96–105.

———. "Two Conceptions of an Environmental Ethic and Their Implications." *Ethics & Animals* 4 (1983): 110–127.

———. "On the Genetic Manipulation of Animals." *Between the Species* 1, no. 3 (1985): 13–19.

———. "The Moral Justifiability of Genetic Manipulation." *Between the Species* 2 (1986): 136–138.

Putnam, Hilary. "Robots: Mechanisms or Artificially Created Life?" *Journal of Philosophy* 61 (1964): 668–691.

Rawls, John. *A Theory of Justice.* Cambridge: Harvard University Press, 1971.

Regan, Tom. "Feinberg on What Sorts of Beings Can Have Rights." *The Southern Journal of Philosophy* 14 (1976): 485–498.

————. "An Examination and Defense of One Argument Concerning Animal Rights." *Inquiry* 22 (1979): 189–220.

————. "Utilitarianism, Vegetarianism, and Animal Rights." *Philosophy and Public Affairs* 9 (1980): 305–337.

————. "The Nature and Possibility of an Environmental Ethic." *Environmental Ethics* 3 (1981): 19–34.

————. *All That Dwell Therein.* Berkeley: University of California Press, 1982.

————. *The Case for Animal Rights.* Berkeley: University of California Press, 1983.

Rodman, John. "The Liberation of Nature?" *Inquiry* 20 (1977): 83–145.

Rollin, Bernard. *Animal Rights and Human Morality.* Buffalo: Prometheus Books, 1981.

————. "On *Telos* and Genetic Manipulation." *Between the Species* 2 (1986): 88–89.

Ross, W. D. *The Right and the Good.* Oxford: Clarendon Press, 1930.

Rousseau, Jean-Jacques. *Emile* (1762).

Ryder, Richard. *Victims of Science.* London: David-Poynter, 1975.

Sagoff, Mark. "On Preserving the Natural Environment." *Yale Law Journal* 84 (1977): 205–267.

Salt, Henry S. "The Logic of the Larder." In *Animal Rights and Human Obligations,* edited by Tom Regan and Peter Singer. Englewood Cliffs, N.J.: Prentice-Hall, 1976.

Sapontzis, Steve F. "The Obligation to Be Rational." *The Journal of Value Inquiry* 13 (1979): 294–298.

————. "Are Animals Moral Beings?" *American Philosophical Quarterly* 17 (1980): 45–52.

————. "A Critique of Personhood." *Ethics* 91 (1981): 607–618.

————. "Must We Value Life to Have a Right to It?" *Ethics & Animals* 3 (1982): 2–11.

————. "Tom Regan, 'The Nature and Possibility of an Environmental Ethic'." *Ethics & Animals* 3 (1982): 33–38.

————. "On Being Morally Expendable." *Ethics & Animals* 3 (1982): 58–72.

————. "The Moral Significance of Interests." *Environmental Ethics* 4 (1982): 145–158.

————. "Moral Value and Reason." *The Monist* 66 (1983): 146–159.

————. "Interests and Animals, Needs and Language." *Ethics & Animals* 4 (1983): 38–49.

————. "Predation." *Ethics & Animals* 5 (1984): 27–38.

————. "J. Baird Callicott, 'Animal Liberation: A Triangular Affair'." *Ethics & Animals* 5 (1984): 113–121.

————. "Some Reflections on Animal Research." *Between the Species* 1, no. 1 (1985): 18–24.

————. "Moral Community and Animal Rights." *American Philosophical Quarterly* 22 (1985): 251–257.

Sartre, Jean-Paul. *The Transcendence of the Ego.* New York: Noonday Press, 1957.

Searle, John R. "How to Derive 'Ought' from 'Is'." *Philosophical Review* 73 (1964): 43–58.

Silverstein, Harry. "The Evil of Death." *The Journal of Philosophy* 77 (1980): 401–424.

Singer, Peter. *Animal Liberation.* New York: Avon Books, 1975.

————. "All Animals Are Equal." In *Animal Rights and Human Obligations,* edited by Tom Regan and Peter Singer. Englewood Cliffs, N.J.: Prentice-Hall, 1976.

————. *Practical Ethics*. Cambridge: Cambridge University Press, 1979.

Sprigge, T. L. S. "Metaphysics, Physicalism, and Animal Rights." *Inquiry* 22 (1979): 101–143.

Steinbock, Bonnie. "Speciesism and the Idea of Equality." *Philosophy* 53 (1978): 247–256.

Stevenson, Charles L. *Ethics and Language*. New Haven: Yale University Press, 1944.

Strawson, P. F. *Individuals*. London: Methuen, 1959.

Swift, Jonathan. "A Modest Proposal for Preventing the Children of Poor Parents from Being a Burthen to Their Parents or Country, and for Making Them Beneficial to the People." In *Animal Rights and Human Obligations*, edited by Tom Regan and Peter Singer. Englewood Cliffs, N.J.: Prentice-Hall, 1976.

Twain, Mark. *The Adventures of Huckleberry Finn*.

VanDeVeer, Donald. "Interspecific Justice." *Inquiry* 22 (1979): 55–80.

Wallace, James D. *Virtues and Vices*. Ithaca: Cornell University Press, 1978.

Warren, Mary Anne. "On the Moral and Legal Status of Abortion." *The Monist* 57 (1973): 43–61.

Watson, Richard A. "Self-Consciousness and the Rights of Nonhuman Animals and Nature." *Environmental Ethics* 1 (1979): 99–129.

White, James E. "Are Sentient Beings Replaceable?" *Ethics & Animals* 3 (1982): 91–95.

Williams, Meredith. "Rights, Interests, and Moral Equality." *Environmental Ethics* 2 (1980): 149–161.

Wreen, Michael. "In Defense of Speciesism." *Ethics & Animals* 5 (1984): 47–60.

Index

Abortion, xvi, 175; and metaphysical person-
hood, 49, 50, 65–66, 68. *See also* Fetus,
human
The Adventures of Huckleberry Finn, 63
Affective needs, 119
Affirmation of life, and environmental ethic,
267–268
Agency requirement for moral rights, 145–151;
sufficient condition analog, 179–180
Agent-dependent moral value, 30–31
Agent-independent moral value, 13, 30–31
Agricultural animals, 86–87; slaughtering and
harvesting, 201–206
Animal(s): equality concept applied to, 78–82,
151–154, 205; liberation rhetoric applied to,
76–78; moral actions in, 28–29, 34–36; moral
sense of "animal," 73–76; reason in, 28–29,
61; virtue rather than moral ideals in, 43–44,
61–62, 217–218. *See also* Exploitation of
animals; Killing animals
Animal Liberation, 159
Animal liberation, xv, 73–87; as affront to
human liberation, 84–87; answering objections to, 111–113; consequences of, 98–103,
197–198; vs. environmental ethics, 259–270;
environmental ethics of, 270–272; equality
concept applied to animals, 78–82; liberation
rhetoric applied to animals, 76–78; the moral
sense of "animal," 73–76; reasons for, 89–
110; rights rhetoric applied to animals,
82–84. *See also* Moral community and
animal rights
Animal research, (im)morality of, xvii, 197–198,
209–228; ability to consent to, 210–213; done
only on those who consent, 213–216; human
interests placed above animals', 286 n.1;
humans as a superior form of life argument,
216–222; morality of superiors exploiting
inferiors, 222–225

Animal rights, xi, 71–72; vs. animal welfare,
209–210; arguments against, xvi, 111–113;
equality concept applied to, 78–82, 151–154,
205; interest requirement for, 73–76, 115–
137. *See also* Animal liberation; Killing
animals; Moral community and animal rights
Animal welfare, vs. animal rights, 209–210
Animal Welfare Act, 90, 209
Anticruelty to animals tradition, 77, 209–210
Aquinas, Thomas, 38, 115
Arbitrariness of the world, and fairness, 108
Aristotle, xi, 109; ethics of, 154; on the moral
value of actions, 14, 273 n.2; practical science
of ethics, 239
Autonomy: and morality, 179–182; and rights,
85–86, 281 n.11

Beauty, in Leopold's environmental ethic, 265,
289 n.46
Belief: and language use, 120–127; and moral
action, 25
Benn, Stanley, 164
Bill of Rights, 79
Biotic community vs. animal liberation, 260–
268; arbitrariness of total holism, 261–264;
environmental ethics vs. personal preference,
264–267; morality and affirmation of life,
267–268
Black, Max, 54
Blatz, Charlie, 111; on moral agency and to
moral rights, 145
Burden of proof, on opposition to animal
liberation, xv, 86–87, 89, 110

Callicott, J. Baird, xviii, 249; criticism of his
ecological holism arguments, 259–270, 289
n.52
The Case for Animal Rights, xi, 89
Cats, consent of, to research, 211–212
Cebik, L. B., 111

297

Character, and moral value of actions, 19–20
Children: defective, 190–194, 284 n.16, 285 n.18; moral rights and interests of, 164; moral rights and personhood of, 51–52; natural contract with, 106
Cigman, Ruth, 78, 111, 133, 159; on the misfortune of death, and animal rights to life, 112, 160–175
Clark, Stephen, xi
Classical act-utilitarianism: concerns in animal research, 223–225; four views of, toward moral value, 182–183; goals of, 62; and moral motives, 18, 273 n.5; moral significance of interests to, 134–135; *reductio* arguments against, 239–240
Community, biotic. *See* Biotic community vs. animal liberation
Community, moral. *See* Moral community and animal rights
Complex issues, taking an interest in, 131–132
Conditioning, and moral actions, 32, 33
Consciousness, and social groups, 74–75
Consent to participation, in animal research, xvii; ability of animals to, 210–213; morality of research based on, 213–216
Consequential defense of humanism, 62–69
Consumption of animals: consequences of eliminating, 98–103, 197–198; as a moral question, 90–92
Contextual absurdity argument against protecting animals from predation, 233–234, 246
"Conventionally moral," defined, 91
Courage and moral value of actions, 19; and out of context actions, 21–22
Culture: embodiment of, argument in environmental ethics, 250, 255–256; taking an interest in, 132–133

Darwin, Charles, 107; on moral actions of animals, 27; on reason in animals, 33
Death, suffering, and awareness of suffering, 170–173. *See also* Killing animals; Right to life
Defective child, total population vs. prior existence utilitarianism applied to life of, 190–194, 284 n.16, 285 n.18
Deliberation, and taking an interest, 132
Deontological point of view, on the moral significance of interests from, 135–136
Descartes, René: on killing/eating animals, 111; on mind/body reality, 33
Descent of Man, The, 33
Desire: language and, 119–129; vs. needs, 116–119

Diamond, Cora, 207
Dogs, moral actions of, 27
Domesticated animals, 86, 93; genetic development of nonsentient, 285 n.4; slaughtering and harvesting, 201–206
Donagan, Alan, 1, 60
Duties and rights, 140–144

Ecological holism, 249, 259–270, 289 n.52; biotic community vs. animal liberation, 260–268; the good of nonsentient things, 268–270
Ecology, term of, 262
Egg production, 202
Embodiment of culture argument in environmental ethics, 250, 255–256
Enjoyment utilitarianism, 182; evaluation of replacement argument, 188–189
Environmental crisis, and inherent value argument, 250–253
Environmental ethics, xviii, 165, 198, 249–259; of animal liberation, 270–272; argument against protecting animals from predation, 235; J. B. Callicott's ecological holism arguments, 259–270; criticism of utilitarianism, 240, 244; and prior existence utilitarianism, 194–195; T. Regan's inherent value arguments, 249–259
Epicurus, on death, 172–173
Equality concept, applied to animals, 78–82, 205; and the relations requirement, 151–154
Ethics, 239
Euthanasia, 49–50
Events, vs. actions, 15
Exploitation of animals, xiv–xv; killing and scavenging unfairly, 206–207; morality of superiors exploiting inferiors, 222–225; slaughtering and harvesting painlessly, 201–206

Factual absurdity argument against protecting animals from predation, 233
Fairness, as a goal, xv, 62; agency requirement and, 149–150; extending moral rights to achieve, 142–144; and liberation of animals, 103–109, 281 n.6
Feinberg, Joel, on moral rights and self-respect, 76
Fetus, human: defective, 190–194, 284 n.16, 285 n.18; interests of, and right to life, 174–175; metaphysical personhood of, 50, 65, 68. *See also* Abortion
Feyerabend, Paul, 6
Fox, Michael W., xi, 111; on origin of values,

283 n.6; on rights of autonomous persons, 281 n.11

Francis, Leslie, 84, 111, 133

Freedom: everyday, 40–41; relationship to morality and rationality, 38–40

Frey, R. G., xv, 111, 174; on consequences of eliminating meat eating, 99–103; critique of his arguments on interests and animal rights, 115–127

Future: human ability to project into, 219–220; prior existence utilitarianism, and obligations to generations in the, 194–195

Galvin, Roger W.: his animal rights proposals, 79; on legal rights, 82

Genetic engineering for animal consumption, 204, 285 n.4

Goals of morality, 62, 89, 148

God, as virtuous rather than moral, 44–45

Good of nonsentient beings, 268–270

Goodness, variety of, and inherent value environmental ethics, 253–259

Grammar, psychological (in)significance of, 120–125

Griffin, Donald R., 66, 74

Guide for the Use and Care of Laboratory Animals, 209

Happiness, xv; liberating animals to increase world, 96–103. *See also* Suffering, goal of minimizing

Hare, R. M., 14

Hart, H. L. A., 82, 160

"Having an interest," xv, 116–119; being rational and, 130–134; in environmental ethics questions, 258; and having rights, 163–166; in life, 161–163; and moral standing, 134–137

Hierarchy argument, humans over animals, 107–109, 216–222, 225–226; and the right to exploit, 222–225, 286 n.1

Humanism, 52–69; consequential defense of, 62–69; humanist requirement for moral rights, 154–156; on interests, 131; logico-linguistic defense of, 54–58; on moral rights of persons, 52–70; phenomenological defense of, 58–60; transcendental defense of, 60–62

Human liberation, animal liberation as an affront to, 84–87

Human rights, xiv; in scientific research projects, 213–215

Humans: enhancing life of, through animal exploitation, 222–225; organ donors for, 227–228; right of, to exploit inferiors,

222–225, 286 n.1; as a superior form of life, 216–222

Hume, David, xi, 107, 108; on reason in animals, 28, 147

Hunting of animals, 206–207, 286 n.5

Ideals, pursuing, vs. the value of virtue, 41–46, 61

Independent valuer, moral value of, 180–181; evaluation of replacement argument, 184–185

Individuals, 48

Inherent value in environmental ethics, 249–259; environmental crisis and necessity for, 250–253; variety of goodness and necessity for, 253–259

Insects, and moral rights, 73–76

Instinct and moral actions, 32, 33

Institutional facts, vs. natural facts, 55–56

Integrity, in Leopold's environmental ethic, 265

Interest(s): having, in environmental ethics arguments, 258; having, vs. having rights, 163–166; having, in life, vs. right to life, 166–170; having, vs. taking, in life, 161–163; holism, to adjudicate conflicts in, 262–263; human, placed above animal's, in animal research, 286 n.1

Interest requirement for moral rights, applied to animals, 73–76, 112, 115–137; language and, 115–129; reason and, xv, 129–137

Interests and Rights, The Case Against Animals, 115, 174

James, William, xv, 73, 110

Judeo-Christian religious values, and relationship to animals, 238

Justification of moral actions, 22–24, 35

Kant, Immanuel, 1, 135, 136; on animals excluded for moral community, 147; on convergence of morality principles and everyday morality, 265; on fitting will to moral law, 42, 45; on God, morality, and virtue, 44–45; on man's faculty of reason, 40; on morality as a way of life, 95; on the moral value of action, 14

Killing animals, xvi, 77; having interest in life and right to life, 166–170; having interests and having rights, 163–166; having vs. taking interest in life, 161–163; rational beings' right to life, 160–161; and scavenging, as a meat source, 206–207; slaughtering and harvesting, 201–206; starvation and need for, 207; suffering loss and awareness of loss, 170–173. *See also* Replacement argument

Laboratory animals, 86
Land ethic, 260–261
Language use, and animals' interests, 115–129; and desire (belief/self-consciousness), 119–129; having an interest (need vs. desire), 116–119
Legal rights, 82
Leibniz, Gottfried Wilhelm, 155
Leopold, Aldo: land ethic, 260–261; values of integrity, stability, beauty, 265–266, 289 n.46
Liberation rhetoric, applied to animals, 76–78
Libertarian argument against protecting animals from predation, 235
Life: affirmation of, in environmental ethics, 267–268; having an interest in, and right to, 166–170; having vs. taking an interest in, 161–163; humans as a superior form of, 216–222; suffering loss of, and awareness of loss, 170–173. *See also* Replacement argument; Right to life
Logical absurdity argument against protecting animals from predation, 233
Logic of the larder. *See* Replacement argument
Logico-linguistic defense of humanism, 54–58

McCloskey, H. J., 111; on interests as necessary for rights, 112; on prescriptive component in interest, 118
Malcolm, Norman, 121
Marginal cases, xii–xiii; rights of humans, applied to animals, 77, 141–142, 281 n.6
Meat eating, 201–207; consequences of eliminating, 98–103
Meditations, 33
Metaphysical personhood: vs. moral personhood, 47, 47–50; and prejudice against extending moral rights, 65–69
Midgley, Mary, xi; on moral actions of wolves, 27
Mill, John Stuart, 219
Mind/body reality, 33
Monkeys, consent of, to research, 210, 212
Moore, G. E., concept of goodness, 253–254
Moral actions: of animals, 27–28, 34–36; freedom and, 38–41; and moral principles, 36–38; pursuing ideals of, vs. the value of virtue, 41–46, 61; and rationality, 30–41; for the right reason, 32–36, 37; value of, xiii, 11–26; value of, and incidentally good actions, 12–17; value of, and justifying moral actions, 22–24; value of, and out of context actions, 21–22. *See also* Virtue
Moral agency view, of moral value, 179–182; evaluation of replacement argument, 183–184

Moral agent(s): agent-dependent moral value, 30–31; agent-independent moral value, 13, 30–31; entitled to moral rights, 145–151; (in)significance of reason in being a, xiii–xiv, 30–41, 60–61; understanding one's actions, 22–26. *See also* Moral actions
Moral character, development of, 62; and the agency requirement, 148; liberating animals and, 90–96
Moral community and animal rights, 139–157; agency requirement, 145–151; humanist requirement, 154–156; reciprocity requirement, 140–144; relations requirement, 151–154
Moral (in)significance of reason, xii–xiv, 1–2, 30–41; and interests, 129–137
Morality: goals of, 62, 89, 148; as a way of life, 95
Moral personhood, vs. metaphysical personhood, 47, 50–52
Moral principles, and rationality, 5–6, 36–38
Moral progress, 62
Moral rights, agency requirement for, 145–151; humanist requirement for, 154–156; interest requirement for, 73–76, 134–137, 163–166; personhood and, 47, 51–52; prejudice against extending, 63–66; priorities of, human and animal, 79–82; reciprocity requirement for, 140–144; relations requirement for, 151–154; rhetoric of, applied to animals, 82–83; sentience, as a condition for, 87, 199–201. *See also* Animal rights; Human rights; Interest requirement for moral rights; Right to life
Moral utopia, 16
Moral value in actions, xiii, 11–26; acting out of context, 21–22; agent-independent/agent-dependent dimensions of, 30–31; incidentally good actions, 12–17; moral agents, philosophers, and judges, and understand one's, 22–26; ulterior motives, 17–20; ways in which lives can acquire, 179–189
Motives, moral, 17–20, 273 n.6
Mounce, H. O., 56

Nagel, Tom, 109, 162
Narveson, Jan, 29, 111
Natural contract, and animal debt to humans, 105–106
Natural facts, vs. institutional facts, 55–56
Natural psychologists, 74
Needs as having an interest, vs. desire, 116–119
Nelson, Leonard, 74
Nonmoral, defined, 91

Nonsentient things, good of, 268–270
Norman, Richard, 84, 111, 133

Organ donors for humans, 227–228
"Ought implies can" principle, and protecting animals from predation, 236–237; as a principle of practical reasoning, 239–245
Out of context actions, moral value of, 21–22

Paternalism, abuses of, in research, 214–215
Patient's Bill of Rights, 163
Patients' rights, 163, 180
Personal preferences, vs. environmental ethics, 264–267
Personhood, xiv, 47–70; denying, 59–60; humanist principles on, 52–70; metaphysical vs. moral, 47–52
Phenomenological defense of humanism, 58–60
Phillips, D. Z., 56
Philosopher, moral, 37
Plato, 1, 239; arguable holistic views of, 260, 262, 289–290 n.52; on moral utopias, 16
Pluhar, Evelyn, criticism of practical reasoning arguments, 242–244
Porpoises, moral actions of, 27
Powerless, moral rights of the, 51–52, 142–144, 149–150, 281 n.7, n.8
Practical Ethics, 159
Practical absurdity argument against protecting animals from predation, 236–237, 239–245
Predation, protecting animals from, xvii–xviii, 198, 229–248; "avoiding" suffering and, 245–247; fairness issue, and human consumption of animals, 106–107; "ought implies can" (practical absurdity) argument, 239–245; *reductio ad absurdum* responses to, 229–233; variety of absurdity arguments against a moral obligation for, 233–239
Preference utilitarianism, 182; evaluation of replacement argument, 185–188
Prejudice, against extending moral rights, 63–69, 127
Preservation of nature argument in environmental ethics, 250
Prior existence utilitarianism, 182; evaluation of replacement argument, 188; and obligations to future generations, 194–195; vs. total population views, 189–194
Priority of rights, animal and human, 79–82, 87, 94
Prudence: vs. morality, 142–143; and the moral value of actions, 20

Racism, 63, 64

Rational(ity): as basis of human superiority, 216–217; and having interests, 130–134; as requirement for right to life, 160–161; and transcendental defense of humanism, 60–62
Rational(ity), and acting morally, 27–46; moral agency limited to rational beings, 30–41; meaning of "rational," 28–30; pursuing ideals vs. the value of virtue, 41–46
Rational(ity), obligation to be, xiii, 3–9; methodology of making decisions on, 6–8; rationality and its alternatives, 4–6; as unproven, and the life of reason, 8–9. *See also* Reason
Rawls, John, xi, 1; on fairness and justice, 104, 108–109, 278 n.13; on moral utopias, 16
Reason: in animals, 28–29; (in)significance of, to morality, xii–xiv, 1–2; (in)significance of, to having interests, xv, 129–137. *See also* Rational(ity)
Reason and the moral value of actions, 11–26; acting out of context, 21–22; incidentally good actions, 12–17; moral agents, philosophers, and judges, 22–26; ulterior motives, 17–20
Reciprocity requirement, for moral rights, 140–144
Reflective ability, and freedom, 40–41, 274–275 n.13
Regan, Tom, xi, xii, xviii, 89, 159; criticism of utilitarianism, 240; on marginal humans' rights applied to animals, 77; on patient rights, 180–181; review of his inherent value environmental ethics, 249–259; on rights of nonsentient beings, 279 n.5
Relations requirement, for moral rights, 151–154
Replacement argument, xvi–xvii, 101–103, 159, 177–196; evaluation of moral standing, 179–189; (in)significance of the replacement article, 178–179; prior existence utilitarianism and obligations to future generations, 194–195; total population vs. prior existence utilitarianism, 189–194
Republic, 239, 260, 262, 289–290 n.52
Research. *See* Animal research, (im)morality of
Rickaby, Joseph, 115
Right reason, moral actions for, 32–36, 37
Rights. *See* Moral rights
Rights, Killing, and Suffering, 99–101
Right to life: having an interest in life, and, 166–170, 174–175; personhood and, 51; rationality prerequisite for, 160–161
Roe vs. Wade court decision, 68
Rollin, Bernard, xi, 261

Rorty, Richard, 89
Ross, W. D., 219; on rights and duties, 140

Sagoff, Mark, 250
Salt, Henry S., 101, 177
Searle, John, his defense of humanism, 54–57
Second-class citizens, 52
Self-consciousness, required for language and
    desires, 127–129
Self-interest, and rationality, 5–6
Self-respect, in human liberation, 85
Sentience, as condition for moral rights, 87
Silverstein, Harry, 173
Singer, Peter, xi, xii, 112, 178, 261; on defective
    child, and replacement argument, 190–194;
    on equality concept, and animals, 79, 82; on
    justifying moral actions, 22–24; on
    preference, 186; on respect for animal life,
    159; on sentient behavior, 199–200
Slaughtering and harvesting animals, 201–206
Slavery, 16, 106, 277 n.9
Socrates, 61
Spinoza, Benedict, 239
Stability, in Leopold's environmental ethic,
    265–266
Steinbock, Bonnie, 77, 79, 111
Stewardship, obligations of, 93
Strawson, P. F., 48
Suffering, goal of minimizing, xv, 62; agency
    requirement and, 149; and animal liberation,
    96–103; obligation to prevent predation and
    "avoidable" suffering, 245–247; obligation to
    prevent predation entailed by, 239–245
Suffering a loss, and awareness of loss, 170–173
Swift, Jonathan, 81 n.14
System of Ethics, A, 74

"Taking an interest," 116–119; in life, 161–163
Temporal events, taking interest in, 131
Theoretical absurdity argument against pro-
    tecting animals from predation, 234–236

Theory of Justice, A, xi
Thompson, Judith Jarvis, 223
Total holism, arbitrariness of, 261–264
Total population utilitarianism, 182; evaluation
    of replacement argument, 185–188, 189; vs.
    prior existence views, 189–194
Transcendental defense of humanism, 60–62
Truman, Harry, 147
Truth, language and, 125–127

Ulterior motives, and moral value of actions,
    17–20
Universal Declaration of the Rights of Man, 71,
    79, 163
Unnaturally absurd argument against protecting
    animals from predation, 237–238
Utilitarianism. *See* Classical act-utilitarianism

Values, origins of, 283 n.6
Vegetarianism, xvii, 98–103, 197, 199–207;
    animal exploitation, killing and scavenging,
    206–207; animal exploitation, slaughtering
    and harvesting, 201–206; entailed in animal
    liberation, 199–201; origin of term, 285 n.2;
    starvation and consumption of animals, 207
Virtue, xv; animals as virtuous, 43–44, 217–
    218; value of, vs. pursuing ideals, 41–46, 61

Wallace, James D., 154, 282 n.19
Watson, Richard, 84; on action initiated by
    animals, 41; on moral actions in animals, 34;
    on reason in animals, 28–29
Well-being feelings, and interests, 74, 117
Wild animals, 93, 105–106; insignificance of the
    replacement argument to, 178–179; killing
    and scavenging, 206–207
Williams, Meredith, 112; on human treatment
    of animals, 111; on interests, 130–131, 132–
    133, 134; on prejudice, 63–64, 137
Wolves, moral actions of, 27
Women, moral rights and personhood of, 51–52